b

THE NEW AUTOCRACY

INFORMATION,

POLITICS,

AND

POLICY IN

PUTIN'S RUSSIA

The New Autocracy

DANIEL TREISMAN
Editor

BROOKINGS INSTITUTION PRESS
Washington, D.C.

The Brookings Institution is a private nonprofit organization devoted to research, education, and publication on important issues of domestic and foreign policy. Its principal purpose is to bring the highest quality independent research and analysis to bear on current and emerging policy problems. Interpretations or conclusions in Brookings publications should be understood to be solely those of the authors.

Library of Congress Cataloging-in-Publication data are available.
ISBN 978-0-8157-3243-3 (pbk.: alk. paper)
ISBN 978-0-8157-3244-0 (ebook)

9 8 7 6 5 4 3 2 1

Typeset in ScalaPro

Composition by Westchester Publishing Services

Contents

Preface

Russia's seizure of Crimea from Ukraine in 2014 shocked observers around the world. It also surprised more than a few professional Russia-watchers. While in retrospect some saw a certain logic in the Kremlin's action—and all knew of Moscow's grievances—few had predicted the move. To many, it suggested the urgent need to reexamine assumptions and gather new evidence about how Russia's leaders currently make high-stakes decisions.

In the fall of 2014, with generous support from the Carnegie Corporation of New York, I recruited a team of experienced, Russia-based political analysts from academia, think tanks, and the press. I matched them up with promising emerging scholars, based mostly in the West, who, in their own work, were applying social scientific techniques to the challenge of understanding Russia. My hope was to capture synergies—between Russian and Western perspectives, accumulated knowledge and fresh approaches, local expertise and scientific method. This book is the result.

The team met at two workshop conferences—in Los Angeles (March 2015) and New York (June 2016)—to plan our research and then to discuss drafts of the chapters. We are grateful to five U.S. scholars—Leon Aron, Timothy Frye, Michael McFaul, Graeme Robertson, and Joshua Tucker—who offered invaluable advice at these events. (Of course, they bear no responsibility for errors or omissions.) For more on members of the team and links to their writings on Russia, see our website at www.russiapoliticalinsight.com.

To say that understanding Russia's political decisionmaking is important is not to say that it is easy. In the more than three years since we began, the process has become—if anything—even more opaque. We have sought evidence from a variety of sources—interviews with current and former insiders, journalistic accounts and memoirs, official records, and data on everything from law production and official meetings to criminal prosecutions and the connections among major business people. Needless to say, we have struggled with problems of inference, knowing that what we see is only part of the picture. Throughout, we were guided by a commitment to questioning conventional wisdom and to reliance on observation and induction rather than to the imposition of any preconceived models.

We thank the Carnegie Corporation—and, in particular, Deana Arsenian and Pat Nicholas—as well as the UCLA Department of Political Science and Social Science Grants office for their help and support along the way. At Brookings, we are grateful to Bill Finan, Valentina Kalk, and two anonymous reviewers.

The book was made possible in part by a grant from the Carnegie Corporation of New York. The statements made and views expressed, however, are solely the responsibility of the authors.

THE NEW AUTOCRACY

ONE

Introduction

Rethinking Putin's Political Order

DANIEL TREISMAN

How are political decisions made in Russia today? The increasingly tense relations between the world's second nuclear power and the West make understanding that process particularly urgent. Yet many images popular in the media and academia, although capturing some element of Russia's political scene, do not seem quite right.

To certain observers, the regime of Vladimir Putin looks like a spruced-up replica of the USSR of Leonid Brezhnev.[1] Once again, the Kremlin is harassing domestic critics and censoring the press. Putin, who once declared the Soviet disintegration a "geopolitical catastrophe," seems intent on reversing it, bringing lands lost in 1991 back under Moscow's control (Shevtsova 2014). Having restored the Soviet national anthem, the Russian president is now said to rule by means of what one analyst, perhaps tongue in cheek, calls a "Politburo 2.0" (Minchenko 2013).

Others see the current regime as an offshoot not of the Soviet Union per se but of its most feared institution—the State Security Committee (KGB), or, more broadly, the security and law enforcement agencies, whose officers

---

1. For instance, Gessen (2012, p. 270).

and veterans are known in Russian as the *siloviki*. Putin, the onetime spy, is cast as the executor of a covert project to establish his former agency's dominance. Analysts portray the siloviki as a cohesive clan, now entrenched within both the Russian polity and the country's corporate boardrooms (Petrov 2002; Kryshtanovskaya and White 2003, 2009; Treisman 2008).

To still others, the Putin regime is essentially a kleptocracy, whose leaders' central aim is "to loot the country without limit" (Dawisha 2015, p. 3). Putin and his cronies—mostly old friends from St. Petersburg—are said to have enmeshed the state in nationwide networks of corruption. To understand Russian politics today, so this argument goes, one simply needs to follow the money.

While these three images emphasize the personal history and choices of Russia's second president, a fourth image sees him as the instrument of something larger. Russian public life, it is said, is governed by *sistema*. What *sistema*—literally "the system"—means depends on who is writing. In one view, it represents informal "power networks that account for the failure to implement leaders' political will" (Ledeneva 2013, p. 4). In another, it is a "style of exercising power that turns the country's people into temporary operating resources" (Pavlovsky 2016, p. 14). The various usages share the notion of something timeless, rooted in culture, that blocks reform and devalues individual rights.

Finally, political scientists who look at Russia often find in it an example of "competitive authoritarianism," a type of regime that converts seemingly democratic institutions into props for dictatorship (Levitsky and Way 2010).[2] In such orders, elections are held not to choose new leaders but to intimidate the dissidents (Magaloni 2006). Legislatures exist not to deliberate over laws but to co-opt potential opposition or to enforce deals between the dictator and other power holders (Gandhi and Przeworski 2006; Boix and Svolik 2013). The façade of democracy is constructed in part to earn respectability and Western aid.

These images point to some recognizable features of Russia under Putin. Yet, as a guide to the country's politics and policy, they seem inadequate. Each highlights one aspect, while neglecting others. Each ignores much of what actually happens, day to day, in Russian government. By emphasizing continuities and cultural stickiness, the neo-Soviet, KGB state, and *sistema* in-

---

2. Steven Levitsky and Lucan A. Way (2010) classify Russia as "competitive authoritarian" until 2008 and then as a fully authoritarian regime.

terpretations create a misleading impression of stasis. They underplay the dramatic ways the country has changed over the past twenty-five years and imply a coherence that is hard to fit with the facts.

Like the Soviet Union, Russia today has a strong leader, a centralized state, superpower ambitions, and an aggressive foreign policy. Yet, unlike the USSR, it lacks a cohesive ruling party and a communist ideology. It has—for the most part—open borders and a market economy. Indeed, many of its leaders are eager capitalists, with their own businesses on the side (Lamberova and Sonin, this volume). The Soviet Politburo after Joseph Stalin, although dominated by the general secretary, contained a number of political heavyweights with their own bureaucratic resources. There is nothing comparable in Putin's Russia. And, for all the propaganda on today's Kremlin-controlled television, the country remains far more open to information than in Soviet times.

Russia is also not a KGB state. In fact, the security services are so fragmented by clan, factional, and interagency rivalries, so divided by generational, bureaucratic, and personal conflicts, that they cannot act cohesively (Soldatov and Rochlitz, this volume). They lack a leader who could make demands on the president. Within government and the higher echelons of the Presidential Administration, the presence of siloviki actually peaked around 2008 and then fell, with individuals from private business mostly filling the gap.[3] In high-stakes battles, top siloviki sometimes lose to big business people or other actors. In 2011, for example, the billionaire Mikhail Fridman fought to prevent the oil company Rosneft, led by Putin's friend Igor Sechin, from partnering with BP to explore the Arctic. Despite Sechin's security service background and personal ties to the president, Fridman won.

Although they have not captured the state, the enforcers have largely captured the criminal justice system, co-opting and weakening the courts (Paneyakh and Rosenberg, this volume). Some key siloviki have participated in top discussions. But they do so not as holders of particular posts but as longtime, trusted confidants of Putin. And their access can end suddenly, as when Putin abruptly retired three of his closest security service colleagues in 2016 (Soldatov and Rochlitz, this volume). Beyond such personal relationships, the influence of the siloviki reflects two factors. First, their vision of a Russia besieged by the West seems—at least judging from

3. See Ananyev (this volume); Rivera and Rivera (2014). The trend might now be changing again (see Soldatov and Rochlitz, this volume).

Putin's public comments—to fit more and more closely with the president's own evolving vision of the world. The Arab Spring and Russia's Facebook protests of 2011–12 appeared to validate the siloviki's warnings that the U.S. Central Intelligence Agency (CIA) was fomenting color revolutions and had plans for one in Moscow. Second, the top security service bosses control most flows of information to the president.

That leading Russian politicians benefit from massive corruption and links to organized crime has been credibly reported more than once.[4] A few close Putin associates—and others connected to them—have become extremely rich during the boom years, although their returns fell sharply when oil revenues sank (Lamberova and Sonin, this volume). But calling Russia a kleptocracy does not help much in understanding its politics. Many key decisions—such as the intervention in Syria or the support for insurgents in Donbass despite the risk of Western sanctions—make little sense in terms of Kremlin bigwigs' mercenary interests. Most state decisions have no direct impact on top officials' offshore accounts. And if corruption and theft are all the Kremlin cares about, it is puzzling how and why some difficult tasks, such as the reform and modernization of the Russian armed forces between 2008 and 2014, still get done.

Accounts of *sistema* sound plausible to anyone who has spent time in Russia. Yet in their vagueness and generality, they explain too little and too much. Too little because such images focus on how decisions are—or are not—implemented and say nothing about what goals decisionmakers choose to pursue. Too much because—although authors of course recognize that some change does happen—*sistema* seems only to explain how it is blocked. That extensive modernization, in fact, has occurred becomes even more mysterious if one sees the society and state as trapped in a premodern matrix of informal codes, cultural norms, and personal relationships. And if formal laws and regulations are routinely subverted, it is puzzling that top leaders invest so much time and effort in enacting them.

Calling Russia a case of "competitive authoritarianism" helps focus attention on what is and what is not unique about its current order. But, as the following chapters suggest, various aspects of Russia's politics do not fit prevailing understandings of how such regimes work. The parliament turns out to be neither a complete façade—a "rubber stamp"—nor a venue for co-opting regime opponents or enforcing bargains between elites and a dictator. Rather, it is a forum for battles over policies among rival

---

4. See, for instance, Duarte and Meyer (2015).

bureaucratic—and occasionally business—actors (Noble and Schulmann, this volume). In most cases, the results represent not some compromise between the parties or some co-optation payoff but rather the relative skill, luck, and persistence of the players in a complicated game.

Elections, rather than intimidating the opposition by means of inflated "supermajorities," seem to have mobilized regime critics, sparking angry demonstrations in 2011–12.[5] Meanwhile, Putin's preservation of superficially democratic institutions is certainly not a bid for Western aid, since Russia receives none and seeks to outlaw international agencies that presume to deliver any. If the point is to win respectability in the West, the defiant openness with which the authorities persecute the political opposition is surprising.

In this book, we attempt to construct a richer picture of how Russian political decisions are made today. Our approach is empirical and inductive. By observing all that can be observed about the role and participation of key actors, we seek to develop a comprehensive understanding of how the system operates, its strengths and weaknesses, and its potential for change. To be clear, this book does not claim to answer all the questions left hanging by previous accounts. And, to be fair, elements of some of the images criticized above also appear in ours. But from an intensive examination of available evidence, a number of new themes emerge.

MORE MODERN

A first theme is that it is impossible to understand Russia's politics today without paying attention to the dramatic change that occurred in society between 1999 and 2011. During these years, Russia was modernizing rapidly. This process both shaped the Putin regime and created the emerging threats to it that prompted the Kremlin's reactionary turn.

Of course, Russia had industrialized—and overindustrialized—already during the Soviet period. As of 1990, 73 percent of the population lived in cities and 40 percent of those employed worked in industry—15 percentage points more than in the United States. The phase of modernization that beckoned, as communism collapsed, was the transition to a postindustrial

---

5. Some might argue that it was the dwindling of United Russia's "supermajority" in 2011 rather than electoral fraud that triggered the protests. But it is hard to believe that the Moscow protesters would have stayed home had the authorities faked an even larger margin of victory.

society. That meant shrinking industry and creating an advanced service sector. Over the next decade, the economy did deindustrialize. By 1999, the employment share of industry had fallen to 28 percent, about the level in Ireland. Meanwhile, service sector employment rose from 46 to 57 percent.[6] This restructuring was accompanied by a wrenching economic contraction and a decline in living standards for much of the population.

When the rebound came, the pace was dramatic. Between 1999 and 2011, Russia's GDP per capita rose from a little under US$13,000 to US$24,000.[7] Living standards surged even faster. Adjusted for inflation, average wages and pensions both increased by 11 percent a year throughout this period. It was during this broad-based boom that Russia experienced the kind of changes in consumption, education, information technology, media, and global integration that sociologists associate with postindustrial society (Bell 1973).

As incomes grew, Russia became a land of consumers, with chain stores and multiplexes spreading across the country. By 2012, Moscow contained more mall space than any other European city; Russia had more than twice as many hotels as it had in 2000 and more ATMs per person than either Japan or the United Kingdom (Kramer 2013; Rosstat 2013b; IMF 2014).

Communications also underwent a revolution. When Putin first took office, only one in every forty-five people had a cell phone subscription. By 2011, Russians had 1.8 subscriptions *per person*. Back in 1999, hardly any Russian families owned a computer and the Internet was virtually unknown. By 2012, three quarters of households contained a computer and 64 million people (55 percent of the population) were logging on to the Internet at least once a month; by 2016 this figure had risen to 81 million people (69 percent of the population).[8] Along the way, Russian edged out German to become the second-most-used language on the web.[9] Social networks—both Russian and Western—had attracted 35 million daily Internet users by September

---

6. All statistics in this paragraph are from the World Bank (2016).

7. World Bank (2016). Estimates at purchasing power parity and in constant 2011 U.S. dollars, accessed August 3, 2016.

8. Public Opinion Foundation (FOM), "Internet v Rossii: Dinamika proniknoveniya, zima 2015–2016 gg. [The Internet in Russia: Dynamics of penetration, winter 2015–2016]," http://fom.ru/SMI-i-internet/12610.

9. W3 Techs, "Historical Yearly Trends in the Usage of Content Languages for Websites," http://w3techs.com/technologies/history_overview/content_language/ms/y.

2013.[10] Simultaneously, the media market boomed. Annual TV advertising revenues rose from US$235 million in 2000 to US$4.5 billion in 2011, while the Internet advertising market grew from nothing to US$1.4 billion.[11]

Amid the crisis of the 1990s, the gross enrollment rate in higher education had actually fallen—from 56 percent in 1989 to 52 percent in 1999. But then it took off, hitting 76 percent in 2011 (World Bank 2016). In this period, the share of the workforce with bachelor's degrees rose from 19 to 30 percent (Rosstat 2003a, p. 42; 2016, p. 114). More and more of the record numbers entering college were studying economics and management or computer science. Meanwhile, Russians traveled abroad more during the Putin years than at any time in the previous century. In 1999 Russians made 13 million trips abroad. By 2011, they were making 44 million a year (Rosstat 2003b, 2013b).

As Russians became more educated, wired, and internationally traveled, their attitudes modernized in some of the ways that theories predict (Rogov and Ananyev, this volume). Ronald Inglehart and his colleagues have shown that in highly educated, information-rich, service sector–dominated postindustrial societies, demands for self-expression, participation, and quality of life become more pronounced (Inglehart and Baker 2000; Inglehart and Welzel 2009). In Russia, the share who favored a "democratic" political system rose from 45 percent in 1995 to 64 percent in 2006 and 68 percent in 2011—although the simultaneous growth in support for unconstrained "strong leadership" suggests a certain ambivalence (World Values Survey 2016). Despite resentment of the West's perceived desire to dictate to Russia, the proportion who favored "Western-style" democracy rose from 15 percent in 2008 to almost 30 percent four years later, for the first time equaling support for a return to Soviet rule (Levada Center 2016, p. 33). Demand for a paternalistic, protective state—although still a majority position—was falling. The proportion who thought the state should guarantee all citizens a decent level of well-being fell from 71 percent in 2001 to 58 percent in 2011. Agreement that the state should only establish

10. FOM, "Dlya chego lyudi ispolzuyut internet? [For what do people use the Internet?]," http://fom.ru/SMI-i-internet/11088.

11. Assotsiatsia Kommunikatsionnykh Agentstv Rossii, "Obem reklamnogo rynka Rossii v 2000–2011 gg. [Volume of the Russian advertising market, 2000–2011]," www.akarussia.ru/node/2085.

and enforce common "rules of the game" jumped from 19 to 34 percent (Rogov and Ananyev, this volume; Levada Center 2016, p. 63).

The late 1990s and early Putin years had seen a strong demand for centralization, unity, and law and order. By 2012 the pendulum was swinging back. By that year, 70 percent agreed that Russia needed a political opposition, up from just 47 percent who had said this in 2000. Only 40 percent backed further centralization of political power, less than the 45 percent who called for political decentralization (Rogov and Ananyev, this volume).

Many parts of the state—corrupt, stagnant, inefficient—looked increasingly at odds with the mood in society. But a few were evolving toward greater effectiveness. Despite the image of Russia's court system as politicized and venal, one subsystem—the commercial *arbitrazh* courts—was thriving (Paneyakh and Rosenberg, this volume). The number of cases that businesses chose to bring to these courts more than doubled between 1999 and 2012, suggesting, if not perfect justice, at least a useful degree of predictability.

Meanwhile, citizens and businesses were increasingly using the regular courts to sue the state, exploiting new powers that—surprising as it might seem—were introduced mostly during Putin's first term. Here the bias against acquittals in Russian jurisprudence worked in society's favor. In 2010 courts ordered the federal government to pay US$220 million to compensate victims of wrongful state actions—seventy times more than in 2001 (Paneyakh and Rosenberg, this volume; Trochev 2012). Even the penal system saw some humanization in the years of Putin and Dmitry Medvedev. The number of Russians sentenced to prison fell from 389,000 in 1999 to 206,000 in 2012. Judges were handing out more probation in place of jail time (Paneyakh and Rosenberg, this volume).

As opinions evolved and online networks spread, a new interest in civic activism began to emerge in some quarters. Participation was low, except for local efforts by homeowners to improve utility services and clean up their neighborhoods (Sobolev and Zakharov, this volume). But, especially in the big cities, attitudes were changing. People began to donate money and clothes to those in need. Local organizations sprang up to defend forests, lakes, and other threatened natural environments or to shield historic architecture from the wrecking ball. When fires destroyed vast tracts of forest around Moscow in the summer of 2010, volunteers mobilized to help the burned villages. Floods in the south elicited a similar reaction. Motorists by the thousands protested the special treatment of privileged drivers, who could cut through traffic with their flashing blue lights. And, as the 2011–12 electoral season approached, thousands of young people with cell phones and Internet accounts signed up to monitor electoral precincts. When they documented ballot stuffing and fraud—and when tens of thousands took to the streets to protest in Moscow and a few other cities—it marked the culmination of this phase of Russia's modernization. It also triggered Putin's reactionary response.

SUDDEN STOP

The dramatic modernization of Russian life that occurred in the 2000s forged the Putin regime. Steadily rising living standards distracted Russians from the political divisions of the 1990s and demobilized the discontented, allowing the Kremlin to concentrate power more and more as the decade progressed. Despite resentment at Russia's shrunken global status, the population was solidly *pro*-Western in the early 2000s, with more than 60 percent favorable toward the United States and more than 70 percent favorable toward the European Union (Rogov and Ananyev, this volume). NATO's bombing of Serbia had outraged most Russians, but pro-Western sentiment bounced back surprisingly fast, especially after the 9/11 terrorist attacks, which won Russians' sympathy. At that time, Russians associated Putin not with assertive nationalism but with Western-style economic and social progress. Support for him was higher among Russians with positive views of the West than among those hostile toward it and among those who said that modernization was necessary than among those who said it was not.[12]

And yet it was alarm at the consequences of this trend that seems to have motivated Putin's abrupt reversal in 2012. The leader who had presided over modernization became the chief obstacle to it. To those in the Kremlin, the new Russia that was emerging posed an unmistakable threat. While hoping to continue the economic progress needed to secure prosperity and sustain the country's military defenses, they acted forcefully to neutralize its social and political spillovers.

12. On attitudes toward the West and Putin approval, see Treisman (2014). In April 2011, among Russians who agreed that modernization was necessary, 76 percent said that they trusted Putin "completely," "mostly," or "partly." Among those who said modernization was not necessary, only 61 percent trusted Putin (FOM, "Penta 15/2011" poll, *Sophist.hse.ru*).

Three tasks were central to the Kremlin's attempt to freeze society. First, it had to demobilize and intimidate the minority that had begun to act on new desires for political participation and responsive government. Second, it had to shake up the business/political elite, reminding those who in the previous decade had grown rich of their vulnerability. Third, with Russia sinking into stagnation, the Kremlin had to replace Putin's old appeal based on surging prosperity and progress with a new one based on national pride, traditional values, and a sense of external threat. In doing so, the authorities could exploit the polarization caused by the unevenness of value change in a rapidly developing society. Putin's team wagered that in the factories of the Urals and the small towns of Siberia, a Soviet-style conservatism survived that could be turned against the city hipsters and other more modernized strata.

To what extent did this counterattack succeed? On the surface, extremely well. A flood of punitive legislation, combined with a smear campaign against leading liberals, and a few politicized trials helped to scare protesters off the streets. The siloviki, set free to hunt, ramped up prosecutions for "extremism" and halted the decline in the number in jail (Paneyakh and Rosenberg, this volume). Business people and technocrats considered close to Medvedev—the figurehead of optimistic modernization—were forced to undergo a kind of vetting, as Putin's silovik friends breathed down their necks.[13] Moderates in the state-controlled media were edged out, and the tone on pro-Kremlin television grew more strident (Lipman, Kachkaeva, and Poyker, this volume). The rhetoric of Orthodox traditionalism and homophobia struck some chords with the public. But it was the Crimean intervention that finally reversed the previous slow slide in Putin's rating, driving it up above 80 percent.

While the new policies certainly reconsolidated power, the research in this book suggests the difficulty of sustaining this strategy. The Kremlin cannot completely abandon economic progress. It faces the challenge of promoting premodern values in a world of postmodern technologies. Development has not stopped. In some ways, it has been temporarily paused; in others, the previous trends in fact have continued.

For example, between 2011 and 2015 the proportion of Russians who used a personal computer every day rose from 36 to 53 percent, and the share logging on daily to the Internet rose from 32 percent in 2011 to 61 percent in

---

13. One businessman reportedly crawled across the floor of Putin's Kremlin office to show his subservience, to the president's amusement (Pavlovsky 2016).

late 2016.[14] The proportion of those employed who had higher education edged up from 30 percent in 2011 to 33 percent in 2015 (Rosstat 2016, p. 114). The number of foreign trips Russians took rose from 44 million in 2011 to 54 million in 2013, before falling back again.[15] Even as the collapsing ruble made such travel more expensive, it was trips to the former Soviet neighbors that suffered; Russians still traveled more to countries beyond the former USSR in 2015 than they had in 2011.

Civic activism has continued, despite the crackdown on nongovernmental organizations (NGOs). Since 2012, citizens have initiated more than five thousand petitions on the online platform Change.org—attracting 17 million signatures (Sobolev and Zakharov, this volume). More than 500,000 Russians signed one protesting the destruction of European food that had been smuggled into Russia after evading Putin's sanctions (*Moscow Times* 2015). Some NGOs organized petitions on their own websites. After 120,000 people signed one promoted by the World Wildlife Fund Russia (WWF Russia) demanding tougher legal penalties against oil spills, the Duma passed a law enacting such penalties in 2013.[16] Activism is found not just on the Internet. When one of Putin's friends, who had won the contract to collect road fees from truck drivers, introduced a new costly system, drivers from forty-three regions held a ten-day strike in protest (*Moscow Times* 2016). And in March 2017 tens of thousands of Russians attended anticorruption protests in ninety-nine cities and towns across the country (Higgins 2017).

At the same time, public opinion may not have moved as decisively toward reactionary nationalism as the immediate response to Crimea implied. In fact, the polling data for this period are mixed and contradictory, suggesting confusion and some discomfort about answering sincerely (Rogov and Ananyev, this volume). In January 2016 fewer Russians than in 2010 favored a political system resembling the current one or Western-style democracy, while very slightly more expressed a preference for the Soviet system (37 percent

14. Levada Center (2016, p. 171); FOM, "Internet v Rossii: Dinamika proniknovenia, zima 2016–2017 gg. [The Internet in Russia: Dynamics of penetration, winter 2016–2017]," http://fom.ru/SMI-i-internet/13300.

15. Data download from Rosstat (www.gks.ru/).

16. WWF Global, "Russian Seas Finally Protected by Robust Law against Oil Pollution," http://wwf.panda.org/wwf_news/?207193/Russian-seas-finally-protected-by-parliamentary-law.

compared to 34 percent in 2010). The big gainer was "don't know," chosen by 19 percent, up from 12 percent in 2010.[17] Yet, in answer to another question posed in November 2016, more Russians said that they would like to live in "a Western-style state with a market economy, democratic institutions, respect for human rights, but with its own character [*uklad*]" (33 percent) than favored "a state with its own unique institutions and path of development" (16 percent).[18] Paternalist expectations continued their decline: between 2011 and 2015, the share who thought the state should guarantee a decent standard of living dropped from 58 to 49 percent, while support for one that would just "enforce common rules of the game" rose from 34 to 41 percent (Levada Center 2016, p. 63).

Anti-Western sentiment soared after the annexation of Crimea, and more and more Russians expressed warm feelings toward Russia's new eastern partner, China (81 percent favorable in early 2015, up from 68 percent in 2011). Yet travel statistics tell a different story. The numbers of trips Russians made to the United States, the United Kingdom, Germany, and France were 42, 18, 16, and 36 percent higher, respectively, in 2014 than in 2011. Over the same years, the number of Russians traveling annually to China fell by half a million.

Interpreting the polls on sentiment toward the West—as well as approval of Putin—presents challenges. One possibility is that the surge in Putin's ratings reflects not a shift in opinion but a change in who agreed to be surveyed. Given relatively low participation rates, even a small increase in willingness to participate among pro-Putin, anti-Western nationalists—along with a decrease in willingness among pro-Western, Putin critics—could produce a large apparent change (Rogov and Ananyev, this volume). If that is the case—and it is difficult to test—then polls might be picking up a change in social cues rather than any real change in attitudes. At the same time, the appearance of broad popular agreement with Putin's agenda may be inflated by the Kremlin's strategic packaging of issues. By combining one issue with broad public resonance—discomfort with homosexuality—and others for which Russians have less enthusiasm—restrictions on civil

17. Levada Center, "Predpochtitelnye modeli ekonomicheskoy i politicheskoy system [Preferred models of the economic and political systems]," www.levada.ru /2016/02/17/predpochtitelnye-modeli-ekonomicheskoj-i-politicheskoj-sistem.
18. Levada Center, "Derzhavnost i osoby put Rossi [Great power status and Russia's special path]," www.levada.ru/2016/12/12/derzhavnost-i-osobyj-put-rossii.

rights—Putin's team created the illusion that Russians backed the whole program (Rogov and Ananyev, this volume).

In short, striking as the post-Crimea rally behind Putin and the surge in national pride have been, they may not signify a public rejection of Russia's previous advances toward globalized modernity. Although less visible than before, tension remains between, on the one hand, a population that has become more educated, Internet connected, international, and eager for responsive government and, on the other hand, a state whose leaders' main concern is to preserve an overwhelming concentration of power. Russia's regime is not a stabilized system. Rather, it has been in constant evolution since the early 1990s, and—for better or worse—that evolution is likely to continue.

INFORMATIONAL AUTOCRACY

That said, how can one best characterize how Russian politics works right now? Another theme emerging from the chapters is the Kremlin's preoccupation with flows of political information. Since soon after his first election, Putin has sought to control such flows. Indeed, he is an almost perfect example of what Sergei Guriev and I call an "informational autocrat" (Guriev and Treisman 2015).

The classic dictators of the twentieth century—whether totalitarians like Joseph Stalin and Mao Tse-tung, military strongmen like Augusto Pinochet and Alfredo Stroessner, or tyrants like Idi Amin and Mobutu Sese Seko—employed mass violence to intimidate the population, killing and imprisoning thousands of their compatriots. Often, they deliberately publicized their violence, staging show trials and public executions. Some indoctrinated citizens into holistic ideologies, demanding ritual demonstrations of loyalty. And most kept a tight—and quite open—grip on the press. Pinochet, for instance, upon taking power, posted military officers in all newsrooms to pre-vet "every item that went into print or on the air" (Knudson 2010, p. 116). The point was to control the population through terror, propaganda, and comprehensive censorship.

Guriev and I argue that Putin and certain other dictators—such as Hugo Chavez and Viktor Orban—are authoritarian leaders of a different, less violent and ideological type (Guriev and Treisman 2015). Even when lacking a commitment to democratic principles and only weakly constrained by institutions, "informational autocrats" recognize that violent repression in modern societies is costly and often counterproductive. Rather than killing and imprisoning thousands to inspire fear, they attempt to convince citizens that they are competent and benevolent leaders.[19]

Such dictators win the sincere support of many of their compatriots, but this support is based in part on the manipulation and distortion of information. Rather than nationalizing the media, they prefer to co-opt journalists and owners to cheerlead on the regime's behalf. When resources are scarce, they do increase censorship, but they usually try to conceal doing so, since competent and benevolent leaders have no need for such methods. Instead of comprehensive bans, they use targeted interventions and smear campaigns to discredit or disable anti-regime sources. When fighting civil wars or insurgencies, such dictators can be brutal (as Putin was in Chechnya). But, outside war zones, violent repression is a last resort since it, too, damages the leader's image.

Having sidelined critics and manufactured popular backing, such regimes can rule via superficially democratic institutions, earning additional credit from the naive. If the president's ratings are high, the president can submit to carefully managed elections without much risk. To sustain the dictator's popularity, the authorities must persuade citizens that any social or economic problems are caused by external enemies or domestic saboteurs rather than the incumbent's own incompetence or corruption. Like democracies, such regimes are preoccupied with opinion polls; however, they use them not to identify public demands to satisfy, but rather to check that their information manipulation is working.

This logic helps in understanding Putin's regime. Inheriting mostly democratic institutions and a relatively free press, he enacted few changes to formal institutions, but he progressively centralized power by recasting informal practice. During the early boom, Putin could dominate without much pressure. The rebounding economy—along with, initially, the fight against Chechen terror—brought him mass popularity, which, given the co-optation of the mass media, was not subjected to serious challenge. Violent repression—outside the Chechen war zone—was rare. As stagnation set in after the global financial crisis, and revenues grew scarcer, the regime moved—as "informational autocrats" do when resources dwindle—toward tighter censorship. The Kremlin also became more repressive toward its

19. Although there were some relatively nonviolent dictators in the past, and there remain some mass killers such as Kim Jong-un, Guriev and I argue that the balance has shifted toward the former (Guriev and Treisman 2015).

critics, but not toward the public at large, which it still hoped to win over with pro-regime propaganda and tales of external enemies.

The chapters that follow document this strategy. Within a few years of coming to power, Putin had established control over all news-reporting national television channels. At first, managing their broadcasts relied almost entirely on co-optation—media "friends" of the regime were happy to trade favors without any compulsion (Lipman, Kachkaeva, and Poyker, this volume). The soaring revenues of media companies during the economic boom enabled cooperative executives to become rich. Yet after Putin's return in 2012—and especially after the war in Ukraine—the methods hardened. The state media adopted a strident anti-Western tone, broadcasted faked news reports, and blocked critical voices almost completely. The remaining islands of independent media came under intense pressure.

The Kremlin's approach to the Internet shows an even starker evolution. Early on, Putin promised web entrepreneurs that he would "opt for freedom" over "excessive regulation," and for much of the next twelve years he did little to tighten controls (Nossik 2014). He may have underestimated the political importance of a medium he dismissed once as "fifty percent pornography" (Kremlin 2010). Things changed after the protests of 2011–12. Declaring the Internet to be a CIA project, Putin licensed the security services and their helpers in the Duma to devise intrusive technical controls and legal penalties to deter online opposition activity (Nossik 2014; Lipman, Kachkaeva, and Poyker, this volume). But the Federal Security Service (FSB) did not seem completely up to the task. It was civilian political consultants who recruited trolls to plant pro-Kremlin comments on blogs and websites. And the Internet companies were pressured to do the censoring themselves (Soldatov 2016).

Like other informational autocracies, Putin's regime invests heavily in opinion polls to monitor the success of its approach (Rogov and Ananyev, this volume). Sources differ on whether these polls ever affect policy decisions; they may, for instance, have persuaded Putin not to remove Vladimir Lenin's embalmed body from the Red Square mausoleum or to raise the retirement age—two unpopular proposals. But polls certainly provide diagnostics to the Kremlin on the effectiveness of its propaganda. "It is as if you have a sick person and you infect him with new viruses and take his temperature," one former official told me. "The thermometer reveals how the viruses are affecting him."[20]

20. Interview with Aleksei Chesnyakov, Moscow, January 2016.

RUSSIA'S TWO SYSTEMS

Several chapters point to a disconnect between two ways that Russian political decisions are made. A useful analogy comes from psychology. Daniel Kahneman argues in his book *Thinking, Fast and Slow* that the human mind operates in two modes or phases. "System 1" refers to the spontaneous and largely unconscious processes by which the brain draws conclusions and makes decisions based on instinct, practice, and routines. A realm of "freewheeling impulses and associations," it "operates automatically and quickly, with little or no effort and no sense of voluntary control." By contrast, "System 2" is "the conscious, reasoning self that has beliefs, makes choices, and decides what to think about and what to do." It monitors proceedings and intervenes episodically. "System 2 takes over when things get difficult, and it normally has the last word" (Kahneman 2011, pp. 21–25).

In similar fashion, one might think of Russian politics as having its own two systems. The first—"normal politics" or "autopilot"—prevails when Putin does not personally get involved. Such cases, which constitute the vast majority of more mundane state activity, are poorly captured by common images of Russia as a centralized dictatorship. In this system, outcomes are determined by an often vicious competition between bureaucratic factions, business actors, regional elites, and powerful individuals. The second system—"manual control" (*ruchnoe upravlenie*) occurs when Putin takes a clear stand. It involves a much more top-down dictation of actions—although the poor preparation of decisions and difficulties of implementation mean that the desired outcome is only sometimes achieved. Both systems involve corruption, power networks, and arbitrary and sometimes inhumane methods. Neither is particularly effective, although both can at times get results.[21]

The rules of "normal politics" are anything but clear and vary with the arena in which the battle occurs. Some are fought out in the Duma, where different actors may propose legislation, insert amendments, block and delay bills, or try to mobilize opposition to them with targeted leaks to the

---

21. This does not correspond to a more common distinction between formal and informal politics; both systems involve both formal and informal aspects. Nor does it correspond to what Richard Sakwa has called Russia's "dual state." For Sakwa (2010, p. 185), the tension is between "the constitutional state, regulated by law and enshrining the normative values of . . . liberal democracies" and an informal "administrative regime" that operates according to its own logic.

press (Noble and Schulmann, this volume). Other issues are fought out through the tortuous process of obtaining "sign-offs" (*soglasovania*) from the multiple bureaucratic principals whose agreement is required before a particular change can be made. Another arena is the media, in which powerful actors, including even top siloviki, float "trial balloons" or plant compromising—and sometimes untrue—stories to discredit their rivals (Lipman, Kachkaeva, and Poyker, this volume). To bring even more pressure, competitors enlist allies in the security agencies to prosecute and jail members of an opposed team. Although bargaining between factions does sometimes occur, the game is not primarily about negotiation. It is a cutthroat, zero-sum contest, in which no methods are ruled out.

Actors always have the option of invoking System 2—that is, appealing to Putin to intervene and decide the outcome. Sometimes they feel obliged to inform him and invite his guidance. But Putin may resent the intrusion or insist that the parties fight it out themselves, assuming all risk and leaving him free to enter later at a moment of his choice, on his terms. One desperate strategy is to appeal to Putin though the press—as his longtime FSB associate Viktor Cherkesov did in 2007, as he battled another silovik faction.[22] But this has never worked. In Cherkesov's case, Putin sharply criticized those who chose to air the regime's dirty laundry in public and demoted his old colleague.

"Manual control" is sometimes necessary to unblock lower-level deadlocks. When it works, it suggests the vitality and crucial importance of the country's top leader. During the global financial crisis, Putin appeared on television bullying industrialists into reopening shuttered plants in the depressed town of Pikalyovo and browbeating retailers about the price of sausages (Treisman 2011). But when it does *not* work—which is surprisingly often—it risks eroding Putin's image of authoritative and effective leadership. That may explain why Putin often rejects appeals to him to take a clear position (Ananyev, this volume). There may also be an element of social Darwinism in letting the bureaucrats and entrepreneurs compete among themselves.

Fear for his credibility may explain Putin's visible frustration at the failures of the bureaucracy to implement even decisions in which he has

---

22. In an article in the newspaper *Kommersant*, Cherkesov (2007) berated those security service members who had become "merchants" rather than "warriors" and warned that fighting among security service factions could undermine the country's stability.

invested his reputation. His occasional *cris de coeur* on this issue sound odd in the mouth of a purported dictator. It sometimes seemed, he remarked acidly in June 2013, that "some agencies live entirely in their own little world" and "look solely to their own narrow problems" (quoted in Monaghan 2014, p. 15). "Will you do your work or not?" he exploded at a meeting of ministers and governors of Far Eastern regions that July.[23]

Such frustration has led to a more informal approach to "manual control." Putin has increasingly taken to bypassing state agencies to rely on parastatal institutions and surrogates. His Russian National Front, created in 2011, is a kind of civil society appointed by the state, with responsibility for mobilizing pro-regime volunteers and criticizing the performance of regional governors. While ordering the Main Intelligence Directorate (GRU) special forces to conduct the military operation in Crimea, Putin enlisted everyone from Cossack vigilantes to the Night Wolves biker group to help out. Even when he uses formal structures, he seeks to hold individuals personally accountable for specific tasks, up to and including the threat of criminal charges.

Manual control went into overdrive in Putin's third term with his "May decrees," a series of orders in which the president committed himself very publicly to specific targets on everything from teachers' salaries to the mortality rate. Many were unrealistic, and the ensemble required fiscal resources many times greater than could plausibly be mobilized (Monaghan 2014). To keep the pressure on, Putin held regional governors personally responsible for their implementation and demanded regular reports on their progress. That may explain a noted increase in Putin's meetings with governors since 2012 (Petrov and Nazrullaeva, this volume).

Of course, neither autopilot nor manual control work well if the vehicle's engine is badly designed, corroded, and out of fuel. Pushing harder on the accelerator does not enable the car to travel faster than its potential or farther than the gasoline in its tank will carry it.

DEGENERATION

Another theme, already mentioned, concerns Putin's increasing tendency, when he does get involved, to opt for informal mechanisms. One should not exaggerate—the state, with its complex bureaucratic routines, has hardly

23. Kremlin (2013), quoted in Monaghan (2014, p. 16).

disappeared. But, more often than before, key decisions seem to be getting made and implemented outside official institutions.

Several types of evidence point in this direction. First, records show that Putin has been doing less of the public, formal things that presidents typically do to make and communicate decisions. After a burst of activity in 2012, he has been issuing fewer and fewer presidential decrees. In 2015 the number of these fell to the lowest level since at least 1994 (Ananyev, this volume; Remington 2014, p. 107). He also meets with the government or heads cabinet meetings far less frequently than in his first two presidential terms (Ananyev, this volume). His official schedule shows fewer meetings with law enforcement and security ministers, who are constitutionally subordinated directly to the president (Soldatov and Rochlitz, this volume). One presumes that more and more of the president's decisions are made in informal settings and encoded in secret decrees or unofficial instructions.

This practice fits with the already noted bypassing of state bodies in favor of non-state institutions and surrogates such as the Russian National Front. Another aspect is the increasing reliance on personal relationships and missions. Putin recruits freelancers—reportedly referred to inside the Kremlin as curators—to manage particular problem areas (Pavlovsky 2016). He lets the individuals assemble their own teams and then, in the president's name, demand assistance and obedience from others. All this is at the agents' risk; if they fail, they can be quietly discarded or even prosecuted for rules broken along the way.

Of course, U.S. presidents also sometimes appoint a "drug czar" or "regulatory czar" to oversee particular policy areas. But in Russia, such curators are informal, personal agents of Putin, with no oversight other than that of the Kremlin itself. The classic case—maybe the first—is that of Ramzan Kadyrov, the president of Chechnya, whom Putin gave virtually unlimited authority to impose stability in the republic. More recently, the businessman Konstantin Malofeev got the Kremlin's go-ahead to organize ultranationalist volunteers to help local insurgents in Donbass. Such use of freelancers may reflect frustration at the ineffectiveness of those with official responsibility. The FSB had failed to prevent—or apparently to predict— Viktor Yanukovych's fall and the events in Ukraine, and it lacked agents on the ground in Crimea (Soldatov and Rochlitz, this volume). So Putin turned to adventurous types who seemed better informed. In a bizarre twist, Putin appeared later to have authorized Malofeev to try his hand at devising Internet controls for the country. In April 2016 Malofeev hosted a meeting in

Moscow with China's "online tsar," Lu Wei, and its "master builder of the country's digital firewall," Fang Binxing, seeking help from the Chinese with filtering technology (Seddon 2016). Such a meeting could not have taken place without the Kremlin's backing. Meanwhile, journalists allege that one of the key organizers of the regime's Internet trolling is another freelancer, a restaurateur who has catered meals for Putin, called Yevgeny Prigozhin (Chen 2015).

When Putin does work through the official channels, he seems happy now to short-circuit the mechanisms, sacrificing expertise to speed. In 2012 he weakened the *soglasovania* system of obligatory sign-offs (Fortescue 2016, p. 430; Ananyev, this volume). In 2014, rather than address disagreements in the cabinet, the Kremlin pressured Prime Minister Medvedev to sign controversial legislation while the relevant ministers were out of town (Gaaze 2014; Fortescue 2016). In 2015 the practice of budgeting for three years at a time, a proud innovation of Putin's second term that had survived the global crisis of 2009, was suspended. And now, rather than let the government work out a budget based on broad priorities defined by the president, as in the past, Putin insists on being personally involved in all spending decisions (Hanson 2015).

In general, however, Putin appears to consult less with his ministers and outside experts. When, in his annual address to parliament in 2014 he unexpectedly announced a "total" financial amnesty, Finance Ministry officials reacted with confusion, wondering whether the president seriously meant to include the legalization of criminal money (Butrin and Visloguzov 2014). Other major decisions seem to have been sprung on the relevant ministers without forewarning.

The reluctance to consult may explain another pathology—an apparent narrowing and deterioration in the quality of information the president receives. Not only are silovik channels ascendant, but even within the security community the FSB has come to dominate the supply of information, unlike in the 1990s and early 2000s when several agencies provided independent reports (Soldatov and Rochlitz, this volume). In recent years, Putin has made a series of embarrassing public misstatements. In January 2016 he told the German newspaper *Bild* that Russia had "more than US$300 billion in gold reserves" as well as US$70 billion and US$80 billion in two government reserve funds. He was off by US$150 billion, as the newspaper *Moskovsky Komsomolets* quickly pointed out (Nemtsova 2016). Then in April Putin had to publicly apologize for falsely claiming that the German newspaper *Süddeutsche Zeitung* was owned by Goldman Sachs; he said that he had been misinformed by an aide (BBC 2016). In justifying Russian intervention in Ukraine, he claimed that Kharkov had been part of the tsarist province of Novorossiya (Kremlin 2014). It had not. After his annual press conference in April 2015, the website *Slon.ru* published a list of eleven inaccuracies in Putin's responses. Among these, he said that the foreign debt to be paid off during the rest of the year was US$60 billion, when in fact it was US$83 billion according to the Central Bank, and he claimed that it was necessary to build a new space station because only 5 percent of Russian territory was visible from the International Space Station. In fact, all Russian territory is visible from the station (Aybusinov 2016).

In part, this pattern resembles the deterioration that sets in when a single authoritarian leader has been in charge for a long time. Such leaders tend to exclude those who bring unwelcome news or views, thus eroding the quality of information and discussion, while simultaneously becoming overconfident in their own judgment.[24] But in part, the administrative mechanism is being undermined by Putin's efforts to improve it. His resorts to manual control and "curators" create confusion, undermine respect for formal procedures, and exacerbate bureaucrats' reluctance to take on responsibility themselves (Stanovaya 2014). They encourage similar manual control and rule bending by governors in the regions. No one quite knows who has the president's special authorization and for what. The constant sense of urgency and the injection of siloviki into civilian policy lead to a contradictory mix of rash decisions and defensive inactivity.

LOOKING AHEAD

To summarize, the Putin order is neither a reprise of the Soviet model nor a security service state. Its leaders are neither single-minded kleptocrats nor hostages to a culture of informal networks. Its institutions do not match

---

24. Erica Frantz and Natasha Ezrow (2009) provide evidence that personalist dictators who control the composition of their advisory group tend to select incompetents and "yes-men" and so suffer from poor intelligence. Historians have noted numerous cases of authoritarian regimes that fell victim to the informational filters they had unwittingly created. Nicaragua's Sandinista party cadres "filtered out the negative from their reports" (Guillermoprieto 1990, p. 89). In Zambia, Kenneth Kaunda "surrounded himself with conmen" (Dowden 1991, p. 23). Venezuela's dictator Marcos Pérez Jiménez "closed his ears and depended for advice on sycophants and third-rate generals" (Burggraaff 1972, p. 157).

the picture that scholars have developed of "competitive authoritarianism." Russia has a regime forged by modernization, whose top officials now seek to reverse the social consequences of development. It is an informational autocracy, in which a ruler aims to concentrate power and secure compliance, but mostly by manipulating information flows and disabling actual and potential challengers rather than through large-scale violent repression. At the same time, it is a political order that operates in two modes: a no-holds-barred contest among rival bureaucratic, business, and other elite actors, fought out in parliament, media, ministries, and the courts, and a pantomime of vertical subordination, which appears when the president steps in to "take charge." It is a state governed by highly formal bureaucratic norms and procedures, some of which resemble those of Soviet times, and which are being eroded by both the clashing interests of "normal politics" and the arbitrary intrusions of a leader who seems increasingly impatient and often misinformed.

The current arrangement is not a stable system—it represents a balance between two forces: the transformational social impact of modernization and the attempt by the Kremlin to enlist modern media and technology to preserve an archaic structure of power. While predicting the timing of crises for such regimes is impossible, no one should be surprised when one occurs. The research in the chapters that follow provides some hints about what form change might take. Of course, the direction would depend on the nature of the transition and on the personality, values, education, and background of the leader who ended up in charge. But one can still distinguish those aspects of the current political scene that are likely to remain important from those that are more fortuitous.

A first point, noted already, is that modernization has stalled but not stopped. Public opinion, although favoring strong leadership and rallying behind Putin after the annexation of Crimea, is less supportive of authoritarian aspects of the current system than might appear. Demands were growing for greater openness, honesty in government, and space for local initiative when Putin's 2012 counterattack struck. Such demands remain just under the surface. Indeed, sustaining the appearance of unity around a program of anti-Westernism and conservative values requires a great deal of work by the media and a continual invention of foreign threats, with costs to the business climate and a constant risk of escalation. Pressure will remain—especially in the event of leader or regime change—for a more open and modern style of government.

The vector before Putin's return was toward not just greater moderniza-tion and openness but also decentralization. Demand for authentic political processes at the local and regional level was growing. Between 2004 and 2010, about 60 percent of respondents favored direct elections of governors, compared to 20 percent who opposed them, which explains Putin's conces-sion on this score, bringing elections back, amid the 2011 protests (Rogov and Ananyev, this volume).[25] Any major political change is likely to be ac-companied by further decentralization, whether deliberate or spontaneous.

On foreign policy, public opinion currently owes much to a media cam-paign that has simultaneously swelled pride in Russia's military might, sown fear, and fanned resentments. These resentments are real and long-standing, but, despite them, Russians have shown a remarkably consistent desire to improve relations with the West, except during relatively brief periods of international tension. As late as May 2013, 71 percent favored "strengthening mutually beneficial ties with Western countries," compared to 16 percent who wanted to "distance [Russia] from the West" (Levada Center 2016, p. 252). Even after the recent barrage of anti-Western television program-ming, 75 percent of Russians in November 2015 thought the country should "improve relations with the USA and other Western countries" (Levada Center 2016, p. 252). There also seems to be a growing desire to define Crimea as a special case. In March 2014, as Russia annexed the peninsula, 58 percent of Russians insisted that their country "had the right" to annex neighboring territories to defend ethnic Russians. By March 2015 that sta-tistic had fallen to 34 percent. At that point, a plurality of 47 percent said that Russia did not have a general *right* to take such actions but that "in the case of the annexation of Crimea Russia [was] behaving decently and law-fully, in accordance with norms of international law" (Levada Center 2016, p. 211). This evolution suggests a disinclination for more adventures, al-though it does not mean that Russians intend to apologize for past ones.

The media—except for small islands of relative independence—have been turned into an instrument of the regime (Lipman, Kachkaeva, and Poyker, this volume). This transformation relied almost entirely on co-optation rather than compulsion. After changes in ownership, new loyal pro-prietors could be rewarded with revenues as markets surged, and employees

25. Of course, this retreat was tactical and changed little in the actual practice of Kremlin control of governors. And the Kremlin has since sought to limit mayoral elections.

could be kept in line with straightforward career incentives. Were political control—along with state subsidies and protections—to weaken, it is easy to imagine media companies changing into primarily profit-seeking businesses. Greater competition and diversity would likely emerge, as entrepreneurs both international and domestic sought to capture part of the multibillion-dollar advertising market.

In business more generally, those favored by the regime would fight to keep their monopolies in the event of political change. But they would be outnumbered by those entrepreneurs and companies that were previously excluded along with those that stayed loyal out of necessity but without enthusiasm. Leader change would prompt a furious contest over the reassignment of rents. Whether that would generate more market competition would depend on the strategy and power of the new leader to enforce market restrictions and on the number and relative lobbying power of the various business groups. At the least, it would break open current arrangements.

Our research suggests at least some desire among judges for a more humane approach to sentencing and reforms to reduce the conveyor-belt-like quality of court proceedings (Paneyakh and Rosenberg, this volume). Of course, those privileged at present would fight to retain their privileges. But, for the most part, judges appear to operate the way they do, not out of choice, but to survive within a system they cannot alter.

These factors point to a Russia, after the next round of political change, with a more modern, open, and decentralized political system and a freer media, a Russia not necessarily friendly toward the West but certainly less hostile. Some other factors are less encouraging. The law enforcement bureaucracies and security services have successfully resisted reform for twenty-five years. They continue to operate in part on the basis of Soviet-era procedures that create perverse incentives. In the event of political change, both leaders and rank-and-file officers are likely to fight to protect their positions and continued access to rents.

Another problem that is unlikely to disappear or improve spontaneously is the situation in the North Caucasus. In any transition, President Kadyrov of Chechnya would be motivated to protect and perhaps increase his power and central leverage. He has demonstrated the ability to deploy thousands of battle-hardened fighters to Ukraine and to stage violent special operations in Russia and abroad. His agents already operate in Moscow and elsewhere in the Russian Federation. A new regime, should transition occur, would face the threat that such an independent and powerful force represents.

Is some transition around the corner? Of course, we cannot say. The record of experts in making such predictions is uninspiring (Tetlock 2009). Putin's ability to maintain control through the hard times that followed the global financial crisis suggests that one should not underestimate his survival skills. Still, the problem is getting harder, while the Kremlin machinery has been gradually degenerating in the ways noted. Gratitude for Crimea will not buy support forever from a society that has continued to evolve, despite efforts to freeze it under a layer of Orthodox conservatism. Internationally, Russia's hopes of coming out of isolation seem remote, as of 2017, amid the Western furor over Moscow-directed election hacking. So far, Putin's team has always managed to figure out what changes are necessary to ensure that things will stay the same. The coming years will reveal whether they still have this ability.

REFERENCES

Aybusinov, Syrlybay. 2016. "Proverka rechi: Odinadtsat netochnostey v otvetakh Putina [Checking the speech: Eleven inaccuracies in Putin's answers]." *Slon.ru*, April 17.

BBC. 2016. "Panama Papers: Putin Sorry for Suddeutsche Zeitung Error." April 15. www.bbc.com/news/world-europe-36053524.

Bell, Daniel. 1973. *The Coming of Post-Industrial Society*. New York: Basic Books.

Boix, Carles, and Milan W. Svolik. 2013. "The Foundations of Limited Authoritarian Government: Institutions, Commitment, and Power-Sharing in Dictatorships." *Journal of Politics* 75, no. 2, pp. 300–16.

Burggraaff, Winfield. 1972. *The Venezuelan Armed Forces in Politics, 1935–1959*. University of Missouri Press.

Butrin, Dmitri, and Vadim Visloguzov. 2014. "Seans voprosov na otvetu [Question-and-answer session]." *Kommersant*, December 10. www.kommersant.ru/doc /2629730.

Chen, Adrian. 2015. "The Agency." *New York Times Magazine*, June 2.

Cherkesov, Viktor. 2007. "Nelzya dopustit, chtoby voiny prevratilis v torgovtsev [We cannot allow warriors to turn into merchants]." *Kommersant*, October 9.

Dawisha, Karen. 2015. *Putin's Kleptocracy: Who Owns Russia?* New York: Simon and Schuster.

Dowden, Richard. 1991. "Profile: The Man Who Was Zambia; Through 27 Years, Kenneth Kaunda Spoke for Black Africa; Last Week's Vote May Mean His Africa Has Had Its Day." *The Independent*, November 3, p. 23.

Duarte, Esteban, and Henry Meyer. 2015. "Putin Allies Aided Russian Mafia in Spain, Prosecutors Say." *Bloomberg*, June 29. www.bloomberg.com/news/articles/2015 -06-29/putin-allies-aided-russian-mafia-in-spain-prosecutors-say.

Fortescue, Stephen. 2016. "Russia's 'Turn to the East': A Study in Policy Making." *Post-Soviet Affairs*, 32, no. 5, pp. 423–54. doi:10.1080/1060586X.2015.1051750.

Frantz, Erica, and Natasha Ezrow. 2009. "'Yes Men' and the Likelihood of Foreign Policy Mistakes across Dictatorships." Paper prepared for presentation at the Annual Meeting of the American Political Science Association, Toronto, September 3–6.

Gaaze, Konstantin. 2014. "Poker dlya odnogo [Poker for one]." *New Times*, September 24.

Gandhi, Jennifer, and Adam Przeworski. 2006. "Cooperation, Cooptation, and Rebellion under Dictatorships." *Economics and Politics* 18, no. 1, pp. 1–26.

Gessen, Masha. 2012. *The Man without a Face: The Unlikely Rise of Vladimir Putin*. New York: Riverhead Books.

Guillermoprieto, Alma. 1990. "Letter from Managua." *New Yorker*, March 26, 83–93.

Guriev, Sergei, and Daniel Treisman. 2015. "How Modern Dictators Survive: An Informational Theory of the New Authoritarianism." Working Paper 21136. Cambridge, Mass.: National Bureau of Economic Research.

Hanson, Philip. 2015. *Putin Adds the Budget to His Growing Portfolio*. London: Royal Institute of International Affairs. www.chathamhouse.org/expert/comment/putin-adds-budget-his-growing-portfolio.

Higgins, Andrew. 2017. "Aleksei Navalny, Top Putin Critic, Arrested as Protests Flare in Russia." *New York Times*, March 26.

IMF (International Monetary Fund). 2014. *Financial Access Survey*. Washington, D.C. http://data.imf.org/?sk=E5DCAB7E-A5CA-4892-A6EA-598B5463A34C.

Inglehart, Ronald, and Wayne E. Baker. 2000. "Modernization, Cultural Change, and the Persistence of Traditional Values." *American Sociological Review*, 65, no. 1, pp. 19–51.

Inglehart, Ronald, and Christian Welzel. 2009. "How Development Leads to Democracy: What We Know about Modernization." *Foreign Affairs*, March–April, pp. 33–49.

Kahneman, Daniel. 2011. *Thinking, Fast and Slow*. New York: Farrar, Straus and Giroux.

Knudson, Jerry W. 2010. *Roots of Revolution: The Press and Social Change in Latin America*. Lanham, Md.: University Press of America.

Kramer, Andrew. 2013. "Malls Blossom in Russia, with a Middle Class." *New York Times*, January 1.

Kremlin. 2010. "Stenografichesky otchet o zasedanii Gosudarstvennogo soveta po voprosam razvitia politicheskoy sistemy Rossii [Speech at State Council meeting on developing Russia's political system]." *Kremlin.ru*, January 22. http://kremlin.ru/events/president/transcripts/6693.

———. 2013. "Stenograficheskii otchet o soveshchanii o kompleksnom sotsialno-ekonomicheskom razvitii Sakhalinskoy oblasti [Transcript of the meeting on the comprehensive socioeconomic development of Sakhalin region]." *Kremlin.ru*, July 16. www.kremlin.ru/transcripts/18824.

————. 2014. "Pramaya linia s Vladimirom Putinym [Direct line with Vladimir Putin]." *Kremlin.ru*, April 17. www.kremlin.ru/events/president/news/20796.

Kryshtanovskaya, Olga, and Stephen White. 2003. "Putin's Militocracy." *Post-Soviet Affairs* 19, no. 4, pp. 289–306.

————. 2009. "The Sovietization of Russian Politics." *Post-Soviet Affairs* 25, no. 4, pp. 283–309.

Ledeneva, Alena V. 2013. *Can Russia Modernise?* Sistema, *Power Networks, and Informal Governance*. Cambridge University Press.

Levada Center. 2016. *Obshchestvennoe mnenie 2015* [Public Opinion 2015]. Moscow.

Levitsky, Steven, and Lucan A. Way. 2010. *Competitive Authoritarianism: Hybrid Regimes after the Cold War*. Cambridge University Press.

Magaloni, Beatriz. 2006. *Voting for Autocracy: Hegemonic Party Survival and Its Demise in Mexico*. Cambridge University Press.

Minchenko, Yevgeny. 2013. "Doklad 'Politbu101 2.0' nakanune perezagruzki elitnykh grup [Report 'Politburo 2.0' on the eve of the rebooting of elite groups]." *Kommersant*, January 21. www.kommersant.ru/doc/2110141.

Monaghan, Andrew. 2014. *Defibrillating the* Vertikal? *Putin and Russian Grand Strategy*. London: Royal Institute of International Affairs.

Moscow Times. 2015. "Russians Protest Destruction of Banned Food Imports." October 11. http://themoscowtimes.com/news/russians-protest-destruction-of-banned -food-imports-50184.

————. 2016. "Russian Truck Drivers Strike for 10 Days against Platon Tax System." February 22. http://themoscowtimes.com/articles/russian-truck-drivers -strike-for-10-days-against-platon-tax-system-51905.

Nemtsova, Anna. 2016. "While Russia's Economy Crumbles, Putin's in Wonderland." *Daily Beast*, January 14. www.thedailybeast.com/while-russias-economy -crumbles-putins-in-wonderland.

Nossik, Anton. 2014. "Russia's First Blogger Reacts to Putin's Internet Crackdown." *New Republic*, May 15. http://newrepublic.com/article/117771/putins-internet -crackdown-russias-first-blogger-reacts.

Pavlovsky, Gleb. 2016. "Russian Politics under Putin: The System Will Outlast the Master." *Foreign Affairs*, May–June, pp. 10–17.

Petrov, Nikolay. 2002. "Seven Faces of Putin's Russia: Federal Districts and the New Level of State-Territorial Composition." *Security Dialogue* 33, no. 1, pp. 73–91.

Remington, Thomas. 2014. *Presidential Decrees in Russia: A Comparative Perspective*. Cambridge University Press.

Rivera, David W., and Sharon Werning Rivera. 2014. "Is Russia a Militocracy? Conceptual Issues and Extant Findings regarding Elite Militarization." *Post-Soviet Affairs* 30, no. 1, pp. 27–50.

Rosstat. 2003a. *Trud i zanyatost v Rossii* [Labor and employment in Russia]. Moscow.

————. 2003b. *Turizm v tsifrakh* [Tourism in figures]. Moscow.

————. 2013a. *Trud i zanyatost v Rossii* [Labor and employment in Russia]. Moscow.

———. 2013b. *Turizm v tsifrakh* [Tourism in figures]. Moscow.

———. 2016. *Rossiisky statistichesky yezhegodnik* [Russian statistical yearbook]. Moscow: Rosstat.

Sakwa, Richard. 2010. "The Dual State in Russia." *Post-Soviet Affairs* 26, no. 3, pp. 185–206.

Seddon, Max. 2016. "Russia's Chief Internet Censor Enlists China's Know-How." *Financial Times*, April 26.

Shevtsova, Lilia. 2014. "Putin's Attempt to Recreate the Soviet Empire Is Futile." *Financial Times*, January 7.

Soldatov, Andrei. 2016. "Once a Defender of Internet Freedom, Putin Is Now Bringing China's Great Firewall to Russia." *Huffington Post*, May 3. www.huff ingtonpost.com/andrei-soldatov/putin-china-internet-firewall-russia_b _982119o.html.

Stanovaya, Tatyana. 2014. "Poslanie prezidenta: Ozhidania i realnost [The President's message: Expectations and reality]." *Politkom.ru*, December 8. http://politcom.ru /18387.html.

Tetlock, Philip. 2009. *Expert Political Judgment: How Good Is It? How Can We Know?* Princeton University Press.

Treisman, Daniel. 2008. "Putin's Silovarchs." *Orbis* 51, no. 1, pp. 141–53.

———. 2011. *The Return: Russia's Journey from Gorbachev to Medvedev.* New York: Free Press.

———. 2014. "Putin's Popularity since 2010: Why Did Support for the Kremlin Plunge, Then Stabilize?" *Post-Soviet Affairs* 30, no. 5, pp. 370–88.

Trochev, Alexei. 2012. "Suing Russia at Home." *Problems of Post-Communism* 59, no. 5, pp. 18–34.

World Bank. 2016. *World Development Indicators.* Washington, D.C.

World Values Survey. 2016. www.worldvaluessurvey.org/WVSOnline.jsp.

TWO

Inside the Kremlin

The Presidency and Executive Branch

MAXIM ANANYEV

W hen the Western media talk about Russia's government, they talk about Vladimir Putin. Journalists and political commentators usually take for granted that understanding the country's political order must involve the analysis of Putin's psychology. The United States–based NPR, CNN, and Fox News and the United Kingdom–based *Daily Telegraph* have all run stories on "what's inside Putin's mind?"—and whether that mind can be changed (NPR 2014; Gingrich 2014; Ablow 2014; Robertson 2015). This preoccupation with Putin's thinking is understandable given that political scientists often classify Russia as a personalist autocracy, in which key decisions cannot be predicted from institutions and procedures (see, for example, Geddes, Wright, and Frantz 2014). Such decisions, it is said, reflect personal calculations that are impenetrable to an outside observer.

Another common image of Russia concerns the "siloviki"—current and former military, law enforcement, and security service agents. In 2003 *New York Times* columnist William Safire proclaimed unequivocally that "Russia today is ruled by Vladimir Putin's siloviki" (Safire 2003). In 2007 Radio Free Europe's Victor Yasmann expressed a similar view: "Virtually all key positions in Russian political life—in government and the economy—are controlled by the so-called 'siloviki'" (Yasmann 2007). Meanwhile, London-based *The Economist*, quoting the Russian analyst Olga Kryshtanovskaya, wrote that "all important decisions in Russia . . . are now taken by a tiny group of men who served alongside Mr Putin in the KGB [State Security Committee]" (*The Economist* 2007).

Along with Putin and his security service friends, Russia's constitution is sometimes blamed for the failure of post-Soviet democratic consolidation. This constitution, enacted in 1993, gives significant powers to the president at the expense of the parliament. Scholars argue that such imbalances in the country's basic law enabled Putin to dominate the legislative and judicial branches. According to political scientists Lilia Shevtsova and Mark H. Eckert, "Mechanisms creating checks and balances to the presidency were deliberately weakened or simply rejected" (Shevtsova and Eckert 2000, p. 33).

Are these views accurate? Accounts of how the Russian executive branch operates are hard to verify because the process is anything but transparent. Data are scarce and rarely reliable. Even officials who served in the administration at the same time sometimes have radically different understandings of how things work. So any attempt to reconstruct the decisionmaking process in the Kremlin is inevitably tentative and incomplete.

Nevertheless, based on a close examination of available data as well as interviews with a number of former Kremlin insiders, some conclusions are possible. After briefly reviewing the recent evolution of Russia's executive branch, I examine the arguments already mentioned. Did Russia's "super-presidential" constitution doom it to autocracy? Is the country governed by a clique of security service veterans? Does Putin personally make all decisions on domestic policy? The answer to all these questions seems to be a qualified no. In fact, changes in de facto political power have had little to do with changes in formal institutions; the political role of the siloviki is more limited than sometimes thought; and the process of decisionmaking is messier and more complicated than is consistent with a view of Putin as the source of all policies.

THE EVOLVING EXECUTIVE

Russia's current constitution was adopted in a referendum held in December 1993, after a violent clash between the president and the parliament. Emerging victorious from this confrontation, President Boris Yeltsin used

Table 2-1. *Presidents and Prime Ministers*

President	Prime minister	Time in office
Boris Yeltsin	Yegor Gaidar	June 1992–December 1992
	Victor Chernomyrdin	December 1992–March 1998
	Sergei Kirienko	March 1998–August 1998
	Yevgeni Primakov	September 1998–May 1999
	Sergei Stepashin	May 1999–August 1999
	Vladimir Putin	August 1999–May 2000
Vladimir Putin	Mikhail Kasyanov	May 2000–February 2004
	Mikhail Fradkov	March 2004–September 2007
	Victor Zubkov	September 2007–May 2008
Dmitry Medvedev	Vladimir Putin	May 2008–May 2012
Vladimir Putin	Dmitry Medvedev	May 2012–

Sources: Lenta.ru; Kodeks (database of legislation and presidential decrees).

the opportunity to rewrite the country's fundamental law to weaken the legislature and strengthen his own position. The constitution was amended in 2008 to lengthen the president's term (from four to six years) and that of the parliament (from four to five years).

Table 2-1 lists all the Russian presidents and prime ministers (except heads of short, caretaker administrations) since 1992. The governments of Yegor Gaidar (1992) and Victor Chernomyrdin (1992–98) are associated with reforms that transformed the Soviet state-run economy into an albeit imperfect market system.[1] In the first five years of Yeltsin's presidency, the state stopped setting prices on most goods, liberalized trade and capital flows, created a national currency, fought inflation, and privatized a large proportion of the country's enterprises. Yeltsin's governments managed to implement these policies, even though regional leaders were defying Moscow's authority and the parliament was from 1995 on dominated by the Communists and other opposition parties.

With Putin's election to the presidency in 2000, the situation began to change.[2] Putin's first term saw the strengthening of the executive branch and the weakening of other political players. The parliament became more

1. See, for example, Shleifer and Treisman (2000) and Aslund (2007) for a detailed description of the first decade of post-Soviet Russia.

2. For more detail on this period, see Baker and Glasser (2005); Taylor (2011); Treisman (2012); Roxburgh (2013); Gel'man (2015); Myers (2015).

docile after the pro-Putin political bloc Unity, which had come a close second to the Communists in the 1999 election, merged with another bloc to form United Russia, thus forging a pro-Putin majority. Pro-Putin parties and candidates went on to win a majority of the seats in the 2003, 2007, 2011, and 2016 elections. Regional governors were weakened in three steps. Putin first created a new institution of presidential envoy to monitor them; he then stripped them of their seats in the parliament's upper chamber and of the associated parliamentary immunity; and finally, in 2004, he abolished gubernatorial elections.

Putin continued consolidating power in his second term, which began in 2004. A fiscal reform in 2004–05 gave the federal government the lion's share of tax revenue. Previously, the regions had retained about half of regional tax receipts, but now the value added tax and the tax on natural resources were reallocated entirely to the center. As a result, the federal share of total revenues surged from 48 percent in 1999 to 62 percent in 2007.

What enabled Putin's governments to recentralize in this way and marginalize other political players that had blocked many decisions of Yeltsin's governments? At least two explanations are possible. First, soaring oil prices helped Putin to stabilize the macroeconomy early in his tenure and provided the revenues needed for the Kremlin to rebuild vertical authority. Under Yeltsin, members of the federal tax service and other enforcement agencies had come to depend on the regional governments for housing subsidies, salary supplements, and other benefits (Shleifer and Treisman 2000). After Putin took office, federal funding of the enforcement agencies rose, boosting the salaries of their employees: from 1999 to 2007, spending on law enforcement and national defense increased from 190 billion rubles (about US$7 billion) to more than 1.6 trillion rubles (US$65 billion).[3] As the central authorities' economic leverage over the enforcement bureaucracies grew, this helped to ensure the loyalty of regional governors and businesses.

A related explanation concerns the leader's popularity. Political scientist Daniel Treisman argues that in Russia the power of the president rises and falls with the president's approval ratings, which are, in turn, driven largely by economic performance (Treisman 2011). Yeltsin, unpopular during most

---

3. National State Statistics Committee (2002). The dollar value is calculated using the official exchange rate on December 31, 1999: US$1.00 = 27.00 rubles. National State Statistics Committee (2010). The dollar value is calculated using the official exchange rate on December 31, 2007: US$1.00 = 24.50 rubles.

of his rule, faced an obstructionist parliament, governors, and business leaders. However, in 1991, at the peak of his popularity, he achieved striking results—such as winning the endorsement of parliament for the dissolution of the Soviet Union and for his plan for radical economic reform. As his approval tanked, so did his ability to enact and implement policies. For Putin, too, although his rating has never fallen very low, the same logic applies. As his approval soared, governors, deputies, and business leaders all pledged loyalty and did little to oppose initiatives that reduced their powers and resources.

Of course, the president's rating is itself influenced by the president's domination of politics. But it is also affected by other things. Putin's initial surge in popularity represented a rally behind him as he sent troops into Chechnya amid a wave of shocking terrorist attacks. Later, his popularity was boosted by the economic recovery. A president's rating can serve as a coordination device for any political opponents. When it is high, defection is dangerous as the government can mobilize its supporters to exclude or punish the disloyal. This logic creates a positive feedback loop—the rating goes up when the government succeeds in marginalizing the opposition, and a high rating ensures that the opposition stays marginalized. The mechanism can also work in the opposite direction, as Yeltsin learned, to his chagrin: a declining rating triggers elite defection. Thus, maintaining high approval is important for political survival.

Within the executive branch, one other player is important: the Presidential Administration (PA). This body, which started as a relatively low-key group of presidential aides, grew into a major institution, especially in the Putin era. Its main task is to oversee the enactment and implementation of presidential decrees, as well as arranging the president's schedule, correspondence, and official activities. Besides these functions, it is the command center from which the Kremlin manages politics at all levels.

Already in 1999, it was shrewd operatives in the PA such as Igor Shabdurasulov and Vladislav Surkov who, together with the politically connected entrepreneur Boris Berezovsky and political consultant Gleb Pavlovsky, created the new pro-Putin political party, Unity (Zhegulev and Romanova 2012). Then, in 2007, PA officials formed the loyal "opposition" party Just Russia out of three small parties—one nationalist, one representing pensioners, and one with obscure positions (Sestanovich 2007; March 2009). While positioning itself to the left of United Russia, Just Russia voted reliably with the government on key issues.

The PA also set about controlling previously independent parties. According to Russia's leading business daily, *Vedomosti*, it demanded in 2007 that all electoral party lists be preapproved by the Kremlin, and PA officials have occasionally told the parties to remove particular candidates (*Vedomosti* 2007). Many experts agree that it is almost impossible to participate in Russian elections without the PA's informal sanction.

A SUPER-PRESIDENTIAL CONSTITUTION?

Is Russia's constitution "presidential," "super-presidential," or "semi-presidential"? On this, analysts of Russian politics disagree. In simple terms, the question is whether the formal powers of the presidency overshadow those of the legislative branch so decisively as to render the former institution dominant.

In some respects, the Russian constitution certainly does seem super-presidential. First, the president can rule by decree, and his decrees are "obligatory for fulfillment." The constitution does not define the scope of permissible decrees, except to say that they must be consistent with the constitution itself and Russian federal laws. This gives the president an opportunity to govern bypassing the parliament, at least on issues on which existing law is silent. If the parliament wishes to override presidential decrees, this requires a two-thirds majority of the votes. Next, it is the president, not the parliament, who appoints the prime minister, subject to the parliament's confirmation. While the parliament may refuse to confirm the president's candidate, if it does so three times in a row, then the parliament is dissolved and new elections are called. Therefore, the price for such parliamentary defiance is quite high.

Nevertheless, one might argue that the balance of power is not tilted as much as it might seem. For one thing, the parliament still has the power of the purse: the annual budget must be confirmed by the parliamentary majority. In practice, the only major clash between the president and the parliament under this constitution occurred in 1998, when the parliament rejected President Yeltsin's nominee for the post of prime minister, Victor Chernomyrdin. In this case, despite the possible cost for the parliament, it was the president who retreated and chose an alternative who was more acceptable to the Communist-dominated legislature, the left-leaning apparatchik Yevgeni Primakov.

Whether or not Russia's constitution gives excessive power to the president, this does not seem to be what explains the authoritarian character of the current regime. After all, the constitution remained unchanged from 1993 to 2008, yet the political system worked in radically different ways during different phases of this period. In the late 1990s, this constitution was consistent with a situation in which the president could accomplish almost nothing because of opposition in the Duma and operated in constant fear of impeachment. Then, after 1999, the same constitution did not prevent the incumbent president from enacting major reforms and consolidating his de facto power, eliminating in practice almost all checks and balances. Moreover, most such changes in the president's de facto power occurred at moments when there was no change in the constitution or any other aspect of formal institutions.

For example, regional elites were extremely powerful in the early 1990s. Some governors declared autonomy from Moscow, and many asserted rights that the center did not recognize. Many successfully lobbied the federal government for subsidies, while helping local enterprises evade taxes (Treisman 2001). Some even threatened to introduce their own local currencies.[4] Curiously, most of the governors in this period—even some of the most assertive and rebellious ones—were Yeltsin appointees. On paper, they should have been subordinate and docile, or so the formal institutions would suggest. They were not.

This situation reversed under Putin, who restored Kremlin dominance over regional governors and legislatures. Again, this had little to do with formal rules. Of course, in the fall of 2004, Putin did abolish gubernatorial elections—a change in the institutions. But the governors had been tamed much earlier. In fact, it was the strong performance of the pro-Putin political bloc, Unity, in the 1999 election and Putin's soaring popularity that, almost immediately, prompted a bandwagon of governors to declare loyalty to him. If any other factor was important, it was the threatened and actual use of the security services and law enforcement to prosecute governors for corruption.

The same pattern—de facto changes first, followed by change in formal rules—appeared in other political arenas as well. In legislative politics, the pro-Putin party, United Russia, first won a crushing victory in the 2003

4. See, for example, the history of the Ural franc in RBC (2015).

election, garnering two-thirds of the seats. Only then were the electoral rules rewritten to make it harder for the opposition: single-member districts were abolished in favor of pure proportional representation, and the threshold for representation was raised from 5 to 7 percent.[5] An amendment to the constitution came in 2008, when the length of the presidential term was extended from four to six years. Yet this came after all other political players had been marginalized and Putin's handpicked temporary replacement, Dmitry Medvedev, had been elected with more than 70 percent of the vote. Of course, such changes clearly strengthened the presidency, but they were possible precisely because the presidency had already become stronger. And they could be reversed in similar fashion were the de facto power of the presidency to weaken.

A SECURITY SERVICE STATE?

Is Russia ruled by the siloviki? This claim can be interpreted in two ways. It might mean that certain individuals with a background in the military or security services have a disproportionate informal influence on President Putin. Or it might mean that the siloviki have taken up a commanding position within key institutions—the government, the PA, and other state bodies. Scholars and commentators often use these interpretations interchangeably.

The first interpretation—informal influence over Putin—has some credibility (see Soldatov and Rochlitz, this volume). Many of Putin's reported confidants have been veterans of the Soviet KGB, such as his former chief of staff, Sergei Ivanov, and the head of the Security Council, Nikolai Patrushev. Indeed, the Security Council is a bastion of top siloviki. For many years, Putin has been meeting with it almost every week.

That security professionals would advise Putin on security is not surprising. Yet on other topics—economics, for instance—their influence is less clear. Especially in his early years, Putin listened to the counsel of a few trusted technocrats on economic matters. The tax reforms of 2001–04 had been prepared by Yegor Gaidar and his colleagues. The idea to create a "sta-

---

5. Political scientists often consider proportional representation more favorable for small parties. The measures in this package of reforms, however, made it harder for small parties to run in the first place. In addition to raising the threshold, burdensome registration requirements were imposed and pre-electoral coalitions were banned in federal elections.

bilization fund" in which to save windfall oil revenues was lobbied insistently by Putin's economic adviser Andrei Illarionov. The fund, created in 2003–04, survived long after Illarionov left the administration. When in 2015 Putin's old friend and silovik colleague Igor Sechin lobbied to have money from this fund transferred to the struggling state-owned oil company Rosneft, Putin refused (BBC 2015).[6]

When asked who has Putin's ear on economic matters today, former Kremlin officials I interviewed mentioned Andrei Belousov, Putin's current economic aide.[7] Belousov, a former head of a macroeconomic think tank, has no reported ties to any of the security agencies.

Even on matters of national defense, Putin sometimes turns to outsiders. In 2007 he surprised many observers by appointing as minister of defense Anatoly Serdyukov, a former furniture salesman and tax official with no military experience besides his two-year mandatory service. Apparently, Putin sought someone independent to implement a far-reaching reform— downsizing the army, modernizing its equipment, and reining in the widespread abuse of recruits. Although Serdyukov was dismissed in 2012, charged with embezzling funds (though never actually prosecuted), his reform achieved considerable results, as the world saw in Russia's Syria campaign of 2015–16.

To test the second interpretation—that siloviki occupy a large proportion of important government posts—I collected data on the biographies of all heads of ministries from 1992 (Chernomyrdin's first government) to the Medvedev government still in office in 2016. The sources consisted of official biographies as well as various press accounts. Figure 2-1 plots the share of people in the government with a siloviki background. Here, I use two definitions of siloviki. The first ("narrow") definition includes people who had a career in the "power agencies"—the armed forces, the Ministry of Internal Affairs, the Procuracy, and the KGB and its successor, the Federal Security Service (FSB). Typically, these people have a military rank not lower than colonel. The second ("broad") definition includes, in addition, people

---

6. Of course, there is plenty of evidence that certain business people with ties to Putin, many of them siloviki, have done well in the Putin era (Treisman 2008; Lamberova and Sonin, this volume).

7. Interview with Vladimir Milov, Moscow, September 28, 2015; interview with Simon Kordonsky, Moscow, December 15, 2015; interview with an expert who chose to remain anonymous, Moscow, September 28, 2015.

Figure 2-1   Siloviki in the Central Government

Percent[a]

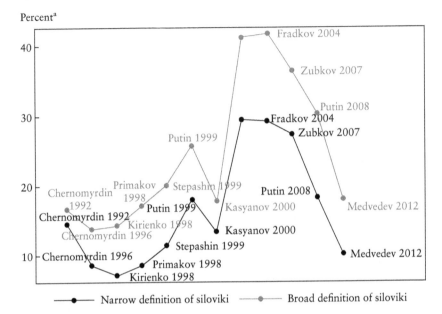

Sources: *Lenta.ru*, Source Online Database of Legislative Information (http://docs.cntd.ru/), and author's calculations.

a. Proportion of total cabinet positions occupied by siloviki under the given definition. Year refers to the first year of the respective government.

who do not have official connections to the power agencies, but whose unofficial connections to those agencies (most often, the KGB) have been reported in the press.

As figure 2-1 shows, the rise in the share of siloviki in government (under either definition) actually starts, not with Putin, but with the premiership of Yevgeni Primakov, in 1998. Yeltsin, in his last two years, was himself seeking out men from law enforcement and the security services, sensing the popular desire for greater "law and order." The presence of siloviki surprisingly *falls* in Putin's first term, but then shoots up in 2004, around the beginning of his second term. Indeed, the all-time peak came with the government of Mikhail Fradkov (2004–07), in which siloviki occupied around 40 percent of cabinet positions (officials of a rank higher than or equal to a minister). From 2007 on, the share of law enforcement and security veterans in the government began to decrease, and the decline continued in all subsequent governments. In Medvedev's government, appointed in 2012, the share of siloviki was lower than it had been in the first Chernomyrdin government of 1992.

If the share of siloviki peaked around 2004, what groups have been on the rise since then? First, the proportion of cabinet members with a background in private business has grown more or less consistently since 1992. From none at all that year, the share of private business executives rose to almost 40 percent in Medvedev's 2012 government—roughly equaling the proportion of siloviki at their high point. In part, this reflected the mass privatization of the 1990s and the gradual replacement of former state sector managers with private business people. Early on, Yeltsin appointed many state enterprise directors to his governments. But there is also a weaker trend toward more economic managers in general: together, former state and private sector business people made up almost half the 2012 Medvedev government, compared to a little more than one quarter in 1992 and about 45 percent in the mid-2000s. At the same time, the presence of intellectuals, think tank analysts, and university professors has declined since the early Yeltsin governments—from more than 40 percent to around 20 percent—and the share of career bureaucrats has risen from about 5 percent to more than 20 percent.

Repeating this analysis for the top three officials in the PA, one finds a similar pattern. The share of siloviki gradually increases in Putin's first two terms (2000–08) and then drops to the initial level, while the share of career bureaucrats and business people from the private sector rises.

What about regional governors? For them, the trend seems slightly different. According to detailed biographical data collected by researchers at the Higher School of Economics in Moscow, the proportion of governors with experience in law enforcement, the military, or the security services rose quite consistently from 1993 to 2008 (see figure 2-2).[8] Thus, the upward trend very clearly predated Putin's arrival on the political scene. After 2008 the proportion begins to fall—as with the government and PA—but it jumps again in 2012, with Putin's return to the Kremlin. Overall, the proportion seems to plateau in 2008–15. Although we see a clear increase since 1990 in siloviki in regional office, it is neither particularly strong nor particularly associated with Putin. Indeed, the annual rate of increase during the Putin-Medvedev years is lower than that during the Yeltsin years.

---

8. I am grateful to Eugenia Nazrullaeva and Andrei Yakovlev for sharing these data.

Figure 2-2 Share of Siloviki among Governors

Percent

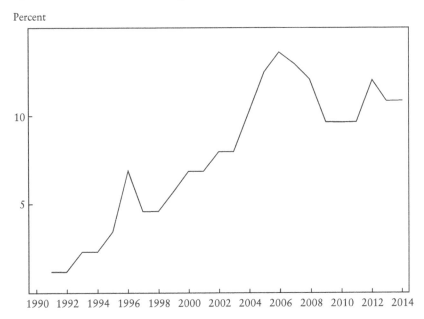

1990 1992 1994 1996 1998 2000 2002 2004 2006 2008 2010 2012 2014

Source: Database of Russian Governors, compiled by Center for the Study of Institutions and Development, Higher School of Economics, Moscow, http://iims.hse.ru/csid/databases/.

And the number of siloviki in gubernatorial office in 2012, the year that Putin restored elections after seven years of presidential appointment, was just thirteen out of a total of eighty-three, hardly an overwhelming presence.[9]

DICTATING POLICY?

In the media and some academic accounts, Putin is presented as a dictator, who has reduced the role of all other state actors to implementing his decisions. The policies that emerge from the Kremlin or the Duma are assumed simply to represent Putin's preferences. Other players—although they may compete for corrupt wealth—are thought to have little influence over other matters.

9. Lack of influence of siloviki as a group in no way means that the regime hesitates to use repression. In fact, as Andrei Soldatov and Michael Rochlitz demonstrate in this volume, the role of siloviki as implementers of policy (though not as deciders) is important for the regime's survival.

In some cases, narrowing attention to Putin may, indeed, make sense. He seems to have made certain key decisions completely autonomously, after sounding out at most a tiny circle of confidants. Ordering special forces to begin the operation in Crimea is one instance (see Treisman, this volume). When in 2008 Medvedev announced "his" initiative to lengthen the presidential term, no one in Moscow seemed to have anticipated this—except for Putin.

But not all decisions are like that. Especially in domestic economic policy, the path is often much slower and messier. Take the issue of mineral deposits. Throughout the 1990s, Yeltsin was unable to reform a perverse system that gave control over subsoil resources simultaneously to the central and regional governments, both of which could grant licenses to firms for extraction (Fortescue 2009). The result was redundancy, conflict, and corruption. In the early 2000s, Putin's administration proposed to overhaul this system, declaring all mineral deposits to be federal property and requiring licenses to be auctioned to the highest bidder. This seems likely to have been a priority for Putin: it would provide vital resources for the federal budget, weaken the governors, and thus help to centralize power.

One might, therefore, expect a leader with dictatorial powers to have enacted the reform quickly. But that is not what happened. Instead, the bill stalled in the Duma for two years, opposed by a range of lobbyists. Only in 2004 did elements of the proposal pass, not as a new bill but as a series of amendments to existing legislation. Although the regions lost control of their mineral deposits and auctions were introduced, these never completely replaced the old system (Fortescue 2009).[10]

How to reconcile the apparently swift and efficient process in some cases with the slow and inefficient one in others? Could the explanation lie in the timing of these two examples? The Putin regime of the early 2000s was hardly that of 2014. In fact, one can find similar cases of Kremlin initiatives that have been blocked and deflected much more recently. One example is President Medvedev's police reform (see Paneyakh and Rosenberg, this volume). After announcing a set of goals and declaring the reform a top priority in 2009, Medvedev ended up in 2011 accepting a watered-down version

---

10. Another prominent example is the debate about environmental regulations, where the executive branch in many ways gave in to the pressures from industry and bureaucracy (see Martus 2017).

that left the police with key opportunities for corruption. Many observers considered the outcome a complete failure.[11]

From these and other cases, one can distinguish two different modes of presidential decisionmaking (see Treisman, introduction to this volume). On the one hand, there are cases in which Putin intervenes directly and commits his prestige to achieving some goal ("manual control"). Decisions then tend to be made expeditiously and quickly passed down the chain of command, although implementation is not always so smooth. On the other hand, there are matters on which Putin does not take a clear position ("normal politics"). In these cases, the process is more complicated.

"Normal politics" manifests itself in different ways in different arenas. Within the executive branch, it is characterized by fierce battles over bureaucratic and corrupt interests, as well as—sometimes—sincerely held intellectual positions. These battles are often hidden, but sometimes leak into the media. The key formal element is the system of "sign-offs" (*soglasovania*). According to the government's procedural regulations, before a given policy proposal can be adopted, each of a list of relevant ministries and other state actors must approve it. Until 2012, the regulations also required that no issue could be raised in a cabinet meeting until it had received the necessary sign-offs.

This mechanism had its advantages. It allowed for some sort of representation of competing interests and militated against hasty actions, in effect giving a veto to those ministers with knowledge of and responsibility for a particular policy area. It could help to build consensus and foster compromises. In democracies, most policy disputes are fought out in legislatures and the media, and policies that do not have enough support are abandoned. In Russia, the opportunities for stakeholders to influence decisions are much more limited. Those with access to some actor in the *soglasovania* loop could at least get a hearing. The great disadvantage of the sign-off system was that it slowed decisions and, in some cases, blocked them completely. In 2012 Putin weakened it significantly, allowing the prime minister to raise issues in cabinet that had not yet been hashed out.

In short, President Putin can push through decisions quickly when he intervenes directly and throws his personal prestige behind them. On matters of urgent concern to him, his powers are quite dictatorial in that sense. Yet, on most issues, on which he takes no strong position, the outcome is deter-

11. On the convoluted politics behind the police reform, see also Taylor (2014).

mined by the clash of bureaucratic and other interests in the sign-off marathon.

Given obvious constraints of time and attention, the president simply cannot take a position on all issues. But Putin sometimes seems surprisingly diffident in this respect. Indeed, he often frustrates subordinates by refusing to take a strong position—even when they urge him to resolve a particular disagreement (Fortescue 2016). According to the former Kremlin insider Gleb Pavlovsky, people often leave the president's office with only a vague sense of what his position is on the issue they discussed (Pavlovsky 2016). Policy proposals that reach Putin's desk often receive the noncommittal resolution "Take this into consideration" (*Rassmotrite*) (Pis'mennaya 2013). One can posit various reasons for this diffidence. It might reflect a lack of interest, expertise, or strong opinions on the issue. It might also indicate a desire to keep his options open, so he can claim credit if the policy succeeds and disavow the agent if it fails. Perhaps he prefers for the interested actors to fight out policy battles among themselves. All these interpretations are possible, but none is consistent with the view that Putin is a decisive leader, surrounded by acolytes with no policy agenda or influence over the outcomes.

If decisionmaking is more complicated than often thought, implementing decisions can be even more problematic. It requires coordination among different government agencies and constant monitoring. In the PA, a set of informal practices emerged to help with this. As one former high-ranking official explained, every written decision (*bumaga*—literally "paper") requires a special overseer to walk from door-to-door pushing for its implementation.[12] This overseer is informally known as the policy's "legs" (*nogi*). Without "legs," a decision risks being delayed or forgotten, even if it originated at the highest level. Another condition for proper implementation is that officials be willing to spend some of their "administrative capital" (*administrativny ves*) to nudge the bureaucratic machine forward if it stalls for some reason. If one of these conditions fails—the person designated as "legs" is insufficiently enthusiastic, say, or "administrative capital" is scarce—the policy may never get implemented.

That seems to be what happened to many of the government's "high-priority" relief measures adopted in response to the economic downturn in 2014. In September 2015 the Russian Government Accountability Office

12. Interview with Kordonsky.

found that only 60 percent of these had made it into actual legislation, and only 30 percent had been fully implemented. Others had been implemented in part or not at all (Schetnaya Palata 2015).

Such problems bedevil even policies to which Putin has committed his own "administrative capital" (see Treisman, introduction to this volume). Frustrated by such failures, he has turned increasingly to alternative, informal channels and bodies. In 2011 he created the Russian National Front (RNF), an umbrella organization that unites nongovernmental organizations loyal to the regime. The RNF's main mission turned out to be to monitor the governors' progress in fulfilling the generous promises that Putin made before the 2012 election—on affordable housing, day-care centers, and so on—which were later pushed down to the regions as unfunded mandates. In May 2016 the government claimed that 70 percent of those policies had been implemented. The RNF claimed the figure was only 15 percent (RBC 2016).

Another informal instrument is the Agency for Strategic Initiatives (ASI), a body Putin created to stimulate innovation. While the RNF checks on social policy, the ASI monitors economic policy and the investment climate. One of Putin's 2012 promises was to reduce red tape on businesses. Since 2012, the ASI has published regular reports on Russia's progress on the World Bank's Doing Business indicators. Whether or not it is thanks to the ASI's efforts, Russia did rise from 120th in the world in 2011 to 51st in 2015. Besides parastatal agencies such as the ASI and RNF, the Kremlin has also taken to encharging particular missions to adventurous freelancers—business people, bureaucrats, or military veterans—who are given leeway to bend the rules as needed so long as they produce results (Treisman, introduction to this volume).[13]

Other evidence also suggests a growing dissatisfaction on Putin's part with formal methods. According to his official schedule, he has been meeting with the government far less frequently than before. In his first and second terms, he held such meetings about forty times a year. Since the start of his third term, the frequency has fallen to about twenty times a year—still higher than under Medvedev's presidency, but only half as often as in his own first two presidential terms. At the same time, he has been issuing far fewer presidential decrees—at least non-secret ones—than in

13. Reliance of the regime on "substitutes for institutions" has also been documented by Petrov, Lipman, and Hale (2014).

Figure 2-3   Presidential Decrees by Month

Number of decrees

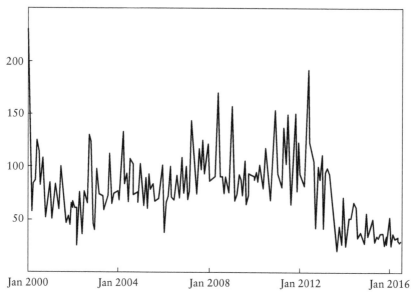

Jan 2000   Jan 2004   Jan 2008   Jan 2012   Jan 2016

Source: Online Database of Legislative Information, http://docs.cntd.ru/.

the past (figure 2-3). The frequency of such decrees is at an all-time low—about thirty-seven decrees per month in 2014–16, compared to an average of eighty-two decrees per month during his first two terms.

One possible explanation is that Putin is focusing more on implementation. Having committed himself to ambitious targets in his 2012 decrees, he is eager now to see these bear fruit. But another—possibly complementary—explanation is that he has taken to enacting and communicating more of his decisions in private and to relying less on the government and more on informal agents to carry them out.

In sum, although his progressive consolidation of power has removed most political constraints, Putin does not resemble the simplistic image of a dictator. Often, he waves his hands and leaves key decisions to subordinates to decide, fighting over them within the game defined by bureaucratic procedures. When he does choose to back a policy strongly, no insider—and few outsiders—overtly oppose it. Yet implementation is another story, and even on issues in which Putin has invested political capital, the "power vertical" often proves unreliable. Frustrated at such failures, he has taken to weakening procedures and bypassing the state more often to work through parastatal organizations and freelancers. Since returning to the Kremlin in 2012, he has met less often than before with his government and has sharply cut back on at least the public subset of presidential decrees.

CONCLUSION

What happens in the Kremlin—and in the White House, home to Russia's government—is far from transparent. Still, based on an analysis of public data as well as interviews with former insiders, some tentative conclusions suggest themselves.

First, changes in the concentration of power in Russia's political system over the past twenty-five years have not coincided with changes in the country's formal institutions; the president's ability to dominate other political actors is more clearly related to economic performance and its effect on the incumbent's popularity. Second, the presence of siloviki in high political offices appears to have peaked in the mid-2000s. What influence key security service veterans have today seems to depend more on personal ties to Putin than on their institutional position (see also Soldatov and Rochlitz, this volume).

Third, political decisions can be divided into two sets—those on which Putin takes a strong position and those that he lets his subordinates work out. The latter are decided by a complicated game of bureaucratic politics, in which backers of a particular proposal must obtain signatures from actors inclined to oppose it. Rather than a decisive leader who sets a clear direction on all issues, Putin often refuses to resolve disagreements among subordinates. Fourth, implementation is a huge problem. Even policies that Putin has strongly supported—especially in economic and social policy—are sometimes delayed or even abandoned. Fifth, dissatisfied with such failures of the official apparatus, Putin has taken to creating parallel structures to monitor implementation and sometimes tasking outside individuals with the organization of key missions. He has cut back sharply on official meetings with the government and the enactment of (at least public) presidential decrees.

REFERENCES

Ablow, Keith. 2014. "Inside the Mind of Vladimir Putin." Fox News, March 11.

Aslund, Anders. 2007. *Russia's Capitalist Revolution: Why Market Reform Succeeded and Democracy Failed*. Washington, D.C.: Peterson Institute for International Economics.

Baker, Peter, and Susan Glasser. 2005. *Kremlin Rising: Vladimir Putin's Russia and the End of Revolution*. New York: Simon and Schuster.

BBC. 2015. "Ulyukaev: Rosnefti otkazalis' vydelyat' dengi iz FNB [Ulyukaev: Rosneft was refused the funds from the Fund for National Welfare]." August 25. www.bbc.com/russian/rolling_news/2015/08/150824_rn_rosneft_ulyukaev.

The Economist. 2007. "Russia under Putin: The Making of a Neo-KGB State." August 23. www.economist.com/node/9682621.

Fortescue, Stephen. 2009. "The Russian Law on Subsurface Resources: A Policy Marathon." *Post-Soviet Affairs* 25, no. 2, pp. 160–84.

———. 2016. "Russia's 'Turn to the East': A Study in Policy Making." *Post-Soviet Affairs* 32, no. 5, pp. 423–54.

Geddes, Barbara, Joseph Wright, and Erica Frantz. 2014. "Autocratic Breakdown and Regime Transitions: A New Data Set." *Perspectives on Politics* 12, no. 2, pp. 313–31.

Gel'man, Vladimir. 2015. *Authoritarian Russia: Analyzing Post-Soviet Regime Changes*. University of Pittsburgh Press.

Gingrich, Newt. 2014. "Inside the Mind of Vladimir Putin." CNN, March 25.

March, Luke. 2009. "Managing Opposition in a Hybrid Regime: Just Russia and Parastatal Opposition." *Slavic Review* 68, no. 3, pp. 504–27.

Martus, Ellen. 2017. "Contested Policymaking in Russia: Industry, Environment, and the 'Best Available Technology' Debate." *Post-Soviet Affairs* 33, no. 4, pp. 276–97.

Myers, Steven Lee. 2015. *The New Tsar: The Rise and Reign of Vladimir Putin*. New York: Alfred A. Knopf.

National State Statistics Committee. 2002. "Finansy Rossii [Russia's finances]." www.gks.ru/bgd/regl/b02_51/IssWWW.exe/Stg/d010/i010050r.htm.

———. 2010. "Finansy Rossii." www.gks.ru/bgd/regl/b02_51/IssWWW.exe/Stg/d010/i010050r.htm.

NPR. 2014. "A View inside the Mind of Vladimir Putin." March 4.

Pavlovsky, Gleb. 2016. "Russian Politics under Putin: The System Will Outlast the Master." *Foreign Affairs*, May–June, pp. 10–17.

Petrov, Nikolay, Maria Lipman, and Henry E. Hale. 2014. "Three Dilemmas of Hybrid Regime Governance: Russia from Putin to Putin." *Post-Soviet Affairs* 30, no. 1, pp. 1–26.

Pis'mennaya, Evgeniya. 2013. *Sistema Kudrina: Istoriya klyuchevogo ekonomista putinskoy Rossii* [Kudrin's system: The story of the key economist of Putin's Russia]. Moscow: Mann, Ivanov i Ferber.

RBC. 2015. "Sam sebe CB: Kto i zachem vypuskaet sobstvennuyu valyutu [DIY Central Bank: Who issues their own currency and why]." June 20. www.rbc.ru /photoreport/30/06/2015/561546bb9a7947095c7dc4c9.

———. 2016. "Obeschaniya tretiego sroka [Third-term promises]." May 17, www .rbc.ru/economics/17/05/2016/573a034a9a7947d189671693a.

Robertson, Ian H. 2015. "Inside the Mind of Vladimir Putin." *Daily Telegraph*, February 24.

Roxburgh, Angus. 2013. *The Strongman: Vladimir Putin and the Struggle for Russia*. London: I. B. Tauris.

Safire, William. 2003. "Siloviki versus Oligarchy." *New York Times*, November 5.

Schetnaya Palata Rossiyskoy Federatsii (Government Accountability Office of the Russian Federation). 2015. *Doklad po rezul'tatam proverki i analiza hoda relalizatsii plana pervoocherednyh meropriyatii . . . za yanvar'–sentyabr' 2015-go goda* [Report on the results of the inspection and analysis of the implementation of the plan of priority measures . . . January–September 2015]. http://audit.gov.ru /activities/control/report-on-the-results-of-the-inspection-and-analysis-of-the -implementation-of-the-plan-of-priority-m.php?sphrase_id=4468750.

Sestanovich, Stephen. 2007. "Putin's Invented Opposition." *Journal of Democracy* 18, no. 2, pp. 122–24.

Shevtsova, Lilia, and Mark H. Eckert. 2000. "The Problem of Executive Power in Russia." *Journal of Democracy* 11, no. 1, pp. 32–39.

Shleifer, Andrei, and Daniel Treisman. 2000. *Without a Map: Political Tactics and Economic Reform in Russia*. MIT Press.

Taylor, Brian D. 2011. *State Building in Putin's Russia: Policing and Coercion after Communism*. Cambridge University Press.

———. 2014. "Police Reform in Russia: The Policy Process in a Hybrid Regime." *Post-Soviet Affairs* 30, nos. 2–3, pp. 226–55.

Treisman, Daniel. 2001. *After the Deluge: Regional Crises and Political Consolidation in Russia*. University of Michigan Press.

———. 2008. "Putin's silovarchs." *Orbis* 51, pp. 141–53.

———. 2011. "Presidential Popularity in a Hybrid Regime: Russia under Yeltsin and Putin." *American Journal of Political Science* 55, no. 3, pp. 590–609.

———. 2012. *The Return: Russia's Journey from Gorbachev to Medvedev*. New York: Simon and Schuster.

Vedomosti. 2007. "Soglasovannaya Rossiya [Approved Russia]." July 26. www.vedo mosti.ru/newspaper/articles/2007/07/26/soglasovannaya-rossiya.

Yasmann, Victor. 2007. "Russia: Siloviki Take the Reins in Post-Oligarchy Era." *Radio Free Europe*, September 17. www.rferl.org/a/1078686.html.

Zhegulev, Ilya, and Lyudmila Romanova. 2012. *Operatsia "Yedinaya Rossiya"* [Operation "United Russia"]. Moscow: Eksmo.

THREE

Not Just a Rubber Stamp

Parliament and Lawmaking

BEN NOBLE and EKATERINA SCHULMANN

Although the Duma formally has the power to discuss and amend laws, its real function is simply to pass laws—it is not an opportunity for influence.

BRIAN TAYLOR

The function of [Duma] deputies has been reduced to stamping bills. And even the refusal to vote in line with the authorities' wishes on important initiatives could well cost legislators their political careers.

SOF'YA SAMOKHINA

Such a parliament may well go through the motions of parliamentary procedure, but the outcomes are foreknown, and the members, although they may use their status as deputies to obtain other benefits of office, have no opportunity to affect policy.

THOMAS REMINGTON

The State Duma—the lower chamber of Russia's bicameral legislature, the Federal Assembly—is often dismissed as a "rubber stamp."[1] This popular

---

1. The comments by Taylor (2014, p. 245), Samokhina (2016), and Remington (2007, p. 123) are remarkably similar to characterizations of the Supreme Soviet of the USSR: "That the Supreme Soviet can neither reject nor amend policy proposals put before it by the government is beyond dispute" (Mezey 1979, p. 42). Indeed,

metaphor for legislatures in nondemocratic regimes portrays such assemblies as completely subservient, slavishly following the orders of their executive principals. These are bodies dominated by the executive, with legislators providing unquestioning support—and a thin veneer of legitimacy—for decisions taken and finalized elsewhere. The executive is the monopoly supplier of bills, all of which become laws without amendment or critical debate; rubber stamp parliaments do not introduce "viscosity" into the policymaking process.[2]

Beyond the rubber stamp moniker, other disparaging labels abound: a "mad printer," furiously churning out repressive legislation inspired by the Presidential Administration; a legal "conveyor belt"; a legislative "Xerox machine"; and an elaborate political "farce," attempting to "divert the attention of citizens from the real mechanisms of adopting decisions."[3] A July 2015 *Gazeta.ru* editorial declared the Duma "no place for work"—a body that had "finally lost its autonomy."[4]

There is, however, evidence inconsistent with these descriptions. For example, bills submitted by the executive to the legislature sometimes fail to become laws, and other, successful bills are occasionally amended beyond recognition during Duma passage. Our first key task, therefore, is to present evidence of these deviations from rubber stamp expectations. The second, more important, goal, however, is to explain *why* these, in fact, take place.

If not merely a rubber stamp, then *what is the Russian State Duma's role in the legislative decisionmaking processes?* In answering this question, we focus on parliamentary lawmaking activity during the State Duma's sixth convocation, running from the very end of 2011 until the middle of 2016, as

---

Thomas Remington (2014, p. 42) argues that "under presidents Putin and Medvedev, parliament has largely reverted to its Soviet-era role as a rubber stamp for the leadership's policy initiatives."

2. On "viscosity," see Blondel (1970). See Noble (2016b) for a detailed discussion of the rubber stamp model and the methods for evaluating its veracity in particular cases.

3. The Russian term for "mad printer" is *vzbesivshiisya printer*. The description of political "farce" is taken from an apparently frank description of contemporary parliamentary practice by a serving United Russia deputy, Evgenii Fedorov—quoted in Ukolov (2014).

4. Editorial, "Ne mesto dlya raboty [No place for work]," *Gazeta.ru*, July 7, 2015, www.gazeta.ru/comments/2015/07/07_e_7597253.shtml.

well as place this period in the longer post-Soviet context.[5] As such, we neither devote much attention to the activities of the Federation Council, nor do we discuss in detail other legislative functions beyond lawmaking, such as executive oversight and constituency representation.[6]

Our argument, in brief, is that rather than always, and simply, providing a seal of approval for initiatives developed fully and finalized elsewhere, the Russian parliament serves as a venue—and the legislative stage of policy-making, more broadly, serves as an opportunity—for *executive, bureaucratic,* and other *powerful non-legislative actors* to contest their competing policy preferences.[7] To be sure, on important policy initiatives, and when elites are united, the Duma is capable of rubber-stamping bills, with initiatives racing through the legislature with little substantive discussion and no amendments. Yet this does not always happen. Although we suggest a number of reasons why this is the case, we underscore the fact that the Duma serves as an "elite battleground" between ministries, departments, executive agencies, and economic interests. Deviations from the rubber stamp model, therefore, result from intra-elite policy squabbling, rather than signifying opposition to, or influence on, executive policy agendas. Although parliamentary activity reflects a cacophony of elite interests, this plethora of voices is largely untethered from societal concerns, with consequential discussions taking place away from public view.

We proceed with an overview of post-Soviet Russian parliamentary politics, lay out evidence of rubber stamp deviations, and discuss the causes of these deviant observations.

5. The first plenary session of the sixth convocation took place on December 21, 2011, with the final plenary session on June 24, 2016.

6. As Joel Ostrow (2001, p. 647, n. 1) argues, "For all intents and purposes, the Duma *is* the Russian legislature"—a claim that is particularly resonant when analyzing the lawmaking process and since institutional reforms have clipped the autonomy of Federation Council members (see Remington 2008).

7. To be sure, we are not the first to make this claim. Remington (2014, p. 42), for example, writes that "parliament has become one of several sites in Russia's political system where bargaining and deal-making among organized interests take place." This chapter, however, builds on these existing insights by updating the empirical picture to the present day, by expanding the range of this evidence, and by providing rich descriptions of episodes to flesh out dynamics that have been intimated but rarely explored in detail.

A BRIEF HISTORY OF POST-SOVIET RUSSIAN PARLIAMENTARY POLITICS

The history of post-Soviet Russian parliamentary politics is not a simple, linear story, moving from chaos to control. To place the Duma's sixth convocation (2011–16) into the longer story of post-Soviet parliamentarism, we provide a brief overview of this historical context, covering institutional details, the shifting partisan composition of the Duma and the executive-legislative balance of power, and an overview of the lawmaking process.

Following the constitutional crisis of 1993—which, at base, was a confrontation between the legislative and executive branches of power, and which culminated in the dissolution of the Congress of People's Deputies and the Supreme Soviet—the new post-Soviet constitution created a new bicameral federal parliament, with 450 seats in the lower house. The 1993, 1995, 1999, and 2003 Duma elections were all conducted using a mixed electoral system, with 225 deputies elected using party-list proportional representation and 225 in single-mandate district (plurality) competitions. By contrast, the 2007 and 2011 elections were conducted using a purely proportional representation system.[8] There is evidence that these institutional changes have affected legislative behavior: Jana Kunicova and Thomas Remington (2008) argue, for example, that deputies elected via single-mandate districts were more likely to defect from the party line when voting on budget bills.

The same formal constitutional structure has hosted very different executive-legislative dynamics in post-Soviet Russia. This variation over time reveals the importance of the *partisan* balance of power in the Duma. Given the stark power asymmetries apparent when this new institutional architecture was forged in 1993—demonstrated most dramatically by Boris Yeltsin's shelling of the parliament building—some commentators predicted legislative subservience to follow. Stephen Holmes, for example, argued that the corollary of Yeltsin's "superpresidential" constitution would be "rubber-stamp," "fig-leaf parliamentarism."[9] Yet the first Duma convocation—sitting from the beginning of 1994 to the end of 1995—was composed of twelve party factions and deputy groups "finely balanced between pro-government and opposition parties."[10]

8. The 2016 Duma elections saw a return to the mixed electoral system.

9. Holmes (1993–94, p. 124).

10. Chaisty (2005, p. 301). The final plenary session of the first convocation took place on December 22, 1995.

The second Duma—running from 1996 to the end of 1999—was an even starker corrective to expectations of legislative quiescence.[11] The Communist Party's seat plurality—in combination with other leftist forces—resulted in frequent clashes between President Yeltsin and the Duma. Yet executive-legislative relations during the second half of the 1990s were not marked exclusively by conflict: Yeltsin sometimes chose to bypass the Federal Assembly completely by using executive decrees (*ukazy*), and politicians were sometimes able to reach policy compromises.[12]

Vladimir Putin's election to the presidency in 2000, along with the success of the Kremlin in crafting a viable "party of power," United Russia, by the end of 2001, ushered in a period with fewer overt clashes between the executive and the legislature. However, the absence of a cohesive, stable, disciplined pro-executive partisan majority necessitated policy bargaining and horse-trading during the third convocation (2000–03), as demonstrated by the substantial—albeit implementable—amendments made by deputies to spending figures during Duma passage of the state budget bill in the early 2000s.[13] Yet the *visibility* of this legislator influence was reduced with the introduction of "zero readings"—consultations between deputies and the government carried out *before* bill introduction to iron out differences before the commencement of formal legislative proceedings.[14]

Executive influence over the Duma was strengthened with United Russia's majority following the December 2003 elections. Although United Russia secured 223 Duma seats on the basis of election results, postelection

11. The first plenary session of the second convocation took place on January 16, 1996, and the final plenary session took place on December 13, 1999.

12. See, for example, Chaisty and Schleiter (2002) on the contrast between the Duma's surprising policymaking *productivity* during this period and its low estimation in the eyes of Russian citizens.

13. That they were implementable is in contrast to the manifestly political changes made to budget bills during Duma passage in the 1990s, which made the final documents poor guides to *achievable* spending levels (see Troxel 2003, p. 159). Interview with an economic correspondent for a major federal newspaper, Moscow, January 17, 2016, transcript. The first plenary session of the third convocation took place on January 18, 2000, with the final plenary session on November 28, 2003.

14. Interview with a former parliamentary reporter for a major federal newspaper, Moscow, January 25, 2016, transcript.

shuffling of deputy partisan ties resulted in the "party of power" commanding more than 300 seats during the fourth convocation, which ran from the end of 2003 to the end of 2007.[15] This numerical dominance further shifted the executive-legislative balance of power. Indeed, newly elected Duma chair Boris Gryzlov suggested on December 29, 2003, that the Duma "is not a venue in which it is necessary to hold political battles, to assert political slogans and ideologies" but "is a venue in which people should be occupied with constructive, effective lawmaking activities."[16] In an October 2005 interview, erstwhile Duma chair Gennadii Seleznev put a less positive spin on the situation, arguing that, because of United Russia's commanding position in the lower chamber, the Duma was now "totalitarian"—a "machine that stamps everything proposed by the president and the government."[17]

The 2007 parliamentary elections cemented executive control over legislative activities, with United Russia achieving a constitutional majority from the very start of the fifth Duma convocation, which ran up to the end of 2011.[18] Thus, the Communist Party secured 57 seats, the Liberal Democratic Party of Russia (LDPR) 40, and Just Russia 38, versus United Russia's 315. However, this numerical dominance for the "party of power" ended following the December 2011 Duma elections, with United Russia officially receiving just under 50 percent of the vote, translating into 238 seats in the lower chamber—a bare majority.[19] Just Russia improved on its previous seat tally, with 64 Duma mandates; LDPR won 56 positions; and the Communist Party secured 92 seats.

15. The first plenary session of the fourth convocation took place on December 29, 2003, with the final plenary session on November 16, 2007.

16. For Gryzlov's remarks, see the transcript of the State Duma's plenary session, no. 1(715), State Duma of the Federal Assembly of the Russian Federation, http://transcript.duma.gov.ru/node/1386/. These comments have since been condensed into the often-cited phrase that the Duma is "not the place for political discussions" (see, for example, Chaisty 2012, p. 97).

17. From an interview by Sergei Tkachuk (2005) in *Novye Izvestia*.

18. The first plenary session of the fifth convocation took place on December 24, 2007, with the final plenary session on November 23, 2011.

19. Unlike previous convocations, the sixth convocation was originally meant to run for five years (instead of four), due to a constitutional amendment adopted in 2008. However, the length of this convocation was shortened by the moving forward of parliamentary elections for the seventh Duma convocation from December to September 2016.

One episode from the first legislative session of the Duma's sixth convocation suggests the brief window available for nonexecutive influence on parliamentary affairs, as well as the institutional changes enacted in response aimed at limiting such opportunities in the future. On May 10, 2012, eight Duma deputies—including United Russia and Just Russia legislators—introduced a bill proposing changes to the Code of Administrative Offenses, markedly increasing administrative responsibility for putative violations of the rules governing public demonstrations.[20] The timing of this proposal was no surprise: May 6, 2012, saw large-scale demonstrations held on the eve of Putin's inauguration to his third presidential term, ending in violence on Bolotnaya Square. Disagreeing with the repressive thrust of this legislative proposal, a group of deputies, including Dmitrii Gudkov, Gennadii Gudkov, Il'ya Ponomarev, and Vadim Solov'ev, planned to hinder the passage of the bill by proposing a vast number of amendments during the bill's second reading on June 5. In Russian, this effort was referred to as an "Italian strike," but, in effect, the goal was to filibuster the bill's reading on the Duma floor. Although this strategy forced the Duma to stay in session until midnight, the opposition deputies were ultimately unable to block the bill, in part because of a violation of the Duma's standing orders regarding the time available for deputies to present particular amendments, reduced by the chair to one minute and then to thirty seconds.[21]

This episode was a brief flowering of oppositional activity on the Duma floor, for which there were consequences. As Eddy Malesky and Paul Schuler have argued, "Authoritarians want reasonable representation of opposition groups, but a process that allows a firebrand or intransigent opposition into the chamber could damage both negotiations and the credibility of revealed bargains to the public."[22] By explicitly setting out to—and apparently succeeding in—humiliating the ruling elite by impeding, and drawing attention to, the passage of a repressive bill, Gennadii Gudkov incurred the

20. An information page for bill 70631-6 is available on the State Duma of the Federal Assembly of the Russian Federation's lawmaking information portal, *Avtomatizirovannaya sistema obespecheniya zakonodatel'noi deyatel'nosti* [Automated system for supporting lawmaking activities] (*ASOZD*), http://asozd2.duma.gov.ru/main .nsf/(Spravka)?OpenAgent&RN=70631-6.

21. A transcript (*Stenogrammy obsuzhdeniya zakonoproekta no. 70631-6*) of the bill's second reading on the Duma floor is available on the lower chamber's online archive, State Duma of the Federal Assembly of the Russian Federation, http://api .duma.gov.ru/api/transcript/70631-6.

22. Malesky and Schuler (2010, p. 485).

ire of the Kremlin: he was stripped of his deputy mandate on September 14, 2012—a move attributed in part to his leading role in the "Italian strike."[23]

In addition to Gudkov's removal, another response came in the form of a raft of changes introduced into the Duma's standing orders, removing the possibility of a repeat of this overt display of opposition. Thus, a Duma resolution (*postanovlenie*) from September 21, 2012, among other changes, reduced the amount of time allowed for the presentation of particular amendments and allowed the Duma leadership to cluster together amendments it considered to be related, therefore removing the possibilities for filibustering; these changes were developed at a closed meeting of the Duma Committee on Regulations.[24]

How does a bill become a law in Russia? All legislative initiatives must be introduced into the State Duma. Article 104 of the 1993 Russian constitution enumerates the actors with the authority to introduce legislative initiatives into the Duma: the president, the Federation Council as a whole, members of the Federation Council, State Duma deputies, the government, the legislative branches of Russian regions, and the Constitutional Court, the Supreme Court, and the Supreme Arbitration Court (before its dissolution in 2014) in areas of their jurisdiction.[25] Most bills are required to pass through three separate readings on the Duma floor in order to progress from the lower chamber. The first reading concerns the general concept of a bill; the second reading concerns the details of a bill, during which amendments can be made; and the third reading is largely used to brush up remaining technical-legal details. During Duma review, in addition to approval, bills can be returned to, or withdrawn by, their sponsors; new coauthors can be added, or they can recall their signatures (this can happen before the first reading has been passed); or bills can be rejected on the floor (under conditions specified in the lower chamber's standing orders).[26] Initiatives can

23. Interview with Dmitrii Gudkov, Duma deputy (Just Russia), Moscow, January 25, 2016, transcript.

24. Makunina (2012). For the draft resolution, see the bill's information page on *ASOZD*, http://asozd2.duma.gov.ru/main.nsf/(Spravka)?OpenAgent&RN=136741-6.

25. For an English-language text of the 1993 Constitution of the Russian Federation, see www.constitution.ru/en/10003000-06.htm.

26. For the Duma's standing orders, see "O reglamente Gosudarstvennoi Dumy Federal'nogo Sobraniya Rossiiskoi Federatsii [On the standing orders of the State Duma of the Federal Assembly of the Russian Federation]," *Consultant.ru*, www .consultant.ru/law/review/lawmaking/reglduma.

also stay in limbo for long periods, as bills are not automatically removed from consideration at the end of Duma convocations.

If adopted by the Duma, a bill (now technically referred to as a "law") moves on to the Federation Council. Following committee review, bills are voted on in a plenary session of the Council. If successful, initiatives move on for presidential signature. If the Federation Council or the president rejects (vetoes) an initiative approved by the Duma, the lower chamber can challenge rejections, or a conciliation commission is created to negotiate a compromise text. Alternatively, the laws rejected by the Federation Council or the president can stay without further consideration for indefinite periods, while officially regarded as being "under discussion" (as opposed to being removed from consideration).

This brief sketch of post-Soviet Russian legislative politics demonstrates the fluctuations in executive-legislative relations, pushing back against a simple narrative moving from the disorder of the early 1990s to complete control under President Putin. The stage is set for our analysis of policy-making processes in the sixth Duma convocation.

REALLY A RUBBER STAMP?

We can test the aptness of the rubber stamp label as applied to the Russian legislature by searching for evidence *inconsistent* with the model's expectations. We can look, in other words, for "black swans."[27] Four observations are inconsistent with this ideal-type model of authoritarian legislative politics: bill introduction into the legislature by nonexecutive actors, the failure of executive-introduced bills to become laws, executive bill amendment, and the vetoing of bills during legislative review. After presenting evidence of these phenomena, we explore the reasons for these puzzling observations.

All Bills Are Introduced by the Executive?
In a recent review of scholarship on "democratic authoritarianism," Dawn Brancati argues that authoritarian legislatures "only rubberstamp government-proposed legislation."[28] Does the State Duma, in fact, only deal with legislative initiatives proposed by the executive, which, in Russia,

---

27. See Noble (2014, 2015, 2016a, 2016b) for a presentation and defense of this approach to evaluating the rubber stamp model of authoritarian legislative politics. On the role of black swans in theory falsification, see Popper (1959).
28. Brancati (2014, p. 317).

consists of both the government and the president? Figure 3-1 presents information on the percentage of all bills submitted to the Duma (by legislative session, spring 2012 to spring 2015), broken down by the introducing actor.

Clearly, the Duma does not simply deal with executive-sponsored bills. Rather, the executive is responsible only for around 20 percent of submitted initiatives (in this period at least), with deputies being the clear leaders, sponsoring around 50 percent of all bills, followed by bills formally sponsored by regional legislatures.[29] (On bills sponsored by regional legislatures, see Petrov and Nazrullaeva, this volume.)

All Executive-Introduced Bills Are Successful?
Executive bills should always receive the endorsement of rubber stamp assemblies; bill failure is inconsistent with perfect legislative subservience. Figure 3-2 presents success rates for bills sponsored by the government, the president, and Duma deputies from the second to the fifth Duma convocations.[30]

Although the success rates of bills sponsored by the government and the president improved over time, in line with greater executive dominance over the legislature, *executive bills continued to fail in the fourth and fifth Duma convocations.* A perfect success rate has been realized only once: by presidential bills in the fifth convocation. Executive bills have also failed in the sixth convocation—for example, bill 42197-6, "On the introduction of changes to various legislative acts of the Russian Federation regarding questions of the implementation of social patronage and of the activities of organs of guardianship and custody," introduced by the government in March 2012 and rejected by the State Duma in second reading in January 2014.[31] In a sense, these data appear to constitute a very weak challenge to the rubber stamp model. After all, the vast majority of executive-sponsored bills do, in fact, become laws. Yet, as we discuss below, the significance of bill failure is

---

29. Figure 3-2 also demonstrates that bills formally sponsored by Duma deputies have been successful, again underlining the fact that the Russian parliament does not simply consider and accept initiatives introduced by the executive.

30. Success rates equal the proportion of executive-introduced bills that are signed into law during the same convocation (excluding bills that are still under consideration).

31. Bill 42197-6's information page on *ASOZD*, http://asozd2.duma.gov.ru/main.nsf /(Spravka)?OpenAgent&RN=42197-6.

Figure 3-1 Submitted Bills, by Initiator and Legislative Session, Spring 2012–Spring 2015

Percent of bills submitted

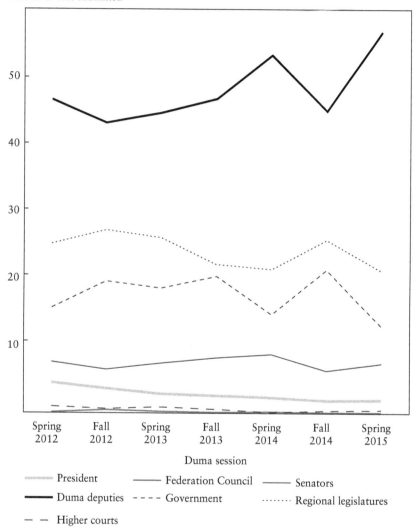

Source: Apparat Gosudarstvennoi Dumy Federal'nogo Sobraniya Rossiiskoi Federatsii (2015, p. 4).

Figure 3-2 Bill Success Rates by Initiator and by Duma Convocation, 1996–2011

Percent of bills that became laws

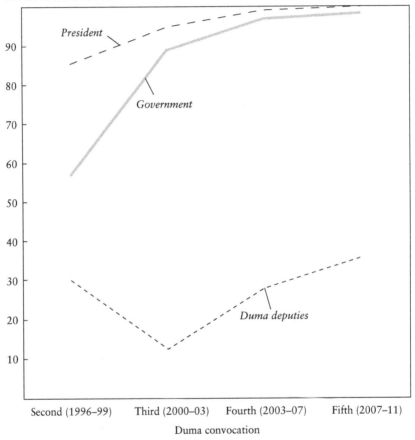

Duma convocation

Source: Apparat Gosudarstvennoi Dumy Federal'nogo Sobraniya Rossiiskoi Federatsii (2015, pp. 7, 9, 13). Unfortunately, Duma lawmaking statistics are not available for the first Duma convocation, 1994–95.

found in the indications it gives regarding the broader, but largely hidden, world of intra-elite conflict.

All Bills Pass through the Legislature without Amendment?
Rubber stamp legislatures are not meant to revise bills. Writing about the fate of a government-sponsored change to the single social tax in the fourth Duma convocation (2003–07), Thomas Remington noted: "[It is] striking that, in contrast to the bargaining that accompanied tax bills in the past,

there were almost no changes to the government's initial version while the bill was going through the Duma."[32] In other words, executive dominance of the legislature resulted in fewer changes to executive-submitted bills. Moving to contemporary practices, Remington has noted that "once a bill reaches the parliament, it usually undergoes only minor revisions."[33]

Some cases, however, jar with this general claim. For example, there is the government-sponsored bill 293332-6, "On the introduction of changes to Parts One and Two of the Tax Code of the Russian Federation and separate legislative acts of the Russian Federation."[34] On introduction to the Duma on June 7, 2013, the bill totaled around two hundred words, but, in its final form, the law consisted of just under ten thousand words. Substantively, whereas the introduced draft concerned simply the registration of aircraft, the final law included numerous changes to legal provisions concerning taxes. There are suggestions, moreover, that such cases are not entirely exceptional: Svetlana Bocharova has gone so far as to claim that "the practice of amending a law [read "bill"] beyond recognition between first and second reading . . . [has become] a tradition."[35]

No Bills Passed by the State Duma Are Vetoed by the Federation Council or the President?

This expectation flows from the assumption that all disagreements are ironed out *before* legislative introduction. Or, if disagreements persist into the Duma, then they will be ironed out by the time of a bill's third reading, including with the involvement of Federation Council members in the drafting and adoption of bill amendments in second reading. Figure 3-3 presents the frequency of vetoes used by the Federation Council and the president by Duma legislative session, 1996–2015.

Although there was a precipitous decline in the number of vetoes used in the shift from the second to the third Duma convocations—in line with the shift in executive-legislative relations discussed above—their use did not reduce to naught in the more recent periods associated with executive dominance over the legislature. And, what is more, these veto episodes include cases of *executive*-sponsored legislative initiatives—for example, bill

---

32. Remington (2008, p. 975).

33. Remington (2016, p. 49).

34. Bill 293332-6's information page on *ASOZD*, http://asozd2.duma.gov.ru/main .nsf/(Spravka)?OpenAgent&RN=293332-6.

35. Bocharova (2013).

Figure 3-3   Number of Bills Vetoed by the Federation Council and the
President by Duma Session, 1996–2015

Number of vetoes

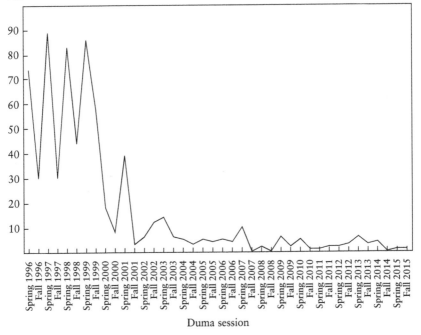

Source: State Duma website (www.duma.gov.ru/legislative/statistics/).

255707-6, on foreign investments in strategically important sectors of the
economy, introduced into the Duma by the government on April 10, 2013.[36]

Although not discussed in detail here, information on voting activity
would tell a similar story. Although the classic, ideal-type rubber stamp image
includes unanimous, slavish voting by automatons, votes in the State Duma
are rarely unanimous. Of the 15,767 votes cast during the sixth convocation
(2011–16), only 5 votes were, strictly speaking, unanimous, where unanimity
applies only to votes in which all 450 deputies voted in favor of a motion.[37]

36. Bill 255707-6's information page on *ASOZD*, http://asozd2.duma.gov.ru/main
.nsf/(Spravka)?OpenAgent&RN=255707-6.
37. This strict interpretation of unanimity does not, however, convey the frequent
occasions on which unanimity is not achieved simply because of the absence of
deputies from the floor, which might not necessarily signal opposition from these
legislators. Voting data are taken from the State Duma of the Federal Assembly

To be sure, many votes are near unanimous. But, more importantly, the executive often relied exclusively on United Russia's 238 votes to pass—or block—initiatives. When the Kremlin wants a show of unity, however, the "Crimean consensus" becomes apparent on the Duma floor, with "opposition" parties joining with the "party of power" to present a united front.[38]

It might be tempting to infer from these deviant observations that, in contrast to the rubber stamp picture of legislative subservience, the State Duma has been able to resist executive lawmaking agendas or that it has been able to realize its own legislative agenda autonomously from executive concerns. This would be premature: the mere fact of these observations tells us very little about their *causes*.

ELITE BATTLEGROUND

What explains these observations that jar with rubber stamp expectations? In this section, we once again look at the four areas discussed in the previous section: nonexecutive bills, executive bill failure, executive bill amendment, and bill vetoing. Although we propose a variety of explanations—including both the use of nonexecutive actors to be the formal sponsors for controversial and repressive legislation crafted by a unified elite, and entrepreneurial activity by Duma deputies—we underscore the legislative stage's capacity to serve as an opportunity for intra-elite policy contestation, particularly between executive and bureaucratic actors.[39] Stephen Holmes provides a vivid account of the

> uncompromising turf warfare, factionalism, and zero-sum competition over vast cash flows inside the Russian elite and the impossibility of imposing discipline or common goals on fragmented, self-dealing bureaucrats. . . . Executive agencies and ministries . . . [that] habitu-

---

of the Russian Federation's online archive of voting information, http://vote.duma .gov.ru/. For an example of a unanimous vote, see the third reading vote on bill 104515-6, which took place on December 20, 2013, http://vote.duma.gov.ru/vote/84183. Bill 104515-6's information page on *ASOZD*, http://asozd2.duma.gov.ru/main.nsf /(Spravka)?OpenAgent&RN=104515-6.

38. Churakova (2015). For a discussion of the "Crimean consensus," see Noble (2017).

39. This argument is redolent of "institutional pluralist" approaches to politics and policymaking in the Soviet Union—see, for example, Hough (1977, 1983) and Skilling (1971).

ally conceal essential information from each other and work at cross-purposes tend to produce incoherent and self-defeating policies, to seize up in periodic deadlocks, to react dangerously slowly to unexpected crises. . . . Such intra-elite warfare reflects massive but hidden state weakness, suggesting strongly that the much talked-of consolidation of vertical power in the age of Putin is more illusion than reality.[40]

Our argument is that these intra-elite dynamics are, in large part, responsible for the rubber stamp deviations presented above. These legislative phenomena occur, not because of legislator autonomy from, or opposition to, executive agendas, but because the executive itself—as well as the bureaucracy and powerful economic interests—is deeply divided on certain policy questions. The legislative stage of policymaking allows these nonlegislative actors both to sneak in policy changes under the noses of their colleagues and to bargain over the details of disputed initiatives.

Nonexecutive Bills

Are bills formally sponsored by nonexecutive actors really the result of nonexecutive policy agendas? There are suggestions that this is not the case: opposition Duma deputy Il'ya Ponomarev has argued that almost 80 percent of bills formally sponsored by parliamentarians are not, in reality, the personal initiatives of these same deputies.[41] Why the disjuncture between formal and real bill sponsorship? This happens for a number of reasons. In certain cases, bills formally sponsored by nonexecutive actors are drafts written by government actors—such as ministries and federal agencies—that have not received the approval necessary from other executive actors in order to be introduced formally as a government initiative.[42] The majority of government-sponsored bills need to pass two formal hurdles: adoption by the government's Commission on Legislative Activities and adoption by the cabinet.[43] Frustrated by this impediment to their initiatives, executive

40. Holmes (2015, p. 37).

41. Gallai and Bocharova (2013).

42. For a discussion of the pre-legislative government sign-off (*soglasovanie*) process, see Fortescue (2012).

43. For information on the commission (Kommissiya Pravitel'stva po zakonoproektnoi deyatel'nosti), see the section "Opisanie [Description]" on the body's Gov-

actors sometimes find "a sympathetic deputy [or another nonexecutive actor with the authority to introduce bills] to introduce legislation on their behalf."[44] And certain powerful state bodies—such as the Central Bank, the Office of the Prosecutor General, and the Investigative Committee— lack the formal authority to submit bills for legislative review, meaning that they have to find other actors to introduce bills into the Duma on their behalf.

In other cases, elite actors do not want to be formally associated with particular bills that they have drafted for fear of popular discontent, including because of these initiatives' repressive character. This concern for disassociation was particularly apparent during the Duma's sixth convocation concerning draconian initiatives developed by the Presidential Administration and the Security Council. Examples of such practices abound. A source within the Presidential Administration admitted, for example, that bill 607554-6—popularly known as the "Rotenberg law," which proposed that Russian citizens be compensated from state budget funds for "unjust decisions of foreign courts," and introduced into the Duma on September 23, 2014—was drafted by lawyers in the State Legal Directorate of the President.[45] Likewise, the law branding those nongovernmental organizations (NGOs) receiving foreign funding and carrying out "political activities" as "foreign agents," although formally sponsored by 243 deputies, was actually drafted by an informal working group in the Directorate of Domestic Policy in the Presidential Administration.[46] Similarly, a bill crafted by the Investigative Committee concerning the controversial reintroduction of the concept of "objective truth" into Russian criminal procedure law was formally sponsored by United Russia deputy Aleksandr Remezkov and introduced into the Duma on January 29, 2014.[47] And a number of anti-extremism and antiterrorism bills, although formally introduced into the Duma on April 7, 2016, by United Russia deputy Irina Yarovaya and senator Viktor Ozerov, were, in fact, drafted by the Security Council—a presidential advisory body

---

ernment of the Russian Federation web page, http://government.ru/department /147/about/.

44. Chaisty (2006, p. 130).

45. Nikol'skaya and Surnacheva (2015).

46. Nikol'skaya and Surnacheva (2015).

47. Berseneva (2014). In fact, Alexander Bastrykin, head of the Investigative Committee, took responsibility for the bill in an interview published in the government newspaper, *Rossiiskaya Gazeta* (Kozlova 2013).

concerned with matters of national security.[48] That *executive* actors were responsible for drafting laws, subsequently interpreted as evidence of Duma deputies being "mad," "rabid," and out of control, should make us cautious when ascribing blame for the stream of repressive legislation promulgated during Putin's third presidency.

Although ascertaining the frequency and precise sources of, and reasons for, such covert introductions is impossible given, for example, the actors' interest in opacity, there is anecdotal evidence of relatively stable agency-deputy linkages, with particular legislators acting as proxies for particular executive or state bodies: the Investigative Committee (Aleksandr Remezkov, United Russia, Legislation Committee); the Ministry of Transport (Evgenii Moskvichev, United Russia, Transport Committee); the Ministry of Health (Nikolai Gerasimenko, United Russia, Health Care Committee; Ol'ga Borzova, United Russia, Committee for Family, Women, and Children); the Ministry of Internal Affairs (Vladimir Vasil'ev, United Russia, Security and Anticorruption Committee; Irina Yarovaya, United Russia, Security and Anticorruption Committee); the Presidential Administration (Leonid Levin, Just Russia, Information Policy Committee); the Presidential Directorate of Domestic Politics (Aleksandr Tarnavskii, Just Russia, Budget Committee; Mikhail Emel'yanov, Just Russia, Economic Policy Committee; Andrei Lugovoi, LDPR, Security and Anticorruption Committee; Aleksei Kazakov, Just Russia, Information Policy Committee; Igor' Lebedev, LDPR, Constitutional Legislation and State-Building Committee; Dmitrii Vyatkin, United Russia, Constitutional Legislation and State-Building Committee); the Supreme, Arbitration, and Constitutional Courts (Pavel Krasheninnikov, United Russia, Legislation Committee); the Office of the Prosecutor General (Aleksandr Khinshtein, United Russia, Security and Anticorruption Committee; Vladimir Ponevezhskii, United Russia, Constitutional Legislation and State-Building Committee); Gazprom (Valerii Yazev, United Russia, Natural Resources Committee); and the Security Council (Irina Yarovaya, United Russia, Security and Anticorruption Committee; Vladimir

48. Interview with a long-serving parliamentary correspondent for a major federal newspaper, Moscow, May 17, 2016, transcript. The council's website is www.scrf.gov.ru/. A source less familiar with the case suggested, in contrast, that the actual initiator of this set of bills was the Federal Security Service (FSB). Interview with a parliamentary, and subsequently, presidential correspondent for two major federal newspapers, Moscow, May 25, 2016, transcript.

Ponevezhskii, United Russia, Constitutional Legislation and State-Building Committee; Igor' Lebedev, LDPR, Constitutional Legislation and State-Building Committee).[49] As this list demonstrates, there is an association between the Duma committee membership of deputies and the policy area of most concern to the represented interests. In sum, although the reasons for obfuscating the "real" sponsors of legislative initiatives vary, nonexecutive actors are used to act as the formal sponsors for bills drafted elsewhere.[50]

There is also evidence, however, of apparently *autonomous*, nonexecutive lawmaking initiatives—something that is not captured by our "elite battle-ground" metaphor. We can point to at least three types. First, in certain cases, it seems that Duma deputies introduce initiatives simply to raise these same legislators' public profile, or to put a particular issue onto the agenda, rather than as sincere attempts to modify the letter of the law.[51] Second, in other cases, Thomas Remington (2008, p. 985) has suggested that United Russia deputies are granted relative autonomy in crafting "regulatory and distributive legislation to reward its supporters" and to ensure "its perpetuation in power." That is, pro-executive deputies are granted the authority to craft policy in certain demarcated areas in exchange for regime fealty. And, third, although decreased in line with the legislature's increased subservience to the executive over time, lobbying by powerful economic actors still takes place during the legislative stage of policymaking (see Chaisty 2013).

Executive Bill Failure

Can the failure of executive bills to become laws be attributed to successful legislative opposition? Again, we argue that this is unlikely to be the

---

49. These deputy links were provided during our interviews with the long-serving parliamentary correspondent and the parliamentary, and subsequently presidential, correspondent.

50. Consistent with this picture, a *Gazeta.ru* editorial from July 2015 argues that, rather than "autonomous politicians, capable of generating and adopting decisions, deputies have turned into an instrument used by different governing institutions for the adoption of their own decisions." Deputies can serve as pawns in proxy skirmishes between non-legislative actors; the State Duma serves as the stage for other people's battles.

51. For suggestions of such a dynamic, see the comments by Deputy Oleg Nilov cited in Ukolov (2014). See also Brunner (2013) for an analysis of similar dynamics in Belgium, France, Germany, and the United Kingdom.

case. For example, the only case of *presidential* bill failure in recent years, which concerned Dmitry Medvedev's electoral reform initiative, was submitted at the end of his presidential term. It did not fail because of resistance from Duma deputies; rather, a rival electoral reform initiative, sponsored by the once-again-president Putin, took precedence, making Medvedev's proposal obsolete.[52] It is unlikely, moreover, to be the only Medvedev-sponsored bill fatality: ten further bills, introduced during Medvedev's presidency, remain formally under consideration in the State Duma—cases we might call Medvedev's "legislative orphans."[53] Since bills can remain formally under consideration indefinitely—that is, bills do not automatically fail at the end of legislative sessions or convocations (see above)—and given the reputational costs associated with bill failure, allowing presidential initiatives to remain dormant appears to be the simplest course of action.

Bill Amendment

The authority to amend bills is conventionally understood as a key *reactive* power of legislatures, used to tailor legislative initiatives to legislators'— and, by extension, the electorate's—policy preferences. However, amendment practices in the Duma do not conform to this idealized picture of legislative practice.[54] An episode from 2014 helps illustrate the gulf between theory and reality. Changes to fees charged to small businesses first appeared among amendments proposed by the head of the Duma's Budget Committee, Andrei Makarov, to bill 605370-6—a government-sponsored initiative on tax policy, introduced into the Duma in September 2014.[55] As noted above, it is an old Duma trick to introduce amendments (conceptually unconnected to the bill as originally submitted) during second reading—an option particularly appealing when actors want to introduce changes quickly and quietly. However, in this case, the proposed changes to the tax bill became known and caused a public uproar (includ-

---

52. See Noble (2014) for an analysis of all cases of executive bill failure, 2008–13, including a discussion of Medvedev's failed electoral reform initiative.

53. View these cases on *ASOZD*.

54. See Noble (2015) for an analysis of data on amendments made to all executive-sponsored bills, 2003–13.

55. Bill 605370-6's information page on *ASOZD*, http://asozd2.duma.gov.ru/main .nsf/(Spravka)?OpenAgent&RN=605370-6. See Schulmann (2014b).

ing protests from the Medium and Small Business Commission of the Public Chamber), prompting legislators to pass the government's bill without the alterations.[56] In a sense, therefore, the Duma was operating well: a negative public reaction resulted in the blocking of a controversial amendment.

This was not the end of the story for small business fees, however. The core policy ideas were included as an amendment made in preparation for the second reading of a different bill, authored by Deputy Andrei Makarov, along with other legislators.[57] As they moved from one bill to another, the proposed amendments changed considerably, so that small business fees no longer applied to all municipalities but applied only to Russia's three cities of federal stature, Moscow, St. Petersburg, and Sevastopol. The fees also became lower, and the range of taxable business activity was reduced from twenty-two areas to just one, distributive trade. The amendments were adopted in this form during the bill's second reading on November 18, 2014. Why this maneuver? Most likely, this was an attempt to shift the responsibility from the government to the parliament. Yet, that same evening, President Putin told a forum of the All-Russia People's Front that the Moscow authorities were behind the idea for the bill amendment, given their unhappiness with how little retail chains were contributing to the city's revenue stream (Kremlin 2014). The Russian Union of Retailers appealed to Putin to veto the law when it reached him;[58] however, the president signed the bill into law on November 29.

This practice of inserting significant changes during second reading to socially resonant bills (albeit without public discussion) is also illustrated by the passage of bill 759895-6.[59] Introduced by the government in April 2015, the original bill concerned the application of Russian civil legislation to transactions completed in Crimea before 2014. The bill was adopted with minor revisions in second reading on May 12, 2015. Rather than moving swiftly on to a third reading on the Duma floor, however, the bill was returned for a *repeat* second reading on July 3, 2015, in order to introduce

56. On the protests, see Sterkin and Churakova (2014).

57. Bill 527250-6's information page on *ASOZD*, http://asozd2.duma.gov.ru/main
.nsf/(Spravka)?OpenAgent&RN=527250-6.

58. See the report by Ishchenko (2014).

59. Bill 759895-6's information page on *ASOZD*, http://asozd2.duma.gov.ru/main
.nsf/(Spravka)?OpenAgent&RN=759895-6.

amendments to the text, as well as to change the title of the bill. Specifically, the chair of the Duma's Legislation Committee, Pavel Krasheninnikov, proposed amendments, which would significantly alter the content of article 222 of the Russian Civil Code—on "unauthorized construction." In spite of the insertion of these provisions completely unrelated to the original bill, and following no discussion on the Duma floor, the bill was adopted by 96 percent of the vote in third reading on July 3.[60] The changes to article 222 of the Civil Code gained particular significance in light of the removal of a large number of retail kiosks and pavilions—alleged to be "unauthorized constructions"—by the Moscow authorities on the night of February 9, 2016—a controversial move labeled the "night of the long shovels."[61] Although clear evidence regarding the reasons for Krasheninnikov's amendment is unavailable, anecdotal evidence from the Duma suggests that the deputy was approached by the constructing lobby connected with the brothers Arkady and Boris Rotenberg.

Again, however, there is evidence of dynamics not captured by the "elite battleground" metaphor. For example, one episode paints Pavel Krasheninnikov in a very different light: as an independent policy entrepreneur, amending a Supreme Court–sponsored bill—concerning the decriminalization of a number of activities—by inserting a change regarding punishment, something he had been championing since 2008.[62] In a sense, this example displays the same pathologies regarding the introduction of changes falling outside the original conception of a bill during second reading and without discussion. And yet this case does serve to demonstrate how legislators—in this case, a loyal United Russia deputy and head of the Duma's Legislation Committee—can, in certain circumstances, act successfully in furthering their own policy agendas.[63]

---

60. For a transcript of the bill's discussion on the Duma floor, including voting results, see *Stenogrammy obsuzhdeniya zakonoproekta no. 759895-6* [Transcripts of the discussion of bill no. 759895-6], State Duma of the Federal Assembly of the Russian Federation, http://api.duma.gov.ru/api/transcript/759895-6.

61. Litvinova (2016).

62. Bill 953369-6's information page on *ASOZD*, http://asozd2.duma.gov.ru/main .nsf/(Spravka)?OpenAgent&RN=953369-6. For Krasheninnikov's championing of the bill, see Churakova (2016).

63. The task remains to specify the conditions under which nonexecutive actors can act autonomously, or as entrepreneurs, in the policymaking process.

Vetoing Bills

Finally, what of bills passed by the State Duma but vetoed by the Federation Council or the president? As noted above, the use of bill vetoes is particularly striking, given the apparent opportunities earlier in the lawmaking process to resolve disagreements between actors. According to one of our interviewees, "If the Federation Council vetoes something, it means that, at the last moment, something happened and they [the authorities] said, 'Do not pass the bill.' "[64] The suggestion is that vetoes from the Federal Assembly's upper chamber do not reflect objections rooted in senators' policy concerns; rather, elite actors can use the veto power to block initiatives.

There are a number of reasons for this late-stage intervention, including the discovery of technical errors and mistakes in the text adopted by the Duma, shifting socioeconomic conditions, and attempts to block initiatives sponsored by nonexecutive actors that clash with executive interests.[65] On the latter, an example is bill 829830-6—an initiative sponsored by the chair of the Duma, Sergei Naryshkin, and the chair of the Duma's Budget Committee, Andrei Makarov. The bill—proposing that changes made to budget spending category figures by the government *between* sessions of the State Duma be subject to review by a joint Duma and Federation Council commission—was introduced and expedited through the lower chamber at the very end of the spring legislative session in 2015.[66] Leaving the Duma on July 4, the bill was taken up by the Federation Council on July 6, with a proposal made by the Council's Budget Committee to adopt the bill on the same day, with the Federation Council's legal department declaring

64. Interview with the parliamentary, and subsequently presidential, correspondent.

65. Of the twenty-one bills that have been vetoed by the Federation Council or the president during the sixth Duma convocation, one bill has been withdrawn from consideration, one is under review in a conciliation commission, two are awaiting reports from the responsible Duma committee, and seventeen have been signed into law following changes made during conciliation commission meetings. For information on vetoed bills, see "Statistika zakonodatel'nogo protsessa [Statistics of the lawmaking process]," State Duma of the Federal Assembly of the Russian Federation, www.duma.gov.ru/legislative/statistics/.

66. Bill 829830-6's information page on *ASOZD*, http://asozd2.duma.gov.ru/main .nsf/(Spravka)?OpenAgent&RN=829830-6. This is a case of a bill being adopted in first reading and in toto, with no separate second and third readings.

only minor objections.[67] However, on July 8, the Council in plenary voted to reject the initiative, with the same Budget Committee supporting this rejection.[68] Why the speedy U-turn? Rather than evidence of Federation Council–specific concerns about the initiative, this veto was motivated, in fact, by concerns raised by the Ministry of Finance regarding the Duma's role in adjusting budget spending levels.[69] Thus, an executive actor used a proxy legislative actor (the Federation Council) to impede the passage of a bill sponsored by parliamentarians.

In Sum

Evidence, which, at first sight, might appear to signify legislative influence, is often, on closer inspection, the result of the Duma serving as a venue for policy bargaining and conflict between a diverse set of largely *non-legislative* interests, including executive and bureaucratic actors with divergent preferences. The State Duma is a "place of action," but legislators as such are not necessarily—and, in most cases, are not likely—the first movers of this activity.[70]

Given strategic considerations—including the reputational costs of airing "dirty laundry" in the relative publicity of parliament—these rubber stamp deviations can be considered particularly puzzling. Would we not expect the Kremlin to ensure that intra-executive and bureaucratic disputes were kept well away from the public gaze? That we do, in fact, observe these phenomena likely speaks to the impaired ability of the core executive to control actors in the policymaking process. The real importance, however, of these deviations lies in the fact that they intimate broader dynamics—

67. For the department's report (*zaklyuchenie*) on the bill, see Legal Department of the Apparat of the Federation Council of the Federal Assembly of the Russian Federation, http://asozd2.duma.gov.ru/main.nsf/(ViewDoc)?OpenAgent&work/dz.nsf/By ID&33216FACEFCAB48C43257E7B0047BD68.

68. For a transcript of the Federation Council's discussion, see records from the 377th meeting (*zasedanie*) of the Federation Council of the Federal Assembly of the Russian Federation, http://council.gov.ru/activity/meetings/56109/transcript, Federation Council.

69. Opposition from the Ministry of Finance was confirmed in an interview with the economic correspondent, Moscow, January 17, 2016. See also Sapozhkov and others (2015).

70. Rory Truex has used the phrase "place of action" when referring in general to legislatures in nondemocratic regimes (see Truex 2014, p. 235).

they are merely the iceberg tips, under which lies a largely hidden world of intra-elite conflict.

CONCLUSION

What role does the Russian State Duma play in the legislative decisionmaking process? In this chapter we have subjected the rubber stamp label—often applied to Russia's Federal Assembly—to empirical scrutiny by disaggregating the various dimensions of this ideal type.[71] The activities of the State Duma can at times appear entirely scripted and at other times farcically theatrical. But they can also involve bitter disputes between influential, *non-legislative* actors, although these conflicts are most often safely tucked away from public view. Rather than an orderly, scripted, simply ceremonial stage in the policymaking process, the picture of the Duma presented in this chapter is largely of a haphazard process of sneaky bureaucratic gamesmanship masquerading as parliamentary politics. The legislative stage of policymaking in post-Soviet Russia has always involved conflict, but the *visibility* of this conflict, and the *actors* involved, has varied over time.

Our aim has been to provide a corrective to representations of contemporary Russian parliamentary politics and practices conforming to the rubber stamp metaphor.[72] The sheer volume of laws produced every year in Russia should, however, caution against making generalizations about the policymaking processes involved. The dynamics concerning high-profile, politicized initiatives—when "System 2" is in operation—are, for instance, likely to differ from those concerning ostensibly technical amendments to the legal landscape.[73] Moreover, the chapter by Nikolay Petrov and Eugenia Nazrullaeva intimates other dynamics relating to the Duma passage of bills sponsored by regional legislatures, which might not reflect intra-bureaucratic battling.

71. Although the rubber stamp label is often used more casually, being applied to legislatures that do not conform perfectly to a model of perfect subservience, we use the concept in this chapter as an ideal type with which to assess the recent functioning of the State Duma.

72. Another approach would be to marshal detailed evidence in *support* of the rubber stamp characterization of contemporary Russian legislative politics.

73. Ideally, we would analyze separately and compare, for example, the legislative passage of bills in different policy areas and of different priorities for the executive. We leave this for future research.

Duma deputies are largely absent from our story—as independent actors, at least. Why would ambitious individuals seek to hold office, given the very limited opportunities for policy influence? This question has been asked regarding other putative rubber stamp nondemocratic legislatures. For example, for deputies in China's National People's Congress, Rory Truex (2014) asks, what are the "returns to office" in a rubber stamp parliament? One likely answer is simple: money. Deputy status comes with its own material perks and privileges, access to patronage, as well as rents (see Remington 2008; Reuter and Robertson 2015). In addition, deputy status confers legal privileges, "such as immunity from prosecution and protection from investigation by law enforcement agencies" (Chaisty 2013, p. 733).[74] United Russia has also largely been absent from our account. In spite of holding a majority of seats in the Duma, the party is not, however, the center of decisionmaking on policy. United Russia serves, rather, as a vehicle for securing electoral victories for the Kremlin, which translate into majority voting blocs in the Duma, as well as the majority of regional and local legislatures.

The fate of Russian parliamentarism inspires particular interest, given the widely held view that there is a relationship between the general health of democracy and the vigor of legislative bodies.[75] The legislative activity from the Duma's sixth convocation cited in this chapter will, however, not likely give succor to those hopeful of seeing democratic politics in Russia. The significance of the Russian parliament does not stem from its role as a check on executive power, responding independently to the legislative initiatives of the government and the president, or as an independent initiator of bills. Our analysis demonstrates that legislative activity need not be animated by democratic, *election*-driven politics; rather, intra-elite politics can provide the impetus for activity in the legislature. To be sure, bureaucratic actors in democracies and non-democracies alike no doubt use the legislative

74. See Blaydes (2011) for a similar argument regarding parliamentarians in the Egyptian parliament during Hosni Mubarak's regime.

75. As David Olson and Michael Mezey (1991, p. xi) argue, "It is important to clarify the policy-making role of legislatures because the strength of a nation's legislature is often viewed as directly related to the strength of that nation's commitment to democratic procedures." And Steven Fish (2006, p. 18) has argued that "would-be democratizers should focus on creating a powerful legislature . . . [and] if politicians fail to establish a national legislature with far-reaching powers, the people will soon find themselves in a polity where their votes do not count (or are not counted properly) and their voices are not heard."

stage of policymaking to further their own interests. What is distinctive about Russia—and possibly other nondemocratic regimes—is how these concerns dwarf the representation of other interests. Instead of the public interest and the electorate's opinion, we have the executive and the bureaucracy talking to itself, competing within itself, and using political institutions to further its interests.[76] This evidence of intra-elite competition highlights yet again the inadequacy of models invoking an all-knowing, all-powerful, all-directing Putin to explain decisionmaking in contemporary Russia. Although the Kremlin has demonstrated an ability to dominate executive bodies on certain issues and at certain times, there remains a great deal of room for individual ministries, departments, and actors to battle against others with competing preferences.

In recognition of parliament's limited capacity to provide a channel for the expression of societal opinions and interests, there has been a proliferation of quasi-parliamentary bodies, such as the Public Chamber and the "public councils" (*obshchestvennye sovety*) under executive ministries. Yet it seems the fear that these institutions—nominally created to improve information flows between society and the authorities—could increase demands for accountability and serve as sites for vocal opposition means that they are not given the very autonomy on which their successful operation depends. As a result, in practice, they appear to perform a very limited information-provision function; any ambition to represent the full range of societal opinions and interests is undermined by opaque methods of membership appointment.[77] At the same time, there are suggestions that "public councils" in some ministries (the Ministry of Health Care and the Ministry of Internal Affairs, for example) do provide meaningful opportunities for consulted NGOs to affect ministerial agenda-setting and decisionmaking. What is of particular note is that NGOs and experts appear to prefer to work with the executive ministries and agencies directly, in preference to going to the respective Duma committees, where the decisionmaking process is

---

76. See Schulmann (2014a, 2015b).

77. Interview with the head of an NGO, Moscow, January 16, 2016, transcript. See also the scandal around the Internet vote for membership of the Public Chamber in 2014 (Rustamova 2014). As Nikolay Petrov, Maria Lipman, and Henry E. Hale (2014, p. 13) argue, "With institutions for interest representation and negotiated compromise gutted for fear of losing political control, policy-making in the Russian system often amounts to a leadership's guessing game as to precisely what society will accept and what it will not, with a significant possibility of misjudgement."

described by them as "less direct" and "unclear," with the results of discussion being uncertain.[78]

Could economic exigencies prompt a renegotiation of executive-legislative relations, including the meaningful diffusion of power to legislative actors, or even simply the incorporation of broader consultation practices into the policymaking process?[79] The Makarov-Naryshkin bill concerning the parliament's role in reapportioning budget spending (cited above) suggests that the legislature is—or, perhaps more accurately, individuals within it are—attempting to shift the executive-legislative balance of power in budgeting.[80] While there are signs that the Ministry of Finance is strongly resisting these attempts, going further to undermine the Duma's role in the budget-making process, there are also signs that this is not a one-way process. On the one hand, amendments prepared by the ministry for the second reading of bill 1055875-6—introduced by Deputy Makarov on April 26, 2016, allowing the government to submit the 2017–19 budget bill up to November 1, as opposed to the conventional deadline of October 1—would allow the government to make certain changes to budget spending figures *without requiring Duma approval*.[81] On the other hand, however, amendments made to the same bill appear to create the body originally proposed by the vetoed Makarov-Naryshkin bill—a Commission of the Federal Assembly for the Reallocation of Budget Spending—which has the ability (on paper, at least) to agree or disagree with government proposals with a seven-day window.[82] Bill 1055875-6 was signed into law by the president on July 2, 2016.[83]

How do electoral dynamics affect the Duma's role in legislative decisionmaking? There have been suggestions that the Presidential Administration has allowed legislators greater freedom to express themselves via legislative initiatives, particularly in the run-up to legislative elections in

78. Interview with NGO head. Likewise, there are indications that lobbyists and experts involved in the budgeting process prefer dealing with the Ministry of Finance, rather than with Duma deputies. Interview with economic correspondent.

79. See Schulmann (2015a, 2015c).

80. Interview with economic correspondent. See Schulmann (2015a).

81. For a discussion of these changes, see Visloguzov (2016).

82. For the bill amendments, see the *Tablitsa popravok no. 1* [Table of amendments no. 1], State Duma of the Federal Assembly of the Russian Federation, http://asozd2.duma.gov.ru/main.nsf/(ViewDoc)?OpenAgent&arhiv/a_dz_6.nsf/ByID&B EEA1F4BB6721B2A43257FB50059E00B.

83. Bill 1055875-6's information page on *ASOZD*, http://asozd2.duma.gov.ru/main .nsf/(Spravka)?OpenAgent&RN=1055875-6.

September 2016.[84] This should not, however, necessarily be regarded as nascent democratization.[85] Insofar as the Kremlin can control the election-focused activities of Duma deputies, then this would appear to be electoral authoritarianism par excellence: rather than the abnegation of electoral politics, the "electoral connection" (Mayhew 1974) is permitted to develop insofar as it benefits the existing regime's hold on power.

Executive control over the legislature is a key component of authoritarian power, something underlined by changes to executive-legislative relations in the regime shifts experienced by other states. For the case of Taiwan, for example, Tun-jen Cheng and Stephan Haggard have pointed to the importance of legislative control: "The apparent strength of the executive *ultimately rested on the capacity of the party to maintain ruling majorities in the National Assembly and particularly in the Legislative Yuan.*"[86] And, regarding the loss of the Institutional Revolutionary Party's hold on power in Mexico, Maria Amparo Casar points to the pivotal role of legislative majorities in bolstering presidential power.[87]

If the Russian executive were to lose command of a disciplined, stable voting majority in the Duma—as well as a compliant body of senators in the Federation Council—then a more fractious executive-legislative relationship would certainly return.[88] In the short to medium term, however, such an outcome is unlikely, even with the changes to electoral legislation allowing somewhat more space for political expression to parties and single-mandate candidates. Even without major change in the Duma's party composition, *external* circumstances—including the ongoing economic crisis and the upcoming 2018 presidential elections—might encourage a less unified and more vocal Duma.[89]

---

84. See, for example, Nikol'skaya and Surnacheva (2015) and Vinokurov (2015).

85. See Schulmann (2015c).

86. Cheng and Haggard (2001, p. 194), emphasis in original.

87. Casar (2002).

88. Indeed, the specter of this scenario has motivated efforts to monitor and shape the electoral prospects of candidates in the September 2016 Duma elections, such as the pro-Kremlin Institute of Socio-Economic and Political Research's series rating politicians, Reiting-2016 (www.politanalitika.ru/).

89. See Schulmann (2016). Given the uncertainty present in the current political system—uncertainty that will only grow in the near future—cautious suggestions of institutional reform to redistribute responsibilities to the legislature have already been voiced in the media (see, for example, Gallyamov 2015 and Trifonova 2016).

REFERENCES

Apparat Gosudarstvennoi Dumy Federal'nogo Sobraniya Rossiiskoi Federatsii [Apparat of the State Duma of the Federal Assembly of the Russian Federation]. 2015. *Analiz prokhozhdeniya zakonoproektov v Gosudarstvennoi Dume po itogam vesennei sessii 2015 goda* [Analysis of the passage of bills in the State Duma following the end of the 2015 spring session]. Moscow.

Berseneva, Tatyana. 2014. "Zakonoproekt ob ob"ektivnoi istine v ugolovnom protsesse obrel vtoruyu zhizn' [Objective truth bill finds second life]." *Pravo.ru*, March 21. http://pravo.ru/news/view/116981/.

Blaydes, Lisa. 2011. *Elections and Distributive Politics in Mubarak's Egypt.* Cambridge University Press.

Blondel, Jean. 1970. "Legislative Behaviour: Some Steps towards a Cross-National Measurement." *Government and Opposition* 5, no. 1, pp. 67–85.

Bocharova, Svetlana. 2013. "Kak zhe vy besite [How annoying you are]." *Lenta.ru*, March 22. http://lenta.ru/articles/2013/03/22/printer.

Brancati, Dawn. 2014. "Democratic Authoritarianism: Origins and Effects." *Annual Review of Political Science* 17, pp. 313–26.

Brunner, Martin. 2013. *Parliaments and Legislative Activity: Motivations for Bill Introduction.* Wiesbaden: Springer.

Casar, Maria Amparo. 2002. "Executive-Legislative Relations: The Case of Mexico." In *Legislative Politics in Latin America*, edited by Scott Morgenstern and Benito Nacif. Cambridge University Press.

Chaisty, Paul. 2005. "Party Cohesion and Policy-Making in Russia." *Party Politics* 11, no. 3, pp. 299–318.

———. 2006. *Legislative Politics and Economic Power in Russia.* Basingstoke: Palgrave Macmillan.

———. 2012. "The Federal Assembly and the Power Vertical." In *Routledge Handbook of Russian Politics and Society*, edited by Graeme Gill and James Young. New York: Routledge.

———. 2013. "The Preponderance and Effects of Sectoral Ties in the State Duma." *Europe-Asia Studies* 65, no. 4, pp. 717–36.

Chaisty, Paul, and Petra Schleiter. 2002. "Productive but Not Valued: The Russian State Duma, 1994–2001." *Europe-Asia Studies* 54, no. 5, pp. 701–24.

Cheng, Tun-jen, and Stephan Haggard. 2001. "Democracy and Deficits in Taiwan: The Politics of Fiscal Policy, 1986–1996." In *Presidents, Parliaments, and Policy*, edited by Stephan Haggard and Matthew McCubbins. Cambridge University Press.

Churakova, Olga. 2015. "'Krymskii konsensus' v Gosdume sokhranilsya, nesmotrya na raznoglasiya po dosrochnym vyboram ['Crimean Consensus' in the Duma stays in place despite differences on early elections]." *Vedomosti*, July 2. www.vedomosti.ru/politics/articles/2015/07/03/599086-krimskii-konsensus-v-gosdume-sohranilsya-nesmotrya-na-raznoglasiya-po-dosrochnim-viboram.

————. 2016. "Soderzhanie pod strazhei pribavit v vese [Pre-trial detention will gain weight]." *Vedomosti*, May 15. www.vedomosti.ru/politics/articles/2016/05 /16/641075-soderzhanie-pod-strazhei.

Fish, Steven. 2006. "Stronger Legislatures, Stronger Democracies." *Journal of Democracy* 17, no. 1, pp. 5–20.

Fortescue, Stephen. 2012. "The Policymaking Process in Putin's Prime Minister-ship." In *Waiting for Reform under Putin and Medvedev*, edited by Lena Jonson and Stephen White. Basingstoke: Palgrave Macmillan.

Gallai, Alla, and Svetlana Bocharova. 2013. "Gosduma vozvrashchaetsya k pere-lomnoi rabote [State Duma returns to ground-breaking work]." *Vedomosti*, March 28. www.vedomosti.ru/newspaper/articles/2013/08/28/gosduma-vozvraschaetsya -k-perelomnoj-rabote.

Gallyamov, Abbas. 2015. "Paralich gosudarstva: Kak raskol v elitakh privodit k pad-eniyu pravitel'stva [Paralysis of the state: How a split in the elites leads to the downfall of the government]." *RBK Daily*, August 12. www.rbc.ru/opinions/politics /12/08/2015/55caf6699a79471e8920eecd.

Holmes, Stephen. 1993–94. "Superpresidentialism and Its Problems." *East European Constitutional Review* 2, no. 4, and 3, no. 1, pp. 123–26.

————. 2015. "Imitating Democracy, Feigning Capacity." In *Democracy in a Russian Mirror*, edited by Adam Przeworski. Cambridge University Press.

Hough, Jerry F. 1977. *The Soviet Union and Social Science Theory*. Harvard University Press.

————. 1983. "Pluralism, Corporatism and the Soviet Union." In *Pluralism in the Soviet Union*, edited by Susan Gross Solomon. London: Macmillan.

Ishchenko, Natalya. 2014. "Prezident podpisal zakon o torgovykh sborakh [Presi-dent signs law on trading fees]." *Vedomosti*, December 2. www.vedomosti.ru /business/articles/2014/12/02/krupnaya-roznica-hochet-skidku-so-sbora.

Kozlova, Natalya. 2013. "Sledstvie vedet Bastrykin [Bastrykin conducts investigation]." *Rossiiskaya Gazeta*, August 27. www.rg.ru/2013/08/26/bastrykin-site.html.

Kremlin. 2014. President Vladimir Putin's speech at the Action Forum of the All-Russia People's Front, Moscow, November 18. Transcript. http://kremlin.ru /events/president/news/47036.

Kunicova, Jana, and Thomas Remington. 2008. "Mandates, Parties and Dissent: Effect of Electoral Rules on Parliamentary Party Cohesion in the Russian State Duma, 1994–2003." *Party Politics*, 14, no. 5, pp. 555–74.

Litvinova, Daria. 2016. "Moscow's Overnight Demolition Blitz Sparks Legal Debate." *Moscow Times*, February 11. www.themoscowtimes.com/news/article/moscows -overnight-demolition-blitz-sparks-legal-debate/559236.html.

Makunina, Svetlana. 2012. "Gosduma snova stanet 'ne mestom dlya diskusii' [State Duma will once again became 'no place for discussion']." *RBK Daily*, September 10. www.rbcdaily.ru/politics/562949984681953.

Malesky, Edmund, and Paul Schuler. 2010. "Nodding or Needling: Analyzing Del-egate Responsiveness in an Authoritarian Parliament." *American Political Science Review* 104, no. 3, pp. 482–502.

Mayhew, David. 1974. *Congress: The Electoral Connection*. Yale University Press.

Mezey, Michael. 1979. *Comparative Legislatures*. Duke University Press.

Nikol'skaya, Polina, and Elizaveta Surnacheva. 2015. "Zakonodatel'naya retseptura: Kak rozhdayutsya na svet rossiiskie zakony [Legislative recipe: How Russian laws are born]." *Kommersant Vlast'*, January 26. www.kommersant.ru/doc/2644727.

Noble, Ben. 2014. "Executive Bill Failure under Authoritarianism: Evidence from the Russian Federation." Paper presented at the Annual Meeting of the American Political Science Association, Washington, D.C., August 28–31.

———. 2015. "Rethinking 'Rubber Stamps': Amending Executive Bills in the Russian State Duma, 2003–2013." Paper presented at the Annual Conference of the Midwest Political Science Association, Chicago, April 16–19.

———. 2016a. "Authoritarian Legislatures, Policy-Making, and Intra-Executive Constraints." Paper presented at the Annual Conference of the Midwest Political Science Association, Chicago, April 7–10.

———. 2016b. "Rethinking 'Rubber Stamps': Legislative Subservience, Executive Factionalism, and Policy-Making in the Russian State Duma." D.Phil. dissertation, University of Oxford.

———. 2017. "The State Duma, the "Crimean Consensus," and Volodin's Reforms." In *A Successful Failure: Russia after Crime(a)*, edited by Olga Irisova, Anton Barbashin, Fabian Burkhardt, and Ernest Wyciszkiewicz. Warsaw: The Centre for Polish-Russian Dialogue and Understanding.

Olson, David, and Michael Mezey. 1991. Preface to *Legislatures in the Policy Process: The Dilemmas of Economic Policy*, edited by David Olson and Michael Mezey. Cambridge University Press.

Ostrow, Joel. 2001. "Chaos in Russian Budgeting as a Product of Institutional Design: The Failure of Unlinked Dual-Channel Institutions." *Journal of Public Budgeting, Accounting and Financial Management* 13, no. 4, pp. 624–52.

Petrov, Nikolay, Maria Lipman, and Henry E. Hale. 2014. "Three Dilemmas of Hybrid Regime Governance: Russia from Putin to Putin." *Post-Soviet Affairs* 30, no. 1, pp. 1–26.

Popper, Karl. 1959. *The Logic of Scientific Discovery*. London: Hutchinson.

Remington, Thomas. 2007. "The Russian Federal Assembly, 1994–2004." *Journal of Legislative Studies* 13, no. 1, pp. 121–41.

———. 2008. "Patronage and the Party of Power: President-Parliament Relations under Vladimir Putin." *Europe-Asia Studies* 60, no. 6, pp. 959–87.

———. 2014. "Parliamentary Politics in Russia." In *Developments in Russian Politics*, edited by Stephen White, Richard Sakwa, and Henry E. Hale. 8th ed. Basingstoke: Palgrave Macmillan.

———. 2016. "Parliament and the Dominant Party Regime." In *Putin's Russia: Past Imperfect, Future Uncertain*, edited by Stephen Wegren. 6th ed. Lanham, Md.: Rowman and Littlefield.

Reuter, Ora John, and Graeme B. Robertson. 2015. "Legislatures, Cooptation, and Social Protest in Contemporary Authoritarian Regimes." *Journal of Politics* 77, no. 1, pp. 235–48.

Rustamova, Farida. 2014. "Internet-vybory Obshchestvennoi palaty ne privlekli oppozitsiyu [Internet elections of the Public Chamber failed to attract the opposition]." *RBK Daily*, May 6. www.rbc.ru/politics/06/05/2014/922151.shtml.

Samokhina, Sof'ya. 2016. "Ukhodyashchaya Duma [Departing Duma]." *Kommersant Vlast'*, April 18. http://kommersant.site/doc/2961577.

Sapozhkov, Oleg, Tatyana Grishina, Maxim Ivanov, and Evgenya Kryuchkova. 2015. "Nepredvidennaya byudzhetnaya kommissiya [Unexpected budgetary commission]." *Kommersant*, July 4. www.kommersant.ru/doc/2761860.

Schulmann, Ekaterina. 2014a. "Patriotichnye termity [Patriotic termites]." *Vedomosti*, September 26. www.vedomosti.ru/opinion/articles/2014/09/26/patriotichnye-termity.

———. 2014b. "Russian Parliament Is Slipping Back to '90s Chaos." *Moscow Times*, November 24. www.themoscowtimes.com/opinion/article/russian-parliament-is-slipping-back-to-90s-chaos/511740.html.

———. 2015a. "Demokratiya otkuda ne zhdali, ili Vozvrashchenie byudzhetnogo protsessa [Democracy unexpected, or the return of the budgetary process]." *Vedomosti*, April 13. www.vedomosti.ru/opinion/articles/2015/04/14/demokratiya-otkuda-ne-zhdali-ili-vozvraschenie-byudzhetnogo-protsessa.

———. 2015b. "Benefitsiary mrakobesiya [Beneficiaries of obscurantism]." *New Times*, July. www.newtimes.ru/articles/detail/100161.

———. 2015c. "Duma-2014 Report: Outcomes and Tendencies." *Russian Politics and Law* 53, no. 5, pp. 57–65.

———. 2016. "Chem zaimetsya novaya Duma [What the new Duma will do]." *Vedomosti*, September 11. www.vedomosti.ru/opinion/articles/2016/09/12/656536-zaimetsya-duma.

Skilling, H. Gordon. 1971. "Groups in Soviet Politics: Some Hypotheses." In *Interest Groups in Soviet Politics*, edited by H. Gordon Skilling and Franklyn Griffiths. Princeton University Press.

Sterkin, Filipp, and Olga Churakova. 2014. "Popravki o sborakh s malogo biznesa snyaty s rassmotreniya v byudzhetnom komitete [Amendments on small business fees withdrawn from consideration in the budget committee]." *Vedomosti*, November 14. www.vedomosti.ru/finance/articles/2014/11/14/popravki-o-vvedenii.

Taylor, Brian. 2014. "Police Reform in Russia: The Policy Process in a Hybrid Regime." *Post-Soviet Affairs* 30, nos. 2–3, pp. 226–55.

Tkachuk, Sergei. 2005. "Eks-spiker Gosdumy RF Gennadii Seleznev: 'U nas seichas totalitarnaya Gosduma' [State Duma former speaker, Gennadii Seleznev: 'We now have a totalitarian State Duma']." *Novye Izvestia*, October 17. www.newizv.ru/politics/2005-10-17/33583-eks-spiker-gosdumy-rf-gennadij-seleznev.html.

Trifonova, Ekaterina. 2016. "Pravozashchitniki zamakhnulis' na formu pravleniya [Human rights defenders aim blow at form of government]." *Nezavisimaya Gazeta*, January 19. www.ng.ru/politics/2016-01-19/1_pravozashitniki.html.

Troxel, Tiffany. 2003. *Parliamentary Power in Russia, 1994–2001: President vs. Parliament*. New York: Palgrave Macmillan.

Truex, Rory. 2014. "The Returns to Office in a 'Rubber Stamp' Parliament." *American Political Science Review* 108, no. 2, pp. 235–51.

Ukolov, Roman. 2014. "Pravila zhizni deputatov v Rossii [Rules of life for Russian deputies]." *Lenta.ru*, December 2. http://lenta.ru/articles/2014/12/02/oniskazali pravdu.

Vinokurov, Andrei. 2015. "Duma stanovitsya ristalishchem, gde rytsari prelomlyayut kop'ya [Duma becomes a stadium where knights compete]." *Gazeta.ru*, April 8. https://www.gazeta.ru/politics/2015/04/07_a_6629877.shtml.

Visloguzov, Vadim. 2016. "Gosduma—ne mesto dlya byudzheta [State Duma is no place for the budget]." *Kommersant*, May 13. www.kommersant.ru/doc/2984550.

FOUR

The *Siloviki* in Russian Politics

ANDREI SOLDATOV and MICHAEL ROCHLITZ

Who holds power and makes political decisions in contemporary Russia? A brief survey of available literature in any well-stocked bookshop in the United States or Europe will quickly lead one to the answer: Vladimir Putin and the "siloviki" (see, for example, LeVine 2009; Soldatov and Borogan 2010; Harding 2011; Felshtinsky and Pribylovsky 2012; Lucas 2012, 2014; Dawisha 2014). *Sila* in Russian means "force," and the siloviki are the members of Russia's so-called force ministries—those state agencies authorized to use violence to respond to threats to national security.

These armed agents are often portrayed—by journalists and scholars alike—as Russia's true rulers. A conventional wisdom has emerged about their rise to dominance, which goes roughly as follows. After taking office in 2000, Putin reconsolidated the security services and then gradually placed his former associates from the State Security Committee (KGB) and Federal Security Service (FSB) in key positions across the country (Petrov 2002, 2005; Kryshtanovskaya and White 2003, 2009). Over the years, this group managed to disable almost all competing sources of power and control. United by a common identity, a shared worldview, and a deep personal loyalty to Putin, the siloviki constitute a cohesive corporation, which has entrenched itself at the heart of Russian politics. Accountable to no one but the president himself, they are the driving force behind increasingly authoritarian policies at home (Illarionov 2009; Roxburgh 2013; Kasparov 2015), an aggressive foreign policy (Lucas 2014), and high levels of state predation and corruption (Dawisha 2013, 2014).

While this interpretation contains elements of truth, we argue that it provides only a partial and sometimes misleading and exaggerated picture of the siloviki's actual role. Based on interviews we conducted with former siloviki, experts on the force ministries, and lawyers and social activists whose work focuses on them, as well as a comprehensive review of written sources and analysis of our own quantitative data, we suggest a different account.

Rather than a coordinated takeover of state institutions, we view the siloviki's ascendance as a result of Putin's reliance—in a highly personalized system—on his own particular network of trusted friends and colleagues. Where others see a cohesive corporation, we see a mosaic of clans and factions that are too divided and lacking in common leadership to advance any collective agenda. What they can do is to compete against each other for budget allocations and corrupt rents, exploiting their freedom from accountability. Although their fragmentation makes it hard to see the siloviki as the driver behind Russia's current policies—domestic and international— they do share a common worldview that is very much aligned with these policies. It is Putin's increasing acceptance of this vision of reality, and his dependence on a few trusted individuals from this world, rather than any institutionalized position or role of the security services, that explains his recent adoption of priorities that have for years been popular in the Lubyanka building in Moscow.

RUSSIA'S FORCE MINISTRIES: FROM SOVIET TIMES TO PUTIN

In the broadest sense, Russia's force ministries comprise the armed forces; the Ministry of Internal Affairs, which until recently had its own internal troops (these were transferred into a new National Guard in the spring of 2016); the Ministry of Emergency Situations, which has its own civil defense troops; the General Procuracy; the Investigative Committee; and the security services—which are our main focus (see Paneyakh and Rosenberg, this volume, for discussion of the Ministry of Internal Affairs and the Procuracy). This landscape has evolved since the end of communist rule in 1991.

Under the Soviet Union, the security and intelligence community was defined by the rivalries and turf wars between two major players, the KGB and the Main Intelligence Directorate of the General Staff of the Armed Forces, the GRU. While the KGB was responsible for foreign intelligence, counterintelligence, and internal security, the GRU focused primarily on military intelligence abroad. Both organizations, the secret police and military intelligence, were essentially part of the large apparatus of the Communist Party of the Soviet Union, which scrutinized and controlled them quite effectively. Under the 1959 KGB guidelines, every party member had the right "to report about shortcomings in the work of the organs of state security to the respective party organs."[1] Each division, department, and office of the KGB had a party cell, a peephole by which the state could monitor its agents. All promotions had to be approved by the Communist Party Central Committee's Administrative Department, which relied on the information gathered by the party cells. This same department also vetted all military intelligence officers of the GRU before they were sent abroad.

In August 1991, as Mikhail Gorbachev's close associates attempted a coup to salvage the Soviet regime, Vladimir Kryuchkov, the KGB head, was among the operation's leaders. By contrast, Vladlen Mikhailov, the GRU director, kept his agency on the sidelines. For this reason, the new, democratically elected Russian authorities led by Boris Yeltsin distrusted the KGB and sought to reform it, while remaining relatively unconcerned about the GRU. As a result, the GRU survived the transition practically untouched. The director was replaced, but the structure and even the name of the organization remained the same.

Although the KGB was expected to undergo substantial reform, it experienced only a simple restructuring. Yeltsin's plan was to break up the agency and delineate the responsibilities of each piece. The largest department—initially called the Ministry of Security, then the Federal Service of Counterintelligence (FSK), and finally the Federal Security Service (FSB)—was put in charge of counterespionage and counterterrorism, with its political section that had tracked and harassed dissidents disbanded; it was also initially stripped of its investigative powers and prisons. But it was this department that inherited the KGB's network of regional branches. The former foreign intelligence directorate was renamed the Foreign Intelligence Service, while the division responsible for electronic eavesdropping, cryptography, and secure government communications became the Committee

1. Soldatov and Borogan (2010, p. 10).

of Government Communication, later called the Federal Agency for Government Communications and Information (FAPSI). A KGB directorate that guarded secret underground facilities was simply renamed the Main Directorate of Special Programs of the President, or GUSP, and the branch that had provided bodyguards for Soviet leaders was renamed the Federal Protective Service (FSO). Finally, the Soviet border guards became an independent Federal Border Service.

During the initial economic and political transition of the early 1990s, the Russian security services went through an unprecedented era of openness. Its officers welcomed into the archives human rights activists searching for files on victims of repression under Joseph Stalin. KGB generals became guests on TV shows, and the agency's leaders invited dissidents to visit its headquarters in Lubyanka Square. Concerned to avoid the fate of the East German Ministry for State Security, or Stasi, the KGB proposed involving prominent political activists in the reform of the agency. Sergey Grigoryants, a famous Soviet dissident who had spent nine years in jail, was invited to join the agency's supervisory committee. He refused, fearing that his name would be exploited. The supervisory committee never produced a reform plan.

Ultimately, Yeltsin's governments failed to create a system of parliamentary oversight over the security services. In a decree issued on December 21, 1993, Yeltsin himself admitted: "The system of the VChK [Cheka]-OGPU-NKVD-MGB-KGB-MB has proved unreformable. The attempts at reorganization that have been made in recent years were basically superficial and cosmetic. . . . The system of political investigation has been mothballed and could easily be recreated" (Waller 2004, p. 349; see also Knight 1994, p. 22). Beneath the surface reorganization, the internal mechanisms and machinery remained largely intact. Bureaucratic procedures, information collection and dissemination, and the rules for approving operations all remained the same, as did the names of most operating units.

Attempts to strengthen accountability were undercut by the security services' control of the necessary information and their assertion of secrecy. In one case, pressure from dissidents and journalists persuaded Andrei Bykov, the FSB's deputy director in 1992–96, to require some outside body to approve surveillance operations—initially the prosecutor's office, but from 1995 onward the courts. Yet the fine print of the regulation made it largely irrelevant. While, in theory, FSB officers had to get a warrant, they were not allowed to show it to the telephone operator for reasons of secrecy. The FSB also had all the necessary equipment to tap directly into telephone conversations by itself, so that in actual practice no one could challenge surveillance orders.

Authority to oversee the FSB and GRU passed from the old Communist Party Central Committee's Administrative Department to a directorate within the Presidential Administration. Yet, lacking the kind of tips and inside information that the communist supervisors had obtained from their party cells inside the security agencies, the new body was operating in the dark, without any real power to control the FSB, the GRU, and other security agencies.

To this day, the widely used Official Secrets Act of the Russian Federation (Zakon o gosudarstvennoi taine) makes it impossible in practice for any independent actor to investigate the dealings of the force ministries. Under the act, the ministries can classify any relevant information as a state secret. Although all security services created special bodies, the so-called internal security directorates, to combat corruption, in fact these bodies were used to protect the reputation of the services. It soon became established practice for police investigators, on discovering employees of the security services complicit in criminal activity, to hand over this part of the investigation to the internal security directorate of the relevant service, which usually shut down the case. In theory, some external control could also have come from the General Procurator's Office, a special body responsible for overseeing all law enforcement agencies including the FSB. Yet a law regulating FSB activities rendered this toothless by stipulating that "information regarding people who provide or have provided FSB organs with confidential assistance regarding the organization, tactics, methods, and means of implementing the activity of FSB organs shall not be subject to oversight by the procurator's office."[2]

Rather than supervising the security services' activities, the parliament has often increased their discretion. The State Duma frequently delegates legislative initiatives on security and intelligence to the concerned agencies and then rubber-stamps the drafts these agencies propose. Both chambers

---

2. Joint Decree of the General Prosecutor's Office and the FSB no. 20-27/10, May 18, 2002. In April 2002, a further decree required that FSB "work-related documents" were to be treated as classified and could, as a rule, only be examined by the prosecutors on the FSB premises. Only in exceptional cases was the Office of the Prosecutor General allowed to demand access to such documents (Soldatov and Borogan 2010).

of the parliament have a committee to deal with the security budget, but it is unclear whether they have ever done more than merely approve the agencies' proposal.

In place of institutionalized oversight of the security services, Yeltsin sought to control them by encouraging interagency rivalries. In the 1990s the foreign intelligence agency remained in direct competition with military intelligence, while the FSB struggled against the communications agency, which also kept a close eye on the social and political situation in Russia. After obtaining a report from the FSB director, Yeltsin could compare it with the report from the FAPSI director. FAPSI was particularly crucial, as it controlled the central electronic vote-counting system, which offered a sneak preview of voting outcomes in real time for the Kremlin.

Interservice rivalry intensified when in 1993 a new agency, the Tax Police, was created to address the problem of Russia's catastrophically low tax receipts. This new body competed bitterly with the department of economic safety within the FSK and later FSB. Meanwhile, the new service charged with protecting the president was transformed by its chief, Alexander Korzhakov, a former Yeltsin bodyguard, into what many described as an updated Praetorian Guard. The agency employed parapsychologists and clairvoyants to draft prognoses and analytical reports for Yeltsin, in parallel with the reports of the communications agency and the FSB.

In short, three main features characterized the security services that President Putin inherited in 2000. First, the two superagencies of the Soviet era—the KGB and GRU—had been replaced by a mosaic of competing services, which Yeltsin's divide-and-rule tactics had mobilized into intense mutual rivalry. Second, the somewhat effective oversight and control that the Soviet Communist Party had exercised had not been replaced by any system of democratic monitoring and accountability. A natural consequence was widespread corruption of all kinds. Third, although now distributed among multiple organizations, the functions, procedures, and authority and even many of the personnel of the security services remained the same as in the late Soviet era.

PUTIN'S RECONSOLIDATION?

Did Putin restore organizational coherence to Russia's security space? At some points, he did seem to be consolidating agencies and strengthening the role of the FSB. In March 2003 he abolished the Tax Police. That same month, he eliminated the communications agency, FAPSI, dividing its personnel and resources between the FSB and the Federal Protective Service. He also folded the border guards into the FSB. In addition, the FSB was permitted to create its own department for gathering foreign intelligence, directly rivaling the Foreign Intelligence Service. And it got the upper hand over the Ministry of Internal Affairs, an agency that combines the national police with an investigations department similar to the U.S. Federal Bureau of Investigation. The FSB placed counterintelligence officers in key posts in the ministry, and in 2003 Rashid Nurgaliev, an FSB general, was appointed to head it. All this made the FSB into the undisputed leader of the country's security services.

Yet there are problems with this image of Putin as the great consolidator. First, the trend toward rebuilding and re-empowering the security services predates him by several years. Indeed, the Russian secret services started to regain the influence they had lost during the fall of the Soviet Union, not with Putin, but already starting in 1995. The main successor of the KGB, the FSK (in which K stands for Kontrrazvedka—"counterintelligence"), was renamed in 1995 as the FSB, replacing "Kontrrazvedka" with the much wider term "Bezopasnost" (security). In 1995 the FSB also managed to regain its investigative department and its own system of prisons. From that time on, the FSB combined the functions of a secret service and a law enforcement agency.

During the late 1990s, Yeltsin began to rely more and more on the siloviki. All three of the prime ministers he chose during the crisis years of 1998–2000—Yevgeni Primakov, Sergei Stepashin, and finally Putin—had security service backgrounds. Thus, Putin's advent to power was not the initial cause of the reconsolidation of Russia's security agencies, but actually a consequence of this already ongoing process.

Second, even as Putin was merging some agencies into the FSB, he was complicating the institutional environment in other ways. All the officers from the abolished Tax Police were redeployed to fill the ranks of a new agency that Putin created to combat the narcotics trade, the Federal Drug Control Service, whose original leader, Viktor Cherkesov, was a former KGB officer from St. Petersburg and Putin's close friend. In April 2016 Putin created a new National Guard out of the internal troops within the Ministry of Internal Affairs. In return, the ministry absorbed the antidrug agency. Despite Putin's reorganizations, the Russian intelligence and security community today consists of nine major agencies. Outside this community,

Putin created another major new silovik institution, the Investigative Committee, which since January 2011 has been the main federal investigative authority in Russia (see also Paneyakh and Rosenberg, this volume). The agency answers directly to the Russian president and is responsible for inspecting the police forces, combating police corruption and misconduct, and investigating local authorities and federal government bodies. Formed within the office of the procurator general in 2007, and given independent status only in 2011, the Investigative Committee does not date back to the KGB, and therefore its employees have a somewhat different mentality; for example, compared with their FSB colleagues, they are slightly more open and ready to talk to the press. It also had relatively high internal cohesion since it was run for years by its founder, Alexander Bastrykin, who could rely on the strong personal loyalty of his top subordinates, most of whom he had appointed himself.

Competition among these many rival agencies remains intense. Yet there is little evidence that Putin uses this rivalry as Yeltsin did to obtain information and maintain control. Only on one occasion is Putin known to have used one agency to check another: in 2007 he asked the Federal Drug Control Service, still led by his friend Viktor Cherkesov, to look into the dealings of the FSB. The result was a bruising defeat for Cherkesov. His leading general in charge of the investigation was jailed, and Cherkesov himself was soon deprived of his position. In the end, the FSB proved too strong even for Putin. Rather than a technique of presidential control, interagency rivalry has largely degenerated into a fight for material benefits, with every service trying to defend its rents and sphere of influence against possible encroachment.

There is only very limited evidence that Putin uses his authority as president to micromanage security service appointments. We know of only two occasions on which Putin directly interfered with personnel decisions to fire or transfer important siloviki. When in the summer of 2004 Chechen guerrilla leader Shamil Basayev invaded Ingushetia and managed to control the republic for two days, Putin fired a group of high-ranking FSB generals. The FSB had temporarily lost control over an entire Russian region, and that was something Putin was not ready to forgive. The second example dates from 2014–16, when Putin started transferring people from the FSO to important positions in the federal agencies and the regions. This last example might indicate the beginning of a new trend, with the number of siloviki in key positions starting to increase again during the past three years, both at the federal center and in the regions.[3]

However, even as he was moving members of his personal bodyguard squad into high political and administrative posts, Putin also began to retire some of his closest longtime associates with a siloviki background. In April 2016 Viktor Ivanov's antidrug agency was disbanded and he was not offered a new post; Evgeny Murov, the head of the FSO, was fired in May 2016; and most dramatic was Putin's dismissal of Sergei Ivanov as head of the Presidential Administration in August 2016. Thus, although the number of siloviki in important administrative positions started to increase again from 2014 onward, the old political heavyweights—who often had their own opinions, sometimes strongly held—were giving way to lower-level service professionals, who are less likely to provide independent input. This is consistent with the continuing tendency to narrow down competing or independent sources of information and limit decisionmaking to an ever smaller group of individuals around the president. One might also see this as a rebalancing of the relative weight of the FSB and FSO.

Thus, Putin only reconsolidated the security services and interfered with personnel appointments to a limited extent. Yet, since coming to power, he has provided the services with a significant increase in resources, in both absolute and relative terms. While spending in absolute terms more than doubled between 2000 and 2007 (Taylor 2011, p. 53), in relative terms the law enforcement and security services increased their share compared to military spending during Putin's first two terms as president.

Another significant increase in financial resources available to both the military and the security services began with Russia's extensive rearmament program, which started in 2011. As a result, the federal budget share for national defense is estimated to have grown from 14 percent of the total in 2011 to 19 percent in 2015, and it is predicted to grow to 25 percent in 2020; spending on security and law enforcement was projected to increase

3. Four examples are Alexander Kolpakov, who became head of the Presidential Administrative Directorate in May 2014; the FSO general Dmitry Mironov, who was first appointed the new head of the Main Directorate of Economic Security and Fighting Corruption within the Ministry of Internal Affairs and then in July 2016 made acting governor of Yaroslavl Oblast; Putin's former bodyguard Alexey Dyumin, who was appointed acting governor of Tula Oblast in February 2016; and another of Putin's bodyguards, Evgeny Zinichev, who was appointed acting governor of Kaliningrad Oblast in July 2016.

from 11 percent in 2011 to 13.5 percent in 2015 (Taylor 2013). By contrast, combined spending on health care and education was set to decline from 9.2 percent of the budget in 2011 to 6.2 percent by 2015 (Taylor 2013). Even though overall spending on rearmament has been readjusted in view of Russia's recent economic crisis, the cuts have been far less significant than in other sectors of the economy (Oxenstierna 2016). This clearly illustrates the changing priorities associated with Putin's return to the presidency in 2012, pointing to a substantial relative increase in power and resources for the force ministries within the Russian government from about 2012 onward.

SECURITY PERSONNEL TAKING OVER THE STATE?

A couple of days before becoming president, Putin addressed his former FSB colleagues. In a speech later cited repeatedly, he announced that "a group of FSB operatives, dispatched under cover to work in the government of the Russian Federation, is successfully fulfilling its task." Some observers, already inclined to see Putin as the frontman for a security service conspiracy, saw this as less a joke than a frank admission.[4] Putin's early personnel appointments seemed to confirm the impression that he was determined to reestablish the dominance of the former KGB. In a widely cited study, Olga Kryshtanovskaya and Stephen White (2003) claimed that by 2003 a quarter of Russia's senior bureaucrats had a background in the force ministries (up from 3.7 percent under Gorbachev in 1988).[5]

Yet there is an alternative explanation for the growing number of siloviki in leading positions that, although somewhat less exciting, is probably closer to the truth. Rather than the result of a coordinated "siloviki project," consciously advanced by Putin, the spread of former KGB officers is a consequence of the informal elite recruitment system that Putin inherited (Renz 2006, 2007). To survive in power, Yeltsin developed a highly

---

4. See, for example, *The Economist* (2007).

5. In a second study, Kryshtanovskaya and White (2009) argue that this group then systematically proceeded to eliminate all alternative sources of power (regional governors, competitive elections, the media, and private business), to build a state where "all important decisions . . . are now taken by a tiny group of men who served alongside Mr Putin in the KGB and who come from his home town of St Petersburg." Kryshtanovskaya, quoted in *The Economist* (2007).

personalized and tactical approach to political appointments. Taking over this system, Putin had little choice but to rely on people he knew and trusted to fill key offices. As many of those he knew, trusted, and had worked with in the past were from either St. Petersburg or the FSB, an increase in the number of such people at the top is not that surprising.

Some scholars have qualified the picture of siloviki dominance. David W. Rivera and Sharon Werning Rivera (2006, 2014) found that while the percentage of siloviki in key positions did rise significantly, after correcting for some methodological inconsistencies the real number of siloviki among the state elite was not around 25 percent but between 15 and 20 percent in 2003, and around 20 percent in 2008, with the numbers then declining again during Dmitry Medvedev's presidency (Rivera and Rivera 2014, p. 44). By looking at all heads of ministries from 1992 to 2016, Maxim Ananyev (this volume) similarly finds a peak in the number of siloviki during the administration of Mikhail Fradkov (2004–07) and then a subsequent decline back to the levels of 1992 for the Medvedev administration from 2012 onward. He identifies a similar pattern for the top-three positions in the Presidential Administration. Comparing these numbers to those for other groups—for example, former business people and career bureaucrats—the siloviki did not occupy an overwhelmingly prominent position. Based on a micro-level study of particular siloviki, Bettina Renz (2006) concluded that the policy role played by many of these individuals was also less important than generally assumed.

In sum, although the number of siloviki in key positions has clearly grown under Putin since the early 2000s, the increase is less dramatic than often thought, and it resulted more from the personalized nature of Russia's recruitment system than from a deliberate strategy adopted by either Putin or powerful forces inside the Lubyanka building.

A UNITED LOBBY FOR FAVORED POLICIES?

Do the various siloviki ministries, agencies, and departments constitute a unified group that is able to coordinate its actions to press for specific policies? The organizational fragmentation already noted renders that unlikely. And institutional divisions are crosscut and exacerbated by factional, personal, and business rivalries (Galeotti 2015, p. 10). The accounts of our interview respondents suggest that, rather than working together to implement a common "siloviki agenda," these different agencies often compete fiercely, for both access to Putin and the control of corrupt income and spheres of influence.

However, the siloviki's increasing presence in the 2000s did have one clear consequence: a visible change in the country's political culture. They brought in the suspicious, inward-looking mind-set of the security services, which had been shaped by Soviet history. This trend is best reflected by one infamous saying of Boris Gryzlov, the parliamentary speaker in 2003–11 and a member of Putin's inner circle (he was a schoolmate of Nikolai Patrushev, then FSB director), who, on his very first day in the State Duma, announced that "the Parliament should not be a ground for political battles." (The quotation became known later as "Parliament is no place for discussion.")[6]

The siloviki do share an interest in the status quo, since any kind of political, institutional, or economic reform would likely limit the size of the corrupt profit streams they enjoy. The force agencies protect each other against outside interference, circling the wagons to prevent the judiciary or anyone else from launching independent investigations into their activities, one respondent told us. Yet, at the same time, they fight furiously among themselves, using "the information and coercive capacities at their disposal" as well as criminal connections to defraud and expropriate targeted businesses (Rochlitz 2014; Galeotti 2015, p. 9).

Another source of conflict that one of our respondents pointed out is the competition for spheres of influence. With different agencies providing protection services for bribes in carefully delimited spheres, an unexpected change in these areas can provoke intense infighting, though it rarely becomes visible to the public.[7]

Yet another source of internal division concerns age. A conflict of generations appears to be emerging, with mid-level officers finding themselves unable to obtain promotions. Putin appointed key allies from his KGB days in St. Petersburg to the FSB's top posts, and most remain in these or other top jobs today, blocking mobility for those below. Frustration has been growing among mid-level officers, leading to a deepening crisis of trust

6. Hearings in the State Duma, December 29, 2003, transcript, www.cir.ru/docs /duma/302/420464?QueryID=3739136&HighlightQuery=3739136.

7. One exception might be the conflict opposing investigator Boris Kolesnikov from the Ministry of Internal Affairs and some allegedly highly corrupt members of the FSB, as documented in Yaffa (2015).

inside the agencies. In a highly unusual move, in 2008 a group of mid-ranking FSB officers appealed first to Moscow military courts and then to the European Court of Human Rights in Strasbourg, with a complaint about the excessive compensation paid to high-ranking FSB generals at a time when mid-ranking officers had difficulties obtaining the benefits to which they were entitled by law. Instead of addressing the complaints, the FSB created a department aimed at protecting high-ranking generals from such lawsuits. As an FSB colonel told us: "This department was established to protect the FSB leadership, not ordinary officers. At one meeting, generals of my section were asked why there was such a big difference in salaries. They answered that the Motherland once had no money. Now, the country has the resources and so they should be paid adequately for their work."

Besides their many divisions, a key obstacle to the siloviki presenting a policy agenda is that—apart from Putin, whose role requires him to arbitrate between them and other political forces—they have no leader. Moreover, there is no setting in which heads of the various services can meet and work out common positions. Thus, rather than a cohesive corporation with a common policy agenda, the siloviki represent a collection of competing agencies, with counterpoised interests and mutual animosities.

A COMMON WORLDVIEW?

Although divided in all the ways already mentioned, the siloviki do appear to share a common view of the world. At least, that is the strong impression we have formed from our recent interviews and from reporting about and studying the force ministries over the past ten years. A good illustration of the way many siloviki think can be found, for example, in a recent interview by Security Council head and former FSB director Nikolai Patrushev or in the official magazine of the FSB, *Za i Protiv* (For and against) (*Rossiyskaya Gazeta* 2015; *Za i Protiv* 2016). Although variation across different agencies and individuals does of course exist, we have tried to summarize the siloviki worldview in three main points.

First, the siloviki favor a strong and highly centralized state that is supported by large and well-financed security and defense structures. This strong state should play a decisive role in the economy and ensure that the economic interests of the nation are defended against the encroachments of globalization. Second, they see Russia as menaced by external forces that envy its economic wealth, natural resources, and status as a great power. The greatest threats come from NATO and the United States. Third, the siloviki tend to see themselves as uniquely competent to understand the dangers Russia faces and to choose appropriate responses. They see the realm of official politics as one of lies and deception, which ordinary people are unable to penetrate. The heads of the security services believe "that they are the only ones who have the real picture and understanding of the world," according to the former dissident Sergey Grigoryants (*Rossiyskaya Gazeta* 2015). A number of our respondents confirmed this point.

Although we observed loyalty to Putin among the former siloviki we interviewed, and a reluctance to find fault with their president at a time of international conflict, there were some nuances. One respondent said that he did not agree with all of Putin's policies, especially with respect to the economy, but added: "We are now under siege, and you do not criticize the commander in chief when the fortress is under siege." Another retired silovik voiced concerns about Russia's recent intervention in Syria, doubting whether those generals and soldiers who had fought in Afghanistan and Chechnya would have been as eager as current leaders to get involved in another conflict. In his view, many of the top siloviki in Russia today never fought in a real war themselves and are therefore more inclined than the older siloviki generation to send soldiers abroad. Some, by emphasizing their professionalism and sense of responsibility to protect the country, implicitly differentiated themselves from others more focused on careerism or corrupt rents. These views reflect the concerns raised by Viktor Cherkesov in a widely cited newspaper article in 2007, where he argued that "warriors should not become merchants" (Cherkesov 2007).

Another common point shared by many siloviki is a close relationship to the Russian Orthodox Church. Leonid Reshetnikov, head of the Russian Institute for Strategic Studies, a think tank that used to be part of the Foreign Intelligence Service, framed the conflict in Ukraine in terms of a conflict between Catholicism and Russian Orthodoxy: "Ukrainism [*ukrainstvo*] from its beginning is an anti-Orthodox concept: it was directed not only against the Russians, against the Muscovites, it was directed against Orthodoxy. This concept was born in the West, in Austria-Hungary, in

Poland, in Catholic countries, and it is now being implemented" (Reshetnikov 2016).[8]

It appears that such views are shared by many members of the security services, especially among the older generation as well as among quite a number of leading generals at the very top. The relationship also goes both ways, with the Russian Orthodox Church maintaining close links with various security agencies. The Moscow Patriarchate even maintains a special department for relations with the siloviki. In a recent letter to the head of the FSB, Patriarch Kirill congratulated the siloviki on their good work.[9]

To reiterate, rather than a united group with the kind of leadership, organization, and shared interests that would make it possible to identify and lobby effectively for favored policies, the siloviki appear today to be a fragmented community of rival services, factions, and personal networks, competing among themselves for budget resources, corrupt rents, and access to Putin. They are united by little other than a general loyalty to the commander in chief and a conservative and nationalistic worldview, although there are divisions here, too. This picture of fragmentation would probably be even more striking if we included a closer look at the armed forces and the police. This raises the question of whether the increasingly authoritarian tendencies in Russian domestic policy and the Kremlin's more assertive international posture reflect the ascendancy of the siloviki as a group or rather the contingent fact that the instincts and understandings of Putin and his close circle were forged over the course of long careers in the force ministries.

8. Reshetnikov was interviewed by Radio Radonezh, a radio station that, according to its website, claims to be "the voice of the Russian Orthodox Church, in Russia and beyond its borders" (http://radonezh.ru/gruppasmi).

9. For example, see this telegram from February 23, 2016, by Patriarch Kirill to Alexander Bortnikov, director of the FSB: "For many years as the head of the Federal Security Service, you always aspire to be an example of professionalism and fidelity to your vocation and the readiness to work selflessly for the good of Russia, performing one of the most important tasks to protect the country from external and internal threats." Moscow Patriarchate, February 23, 2016, www.patriarchia.ru /db/text/4383916.html.

EXPLAINING THE AUTHORITARIAN TURN

At first glance, what happened in Russia during the past four years seems to come close to realizing what many researchers would characterize as a "siloviki agenda" (see, for example, Bremmer and Charap 2007; Staun 2007), namely, a "tightening of screws" for the political opposition at home and an increasingly aggressive foreign policy abroad. One might take this as a sign of the siloviki's final victory in the bureaucratic struggle against all other powerful actors. Yet there are problems with this view.

Most important, it does not explain the timing of the change. It appears that Putin's greater reliance on the siloviki and adoption of their agenda was a reaction to events rather than the result of any lobbying or prior bureaucratic strengthening of the force ministries. Indeed, Rivera and Rivera (2014) argue that the share of siloviki in top positions declined during the Medvedev presidency. A recent increase of siloviki in leading positions both at the federal level and in the regions occurred only after the onset of the Ukraine crisis in 2014. Similarly, although Russia's extensive rearmament campaign was initiated in 2011, the fact that defense and security-related spending was reduced much less than spending on other sectors of the economy during the recent economic crisis was due to the perception of new risks and threats, rather than a result of successful lobbying by the force ministries (Oxenstierna 2016).

Two key events had a major impact on the change of the direction of Russian domestic policy after Putin returned to the presidency in 2012—the Arab Spring in early 2011 and then the mass protests that broke out in Moscow after Russia's parliamentary and presidential elections in December 2011 and March 2012. Even more than during the mid-2000s, when a series of "color revolutions" toppled a number of regimes in the post-Soviet world, Russia's elites during and after Putin's return to the presidency were frightened by the prospects of increased social unrest and the specter of potentially violent regime change (see below).

On February 22, 2011, Dmitry Medvedev, then the Russian president, urgently convened a meeting of the National Antiterrorism Committee, which consisted of leaders of the security and law enforcement agencies. Medvedev chaired the event and in his opening remarks soon turned to the Arab Spring. "Look at the current situation in the Middle East and the Arab world. It is extremely difficult and great problems still lie ahead," he said.

"We must face the truth. That scenario was harbored for us, and now attempts to implement it are even more likely."[10]

These events strengthened the siloviki's influence primarily because they seemed to confirm the narrative that siloviki leaders had been expounding for years—and to which Putin appears increasingly committed. In this narrative, the United States has been working consistently to topple political regimes on the soil of the former Soviet Union. The color revolutions of the early 2000s in Georgia and Ukraine are understood as part of this effort. They demonstrated not just the covert aggression of the United States but also its grasp of a new technology—social networks—that could mobilize revolutionary crowds into the streets even without traditional instruments such as trade unions and opposition parties.

In the past, Putin had turned mostly to his civilian political operatives, led by Vladislav Surkov, to manage such threats. It had been Surkov who, in the mid-2000s, set up youth movements such as Nashi (Ours), to combat potential anti-regime crowds; mobilizing such pro-Putin groups was chosen as the main strategy to counter color revolutions. The 2011–12 Moscow protests were seen as a failure of Surkov's team, and instead law enforcement leaders were authorized to use harsher methods. Surkov was replaced as the top Kremlin official in charge of domestic policy by Vyacheslav Volodin, who took care to coordinate with the siloviki. While Surkov was bold enough to pick a fight with the Investigative Committee, Volodin had no intention of challenging the force ministries, warning one regional governor: "If you get in a fight with the siloviki, don't expect support from us."[11]

The increasing reliance on the use of law enforcement was evident in the arrest of thirty protesters after a demonstration on Bolotnaya Square on May 6, 2012. Many of those arrested were detained until late 2013, and six were sentenced to prison terms of 2.5 to 4.5 years. Yet the siloviki have not

10. "Transcript of the Meeting of the National Antiterrorism Committee," February 22, 2011, http://eng.kremlin.ru/transcripts/1804.

11. In a speech at the London School of Economics on May 1, 2013, Surkov criticized the Investigative Committee for being too aggressive in its investigation against the innovation hub Skolkovo, the promotion of which was one of his responsibilities. The speech led to harsh criticism from the side of Vladimir Markin, press secretary of the Investigative Committee, and is believed to have triggered Surkov losing his post as deputy prime minister a week later. See, for example, *The Interpreter* (2013). On Volodin's warning to the regional governor, see *Republic* (2013).

always seemed up to the new challenges. The vigorous propaganda campaign that the Kremlin unleashed, both on national TV (see, for example, Pomerantsev and Weiss 2015) and on the Internet (Soldatov and Borogan 2015), appears to have been managed by civilians. At first, Putin had turned to the siloviki for help combating the new dangers associated with social networks. But FSB generals complained that they had no effective techniques to address these threats (Soldatov and Borogan 2015). Besides a few new measures to filter the Internet, they did not come up with much, so it was left to civilian operatives to mount the main counteroffensive. From offices in several cities, an army of publicly funded Internet trolls together with some pro-Kremlin bloggers were assigned to dominate discussion forums and social networks frequented by the opposition (Chen 2015).

To the Kremlin, the political protests that started in Ukraine in late 2013 seemed just another Western attempt at regime change. The FSB, tasked with providing information about political developments in Ukraine since the late 1990s, utterly failed to predict the crisis. The reasons for the failure were primarily the agency's lack of interest in grassroots mass movements. Instead, the FSB focused almost exclusively on the corrupt elites in power, following the old idea "If we control the shah, we control the country." The problem was exacerbated by a shared background: former KGB generals now serving in Ukraine's security service told a different group of former KGB generals now serving in Russia's FSB what was happening in the country. As a result, odd ideas defined the FSB's approach. According to some sources, the FSB invested heavily in gathering information about ultranationalist groups in the West of the country, fearing a merger between Ukrainian and Polish nationalist movements, even though in fact such a merger was highly unlikely given the history of the relations between the two movements. When the crisis erupted, the only option for the FSB to explain what was happening in a country supposedly under full control and to justify its failure to forecast the crisis was to blame some powerful player beyond the borders, that is, beyond the reach of the FSB—the West.

Putin enlisted both the siloviki and his civilian political team to counter the crisis. He brought back Surkov with the mission, according to the journalist Mikhail Zygar (2015), to liaise with Viktor Yanukovych and keep him in power. Simultaneously, he sent a number of high-ranking FSB officers to Kiev to advise on how to suppress the street demonstrations. Both failed, and Yanukovych ultimately fled the country. Putin then switched to a more aggressive policy, based almost entirely on the siloviki. This meant first the occupation of Crimea, then support for pro-Russian separatists in eastern Ukraine, and eventually intervention in Syria's civil war in September 2015 to defend the pro-Russian leader Bashar al-Assad against Western-backed opposition forces and Islamist extremists.

The Crimean events are instructive. On the one hand, the relevant siloviki—in this case, the GRU—managed the military operation competently, limiting bloodshed. On the other hand, as Daniel Treisman documents (this volume), the political management of the intervention was poorly prepared and chaotic. The commander of the operation, Oleg Belaventsev, a former spy and longtime associate of the defense minister, Sergei Shoigu, arrived in Crimea with practically no intelligence about the prevailing political situation.

The reason was that, because the FSB had been focusing on western Ukraine, it hardly had any intelligence positions or people at hand in Crimea. That prompted Putin to rely more on people who had at least some local knowledge and were adventurous enough to spring into action, people with connections in ultranationalist and radical Orthodox movements. One example is the Russian Orthodox billionaire Konstantin Malofeev, who became a power broker in Crimea and later in eastern Ukraine (Weaver 2014).

In Moscow, key decisions appear to have been made by Putin alone, in the heat of the crisis.[12] Within a few days after the initial Russian intervention, the Kremlin's plan for the region's future evolved from autonomy within Ukraine to outright annexation by Russia. Remarkably, the failures of the FSB did not shake Putin's confidence in people from the security services and the army: throughout, Putin appears to have consulted only a handful of top officials, most of them siloviki, including Alexander Bortnikov, head of the FSB, and Shoigu, the defense minister.

In the subsequent uprisings in the Donbass and Lugansk regions of eastern Ukraine, Russia's security services seem to have been secondary players until quite late in the game. Volunteers from nationalist networks,

12. Putin himself claimed in March 2015 that he had made the decision to take over Crimea alone and then summoned the chiefs of the security services to work out details (BBC 2015). Putin gave a similar account to Treisman when asked about this at a reception in Sochi in October 2015. Asked whether he had consulted aides before deciding on the Crimea operation, he answered: "No, I told them we will do this and then that. I was even surprised at how well it went!" (Treisman, personal communication).

funded by patriotic business people, took the lead, stirring up locals and organizing militias, before the Kremlin had taken any clear position. Although the Kremlin provided military support, it was only after the shooting down of a Malaysia Airlines passenger jet in July 2014 that the Kremlin sought to impose more direct control over the rebellion.

All this suggests that the siloviki, as a group, were more the implementers of policies than a determinant of policy choices. Certain key siloviki played a much greater role because they happened to be important members of Putin's small circle of close associates. The policies Putin chose fit with the conservative, anti-Western, and action-prone worldview of the siloviki. But this reflected not security services lobbying but the fact that unexpected events—the Arab Spring and Moscow protests—seemed to validate this worldview.

Even those in Putin's close network probably influence him more by shaping the flow of information to him than by direct persuasion. Under Yeltsin, a number of competing security services provided information to the president, with the FSB, the Federal Agency for Government Communications and Information (FAPSI), and the Presidential Security Service (part of the FSO) focusing on internal intelligence and the Foreign Intelligence Service and the GRU providing information about the outside world. This changed in 2003, when Putin split FAPSI between the FSO and the FSB. Simultaneously, the Kremlin began to rely less and less on information provided by the Presidential Security Service, while the department of analysis, forecasting, and strategic planning of the FSB was strengthened and also started to provide information on developments abroad.

By the mid-2000s, much of the information received by the Kremlin was thus provided by the FSB, putting the agency into a position the Soviet KGB had never enjoyed. The Soviet Politburo, traumatized by Stalin-era purges, was determined to keep the secret police in check and deprived the KGB of any analytical function. The KGB was tasked to supply raw data to a group of consultants under the KGB chair, all of them civilians, and it was their task to prepare analytical reports. Today, the FSB not only enjoys a near monopoly with respect to the provision of intelligence to the Kremlin, but the hierarchical organizational structure of the agency puts enormous power into the hands of its director, who has to countersign every document before it is presented to the president. The FSB director thus effectively controls what kind of information reaches Putin.

The importance of Putin's informal interactions with trusted siloviki friends, as opposed to his more formal contacts with force ministry officials, is also suggested by the details of the president's schedule. Using the official

Figure 4-1 Personal Meetings of the Russian President or Prime Minister with People Who Either Had a Siloviki Background or Were Working in a Field Related to the Security Services

Percent of all meetings

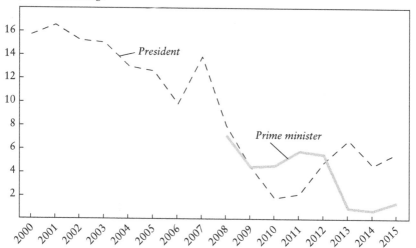

Sources: Kremlin.ru and Premier.gov.ru.

listing on the Kremlin's website, we analyzed data on all the personal meetings held by Putin since January 1, 2000 (as well as those of Dmitry Medvedev since May 2008).[13] These listings show a decline in the percentage of official meetings that Putin held with members of the force ministries since about 2008. While in 2000–07 about 14 percent of the president's meetings were with siloviki, the percentage declined to around 5.5 percent in 2008–15. Medvedev, both as president and as prime minister, hardly met with the siloviki at all: only 2 percent of his official meetings were with members of the force ministries between 2008 and 2015 (figure 4-1). Of course, the Kremlin website lists only official meetings and those that the authorities have no reason to conceal. We interpret the patterns as suggesting that the key meetings on security—domestic and international—were increasingly held informally, between Putin and his trusted personal advisers, and thus not recorded on the public schedule (see also Ananyev, this volume).

As early as 2005, two scholars concluded, based on a series of interviews with Russia's governmental elite: "The authority of the central execu-

---

13. As listed on the official website of the Russian president, http://kremlin.ru /events/president/news.

Table 4-1. *Key Siloviki Close to President Vladimir Putin and Their Positions*

Nikolai Patrushev	Federal Security Service (FSB) director (1999–2008) Head of the Security Council of Russia (2008–present)
Sergei Ivanov	Background in the First Chief Directorate of the State Security Committee (KGB), the Foreign Intelligence Service (SVR), and the FSB. Minister of defense (2001–07) First deputy prime minister (2007–08) Deputy prime minister (2008–11) Head of the Presidential Administration of Russia (2011–16) Member of the Security Council
Igor Sechin	Deputy head of the Presidential Administration (2000–08) Chairman of Rosneft (2004–present)
Alexander Bortnikov	KGB/FSB in Leningrad/St. Petersburg (1975–2004) Deputy director of the FSB (2004–08) Director of the FSB (2008–present)
Alexander Bastrykin	Head of the Investigative Committee (2011–present)
Viktor Zolotov	Director of the Russian president's personal security service (2000–14) Deputy minister of internal affairs and commander of the internal troops of Russia (2014–15) Chief of the National Guard (2015–present)

tive is in practice devolved to a series of small and informal groups around the President himself. Putin prefers to work not with formal institutions but with ad hoc groups that are not defined by institutional boundaries" (Kryshtanovskaya and White 2005, p. 1066). This tendency appears to have intensified.

While for most of the 2000s Putin's inner circle included a balance of siloviki and economically knowledgeable technocrats such as Alexei Kudrin and German Gref, the latter group appears to have been sidelined in recent years. Even members of the government understand that they are on a short leash. In an interview in early 2015, the president of a major foreign business association described the strange atmosphere he had witnessed at a recent high-level meeting on economic policy. At this event, the finance minister, the minister of economic development, and the head of the Duma budget committee had all agreed on urgent priorities, the respondent recalled, but hinted at their powerlessness. It was as if they were saying, "If only we were in power, we would know what to do."[14]

Although experts debate the exact composition of the inner circle, the siloviki listed in table 4-1 are highly likely to be members.

CONCLUSION

Upon coming to power, Putin sought to turn the officers of the FSB—along with various KGB veterans—into what his associate Nikolai Patrushev termed a new nobility. These top siloviki were to provide a recruitment base to fill key positions in the government and state-controlled corporations. They would formulate a new Russian "national idea" and plan for the country's future. In short, they would become guardians of the regime. Far from being a return to Soviet practice, this actually represented something quite new to Russia. The old KGB had been not a ruling caste but a bureaucratic tool, always under the firm control of the Communist Party.

But this project failed. The "new nobles" could not find solutions for the political challenges confronting the Kremlin in the 2000s, forcing Putin to turn to others. His responses to color revolutions—that is, pro-Kremlin youth movements and repressive legislation against nongovernmental organizations—were conceived not by the siloviki but by Vladislav Surkov, a civilian spin doctor. Nor did the FSB thinkers come up with a common vision for Russia's future. Indeed, the siloviki proved remarkably ineffective at political tasks. Divided among themselves on multiple dimensions, they spent a great deal of time and effort fighting each other.

Despite this disappointment, Putin nevertheless kept certain leading siloviki close to him in top posts and continued to listen to their reports and advice. These individuals were highly influential, but not because of their formal positions. Two things won them the president's ear. First, they benefited from close personal ties to Putin that often went back decades and that cut through his usual distrust. Second, the traditional silovik narrative of U.S. hostility and covert subversion came to seem more and more plausible to him as the years passed.

However, even these factors did not keep Putin from eventually demoting these insiders. In 2016 he began to push aside his old silovik comrades,

14. The interview was conducted by Michael Rochlitz, together with two other colleagues from the Higher School of Economics; see Rochlitz (2016, p. 21).

firing Viktor Ivanov, whose antidrug agency was absorbed by the Ministry of Internal Affairs, and dismissing Sergei Ivanov as head of the Presidential Administration. In place of FSB officers, he increasingly recruited new aides from the Foreign Ministry or his bodyguard service. At the same time, he began to refocus the FSB on tasks that had been central for the Soviet KGB—hunting down spies and conducting selective repression. While spy mania serves to intimidate the population, selective repression keeps the elites in line.

The younger professionals whom Putin has taken to hiring are unlikely to acquire the status and stature of Putin's first-generation siloviki. They certainly do not think of themselves as a new nobility. More subservient than their predecessors, these new aides are less likely to offer independent ideas or to challenge Putin's views. This will exacerbate the apparent narrowing of competing information sources.

Yet, while losing faith in the personal capacities of his silovik contemporaries, Putin seems increasingly sold on the tool kit of silovik techniques. Inside the country, that means, for instance, repression against governors and federal officials; outside it, techniques include so-called active measures, hacking, and cyber operations. Increasingly, it is freelancers outside the security agencies—such as the nationalist businessman Konstantin Malofeev, with his Donbass volunteers, or squads of hackers and Internet trolls—who are entrusted with sensitive missions.

Putin's switch, starting in 2012, to harsher methods of domestic control and a more assertive international line did not result from lobbying by the siloviki—or even by Putin's top silovik associates. Rather, it reflected the new challenges thrown up by the Arab Spring and the Moscow protests, which he interpreted as cases of Western subversion. This conviction hardened with the events in Ukraine in 2013. The combination of a heightened belief in U.S. hostility and the licensing of the silovik tool kit to adventurous freelancers promises to make Russian actions, especially in foreign policy, even more risk seeking and unpredictable than before.

REFERENCES

BBC. 2015. "Putin Reveals Secrets of Russia's Crimea Takeover Plot." March 9. www.bbc.com/news/world-europe-31796226.
Bremmer, Ian, and Samuel Charap. 2007. "The Siloviki in Putin's Russia: Who They Are and What They Want." *Washington Quarterly* 30, no. 1, pp. 83–92.

Chen, Adrian. 2015. "The Agency." *New York Times Magazine*, June 2.

Cherkesov, Viktor. 2007. "Nelzya dopustit, chtoby voiny prevratilis v torgovtsev [We cannot allow that warriors turn into traders]." *Kommersant*, October 9.

Dawisha, Karen. 2013. "Is Russia's Foreign Policy That of a Corporatist-Kleptocratic Regime?" *Post-Soviet Affairs* 27, no. 4, pp. 331–65.

———. 2014. *Putin's Kleptocracy: Who Owns Russia?* New York: Simon and Schuster.

The Economist. 2007. "Russia under Putin: The Making of a Neo-KGB State." August 23. www.economist.com/node/9682621.

Felshtinsky, Yuri, and Vladimir Pribylovsky. 2012. *The Putin Corporation: The Story of Russia's Secret Takeover.* London: Gibson Square Books.

Galeotti, Mark. 2015. "Putin's Spies and Security Men: His Strongest Allies, His Greatest Weakness." *Russian Analytical Digest*, no. 173 (October), pp. 8–10.

Harding, Luke. 2011. *Mafia State: How One Reporter Became an Enemy of the Brutal New Russia.* London: Guardian Books.

Illarionov, Andrey. 2009. "The Siloviki in Charge." *Journal of Democracy* 20, no. 2, pp. 69–72.

The Interpreter. 2013. "Why Vladislav Surkov Was Fired." May 13. www.interpreter mag.com/why-vladislav-surkov-was-fired.

Kasparov, Garry. 2015. *Winter Is Coming: Why Vladimir Putin and the Enemies of the Free World Must Be Stopped.* London: Allen and Unwin.

Knight, Amy. 1994. *Russia's New Security Services: An Assessment.* Federal Research Division, Library of Congress.

Kryshtanovskaya, Olga, and Stephen White. 2003. "Putin's Militocracy." *Post-Soviet Affairs* 19, no. 4, pp. 289–306.

———. 2005. "Inside the Putin Court: A Research Note." *Europe-Asia Studies* 57, no. 7, pp. 1065–75.

———. 2009. "The Sovietization of Russian Politics." *Post-Soviet Affairs* 25, no. 4, pp. 283–309.

LeVine, Steve. 2009. *Putin's Labyrinth: Spies, Murder, and the Dark Heart of the New Russia.* New York: Random House.

Lucas, Edward. 2012. *Deception: Spies, Lies and How Russia Dupes the West.* London: Bloomsbury Publishing.

———. 2014. *The New Cold War: Putin's Threat to Russia and the West.* Basingstoke: Palgrave Macmillan.

Oxenstierna, Susanne. 2016. "Russia's Defense Spending and the Economic Decline." *Journal of Eurasian Studies* 7, no. 1, pp. 60–70.

Petrov, Nikolay. 2002. "Seven Faces of Putin's Russia: Federal Districts and the New Level of State-Territorial Composition." *Security Dialogue* 33, no. 1, pp. 73–91.

———. 2005. "*Siloviki* in Russian Regions: New Dogs, Old Tricks." *Journal of Power Institutions in Post-Soviet Societies*, no. 2. http://pipss.revues.org/331.

Pomerantsev, Peter, and Michael Weiss. 2015. "The Menace of Unreality: How the Kremlin Weaponizes Information, Culture and Money." *The Interpreter*, November. www.interpretermag.com/the-menace-of-unreality-how-the-kremlin -weaponizes-information-culture-and–money.

Renz, Bettina. 2006. "Putin's Militocracy? An Alternative Interpretation of *Siloviki* in Contemporary Russian Politics." *Europe-Asia Studies* 58, no. 6, pp. 903–24.

———. 2007. "The *Siloviki* in Russian Politics: Political Strategy or a Product of the System?" *Russian Analytical Digest*, no. 17 (March), pp. 2–4.

Republic [formerly *Slon*]. 2013. "Bastrykin vmesto Surkova [Bastrykin instead of Surkov]." http://republic.ru/russia/bastrykin_vmesto_surkova-945953.xhtml.

Reshetnikov, Leonid. 2016. Interview, Radio Radonezh, January 15. http://riss.ru/smi/25386.

Rivera, David W., and Sharon Werning Rivera. 2006. "The Russian Elite under Putin: Militocratic or Bourgeois?" *Post-Soviet Affairs* 22, no. 2, pp. 125–44.

———. 2014. "Is Russia a Militocracy? Conceptual Issues and Extant Findings regarding Elite Militarization." *Post-Soviet Affairs* 30, no. 1, pp. 27–50.

Rochlitz, Michael. 2014. "Corporate Raiding and the Role of the State in Russia." *Post-Soviet Affairs* 30, nos. 2–3, pp. 89–114.

———. 2016. "Collective Action Abroad: How Foreign Investors Organize—Evidence from Foreign Business Associations in the Russian Federation." Working Paper 32. Moscow: Higher School of Economics.

Rossiyskaya Gazeta. 2015. December 22. http://rg.ru/2015/12/22/patrushev-site.html.

Roxburgh, Angus. 2013. *The Strongman: Vladimir Putin and the Struggle for Russia.* London: I. B. Tauris.

Soldatov, Andrei, and Irina Borogan. 2010. *The New Nobility: The Restoration of Russia's Security State and the Enduring Legacy of the KGB.* New York: Public Affairs.

———. 2015. *The Red Web: The Struggle between Russia's Digital Dictators and the New Online Revolutionaries.* New York: Public Affairs.

Staun, Jørgen. 2007. "Siloviki vs Liberal-Technocrats: The Fight for Russia and Its Foreign Policy." Danish Institute for International Studies (DIIS) Report 2007:9. Copenhagen: DIIS.

Taylor, Brian D. 2011. *State Building in Putin's Russia: Policing and Coercion after Communism.* Cambridge University Press.

———. 2013. "Kudrin's Complaint: Does Russia Face a Guns vs. Butter Dilemma?" PONARS Eurasia Policy Memo 254. George Washington University.

Waller, J. Michael. 2004. "Russia: Death and Resurrection of the KGB." *Demokratizatsiya* 12, no. 3, pp. 333–56.

Weaver, Courtney. 2014. "Malofeev: The Russian Billionaire Linking Moscow to the Rebels." *Financial Times*, July 24.

Yaffa, Joshua. 2015. "The Double Sting: A Power Struggle between Russia's Rival Security Agencies." *New Yorker*, July 27.

Za i Protiv. 2016. http://osfsb.ru/materialy/zhurnal-fsb-za-i-protiv/.

Zygar, Mikhail. 2015. *Vsya Kremlevskaya rat* [All the Kremlin's men]. Moscow: Intellektualnaya Literatura.

FIVE

Regional Elites and Moscow

NIKOLAY PETROV and EUGENIA NAZRULLAEVA

President Vladimir Putin is widely believed to have fundamentally recast relations between Russia's central authorities and the country's regional elites. He is seen as having reversed a disastrous slide into anarchic decentralization that began with the disintegration of the Soviet Union and lasted through the 1990s. Rather than merely redressing the balance, however, Putin is accused by critics of having completely neutered the institutions of federalism, replacing almost all elements of local and regional self-government with his "vertical of power." Along the way, analysts add, he has used the centralized bureaucracies of the security services and police to re-impose control through fear. Regional elites have been eliminated as a significant autonomous political actor.

Elements of this conventional wisdom certainly ring true, but the Kremlin's centralization efforts were not the same in all regions. As it tried to constrain and co-opt strong regional elites, especially in the national republics, it faced constant political trade-offs. Paradoxically, by incorporating regional officials into his hierarchy of command, Putin at times gave them new opportunities—or enhanced old ones—to pursue local or corporate interests at the center. Regional actors continued to introduce bills in the

Duma and even achieved greater success at getting them enacted as the 2000s wore on. At the same time, regional governors continued to lobby in the executive branch, and their meetings with the president elicited discretionary payouts from federal funds.

While we share the view that federalism has been virtually eliminated, it has not been fully replaced by authoritative centralization. Rather than forging a stable, centralized political order, President Putin has presided over one swing of a pendulum that has cycled periodically between centralization and decentralization. These swings have both an economic and a political nature. They are caused by the fluctuations in oil prices and the windfall revenues that periods of high prices produce for the Kremlin. When the oil market booms, the center can use its hydrocarbon rents to co-opt and intimidate regional elites, centralizing power. When revenues fall, pressures for decentralization reappear. Still, this logic is not all-determining: even in the current period of recession, regional elites remain much more constrained than in the 1990s. And, recognizing the dynamic, Putin has been making great efforts to block another pendulum swing that would re-empower the regions. To prevent this, he has tried to centralize even further. Yet, inadvertently, by restoring the old electoral system for the Duma in 2016, he may have strengthened representation of regional elites in Moscow, which will complicate his task.

CENTER AND REGIONS SINCE THE SOVIET DISINTEGRATION

Relations between Russia's central government and those of the country's regions have passed through several phases during the past twenty-five years. The pendulum has swung back and forth between greater central power and more regional autonomy.

After the Soviet system collapsed, the newly independent Russian state consisted of eighty-nine regions, each of which had the status of a "subject" of the federation. These came in several varieties—ethnic republics, of which there were twenty-one in 1993; fifty-five *oblasts* (provinces); six *krais* (territories); five autonomous *okrugs* (districts); and two cities of federal significance (Moscow and St. Petersburg).[1] Under a "federation treaty" that President Boris

---

1. However, only in nine republics—Dagestan, Tatarstan, Kabardino-Balkaria, Tuva, Chechnya, Ingushetia, North Ossetia, Kalmykia, and Chuvashia—is the non-Russian ethnicity a majority (Petrov and Slider 2016).

Yeltsin signed in 1992, the ethnic republics received special treatment: they could have their own constitution and a supreme court and could elect their top official, who, unlike in other regions, was called a "president."

The first years saw a dramatic, spontaneous decentralization of power and resources as regional elites lobbied a weakened and distracted center, backing up demands for preferential treatment with threats of secession or lesser forms of disruption (Hale 2003; Stoner-Weiss 1997; Treisman 1996, 2001). Through a variety of pressure tactics and agreements, the ethnic republics— and, following their example, many ordinary *oblasts* and *krais*—extracted privileges and material benefits from Moscow. These included everything from subsidies, credits, and larger retained shares of tax revenues to property rights over local natural resources (Treisman 1996).

Besides such concessions, regional elites were also granted representation in the federal legislature. In 1993–95 members of the upper house of parliament, the Federation Council, were elected in the regions, and many of the first crop of "senators" were governors (37 percent) or regional legislators (9 percent). From 1995 on, Federation Council elections were replaced by a system in which the governor and chair of the legislature of each region served ex officio as the region's senators (Slider 1996; Treisman 2001). Besides this role, governors extended their influence into the lower house, the State Duma. They could ensure that candidates running on different party lists or as independents in the mixed-member system came from their networks (Reuter 2017). The strong regional representation in the 1990s meant that regional elites could push through bills in the central parliament that served their interests.

For the Yeltsin administration, struggling against multiple simultaneous crises, co-opting the regional elites became a strategy to hold on to power. The one exception was the republic of Chechnya, the only region that had insisted on complete independence. In this case, Yeltsin sought to restore central authority by force, ordering Russian troops to invade the southern republic on December 11, 1994. The war dragged on until August 31, 1996, and in the following three years the republic degenerated into a kind of warlord-dominated failed state.

While initially, under a grant of power from the parliament, Yeltsin appointed the heads of administration of nonethnic regions, he gradually allowed these regions also to hold elections for their governors. By the summer of 1996, the practice had expanded to the whole country, giving the elected regional heads considerable local legitimacy.

Who were the regional elites in the early 1990s? In large part, they emerged from the old Soviet-era *nomenklatura* (Kryshtanovskaya and White 1996; Moses 2008). Communist professionals were supplemented by new economic, business, military, and law enforcement elites (Moses 2008). While gubernatorial elections led to some turnover, other subnational officials such as city mayors, deputy mayors, and deputy governors often survived in office for long periods. In the 1990s, a number of regional political entrepreneurs built strong political machines out of the local remnants of the Communist Party (Hale 2003). Mostly informal and nonpartisan, these machines could mobilize networks of supporters either to challenge or support central incumbents (Golosov 2013; Ross 2000). Central officials, starting with Yeltsin, sought to co-opt such regional bosses and enlist their help at election times.

The regional machines could be seen in action during the critical 1996 presidential election, in which a depleted and unpopular Yeltsin sought to overcome a credible challenge from the Communist leader Gennady Zyuganov. Some ethnic republics voted overwhelmingly for Zyuganov in the first round, but then swung to a majority vote for Yeltsin in the second round, which included only the two top vote-getters from the first. In some regions, fewer voted for Zyuganov when the choice was between just two candidates than voted for him in the first-round ballot between ten! Such swings strongly suggest a coordinated flip on the part of local voters, informally orchestrated by the regional leader after he guessed what the election's outcome would be. In Dagestan, for instance, Zyuganov received 63 percent in the first round—but then only 45 percent in the second. Yeltsin's share rose from 29 percent to 53 percent.

By the end of the decade, the process of spontaneous decentralization had reached an extreme. In the view of some analysts, the regional elites had become collectively stronger than their central counterparts, and the only thing that prevented a regional alliance from winning the presidency in 2000 was the inability of the governors to coordinate (Reuter 2017).

Under Putin, the pendulum swung back toward recentralization. The recovery of the Russian economy, along with rapidly increasing oil prices (see figure 5-1), and the re-initiation of war in Chechnya prompted a surge in Putin's popularity that enabled him to rewrite the rules of federal politics (Reuter 2017; Treisman 2011). One key instrument was the Kremlin-controlled United Russia party. Before the 1999 Duma election, several governors had tried to form their own parties based on subsets of regional

Figure 5-1   The Dynamics of Oil Prices and Subnational Revenues

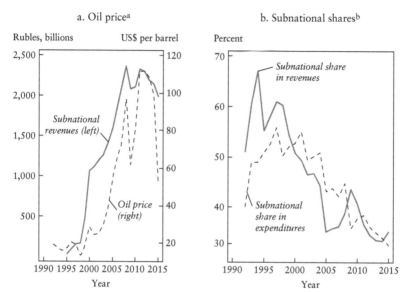

a. Oil price[a]

b. Subnational shares[b]

Sources: Annual Statistical Bulletin, Rosstat (www.gks.ru/); Federal Treasury
(www.roskazna.ru/); Thomson Reuters; authors' calculations.

a. Oil price = Europe Brent Spot Price FOB (dollars per barrel), which serves as the
benchmark for Russia's Urals crude. Subnational revenues = total subnational revenues,
from consolidated regional budgets (billion rubles; trillion rubles before 1998), inflation
adjusted using consumer price index (CPI) (since 1995).
b. Subnational shares (consolidated regional budgets) in expenditures and revenues
of Russia's consolidated budget.

elites. Moscow's mayor Yuri Luzhkov had founded Otechestvo (Fatherland),
Tatarstan's president Mintimer Shaimiev had organized Vsya Rossia (All
Russia), and Samara Oblast governor Konstantin Titov had started Golos
Rossii (Voice of Russia) (Reuter 2017). Otechestvo and Vsya Rossia soon
merged to form Otechestvo–Vsya Rossia. Faced with this hostile regional
coalition, the Kremlin created the Unity party to back its presidential candidate, Putin. Although Unity won endorsements from a few regional governors, they were mostly weak ones; the Kremlin hoped at this point only to
split the regional elites rather than to absorb them.

After Putin's victory, Unity and Otechestvo–Vsya Rossia merged in 2001
to form the pro-Kremlin United Russia, which dominated politics from
then on. United Russia managed to unite central and regional political
elites in one organization (Reuter and Remington 2009; Reuter 2010). By

2005 almost half of the serving regional governors had joined the party, and by 2007 only eight remained unaffiliated with it (Reuter 2017). Those with longer tenure in office and in regions with more concentrated economic structure were the fastest to join (Reuter 2010). In the 2007 election, the mixed-member system—with half of Duma members elected in single-mandate constituencies and others elected on party lists—was replaced by one of pure proportional representation, which enhanced the power of parties, most important, United Russia.

Other changes also reduced the power of regional elites. From 2001 on, governors and regional legislature chairs no longer served ex officio in the Federation Council but instead got to choose representatives to it. Rather than being regional representatives at the federal center, governors eventually became Moscow's representatives at the local level. They also became members of the State Council, a new consultative body formed by Putin in September 2000, which met at the president's discretion to discuss an agenda set by the Kremlin. The Presidium of the State Council, made up of one member from each of the federal districts, met monthly with the president.

Rising oil prices boosted Russia's consolidated budget revenues. Adjusted for inflation, subnational revenues doubled over the period 2000–08 (see figure 5-1a). Fiscal reforms enacted in the early 2000s eliminated most regional tax privileges, leaving regional budgets more dependent on federal transfers (Treisman 2007). The subnational share of total revenues, which had peaked at 67 percent in 1994, fell to 35 percent in 2005 (see figure 5-1b). In the early 1990s, regions had been rewarded fiscally for threatening the center with disruptions (Treisman 2001). Despite Moscow's centralization efforts, regional efforts to extract resources from the federal authorities did not end completely. In the 2000s, governors continued to compete for financial support, lobbying regional projects at the federal level (Sharafutdinova and Turovsky 2016).

Another major step toward recentralization was the abolition of gubernatorial elections in 2004. From then on, governors were essentially appointed by the president. Regional heavyweights were replaced by outsider technocrats loyal to Moscow (Buckley, Frye, and others 2014; Huskey 2010). The new governors appointed by Putin tended to have less experience working in the given region and more often came from the federal bureaucracy or from other regional administrations (Buckley, Frye, and others 2014). To the extent that local experience meant greater expertise and Moscow careers signified loyalty to Putin, this fits with the argument that authoritarian leaders tend to sacrifice competence to loyalty (Egorov and Sonin 2011).

Putin also reduced the governors' power by creating other channels of control that bypassed them. He imposed seven presidential envoys above the governors, with staffs recruited mostly from Moscow (Petrov 2005). (Although presidential envoys to regions had existed in the 1990s, their role was greatly enhanced: they were built into the "power vertical" and became less dependent on governors and regional elites.) The envoys were assisted by a chief federal inspector in each region, many of whom had previously worked in military and security structures such as the State Security Committee (KGB), the Ministry of Internal Affairs, or control departments of the regional administrations (Petrov 2005). While these were often local natives, the inspectors appointed to important spots such as the republics of Bashkortostan and Tatarstan, Kemerovo Oblast, and Krasnoyarsk Krai had most recently worked in Moscow (Petrov 2005).

As governors became less regional representatives than central agents, the legislature speakers and elected mayors of the regional capital cities took over the role of speaking for the regional elite. But over the 2000s, the autonomy and the power of mayors were also eroded. A federal law in 2003 stripped them of direct responsibility for the city budget and administration, assigning these to city managers (Moses 2013, p. 13). They were also weakened by frequent clashes with the governors—such conflicts occurred in almost two-thirds of regions in 2000–10.[2] As a result, some 30 percent of regional capital mayors in 2010–13 did not serve their full terms, resigning early or in some cases being prosecuted and jailed (Moses 2013). Meanwhile, direct mayoral elections have been canceled in half of Russian cities since 2005 (Buckley, Garifullina, and others 2014). In 2012 over 80 percent of mayors were elected indirectly by municipal councils (Moses 2013, p. 13). Regional legislature speakers were also weakened.

The next swing of the pendulum came in 2011, when protests after the State Duma election prompted the central authorities to move again toward regionalization. However, the change was limited. Gubernatorial elections were reinstated and held in seventy-one regions in 2012–16.[3] But these elections proved less competitive (in terms of the closeness of the victor's

2. Estimates from Alexander Kynev, International Center for the Studies of Institutions and Development (ICSID, http://iims.hse.ru/csid/).

3. As of September 18, 2016.

Table 5-1. *Differences between Elected Governors: Before 2005 and after 2012*

Variable	Elected before 2005	Elected after 2012[a]	Difference, Δ[b]
Average turnout[c] (%)	54.14	45.77	−8.37*
Average vote margin[d] (%)	37.74	61.09	23.35*
N[e]	212	71	

Sources: ICSID database on governors (http://iims.hse.ru/csid/), Central Electoral Commission (www.cikrf.ru/).

* The null hypothesis of no difference in means is rejected at the 1 percent significance level.

a. Gubernatorial elections after 2012: data collected up to September 18, 2016.

b. "Difference" is the difference in means *t* statistic.

c. The alternative hypothesis: for turnout the difference Δ < 0; for vote margins the difference Δ > 0.

d. Vote margin = the winning candidate's share minus the runner-up candidate's share.

e. Total number of election events before 2005 is 232; data are missing in the 1990s.

margin) and attracted lower voter turnout than those held in 1992–2004 (see table 5-1). In only twenty-nine cases was a new governor elected, and twenty-eight of these "new" governors were actually acting governors whom Putin had recently appointed.[4] Only five non–United Russia members won— and Putin later fired two of them, one for failing to meet a federal policy benchmark and the other (Nikita Belykh, a former liberal party leader, originally appointed governor of Kirov Oblast by Dmitry Medvedev) to stand trial, accused of accepting bribes (Gessen 2016). In 2016 alone, eight governors (including Belykh) were dismissed by Putin, replaced with acting governors sent from Moscow.

While some governors have strong ties to the regions where they serve and are embedded into the regional elite network, others are complete outsiders. Moscow appears to have wanted loyal managers rather than strong regional candidates.[5] Since June 2012, around 40 percent of new governors (including acting governors) have been outsiders, with no prior regional ties.[6] Some even choose to live in Moscow on weekends and, together

4. The single exception was the victory of challenger Sergey Levchenko in Irkutsk in 2015.

5. See commentary by Mikhail Vinogradov in Petersburg Politics (2016a).

6. Petersburg Politics (2016a), updated as of December 2016 based on Petersburg Politics (2016c). From March 10 to December 2016, governors were changed in four regions: in Kirov Oblast, Yaroslavl Oblast, Sevastopol, and Kaliningrad Oblast (twice).

with close aides, commute to the region for workdays. For instance, Alexander Khloponin, who served as governor of Krasnoyarsk Krai in 2002–10, divided his time between his local office and his family in the capital. Conflicts often break out between such "helicopter governors" (or presidential envoys) and the regional elites. A local populist, Yevgeny Roizman, running as an independent, defeated the Moscow-backed candidate in the 2013 election for mayor of Yekaterinburg, Russia's fourth-largest city, located in Sverdlovsk Oblast. Roizman, supported by local elites, has a history of conflict with the outsider governor of Sverdlovsk Oblast, Yevgeny Kuivashev.

Perhaps recognizing this issue, Putin reappointed some strong, regionally rooted governors. Two managed to survive the turbulence of the 2000s and preserve their political machines—Yevgeny Savchenko in Belgorod Oblast (in office since 1993) and Aman Tuleev in Kemerovo Oblast (since 1997). At the same time, some regional politicians moved up to federal legislative and executive bodies, more often the latter. The elites of St. Petersburg, Krasnoyarsk Krai, the Tatarstan Republic, Perm Krai, and Kaluga Oblast have all established significant networks in Moscow.

Besides reintroducing gubernatorial elections, the Kremlin sought to deflect popular anger after the 2011 election by restoring the mixed-member electoral system for the State Duma that had been replaced by pure proportional representation. The results of the September 2016 election show that this has reinvigorated regional representation. For example, candidates from Sverdlovsk Oblast alone won a total of 14 seats in the new Duma (out of 450), which is comparable to the 15 received by the Tatarstan Republic, known for its lobby. Single-member district legislators, elected with the support of regional and business elites, may reestablish the kind of presence at the center that had largely disappeared since 2007. Meanwhile, those regional politicians elected to central bodies with strong popular support may, back home, compete with governors who remain dependent on Moscow.

Of course, the Kremlin has worked to limit the impact of concessions made to regional elites since 2011—and has largely succeeded (see table 5-2). First, whereas two former governors (Alexander Khloponin and Viktor Tolokonskiy) served as presidential envoys in 2010, no governors remained in this role as of 2014. Second, despite being elected, governors can still be

Five of the nine acting governors appointed in 2016 not only were from the central elite but also had law enforcement backgrounds.

Table 5-2. *Regional Elite Power since 2012: Important Changes*

Positive developments	Additional constraints
Reinstatement of gubernatorial elections (2012)	Increasing practice of dismissing incumbent and appointing an acting governor shortly before the region's election, with a view to getting the appointee elected
Reinstatement of the mixed-member parliamentary system and introduction of a lower electoral threshold (5 percent instead of 7 percent) (2016 election)	Increasing appointment of outsiders as acting governors (since 2012)
Inclusion of 85 representatives from regional civic chambers in the Civic Chamber of the Russian Federation (2013)[a]	Increasing appointment of former law enforcement agents as presidential envoys (since 2014) and recent appointments of acting governors with law enforcement backgrounds (since 2016)
Governors given the right to negotiate with the federal center about the appointments of federal representatives in the region and to reject Moscow's candidates (2015)	Reduction in mayors' responsibilities and in direct mayoral elections (since 2012)
	Regional policy and budgetary autonomy constrained by detailed targets in presidential "May decrees" (2012), adding to the long list of subnational responsibilities (600 of these added since 2005[b])
	Federal ministers can file complaints to have a governor dismissed (2013)
	Growing pressure of law enforcement on governors; several governors arrested (since 2014). Formation of new executive body, the National Guard (2016)
	Law to abolish the Ministry of Regional Development (2014)

Source: Authors' analysis.

a. According to the Civic Chamber, it was formed in 2005 to help cooperation between citizens, NGOs, and federal and local elites. See the official website of the Civic Chamber of the Russian Federation, oprf.ru/en/about.

b. Sergey Fedeichev, "Regions Were Reminded of the Reform of Powers and Responsibilities," *Kommersant*, June 6, 2016, www.kommersant.ru/doc/3013959.

fired, not only by the president but—since 2013—on the basis of complaints filed by federal ministers (Petrov 2015). In extreme cases, governors can be pressured by law enforcement officials. Since 2014, six governors have faced criminal charges (compared to four cases in 1996–2013).[7]

7. See commentary by Mikhail Vinogradov in Petersburg Politics (2016b).

THE PARADOX OF THE CHECHEN REPUBLIC

Although the Chechen Republic with its personalistic regime can be considered an extreme case, it contributes to our understanding of center-region relations since the 1990s. The republic's current leader, Ramzan Kadyrov, unlike all other regional leaders, has legitimacy that is independent of Putin's (Petrov 2016). The interaction between Moscow and Kadyrov fits into a vassal-type model, in which in return for maintaining the center's control over the unstable territory the warlord is rewarded with absolute control over the region. The Chechen Republic receives large amounts of fiscal grants from the center and has representative offices abroad, as well as, de facto, its own military forces and siloviki—"force ministries," law enforcement agencies authorized to use violence against threats to the region's security (Soldatov and Rochlitz, this volume)—who operate not only in the region but also in Moscow.

The current model of relations between the Chechen Republic and the center was largely determined by the second Chechen war (August 1999–May 2000), which marked Putin's rise to power and coincided with the surge in his approval rating (from 31 percent in August 1999 to 84 percent in January 2000; see Treisman 2011). This war resulted from intra-elite tensions and the weakening authority of the republic's president, Aslan Maskhadov, elected in 1997. In 2000 Putin supported a former guerrilla leader, Akhmat Kadyrov, as the next president of the Chechen Republic. This decision caused tensions in both federal and Chechen elite circles (Russell 2011). Following the assassination of Akhmat Kadyrov in 2004, his son, Ramzan Kadyrov, de facto inherited the office (he became the president de jure in 2007).

During his time in office, Ramzan Kadyrov has been able to create a power pyramid in the republic, based on personal loyalty. He co-opted or neutralized elites in the region. Even federal elites in the region were subordinate to Kadyrov and not to the federal center (Russell 2011). In turn, he has repeatedly demonstrated personal loyalty to Putin, for instance, calling for the renaming of "presidents" in the ethnic republics "heads of republic" so that there would be just one president in Russia.

The model has relied on massive flows of funds from Moscow to Grozny. Like other North Caucasus republics, Chechnya receives large subsidies. The share of fiscal grants in the region's budget is over 80 percent (see figure 5-2a)—higher than that of any other region except neighboring

Figure 5-2 The Dynamics of Fiscal Grants, 2000–15[a]

a. Region's fiscal grants relative to total budget income[b]

b. Fiscal grants adjusted for inflation[c]

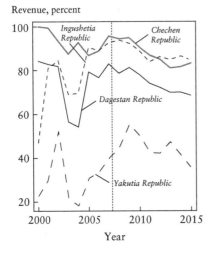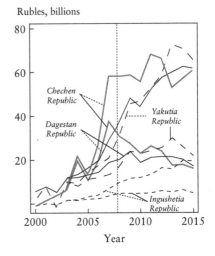

Sources: Federal Treasury (www.roskazna.ru/); Moscow State University database
UIS Russia (http://uisrussia.msu.ru/); authors' calculations.

a. Grants to the Chechen Republic compared to the Republics of Dagestan, Ingushetia, and Yakutia.
b. The 2003–04 changes were caused by an increase in total revenues due to a higher share of taxes from natural resources, which went into regional budgets to compensate losses from the tax reform of 2000–04.
c. Fiscal grants adjusted for inflation using CPI since 2004 (CPI for the Chechen Republic is officially available only since 2004). Dotted lines point to nominal grants, for comparison.

Ingushetia. In absolute terms, only the republics of Yakutia and Dagestan received larger grants in 2013–14 (see figure 5-2b). Such transfers—which include both formula-based equalization grants and other more discretionary ones—increased sharply from 2004 to 2007, the years of Ramzan Kadyrov's de facto rise to power (Zubarevich 2011). While the republic received similar levels of support in nominal terms after 2007, inflation eroded the value of the subsidies, and the high birthrate reduced their value per capita (see figure 5-2b).[8]

8. According to the official statistics published by Rosstat (www.gks.ru/), the Chechen Republic demonstrates both high inflation and a substantive population growth. In terms of per capita fiscal grants, adjusted for inflation, the decrease after 2007 is even more pronounced.

However, fiscal grants are not the only income the republic receives from the federal center. In 2015 federal authorities seized the oil company Chechennetekhimprom and gave it to the region. Moreover, Chechnya has its own fund under full discretion of Kadyrov, the nongovernmental organization (NGO) Akhmat Kadyrov Regional Fund, with officially undisclosed sources of income. According to a 2016 Russian Business Consulting (RBC) report, the NGO has founded several companies in the region—including a large construction firm, Megastroyinvest, which has received 4.8 billion rubles in public procurement contracts since 2012 (as of February 2016) (Nikolskaya and others 2016). According to Gulnaz Sharafutdinova and Rostislav Turovsky (2016), Kadyrov has also looked to improve his agents' lobbying skills, sending working groups to Tatarstan to study that republic's model of interactions with the federal center.

Putin's recent "interventionist" policies seem to have contributed to Kadyrov's popularity, despite his conflict with the federal elites, especially with the Federal Security Service (FSB) chief Alexander Bortnikov. Bortnikov implicated Chechen siloviki in the assassination of the opposition leader Boris Nemtsov in 2015. A year after Nemtsov's murder, on February 27, 2016, Kadyrov announced that he was ready to leave office. However, he was reelected with around 98 percent of the vote in September 2016. Kadyrov appears to be quite popular also outside the republic. According to a 2017 nationwide poll by the Russian Public Opinion Research Center (VCIOM), 55 percent of Russian respondents said that they consider his actions beneficial for the country (VCIOM 2017).

The decline in fiscal support (in real terms) and the creation in 2016 of a new law enforcement body, the National Guard, which consolidates all domestic security troops—including Kadyrov's—suggest that the special relationship that the Chechen Republic has enjoyed since 2007 could be changing. However, Moscow is still clearly ready to make some concessions, such as the transfer of Chechennetekhimprom to the republic.

SUBJECTIVE RATINGS OF REGIONAL LOBBYING

We approach the challenging task of assessing the political influence of regional actors in several ways. First, we consider a measure of the effectiveness of regional lobbying efforts based on the subjective evaluations of a large number of Russian experts on regional politics. Since 1999, the newspaper *Nezavisimaya Gazeta*, along with the Agency of Economic News, has published ratings of "Russia's best lobbyists" at the national level, including a section on the best lobbyists among regional governors. Specifically, experts are asked to estimate how successful the various governors are in lobbying their region's interests—for instance, by influencing the center's decisions related to regional projects, financial support, and regional budgets. The experts can assign scores of 0–5, where 5 stands for the most successful lobbyist (0–1: very weak lobbying power; 1–2: weak; 2–3: average; 3–4: strong; and 4–5: very strong).[9]

Up to fifty experts from different backgrounds—economic news outlets, research centers, and NGOs—are surveyed. Experts are asked to evaluate the lobbying efforts of each person from the list of up to two hundred candidates known to be involved in lobbying.[10] Regional leaders represent one of the three categories, along with business people and professional lobbyists. The overall methodology remains unchanged over the years, but the list of experts seems to change over time. Consistency in methodology is important, allowing us to treat the scoring in different years as comparable.

For every year since 1999, *Nezavisimaya Gazeta* has published the names and scores of the twenty-five "best lobbyists" among the governors. Since the 0–5 scale is the same each year, and the descriptions of what each number represents have not changed, we can gauge the experts' average assessment of the power of regional lobbyists by comparing the scores of the median governor among the top twenty-five in each year. Figure 5-3 shows these median scores. (To give a sense of the consistency of the experts' estimates, the bands show the interquartile range within which the experts placed the governor's score.) As can be seen, the median (included) governor's rating starts quite high—at 3.5—and trends downward until 2005, reaching a low point of around 2.75. It then trends upward, reaching a high of 3.4 in 2015. This is consistent with the view that Putin reduced the power of regional governors to lobby Moscow for benefits in the early 2000s but that, after gubernatorial elections were replaced with central appointment, the regional governors— or, at least, the strongest among them—gradually acquired greater leverage to lobby for their regions. Still, one should not read too much into these figures given their subjective nature and the high degree of variance observed in the experts' estimates.

9. See the details on methodology discussed in *Nezavisimaya Gazeta* (1999).

10. *Nezavisimaya Gazeta* (1999). In recent years *Nezavisimaya Gazeta* mentions around ten experts "and others."

Figure 5-3   Russia's Governors—Best Lobbyists in the 2000s

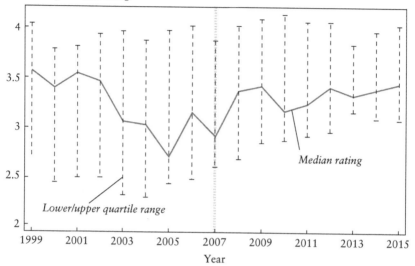

Nezavismaya Gazeta rating

Year

Sources: Nezavisimaya Gazeta (www.ng.ru/); authors' calculations. In 1999–2006 the December ratings are used; in 2007–15 the official average ratings over the year are used.

The *Nezavisimaya Gazeta* ratings offer insight into what kind of regions—and governors—are seen as most effective in the game of inter-level politics. The mayors of Moscow, Yuri Luzhkov and then Sergei Sobyanin, as well as Valentina Matviyenko, the governor of St. Petersburg, an old Putin associate, have consistently placed near the top of the list, as have the successive presidents of the Republic of Tatarstan, first Mintimer Shaimiev and then Rustam Minnikhanov. For a few years after Minnikhanov replaced Shaimiev, he was considered a weaker lobbyist, but his rating soon grew to equal his predecessor's. The Chechen president Ramzan Kadyrov's rating has increased sharply since he first officially took office in 2007; by 2009 he was among the top lobbyists.

SUCCESSFUL LOBBYING IN THE REGIONS

What mechanisms could explain variation in regional elites' lobbying power? *Nezavisimaya Gazeta* ratings experts evaluate regional elites' success taking into account multiple dimensions, including whether a region received increased federal support (for example, fiscal grants from the federal budget to Chechnya) or whether a region secured implementation of a federal project (for example, the 2013 Summer Universiade in Kazan, Tatarstan).

With the descriptive nature of the data we have, it is difficult to make causal claims. We see several patterns that could define a successful lobbying game under Putin. In most notable cases, lobbying power is affected not by the personality of a governor but by the importance of the region itself. Economically powerful regions like the two national capitals seem to do best in lobbying. Ethnic republics that could either threaten the regime with disruptions (Chechnya) or that managed to keep their political machines despite the pendulum swing toward recentralization (Tatarstan) continue to enjoy preferential treatment. In other cases, governors' personalities seem to matter, which is harder to measure and generalize. One dimension is the length of tenure in office. Aman Tuleev in Kemerovo was consistently placed among the top lobbyists throughout the 2000s, with a score close to 4 out of 5. Governors' business ties to oligarchs are another dimension—which overlaps with the economic importance of a region. A famous example is Chukotka's governor—an oligarch, Roman Abramovich—who had a lobbying score of over 4 (except for 2004) while he was in office.

HOW REGIONAL ELITES LOBBY

Governors and other elite members may lobby for their region's interests in both the parliament and the executive branch. We consider both in turn.

Lobbying in Parliament

One way regions can influence central policy is by initiating bills in the central parliament and lobbying for their passage. In theory, regional legislatures have the right to initiate federal legislation. One might assume that, after Putin consolidated power over both the governors and the Duma in the early 2000s, such regional initiatives would have become much rarer. To test this, we collected data on all bills introduced in the State Duma since 1996 from the Duma's website (http://duma.gov.ru/). We identified all bills introduced by a regional legislature ("regional bills") and recorded which had been passed and signed into law by the president. Of course, as Ben Noble and Ekaterina Schulmann (this volume) point out, the State Duma works as the battleground where regional elites (and nonexecutive agents in general) can be siding with deputies to get their bill through the Duma.

Therefore, by looking only at the bills formally introduced by regional legislatures, we may underestimate the number of bills that advance regional interests.

Figure 5-4 shows the dynamics. The share of regional bills in all bills considered by the Duma increases from about 20 percent in 1995 to 50 percent in 2004 and stays around that level until 2008, after which it falls. This is not what was expected. In precisely the period of Putin's consolidation, regions appear to have had the greatest ability to promote their legislative initiatives in Moscow. Although regional legislatures seem to be more active than the executive branch in introducing new legislative initiatives in the mid-2000s, they are still less successful than the executive branch and the Duma deputies in getting bills passed. The consolidation under Putin is visible in the enactment dynamics: the share of bills introduced by the president or the government rapidly increases after 2006 (figure 5-4a), and, most important, the share of successful bills introduced by the executive branch gradually increases throughout the 2000s (figure 5-4b) (for more discussion of these trends, see Noble and Schulmann, this volume).

How many of the regional bills make it into law? Through the early 2000s, most failed: far fewer than 10 percent of the regional bills introduced ended up signed by the president. But from then on, the rate picks up, reaching 14 percent in 2009 and peaking at 17 percent in 2010. After that year, the rate falls again, returning to the rate of the late 1990s by 2015. Again, we see a surprising surge in regional legislative activity—and success—during the pendulum swing toward recentralization between about 2005 and 2010. This pattern presents a puzzle that challenges the common wisdom "mad printer" concept associated with the State Duma (Noble and Schulmann, this volume). Legislative lobbying continued to exist despite the center's efforts to strip power from regional elites. The wave of regional legislative activity subsided toward the end of the 2000s.

On what topics do the regions lobby? Figure 5-5 disaggregates the regional bills in terms of the most common topics. Tax issues are important throughout, reaching a sharp peak in 2003, just as the federal authorities were passing major reforms to Russia's tax system. We also see a significant number of bills related to social policy (education, health care, pensions, and so forth) and economic policy (agriculture and fisheries, mining, manufacturing, trade, including the alcohol market, and so forth). Another major

Figure 5-4 The Dynamics of Regional Legislative Initiatives in the State Duma

a. Bills introduced by initiator[a]

b. Bills signed into law by initiator[b]

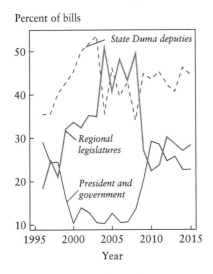
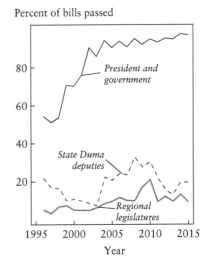

Sources: State Duma (http://duma.gov.ru/); authors' calculations.

a. Regional legislatures = total number of bills introduced by regional legislatures divided by total number of all bills introduced. President and government = total number of bills introduced by the president and the government divided by total number of all bills introduced. State Duma deputies = total number of bills introduced by State Duma deputies divided by total number of all bills introduced.

b. Regional legislatures = number of regional bills that were signed by the president divided by the number of relevant bills that were signed, declined, or removed. President and government = number of executive bills that were signed by the president divided by the number of relevant bills that were signed, declined, or removed. State Duma deputies = total number of bills introduced by State Duma deputies that were signed by the president divided by the number of relevant bills that were signed, declined, or removed.

category, state capacity, consists largely of changes in the constitution and law enforcement practices and includes bills related to courts and criminal and administrative processes. The peak of law enforcement bills after 2010 is caused by a series of reforms of the criminal and administrative codes.

Given the topics in figure 5-5a, what regional bills are the most successful, that is, end up being signed into the law? Similar to figure 5-4b, in figure 5-5b we calculate success rates for regional bills by the most common topics. We see a peak in 2010 for the bills on state capacity, in contrast to the 1990s when the most successful bills tended to be about social policies.

Figure 5-5   The Dynamics of Regional Legislative Initiatives by Topics

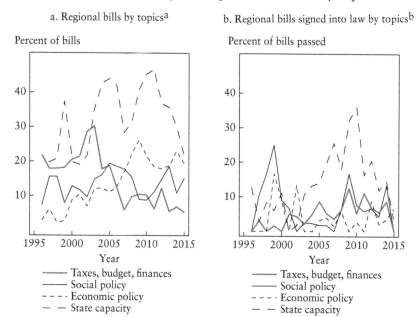

a. Regional bills by topics[a]

Percent of bills

b. Regional bills signed into law by topics[b]

Percent of bills passed

Year

———— Taxes, budget, finances
———— Social policy
- - - - Economic policy
— — State capacity

Sources: Authors' calculations; State Duma (http://duma.gov.ru/); api.duma.gov.ru/pages /dokumentatsiya/spisok-tematicheskih-blokov.

a. Ratio of regional bills by topic = total number of regional bills related to a topic divided by total number of all regional bills. Categories are not mutually exclusive and exhaustive, defined using keywords before 2003 and based on official classification since 2003.
b. Number of regional bills by topics that were signed by the president divided by the number of relevant bills that were signed, declined, or removed.

For the tax-related laws, despite the lobbying activity aimed at retaining regional tax privileges, the number of bills approved by the president remained unsurprisingly low.

Which regions get their bills signed into law most often? It turns out that the highest success rate for regional bills is observed for Russia's new regions—the Republic of Crimea and the city of Sevastopol (80 and 50 percent, respectively, since 2014). Without these two clear outliers, the highest success rates (over 20–25 percent on average for the whole period, with a median rate of 10 percent) are observed for the legislatures from Irkutsk Oblast, Tula Oblast, Buryatia, Dagestan, and Tver Oblast. Interestingly, Tatarstan has a bills success rate of 13 percent, and Chechnya around 6 percent.

Overall, the regions with high success rates in legislative lobbying are not placed high on *Nezavisimaya Gazeta*'s list of top lobbyists, which can be partly explained by the rating better capturing the executive lobbying channel.

Lobbying the Executive

Regions lobby the federal executive through various channels. They maintain special representative offices in the capital, which can cultivate the necessary relationships in the ministries on a day-to-day basis. Such regional representative offices (*predstavitelstva*) and national communities (fellow-countrymen's associations, or *zemlyachestva*) help governors promote initiatives with the president and central government. While almost all regions have such offices, their size and status vary. The ethnic republics' representative offices interact with the Presidential Administration, while those of other regions are affiliated with the government. Even among ethnic republics, there is variation. Tatarstan's office is particularly elaborate, including two subdivisions—one for international and economic coordination and another for domestic issues relevant to the republic. In addition, Tatarstan has offices in a number of other Russian regions (Crimea, Sverdlovsk Oblast, St. Petersburg and Leningrad Oblast, the Bashkortostan Republic, Khanty-Mansi Autonomous Okrug, Saratov Oblast, and Nizhegorod Oblast) as well as trade and economic representative offices overseas.

While such bureaus in the capital manage lower-level contacts, much of the most important lobbying occurs during meetings with the president—either in Moscow or in the regions. In the early 1990s, visits to particular regions by senior officials—the president, vice president, prime minister, or speaker of the Duma—led to intense lobbying. President Yeltsin's aides knew never to leave him alone during his visits outside the capital, as regional elites would exploit any opportunity to bargain for benefits (Treisman 1996). Regions that Yeltsin visited personally during his campaign for reelection in 1996 received significantly more in net transfers that year (Treisman 2011). In 2002–12 this trend continued: regions visited by federal executives—the president, the prime minister, deputy prime ministers, certain ministers, and others—enjoyed larger discretionary transfers from the center (Sharafutdinova and Turovsky 2016). Tatarstan's regional elites are said to "cultivate" their relations with federal officials—inviting them to join local events and celebrations and stay for holidays (Sharafutdinova and

Figure 5-6   The Dynamics of Presidential Meetings with Regional Elites

Percent of all meetings   Number of visits

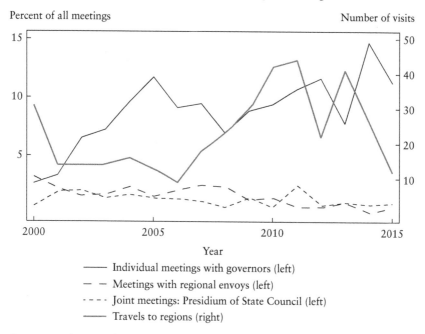

Year

———— Individual meetings with governors (left)
— — Meetings with regional envoys (left)
- - - - Joint meetings: Presidium of State Council (left)
———— Travels to regions (right)

Sources: Kremlin.ru; authors' calculations.

Notes: All indicators, except for travels, are calculated as a proportion of the president's total scheduled meetings (left axis). Presidential travels are measured as the number of visits (right axis). St. Petersburg and Moscow visits are not accounted for in presidential visits.

Turovsky 2016). In some cases, regional notables get to join the president's delegation during his visits abroad. Representatives from other regions, including the Chechen Republic, have traveled to Tatarstan to study its techniques for attracting federal support (Sharafutdinova and Turovsky 2016).

Thus, access to federal officials may be a good proxy for a region's lobbying capacity. Examining the frequency of governors' meetings with the president, based on the official reports from the Kremlin website, we see an upward trend since 2008, although such meetings constitute a small proportion of the president's total scheduled events (figure 5-6). Presidential visits to the regions trended upward from 2006 to 2011. Of course, not all of the president's meetings with governors are reported on the website, while some meetings that get reported may be window dressing. For the dynamic of meetings to be meaningful, we must make an explicit assumption that any bias in reporting did not change much over time. The president's meetings with his regional envoys remained relatively stable over the past fifteen years, as did the frequency of his meetings with the Presidium of the State Council.

Of course, meetings not only enable regional actors to lobby the president; they also provide an opportunity for the president to give orders to the governors. These figures do not reveal anything about the power balance. In fact, reviewing the officially reported topics of the meetings over time, we see that the increase in meetings in 2013 relates to the president's May decrees of 2012. Such discussions had to do more with the president checking up on how his decrees were being implemented than with governors bringing up their own regional problems.

Do meetings with the president lead to material benefits for a region? One channel through which this might occur is via the president's reserve fund, a special pot of money totaling up to 1 percent of the state budget that can be allocated at the president's discretion. Out of 767 presidential meetings with the governors in 2000–15, a subsequent decision was made to allocate money from the president's reserve fund to the relevant region in approximately 15 percent of cases.

Figure 5-7 shows the geography of presidents' travels, with the main destinations being North Caucasus, the Far East, and the Volga-Ural region. The regions most visited by both Putin and Medvedev over the 2000–15 period include the Rostov Oblast (twelve times), Tatarstan Republic (ten times), Bashkortostan Republic (nine times), and Chechen and Ingush Republics (eight times total). This suggests a concern with the potential instability of the country's southern regions and the Muslim areas on the Volga.

There is a positive correlation between the amount of federal support a region receives, in inflation-adjusted fiscal grants per capita, and the number of times a governor met with the president. In 2000–15 total federal grants to each region were 5 percent higher in a given year for each meeting between the governor and the president that year, and 14 percent higher for every presidential visit to the region.[11] (Of course, we cannot say whether

---

11. Correlation estimates are based on longitudinal models, controlling for regional heterogeneity (fixed effects) and for the lagged level of transfers per capita (to take into account the cumulative effect). The following outliers were omitted from the

Figure 5-7   The Geography of Presidents' Travels in 2000–15

Number of visits
- Four or less
- From five to six
- More than six
- Omitted regions

Sources: Prostocifry.ru, based on information from Kremlin.ru; authors' calculations.

Notes: Total number of times the presidents visited a region. The seemingly detached region on the left is Kaliningrad Oblast. St. Petersburg with Leningrad Oblast and Moscow with Moscow Oblast are omitted from the analysis. Another omitted outlier is Krasnodar Krai, which contains the president's summer residence in Sochi, a third unofficial capital city, after Moscow and St. Petersburg. The region also frequently hosts major domestic and international events, for example, the Winter Olympics in 2014. The Crimea Republic and Sevastopol were also omitted. The legend denotes the number of visits: less than four visits (bottom 25 percent of regions, i.e., rarely visited); from four to six visits (25–75 percent of regions, i.e., frequently visited); more than six visits (top 25 percent of regions, i.e., visited very often). "Omitted regions" are outliers specified above. The median number of visits is five.

the meetings caused the additional grants or whether both were caused by something else.)

Implementation of Federal Decisions

A final way that governors can affect central policy is by simply not implementing it. One notable example is the federal law, updated in 2010, which removed the status of "president" formerly enjoyed by the leaders of ethnic republics. The law allowed for a four-year transition period. Bashkortostan stretched this to the limit, formally changing the leader's status only in December 2014. Tatarstan managed to extend the transition period for an additional year and did not comply even after that year ran out at the end of 2015. Asked about Tatarstan's situation during a press conference on December 17, 2015, Putin said that the decision was at Tatarstan's full discretion and that it did not matter to him what the head of the republic was called.

___

sample: Moscow and Moscow Oblast, St. Petersburg and Leningrad Oblast, Krasnodar Krai (Sochi-related fiscal grants), and the Chechen Republic.

CONCLUSION

Assessing the degree to which regional elites influence central decisions is challenging given the non-transparent and informal nature of this relationship. Still, the information we reviewed suggests something more complicated than the common image of an ever more centralized and hierarchical "vertical of power." On the one hand, the period in which governors were appointed by the president saw an influx of outsiders and Moscow bureaucrats into the country's regional administrations. Other reforms strengthened the role of security service and law enforcement personnel in the regions.

On the other hand, various evidence suggests that regional elites still managed to achieve their goals in relations with the center after 2004. The influx of outsiders, who were expected to have less bargaining power, was accompanied by an outflow of regional notables into the federal elite. New governors, sent out from the capital, used their clientelistic networks—and connections to corporations—to lobby the Kremlin. Experts on regional politics saw a gradual growth in the lobbying power of governors from 2005 to 2015. The share of regionally initiated bills in the Duma's workflow peaked between 2004 and 2008, and the proportion of these signed into law continued to increase until 2010. (Still, the success rate of such bills remained much lower than that of government and presidential bills.) Presidential meetings with the governors grew more frequent after 2008. Although the function of these may have been to allow the president to instruct his regional agents rather than to allow them to lobby him, he did, nevertheless, subsequently deliver additional funds to the region in question in a significant number of cases. Presidential visits continued to be associated with higher fiscal support throughout the 2000s.

Regional elites differ in their power to affect the center's decisions. Ethnic republics are among the most successful lobbyists, while other regions' influence varies with the personality of the governor, the strength of corporate interests in a region, and how well the region is represented in Moscow. The Chechen Republic has remained an extreme outlier. It was allowed to become practically autonomous and bought off with lavish aid. Personal loyalty and individual negotiations characterize how political business is done, both with the center and inside the republic.

Since 2011, pressures to decentralize have led to the reinstatement of gubernatorial elections and the mixed-member electoral system. Clearly, Putin calculated that such concessions could be neutralized by additional checks imposed in the implementation. This may turn out to be true. But, in the short run, the return of locally popular elected representatives to the Duma may enhance regions' ability to play the central political game in their own interest.

REFERENCES

Buckley, Noah, Timothy Frye, Guzel Garifullina, and Ora John Reuter. 2014. "The Political Economy of Russian Gubernatorial Election and Appointment." *Europe-Asia Studies* 66, no. 8, pp. 1213–33.

Buckley, Noah, Guzel Garifullina, Ora John Reuter, and Alexandra Shubenkova. 2014. "Elections, Appointments, and Human Capital: The Case of Russian Mayors." *Demokratizatsiya* 22, no. 1, pp. 87–116.

Egorov, Georgy, and Konstantin Sonin. 2011. "Dictators and Their Viziers: Endogenizing the Loyalty-Competence Trade-Off." *Journal of the European Economic Association* 9, no. 5, pp. 903–30.

Gessen, Masha. 2016. "The Non-Political Political Arrest of Nikita Belykh in Russia." *New Yorker*, July 1.

Golosov, Grigory. 2013. "The Territorial Genealogies of Russia's Political Parties and the Transferability of Political Machines." *Post-Soviet Affairs* 30, no. 6, pp. 464–80.

Hale, Henry E. 2003. "Explaining Machine Politics in Russia's Regions: Economy, Ethnicity, and Legacy." *Post-Soviet Affairs* 19, no. 3, pp. 226–61.

Huskey, Eugene. 2010. "Elite Recruitment and State-Society Relations in Technocratic Authoritarian Regimes: The Russian Case." *Communist and Post-Communist Studies* 43, no. 4, pp. 363–72.

Kryshtanovskaya, Olga, and Stephen White. 1996. "From Soviet *Nomenklatura* to Russian Elite." *Europe-Asia Studies* 48, no. 5, pp. 711–33.

Moses, Joel. 2008. "Who Has Led Russia? Russian Regional Political Elites, 1954–2006." *Europe-Asia Studies* 60, no. 1, pp. 1–24.

———. 2013. "Russian Mayors Embattled." *Russian Analytical Digest*, no. 139, pp. 12–15.

Nezavisimaya Gazeta. 1999. "Best Russia's Lobbyists." October 21. www.ng.ru/ideas/1999-10-21/lobby.html.

Nikolskaya, Polina, Vyacheslav Kozlov, Anastasia Yakoreva, Elena Myazina, and Anna Kozhukhar. 2016. "RBC Research: 20 Main Facts about the Chechen Republic." Russian Business Consulting. www.rbc.ru/research/society/01/02/2016/56ae68679a7947d73142182d.

Petersburg Politics. 2016a. "Reiting Fonda 'Peterburgskoi Politiki' za fevral' 2016 goda [Rating of the Petersburg Politics Fund in February 2016]." March 10. http://fpp.spb.ru/fpp-rating-2016-02.

———. 2016b. "Reiting Fonda 'Peterburgskoi Politiki' za iun' 2016 goda [Rating of the Petersburg Politics Fund in June 2016]." July 7. http://fpp.spb.ru/fpp-rating -2016-06.

———. 2016c. "17-i reiting politicheskoi vyzhivaemosti gubernatorov [17th Governors' Political Survival Rating]." December 12. http://fpp.spb.ru/rate17.php.

Petrov, Nikolay. 2005. "*Siloviki* in Russian Regions: New Dogs, Old Tricks." *Journal of Power Institutions in Post-Soviet Societies*, no. 2. http://pipss.revues.org/331.

———. 2015. "Heavyweights Are Not Needed: Will the New Crisis Cause a Parade of Sovereignties?" *RBC Daily*, May 26. www.rbc.ru/newspaper/2015/05/26 /56bcd5159a7947299f72bfa8.

———. 2016. "Making Sense of Kadyrov's Political Posturing." European Council on Foreign Relations, March 3. www.ecfr.eu/article/commentary_making_sense _of_kadryovs_political_posturing_6018.

Petrov, Nikolay, and Darrell Slider. 2016. "Regional Politics." In *Putin's Russia: Past Imperfect, Future Uncertain,* edited by Stephen Wegren. 6th ed. Lanham, Md.: Rowman and Littlefield.

Reuter, Ora John. 2010. "The Politics of Dominant Party Formation: United Russia and Russia's Governors." *Europe-Asia Studies* 62, no. 2, pp. 293–327.

———. 2017. "The Emergence of a Dominant Party in Russia: United Russia, Putin, and Regional Elites, 2000–2010. In *The Origins of Dominant Parties: Building Authoritarian Institutions in Post-Soviet Russia.* Cambridge University Press.

Reuter, Ora John, and Thomas Remington. 2009. "Dominant Party Regimes and the Commitment Problem: The Case of United Russia." *Comparative Political Studies* 42, no. 4, pp. 501–26.

Ross, Cameron. 2000. "Federalism and Democratization in Russia." *Communist and Post-Communist Studies* 33, no. 4, pp. 403–20.

Russell, John. 2011. "Chechen Elites: Control, Cooptation or Substitution?" *Europe-Asia Studies* 63, no. 6, pp. 1073–87.

Sharafutdinova, Gulnaz, and Rostislav Turovsky. 2016. "The Politics of Federal Transfers in Putin's Russia: Regional Competition, Lobbying, and Federal Priorities." *Post-Soviet Affairs* 33, no. 2, pp. 161–75.

Slider, Darrell. 1996. "Elections to Russia's Regional Assemblies." *Post-Soviet Affairs* 12, no. 3, pp. 243–64.

Stoner-Weiss, Kathryn. 1997. *Local Heroes: The Political Economy of Russian Regional Governance.* Princeton University Press.

Treisman, Daniel. 1996. "The Politics of Intergovernmental Transfers in Post-Soviet Russia." *British Journal of Political Science* 26, pp. 299–335.

———. 2001. *After the Deluge: Regional Crises and Political Consolidation in Russia.* University of Michigan Press.

———. 2007. *The Architecture of Government: Rethinking Political Decentralization.* Cambridge University Press.

———. 2011. "Presidential Popularity in a Hybrid Regime: Russia under Yeltsin and Putin." *American Journal of Political Science* 55, no. 3, pp. 590–609.

VCIOM. 2017. "Ramzan Kadyrov: portret politika [Ramzan Kadyrov: The portrait of a politician]." Press release no. 3372, May 12. http://wciom.ru/index.php?id =236&uid=116195.

Zubarevich, Natalia. 2011. Socio-Economic Development of the Republics of North Caucasus: Quantitative and Expert Estimates (2000–2010)." *Social Atlas of Russian Regions.* www.socpol.ru/atlas/portraits/r_sk.shtml.

SIX

The Role of Business in Shaping Economic Policy

NATALIA LAMBEROVA and KONSTANTIN SONIN

By 2016 the Russian economy found itself in a dire state—in 2015 GDP contracted by 3.5 percent, and inflation rose to about 13 percent for the year. Real incomes fell—for the first time in the sixteen years since 1999— by about 10 percent. Two reasons are immediate: first, the collapse of the world price of oil, the main Russian export product, and, second, Western sanctions imposed as a result of Crimea's integration into Russia. However, the more troubling aspect is the medium- to long-term perspective: the Russian economy has already stagnated for half a decade, and with Vladimir Putin firmly entrenched and unwilling to entertain any institutional reform, it is likely to stagnate further.

By the year 2016, the common picture of Putin's Russia was that it is a thoroughly corrupt police state, with the president set to stay indefinitely and interested mostly in projecting his power in the international arena, with his cronies preoccupied with self-enrichment. Documents leaked by government officials or international news agencies have corroborated

Figure 6-1   Russia's GDP per Capita[a]

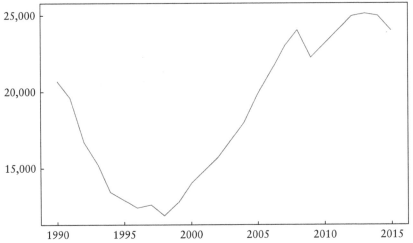

GDP per capita, PPP, USD

Sources: Trading Economics (http://tradingeconomics.com); World Bank.

a. As of 2016, Russia's GDP per capita had stagnated for nine years at levels not far above the highest point reached by the Soviet economy in 1990. (As Soviet output had a disproportionate level of military production, the current level of per capita consumption is arguably significantly higher.)

and expanded this view.[1] This situation is considered to be the final point of the following well-established narrative. The oligarchs who emerged in the mid-1990s, largely due to shady privatization deals, used their money to corrupt and dominate the president and parliament, dictating policy. Putin, upon coming to power, used his popularity associated with the Chechen war and the fast growth of the early 2000s (figure 6-1) to implement a variety of liberal and progressive policies (deregulation, lowering inflation, building reserve funds, lowering tax rates, and so forth). However, the same popularity allowed a progressive expropriation of assets from the oligarchs and a transfer of these assets into formal state

1. The websites Navalny.com and fbk.info contain a number of government materials discovered by social media activists, including Alexey Navalny and his Anti-Corruption Foundation. For the so-called Panama papers, see International Consortium of Investigative Journalist (ICIJ), http://panamapapers.icij.org/. Reuters published an extensive investigation of corruption in Russian government: www.reuters.com/investigates/section/comrade-capitalism.

ownership. Finally, the formal state ownership of industrial assets generated a new cohort of superrich oligarchs, drawn predominantly from the circle of Putin's close friends and former State Security Committee (KGB) officers.

Our view is that the picture is far more complex. First, while internal security and foreign affairs priorities took precedent over economic concerns throughout the seventeen years of Putin's rule, the influence of business on economic policy was substantial. Second, on some critically important policy issues, such as monetary policy, the government has consistently been on the progressive, liberal side—even in the twilight years of economic turmoil. Third, the most significant economic change of the Putin years, the large-scale nationalization of industrial assets, has not met stiff, if any, resistance from the business community, as a naïve theory might predict. Instead, many business people have welcomed these developments and exploited the opportunities provided by the nationalization drive. Fourth, while the number of individuals with security and military background in government and state-controlled business has increased dramatically under Putin (as figure 2-2 in Ananyev, this volume, shows, it peaked in 2006 in the central government, yet continues to rise at the regional level), the main beneficiaries are early personal connections of the president. Fifth, while cronyism has become an important input in economic policymaking, it can be defeated, at least on occasion, by loosely organized small-business protests.

That business and politics are interrelated in Putin's Russia to an extent rarely seen in the developed world creates a major methodological problem. The main complication is that being a business person or a politician is not an innate personal characteristic but an occupation of choice. The same people who started their private businesses in the early 1990s ran for governorships a decade later and joined the government or state-controlled companies in the Putin years. By the 2010s, many, if not all, members of the cabinet either themselves operated a medium-to-large business or had a spouse who operated a business in the field for which they were responsible as government officials. Most members of the parliament and nearly all members of the upper chamber of the parliament run large or extra-large businesses as their full-time occupation.[2] Many top bureaucrats in the

2. In 2008 the *Forbes* billionaires list included nine members of the upper chamber (senate) of the Russian parliament, none of whom had any significant political

Presidential Administration, military, law enforcement, and security services or their immediate relatives are heavily involved in business.[3] As we demonstrate below, those personally connected to President Putin form a distinctive group that is more successful than any other.[4] We rely on different analytical tools to examine business and its impact on economic policy.

From the viewpoint of 2016, Putin's seventeen years in power can be subdivided into three periods, marked by two major events of Putin's presidency. The first is 1999–2003, the "liberal agenda by inertia" period, when Putin's quest for consolidated power was accompanied by attempts at institutional reforms. The reforms of this period, most of them announced through 2000–01, addressed mainly the ills and problems of the 1990s. Their liberal, market-oriented agenda was in stark contrast to the agenda pursued in later years; most of them were abandoned or died quietly by the mid-2000s. During this period business influence over policy followed both conventional and unconventional patterns. Conventionally, business and industrial groups provided campaign donations or outright sponsored parliament members. Less conventionally, a number of big business people ran for elected offices themselves. This period ended with the infamous Yukos case when Mikhail Khodorkovsky, a businessman who had tried to use his economic resources to compete with Putin politically, was prosecuted for tax evasion. With the onslaught "ratified" by the 2003 parliamentary elections, the Yukos corporation was disbanded and huge parts were absorbed by Rosneft—a newly formed government corporation with Igor Sechin (a longtime connection of Putin) as chair of its board (and subsequently also the CEO).

---

experience before joining the chamber. The extent is unparalleled in both pre-Putin Russia and elsewhere (see Gehlbach, Sonin, and Zhuravskaya 2010).

3. Not surprisingly, attempts to identify channels and consequences of business influence on Russia's economic policy produced largely inconclusive results (Pyle 2011; Pyle and Solanko 2013; Yakovlev, Sobolev, and Kazun 2014).

4. In March 2016 *Forbes Russia* compiled official data on main beneficiaries of state procurement contracts in 2015. Of the top five recipients, who received more than 1 trillion rubles (US$15 billion), four are personal connections of Putin: his former judo coach, his summerhouse co-op partner, a son of his judo coach, and a son of another member of the summerhouse co-op. The fifth person is a minority partner of one of the above four.

In the second period, 2003–08, world oil prices stayed high, and the government used the budget surplus to pay down the state debt and increase spending—spending on its own employees above all. In these circumstances, there was no pressure to push forward reforms that increased efficiency. Instead, the government used windfall oil revenues to nationalize large enterprises—either by force (see the Yukos case below) or by paying off the former owners (see the TNK-BP case below). As the regional elections were canceled, big business people stopped running for governorships, yet their number in the nonelected upper chamber of the parliament increased. This period was characterized by the rise of longtime connections of Putin to the heights of economic and political influence. They entered the *Forbes* list and occupied prominent positions in the government apparatus and state corporations. At the same time, the number of official presidential meetings with the business community hit its low point (as suggested by analysis of the protocol of meetings of the Russian president). The lobbying efficiency of private companies also dipped during this period (as suggested by analysis of lobbying efficiency based on the "best lobbyists" rating).

The 2008–09 financial crisis hit Russia hard: the fall in GDP was the largest in the Group of Twenty (G-20) industrialized nations, and, according to a survey by the European Bank for Reconstruction and Development (EBRD), almost half of households had to reduce consumption of basic goods (EBRD 2011). Yet the crisis did not reverse the nationalization drive: instead, state control of the economy increased as the government encouraged state banks to bail out major private enterprises (in return for equity, which put shares of these enterprises into state hands).

The return of high oil prices in 2009–14, the third period, allowed the government to spend more and more money on internal security and the military and to replace any attempts at institutional reforms with individual projects financed and structured outside the traditional channels. The huge government contracts of 2010–15 also followed personal connections with Putin. We analyzed the data of the "kings of government contracts" rating collected by *Forbes Russia* and data about political connections and found that the members of Putin's inner circle and their immediate connections tended to receive significantly more funds in government contracts (among the top recipients). The magnitude of the effect of such connections is striking: members of the inner circle receive 142 times more money in contracts than unconnected individuals.

BUSINESS POLICY INPUT IN THE EARLY PUTIN YEARS

The 1990s left Putin, who came to power in the summer of 1999, with idle labor resources, spare industrial capacity, newly installed market institutions, and an emerging entrepreneurial class. They also left him with a mood of popular discontent with previous policies on which to build his power. These two defining features of the political and economic landscape at the turn of the century were related to the mass privatization of the 1990s. First, at the turn of the new century the Russian economy was largely private—in stark contrast to early 1990, when there were few private enterprises—and in some contrast to 2015, when most of the economy was, at least formally, back under direct state control. Second, though privatized enterprises would eventually prove to be more efficient than those that remained in state hands (see, for example, Brown, Earle, and Telegdy 2006), the popular attitude toward privatization was starkly negative.[5] That is, the positive effects of privatization came too late to be properly registered by the populace.[6] Not surprisingly, the influence of business interests on economic policy had to be channeled outside the institutions of electoral

5. In a series of papers, J. David Brown, Scott Gehlbach, John Earle, and Almos Telegdy analyzed productivity performance of private enterprises, documenting a positive impact of privatization on both productivity and employment in several postcommunist countries (e.g., Brown, Earle, and Gehlbach 2012). In all of these countries, in the period spanning five to seven years after privatization, the effect of privatization by foreigners—that is, privatization in the most well-organized industries—was significant. In contrast, privatization by natives had a small (Romania and Hungary), zero (Ukraine), or negative (Russia) effect. Additional analysis of survey data demonstrated that this effect cannot be due to tax avoidance by large firms (relative tax avoidance by private versus state-owned enterprises in Hungary and Lithuania was twice as large as in Russia). In subsequent studies (for example, Brown, Earle, and Telegdy 2006), the same group of authors documented a sharp rise in privatization's impact on productivity in the 2004–5 Russian data (ten years after privatization).

6. A study of attitudes toward privatization that used a survey of twenty-eight thousand individuals from twenty-eight transition countries conducted by the World Bank and EBRD in 2006 demonstrated that the ex post support for liberal economic reforms was low even among those that benefited from them (Denisova and others 2009).

politics—attempts to organize a party that would embrace pro-business, liberal attitudes consistently failed.

In 1999 the need for improvement of the business climate was very much on the agenda of the new president's economic team. Initially, the idea was to co-opt the business community into a kind of corporatist relationship, in which the Kremlin would deal with four officially sanctioned business organizations—the Russian Union of Industrialists and Entrepreneurs, the Chambers of Commerce and Industry, Opora Rossii (All-Russian Public Organization of Small and Medium-Sized Enterprises), and Delovaya Rossia (Business Russia). This seems to have given these groups considerable influence over the details of economic policy. In contrast to the 1990s, when most business-friendly reforms were pushed through by a group of liberal ministers in President Boris Yeltsin's successive cabinets, there is a long list of legislation and regulations that these organizations take credit for (for details, see Markus 2015; Yakovlev, Sobolev, and Kazun 2014). As suggested by a study by Andrei Yakovlev and others (2011), Russian business people perceived the membership in such organizations as efficient in promoting their interests. Mostly, they helped companies to negotiate their preferred policies in return for corporate sponsorship of various social and government projects.

In the early 2000s, another important channel of influence was regional and federal politics. Dozens of big business people ran for electoral office—mostly for powerful regional governorships. In contrast to modern U.S. politics, where business people, once in office, discontinue their hands-on involvement in the business they own or manage, in Russia they ran for public office to protect and expand their businesses (Gehlbach, Sonin, and Zhuravskaya 2010). By 2005 regional governors were stripped of their influence and were appointed by Moscow, rather than elected locally.

At the federal level, business people provided campaign finance to parliament members. In 2003 Mikhail Khodorkovsky, the majority owner and CEO of Yukos, the largest Russian oil company, cultivated a large faction of deputies in parliament—more than one hundred in the Duma, by some estimates. He was personally financing the Union of Right Forces party and had promised to single-handedly pay all the bills of another political party, Yabloko, for the 2003 campaign. Yukos executives were contributing to the Communists, and some were themselves at the top of the Communist

Party list.[7] Khodorkovsky even paid some deputies in Putin's own United Russia party, calling into question their ultimate loyalty.

In the Duma, the "Yukos faction" faithfully protected the company's interests (Volkov 2008, p. 260). The lobby blocked a bill to eliminate the offshore zones within Russia that corporations used to avoid taxation (see also box 6-1). "First they buy loopholes in legislation, then they buy officials, and then they optimize taxes," the economics minister German Gref asserted (quoted in Volkov 2008, p. 260). A proposed law to create a tax on "supplementary income from the mining of hydrocarbons" was rewritten by the Duma in a way that benefited Yukos but created huge problems for the state enterprises Rosneft and Tatneft. These changes, Gref complained, would cost the government US$2 billion a year (Pluzhnikov and Shevchenko 2008, p. 346). An amendment capping export tariffs on oil products was slipped into a critical economic package in 2002, leaving Putin little choice but to sign it (White and Whalen 2003).

The Yukos affair—the company was nationalized by force, while Khodorkovsky and his top deputy spent ten years behind bars and other big shareholders fled the country—completed the transformation toward a political system in which, as envisioned by the Kremlin, business people were supposed to be represented by associations. However, while these associations played a significant role before the Yukos affair, their influence grossly diminished afterward. In figure 6-2, there is a sharp fall in the number of the president's meetings with business people following the Yukos affair; when the number of meetings increased again years later, these were predominantly with CEOs of state-owned or state-controlled corporations.

Over the years, there have been persistent attempts, mostly unsuccessful, to soften the antibusiness stance of the political leadership. In one instance in 2009 "a group of entrepreneurs who were deputies of the State Duma" introduced amendments to the Criminal Code "prohibiting pretrial arrests of persons accused of economic offenses and restricting other forms of violent pressure on business" (Yakovlev, Sobolev, and Kazun 2014). These amendments were initially opposed by the police and secret services, then adopted by the parliament in a watered-down form, and gradually

---

7. In July 2009 former prime minister Mikhail Kasyanov said that Putin had given Khodorkovsky's financing of the Communist Party without the Kremlin's agreement as a reason for the legal campaign against Yukos when Kasyanov asked him about this in July 2003 (Belton 2009).

BOX 6-1   The Oil Tax: The Permanent Reform

For any country with substantial oil reserves, control over the resources is a major political issue. Countries that had mature political institutions before the discovery and use of major oil reserves, such as the United States, Great Britain, Norway, or the Netherlands, have not had serious problems, either taxing private companies or managing their oil through state monopolies. Countries with weak political institutions typically follow cycles of nationalizations, which end up in the development of inefficient and corrupt behemoths, and privatizations, which end up with companies growing too strong to be properly taxed (see Guriev, Kolotilin, and Sonin 2011).

By the late 1990s, Russian oil and gas companies, privatized in the mid-1990s, were especially hard to tax. In a showcase confrontation in summer 1998, Gazprom's private security guards did not allow the tax service to enter the company's headquarters; many attempts to increase the government take of natural-resource income were repeatedly denied, as gas and oil industries had significant leverage over members of the parliament. The first efforts of Putin's government to raise taxes on oil culminated in the arrest and trial of Mikhail Khodorkovsky and nationalization of the Yukos. The company's heavy investment in maintaining a strong oil lobby in the parliament was considered a major obstacle for government collection of oil revenues.

The period 2003–08 witnessed a number of changes in the way oil revenues were taxed, with the government in the post-Yukos era having the upper hand. Even though the duties and taxes on oil companies rose significantly (a new formula linked the rate to the oil price in the world market), the procedures became more transparent (the burden was shifted onto easier-to-collect export duties), and enforcement improved, the steep rise of oil prices nevertheless left the oil companies with huge profits.

With oil prices reaching US$100 per barrel in 2006–08, the main state-controlled companies, Rosneft and Gazprom, became vehicles through which President Putin financed his pet projects, such as the support of sports leagues and clubs; major projects, such as the Sochi Olympics; and many others. Both companies were extensively used in foreign affairs (for example, Gazprom's gas was a major source of leverage in negotiations with Ukraine). In exchange, the management was allowed to control more and more of retained earnings—via various tax and investment exemptions.

phased out when the regime became more repressive in the wake of the 2011–12 protests.

A major liberal reform that has generated a stream of positive coverage around the world, and has long served as a stamp of Putin's free-market inclinations, was the tax reform of 2001. First, the progressive personal

Figure 6-2   Official Meetings with Business Leaders as a Share of Total
Official Meetings of President Putin

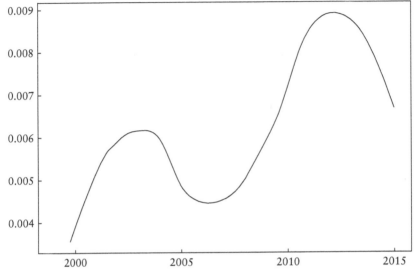

Share of meetings with businessmen

Sources: Calculated by authors from the official data on Putin's Kremlin website
(http://Kremlin.ru/). We thank Anton Sobolev and Maxim Ananyev for these data.

income tax with 30 percent at the top margin was replaced with a flat income tax of 13 percent. The corporate profit tax was reduced from 35 to
24 percent, most common business costs became deductible, and the top
bracket of the (regressive) social security tax fell from 39.5 to 26 percent.
Tax collection was unified in one agency, putting an end to the perennial
intergovernmental struggles of the Yeltsin years. Finally, small-scale tax
violations were decriminalized.

In 2000–04, Putin's government attempted a deregulation reform. Registration, licensing, and standardization procedures were simplified; the
amount of required reporting was reduced; and inspections by regulators were restricted. Despite some modest initial success as documented
by the biannual monitoring of the World Bank and the Centre for Economic and Financial Research (CEFIR), the reform failed to bring substantial relief to small and medium-size business (Schetinin and others
2005).

If the tax reform was real enough, and the deregulation effort visible,
privatization was a bogus part of Putin's liberal agenda. While mentioned

as a policy priority in almost any major leader's address on economic matters, there has been no consequential attempt at any privatization since 2002. Frustrated by the total absence of progress, government officials started to call "privatization" the selling of small tranches of minority shares in a few big-name companies, at the same time ensuring that the minority shareholders have negligible influence or oversight over the company's operations.

Another major project—opening the Russian economy to world trade and integrating it into the world economy—followed the same familiar pattern, from early attempts at reform to lost interest, stagnation, and then failure. Accession to the World Trade Organization, formally completed in 2012 after more than fifteen years of negotiation, was a mere formality. Since 2008, foreigners have been barred from making investments in thirty industries designated "critical for national security" by the government; by 2014, this number had reached forty-five. In 2014, following Western sanctions, and in 2015, following conflicts with Egypt and Turkey, the government initiated new sweeping rounds of trade restrictions. As Microeconomics 101 would predict, the major beneficiaries of trade restrictions are domestic producers. Fittingly, the family of the minister of agriculture, Alexander Tkachev, the main public proponent of the ban on food imports from the United States and the European Union, was a major beneficiary of the ban (Vinokurova 2016).

BUSINESS INFLUENCE IN THE AGE OF NATIONALIZATION

The emphasis on nationalization has been as consistently characteristic of Putin's policy during his seventeen years in power as the emphasis on privatization has been in his presidential addresses of the same period. A naïve theory would suggest that nationalization, the single most important economic policy in Russia implemented under President Putin, should be (1) conducted as a coherently formulated policy by the political leadership and (2) opposed by private entrepreneurs. In reality, it has never been formulated as a policy goal; rather, it was conducted via ad hoc decisions, sometimes with the pretense that it is a temporary measure. Even more surprising, private business people have rarely displayed significant resistance to what would, at first glance, look like an attack on their interests. The explanation is simple: in many cases, the former private owners were major beneficiaries of nationalization.

The hostile nationalization of Yukos (box 6-2), completed largely by late 2004, was preceded by the acquisition, at an inflated price, of Severnaya Neft, a relatively small oil company. In 2005 the state-owned natural gas giant Gazprom acquired Sibneft, privatized in 1996–97 in the last installment of the loans-for-shares auctions, in what was the largest corporate takeover in the history of Russia to this date. The takeover was peaceful, with the price tag determined by the market.[8] In 2006 Western companies such as Royal Dutch Shell were intimidated into selling their stakes in major oil development projects such as Sakhalin and Kovytka to Gazprom.[9]

Over the years, the operational ways that major companies were nationalized varied significantly. Nationalizations in 2001–04 of the media companies Russian Public Television (ORT) and Media-Most, and later Yukos, wiped out their former owners' fortunes and left them with criminal prosecution on their hands. The assets were taken from vocal critics of Putin—Boris Berezovsky, Vladimir Gusinsky, and Mikhail Khodorkovsky, "the oligarchs" of the Yeltsin era—and transferred to state corporations where Putin's connections were top managers. By contrast, in 2013 the owners of TNK-BP, the largest private oil company in Russia, were paid US$55 billion dollars (in February 2016 the acquired assets were worth from US$20 billion to US$30 billion at best). In 2015 the owner of the oil company Bashneft went to jail and was released only after acquiescing to the nationalization deal offered by the Kremlin; reportedly, he was not paid anything close to the market price, yet kept significant stakes in other businesses.

Nationalizations were not focused exclusively on oil. VSMPO-AVISMA, the world's largest producer of titanium, was acquired by a state holding company, the vehicle to manage Russia's production in export-oriented military industry, in 2006. Before that, in 2005, the same holding structure acquired a controlling stake in AvtoVAZ, the largest car producer. The aviation, shipbuilding, and nuclear industries were consolidated under state control as well, using both coercion and compensation to the private owners. While coercion led to undercompensated acquisitions, in almost any case involving compensated nationalization, there were suspicions of

8. Some government officials bragged that the actual payment to the previous private owners was a tiny fraction of the announced amount.

9. In the 1990s the Sakhalin project was established as a production-sharing agreement, a common contract form that protects foreign investors in weakly institutionalized countries.

Figure 6-3   Expert Estimates of Lobbying Efficiency

Index of lobbying efficiency

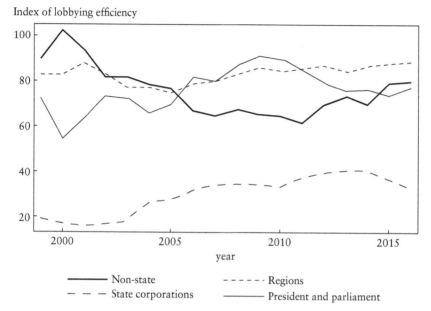

Sources: *Nezavisimaya Gazeta*; authors' calculations.

the state company overpaying for the acquisition, with the premium going to the bureaucrats overseeing the transaction. In 2010 the state-owned Sberbank, Russia's largest retail bank, acquired Troika Dialog, the largest Russian private investment bank.

As the number and size of state corporations grew, so did their influence, as measured by lobbying efficiency. By contrast, the influence of privately held companies declined. Figure 6-3 uses the ranking of the "best lobbyists of Russia" published annually by the newspaper *Nezavisimaya Gazeta*, based on the estimates of up to six dozen experts. The lobbying efficiency score (on a scale from 0, least efficient, to 5, most efficient) increases if the individual secures an important post for an ally, wins a major court case, receives a large government contract, or gets an important piece of regulation passed.[10] Figure 6-3 contrasts the total lobbying efficiency scores for all non-state organizations, companies at least 50 percent

10. The data cover seventeen years, but for 1999–2006 many monthly scores are missing, and therefore we averaged and normalized available monthly scores to be consistent with the yearly averages.

owned by the state, regional leaders, and members of the federal parliament, Presidential Administration, or cabinet of ministers. As can be seen, the total influence of the state companies rises until 2014, while that of non-state organizations falls from a peak in 2001 to a low point around 2011, before recovering somewhat.

The impact of nationalization is extremely hard to estimate. The major studies of post-socialist privatization by John Earle and his coauthors required years of data cleaning, with their first results published a decade or more after the events. With Putin-era nationalization, an additional difficulty is that, unlike privatization, it has been happening on a case-by-case, idiosyncratic basis. Nationalized assets are often held by state-controlled holdings with a complicated cross-ownership structure. Still, a simple exercise suggests how nationalization may affect business behavior. Examining a random sample of 125,786 Russian companies in 2003–13, we found that companies tended to invest less after a major nationalization had occurred within their industry.[11] Observing such nationalizations, owners apparently fear that their assets will also be expropriated.

The TNK-BP acquisition by Rosneft—the largest-ever purchase, at a market price, of a highly profitable private company by a state-owned company—has little historical precedent. Many governments have nationalized oil companies through the course of the twentieth century, primarily because of their inability to properly tax large, politically influential private companies (for the list of all nationalizations, see Guriev, Kolotilin, and Sonin 2011). The unprecedented nature of the Rosneft nationalization lies in the fact that the transfer of assets was peaceful, and the previous owners received a market-based compensation for their assets.

The TNK-BP nationalization resulted from two factors, which are typical for oil company nationalizations (see box 6-3). First, the government decision to go forward was made possible by the windfall oil revenues in the period of historically high oil prices. Though formally financed through, in part, retained earnings, and, in part, issuance of debt by a public company, an acquisition by an 80 percent state-owned and 100 percent state-controlled company is equivalent to nationalization, fully paid from state coffers. Second, though some observers attribute the project to the personal ambitions of the Rosneft chairman, Igor Sechin, a Putin confidant of two decades and a major architect of the Yukos takeover, the project would not

11. Company data are from the Ruslana database (http://ruslana.bvdep.com/).

BOX 6-2 The 2003 Nationalization: A Hostile Takeover

Yukos was created by the Russian government in April 1993 to integrate a number of parts of the former oil industry, and it was subsequently privatized through one of the infamous loans-for-shares auctions (Treisman 2010). Until Yukos's core shareholder group had accumulated an absolute majority of shares, minority shareholders, including foreign institutional investors, were treated poorly. After 1999, however, Yukos often surpassed other large Russian companies in developing new standards of corporate governance and transparency. In August 2001 the *New York Times* reported, "Mr. Khodorkovsky has concentrated on recasting Yukos to look more like a company that investors can trust" (Tavernise 2001).

Between 1998 and 2003, thanks to rising oil prices, improved corporate standards, and the increasing attractiveness of emerging markets, the company's market equity capitalization grew more than tenfold. By 2003 Yukos was the largest oil company in Russia and second only to Gazprom among all Russian companies by capitalization. On July 2, 2003, Platon Lebedev, a major shareholder and director of Menatep, a holding and investment company that owned 61 percent of Yukos's common stocks, was arrested and charged with embezzling state assets in the 1994 privatization. On October 25, 2003, Mikhail Khodorkovsky, the CEO and the largest shareholder of Yukos, was arrested and charged with tax evasion, fraud, forgery, and embezzlement (all initial charges were unrelated to Yukos).

On December 2, 2003, the Ministry of Taxation informed the prosecutor's office that Yukos had underpaid at least US$5 billion in taxes in 1998–2001. (Before, Yukos had won trial judgments over these cases and the ministry had publicly agreed that there were no overdue taxes.) Eventually, the amount of back-dated taxes and fines due to the allegedly illegal exploitation of regional tax-incentive schemes reached US$27.5 billion. In 2004–06 the company's core assets were transferred to the state-owned Rosneft, while the majority of owners, managers, and representatives fled the country. The former owners succeeded in asserting control over some of the company's assets that remained outside Russia; by 2016 they had secured a number of court rulings, including that of the Permanent Court of Arbitration and the European Court of Human Rights, awarding them billions of dollars in compensation of their losses and damages.

For the post-Yukos life of its core assets, see the case of TNK-BP, which was bought by Rosneft, a company composed primarily of former Yukos assets, in box 6-3.

BOX 6-3   The 2013 Nationalization: A Mutually Beneficial Deal

TNK-BP was created in 2003 as a vertically integrated company that united oil-related assets belonging to BP, a major world oil company, and a group of Russian business people. The result was an oil company that was the third largest in Russia and among the ten largest in the world. It combined upstream and downstream operations in Russia and Ukraine, belonging, in equal shares to BP and the Alfa-Access-Renova (AAR) consortium, the group of Russian investors. Though significant tensions emerged at times between the British and Russian shareholders (generating worldwide news coverage in 2008), the company was considered very successful and was expanding worldwide, acquiring operations in Vietnam and Venezuela.

In 2011 the Russian state corporation Rosneft attempted to form a strategic alliance with BP to explore the Arctic. This involved a US$16 billion share swap, which was interpreted as a preliminary step toward a takeover of the British part of TNK-BP. AAR succeeded in blocking the partnership via the Stockholm arbitration court. Instead, an agreement was reached in 2013, under which Rosneft paid US$55 billion for TNK-BP in a deal that gave BP a 20 percent share of Rosneft.

The deal was the largest corporate acquisition in the history of Russia, and the largest peaceful, market-based nationalization in history. It created the largest publicly traded oil company in the world in terms of proven reserves. However, by 2016 the total market capitalization of Rosneft was as low as US$36 billion, and it was on the path to posting one of the largest losses due to a market-based acquisition in history.

have been possible without strong popular support for nationalization. At the same time, if not for the political power of the existing private owners, they would not have been compensated in full.

PERSONAL CONNECTIONS AS A BUSINESS ASSET

While by 2016 corruption and cronyism had become, in the opinion of the Western public and media, a defining feature of Putin's administration, there have been few systematic attempts to study the phenomenon.[12] The

12. See Steven Lee Myers's *The New Tsar: The Rise and Reign of Vladimir Putin* (2015) for an excellent journalistic account and Dawisha (2014) for an academic study of "Putin's kleptocracy."

obvious problem in analyzing cronyism is how to determine whether a billionaire associate of the president is, in fact, a gifted entrepreneur, whose talent has brought both wealth and closeness to power, or a mere acquaintance of the president, whose wealth and power owe nothing to talent and everything to the president's whims.

To deal with this problem, we focus on Putin's associates from before his rise from relative obscurity. In 1996, when Putin was a vice governor of St. Petersburg, eight people established the Ozero cooperative of country house owners in the beautiful countryside near the city. Besides Putin, the other seven were Vladimir Smirnov, Nikolay Shamalov, Vladimir Yakunin, Yuri Kovalchuk, Vladimir Myachin, Sergey Fursenko, and Andrey Fursenko. We added to these a number of Putin's university friends, former colleagues, and relatives, all of whom were close to the future president before his career took off.[13] The resulting list of Putin's "inner circle" is conservative and not exhaustive. However, the fact that we have probably missed some members should make it harder to detect effects of connections— and even more believable if we do.

Of these twenty-four members of Putin's inner circle, four were featured at least once in 2005–15 on the Russian edition of *Forbes*'s annual list of the country's "200 richest people." To avoid confounding, we look at these four people as "treatment" and do not investigate the changes in their wealth. We call those 253 people who appeared at least once on this list the "super-wealthy."[14] Perhaps more surprising, the direct connections of "Ozero" members also did well. We judge two people to be "connected" if

---

13. Individuals' biographies and connections to Putin are derived from *Forbes Russia* yearly publications.

14. In the first ten years of Putin's rule, 1999–2008, the economy was growing at 7 percent per annum, which meant that the country's GDP nearly doubled. With the appreciation of the ruble, the income and the wealth of Russian people have increased even more dramatically. In 2008, the last year of fast growth, *Forbes* listed eighty-seven Russian billionaires (it excluded those who were in the executive branch yet were allegedly worth billions). While some of the billionaires owed their fortunes to genuine start-ups, of the twenty richest people in Russia, nineteen (95 percent) became rich as a result of a dramatic increase in world prices of raw materials, oil and metals. Most obtained their assets through privatization; at least seven of them were CEOs of Soviet industrial dinosaurs who, in the crisis years of the 1990s, accumulated ownership using the cash flows of enterprises that they led.

their names appeared together in at least one article in the News section of Yandex, Russia's most popular search engine. It turns out that, among the super-wealthy, those who were personally connected to a member of Putin's inner circle saw their wealth exceed the wealth of others—at least, in years when the oil price was above US$70 a barrel. The effect was enormous: these connections of connections received an additional US$800 million a year on average in high oil price years. Such connections did not help—and could even hurt—in years when oil fell below US$70 a barrel. More distant connections to the inner circle had no detectable effect.

Just as the "right" political connections benefited business people, the "wrong" political connections harmed them. We used a similar methodology to access the role of business connections to Khodorkovsky—the famous head of Yukos who was prosecuted—and find that the wealth of those connected to him tends to be lower than the wealth of other "super-wealthy." Nor did connections to other rich business people correlate with greater wealth. One might expect that the most connected members of the super-wealthy would be the richest. However, that was not the case once we adjusted for connections to Putin's inner circle. The only way general connectedness mattered was that it attenuated the negative effect of connections to the "wrong" people.

Though personal connections play a huge role in Putin's Russia, their power is not unlimited. In one recent episode, one of Putin's closest cronies was defeated by a mass protest of truck drivers. In 2015 the government introduced "Plato," a system that helps to collect a newly established toll that charges truckers for use of federal highways. The system is managed by a company partly owned by Igor Rotenberg (a son of Putin's longtime friend and judo sparring partner turned billionaire); the concession conditions were specifically tailored to insure the company against almost any possible losses. The new toll imposed a significant cost on transportation companies and truck drivers, threatening to throw many of them out of business.

The Plato system started operating in November 2015, with many computer glitches, and collected 800 million rubles (US$11.9 million) in just three weeks. At that point, truck drivers and transportation companies tried to stop implementation, first with petitions and then with public protests and by blocking roads. On December 15, the government backed down: the president signed a law that reduces the penalties for noncompliance by ninety times: 5,000 rubles instead of 450,000 rubles for legal entities and 5,000 rubles for individuals. The size of the toll itself was also significantly cut.

Interestingly, the Business Association of Truck Drivers did not support the protesting truckers, accusing them of "an act of sabotage." This episode demonstrates that small businesses can—although they do not always do so—cause the government to make major (and public) policy changes. It also shows how grassroots protests sometimes circumvent the formal business associations that, by this point, the authorities have co-opted.

REFORM BY STATE CORPORATIONS

Personal connections are also key to the Kremlin's current approach to economic management. From 2007 on, perceiving previous attempts at institutional reform to have failed, Putin tried a new tack. He began creating ad hoc corporations, each under a trusted individual, to administer whole industries or large-scale projects. Such state corporations were exempt from some (sometimes a lot of) government regulation and oversight and received a mix of state and quasi-state financing, including loan guarantees from state-owned banks.

Examples abound. The Rosnano corporation was established to spur innovation in an environment with insecure property rights and thus low incentives to innovate. Instead of institutional protections, Anatoly Chubais, the legendary reformer of the pre-Putin era and Rosnano's chairman, promised to provide personal protection to projects in which Rosnano invested. Another example, the International Financial Center project, aimed to carve out an island of better law and enforcement for selected international investors. The Skolkovo Foundation sought to lure technology companies with promises of special tax and legal treatment. A group of select universities, designated "national research universities," were protected from archaic regulation. In perhaps the biggest project of all, the government established a holding company, Rostec, in 2007 to promote the development and production of modern products in both defense and civilian industries.

As a rule, such projects were headed by someone personally appointed by and reporting directly to Putin. In contrast with the Ozero-style cronies, such executives have typically been drawn from a pool of industry insiders. Sometimes, the projects would bring visible improvements over the archaic status quo. Yet another result of this anti-institutional approach was a proliferation of dubious projects that received government financing and preferential treatment. Projects to create a "national browser" and a "national search engine" are typical, though somewhat bizarre, examples.

At the same time, some of these projects have proved relatively efficient within a system in which even the supreme leader could not complete much-needed institutional reforms.

CONCLUSION

In 2016 Russia entered its seventeenth year under Putin's leadership and its ninth year of economic stagnation. On the positive side, macroeconomic policy under Putin has been consistently conservative. Over the years, the efforts of private business people, supported by professionals within the government, have led to some limited reforms and improved the quality of life of Russians. In 2016 Russians drive more cars over better roads, have access to a far wider spectrum of financial services, and enjoy more streamlined bureaucratic procedures than they did in 1999.

However, the negative side is no less apparent. Russia's windfall oil revenues financed the formation of a personalized, archaic political regime. Large private businesses have become inseparable from the state administration. Attempts to create better institutions—never particularly effective—have been replaced by a proliferation of ad hoc, individual projects. With political arrangements set up to keep the current leadership in power, and tiny elites busy exploiting connections to the leader to enrich themselves, there is no reason to expect much-needed economic and institutional reforms to come from above. Whether such reforms might occur under pressure "from below" without a serious disruption remains an open question.

REFERENCES

Belton, Catherine. 2009. "Kasyanov Reveals Putin's Pursuit of Tycoon." *Financial Times*, July 20.

Brown, J. David, John Earle, and Scott Gehlbach. 2012. "Privatization." In *The Oxford Handbook of the Russian Economy*, edited by Michael Alexeev and Shlomo Weber. Oxford University Press.

Brown, J. David, John Earle, and Almos Telegdy. 2006. "The Productivity Effects of Privatization: Longitudinal Estimates from Hungary, Romania, Russia, and Ukraine." *Journal of Political Economy* 114, no. 1, pp. 61–99.

Dawisha, Karen. 2014. *Putin's Kleptocracy: Who Owns Russia?* New York: Simon and Schuster.

Denisova, Irina, Markus Eller, Timothy Frye, and Ekaterina Zhuravskaya. 2009. "Who Wants to Revise Privatization? The Complementarity of Market Skills and Institutions." *American Political Science Review* 103, no. 2, pp. 284–304.

EBRD (European Bank for Reconstruction and Development). 2011. *Transition Report 2011—Crisis and Transition: The People's Perspective*. London.

Gehlbach, Scott, Konstantin Sonin, and Ekaterina Zhuravskaya. 2010. "Businessman Candidates." *American Journal of Political Science* 54, no. 3, pp. 718–36.

Guriev, Sergei, Anton Kolotilin, and Konstantin Sonin. 2011. "Determinants of Nationalization in the Oil Sector: A Theory and Evidence from Panel Data." *Journal of Law, Economics, and Organization* 27, no. 2, pp. 301–23.

Markus, Stanislav. 2015. *Property, Predation, and Protection*. New York: Cambridge University Press.

Myers, Steven Lee. 2015. *The New Tsar: The Rise and Reign of Vladimir Putin*. New York: Alfred A. Knopf.

Pluzhnikov, Sergey, and Dmitry Shevchenko. 2008. *Zyuganov.net: Tainaya istoria KPRF 1990–2008* [Zyuganov.net: The secret history of the Communist Party of Russia 1990–2008]. Moscow: Stolitsa-Print.

Pyle, William. 2011. "Organized Business, Political Competition, and Property Rights: Evidence from the Russian Federation." *Journal of Law, Economics, and Organization* 27, no. 1, pp. 2–31.

Pyle, William, and Laura Solanko. 2013. "The Composition and Interests of Russia's Business Lobbies: Testing Olson's Hypothesis of the 'Encompassing Organization." *Public Choice* 155, nos. 1–2, pp. 19–41.

Schetinin, Oleg, Oleg Zamulin, Ekaterina Zhuravskaya, and Evgeny Yakovlev. 2005. "Monitoring the Administrative Barriers to Small Business Development in Russia: 5th Round." Policy Paper 22. Moscow: Centre for Economic and Financial Research (CEFIR).

Tavernise, Sabrine. 2001. "Fortune in Hand, Russian Tries to Polish Image." *New York Times*, August 18.

Treisman, Daniel. 2010. "'Loans for Shares' Revisited." *Post-Soviet Affairs* 26, no. 3, pp. 207–27.

Vinokurova, Ekaterina. 2016. "Even the Military Industrial Complex Does Not Have Such a Lobby." *Znak*, May 31. www.znak.com/2016-05-31/v_chih_interesah _rossiya_prodolzhaet_prodovolstvennuyu_voynu_s_zapadom.

Volkov, Vadim. 2008. "Standard Oil and Yukos in the Context of Early Capitalism in the US and Russia." *Demokratizatsiya* 16, no. 3, pp. 240–64.

White, Gregory, and Jeanne Whalen. 2003. "Behind Moscow's Big Showdown: Putin Thought He Had Cut a Better Deal with Oil Barons." *Wall Street Journal*, August 1.

Yakovlev, Andrei, Anton Sobolev, and Anton Kazun. 2014. "Means of Production versus Means of Coercion: Can Russian Business Limit the Violence of a Predatory State?" *Post-Soviet Affairs* 30, nos. 2–3, pp. 171–94.

Yakolev, Andrei, Andrei Zudin, and Victoria Golikova. 2011. "Biznes-assotsiatsii i ikh rol' v protsessakh modernizetsii v Rossii [Business assoctions and their role in the modernization processes in Russia]." *Obshchestvennie Nauki i Sovremennost'* 3, pp. 26–35.

SEVEN

Media in Russia

Between Modernization and Monopoly

MARIA LIPMAN, ANNA KACHKAEVA, and MICHAEL POYKER

Two trends have transformed the Russian media since the end of Soviet rule. The first is the modernization of the sector. Starting in the late 1980s, what had been a tightly controlled instrument of communist agit-prop evolved into something closer to the Western concept of professional journalism based on editorial independence. Then, the 2000s saw the transformation of what had been an economically struggling sector into a multibillion-dollar business, boasting new technologies, state-of-the-art formats, and a broad range of broadcasts and publications to meet a variety of tastes.

The second trend, evident from the early 2000s, is the increasing effort of the central authorities to concentrate all major media assets in the hands of a few loyalists of Vladimir Putin. By the end of Putin's first presidential term, all three mass-audience TV channels with news coverage were securely

Authors are grateful to Leon Aron, Daniel Treisman, Joshua Tucker, and the participants at the UCLA seminar for excellent suggestions. We thank TNS Global and the Levada Center for providing data. Whatever errors remain are our fault.

under Kremlin control. By the decade's end, nearly all of about two dozen national television stations were under control of just three entities—the state itself, the media subsidiary of the state gas company Gazprom, and a range of business structures controlled by Yuri Kovalchuk, a member of Putin's innermost circle.

These transformations raise several questions. How did the media's modernization and growing profitability interact with the Kremlin's campaign for political mastery? Was the redistribution of ownership governed by primarily political motives, or was the purpose to grant lucrative assets to Putin's friends? After Putin's return to the presidency in 2012, and especially after the annexation of Crimea in 2014, the Kremlin switched to a more overtly propagandistic use of the media. The extreme character of much of this propaganda raises another puzzle. To achieve propaganda goals or profits, broadcasters need to retain viewers; distortions that are too blatant risk driving them away (Gehlbach and Sonin 2014). Yet after the annexation of Crimea, Russian television pulled out all the propaganda stops, and, despite this, audience size went up, not down.

Our review of the evidence suggests a complicated mix of political and commercial motives in the Kremlin's media strategy—but with political motives clearly dominating. It should be pointed out that in orchestrating or overseeing the redistribution of media properties the Kremlin entrusts business magnates with major political resources. All of them have other business interests—in banking, metals, or energy—on which they rely for most of their profits. To some, holding a stake in media properties is a service they do for the Kremlin, rather than a major business interest. Major holders, of course, seek to profit from their media operations, but sometimes doing this service and assisting the Kremlin's political goals may reduce profits. According to some reports (see below), such loyal holders find ways to make up for their losses, including obtaining compensation from the government.

We argue that the Russian case challenges certain premises of previous work on media persuasion. Contrary to the claim that inaccurate "news" drives viewers away, the raw and aggressive propaganda on pro-Kremlin TV attracted larger audiences than before. Our explanation is that what the state channels were selling was not accurate information but emotional gratification. They offered versions of reality that—although not infrequently untrue—made Russians feel good about themselves and their country. Finally, although it is hard to disentangle the effects of pro-Kremlin media from those of the Putin team's political monopoly and repressive policies, we provide some evidence that the recent propaganda offensive did influence both attitudes and beliefs.

MEDIA MODERNIZATION

Since the fall of the Soviet Union, Russia's media have been in continuous evolution. The early 1990s saw a surge of idealism as reporters and editors embraced Western standards and practices. The new Russian Media Law, drafted in late 1991, emulated the best U.S. and European models of editorial independence and objectivity. Across the country, journalists struggled to learn how to find out the news first, to get the best sources, and, most important, to keep the state at arm's length.

Around the same time, Russia's new entrepreneurs began to take seriously the business aspect of media. The most prominent among them was Vladimir Gusinsky, who founded Russia's first fully fledged private media holding, Media-Most, whose crown jewel was NTV, a national TV channel with news coverage. Hundreds of independent newspapers, magazines, and other publications sprang up within a few years.

Starting from the Soviet system, in which all media were state owned and subject to prepublication vetting by communist censors, the transition was spectacular. Yet the early advances were, in some ways, fragile. Emerging media tycoons proved as susceptible as others to what one Moscow-based Western diplomat called the "incestuous" relationship between business and government.[1] Journalists failed to develop an efficient professional association or an environment of solidarity and shared ethical standards that could protect them against state incursions. And, arguably, the weak commitment in Russian society to liberal values such as freedom of speech left journalism vulnerable.

The economic boom of the 2000s turned what had been a financially struggling industry into a lucrative business. The TV advertising market grew from US$235 million in 2000 to US$4.7 billion in 2008.[2] By then,

---

1. Glenn Waller, an Australian diplomat, quoted in Hoffman (2002, p. 322).

2. See Association of Communication Agencies of Russia, "Ob'em reklamnogo rynka v Rossii v 2000–2011 gg [The size of the Russian advertising market in 2000–2011]," www.akarussia.ru/node/2085. On the development of media as business, see Kachkaeva (2008); Lipman (2009).

even the print press was selling US$2.6 billion worth of ads a year. Total advertising revenues on all media grew from US$807 million in 2000 to US$10.3 billion in 2008. Competition for these revenues became fierce.

During the political turmoil of the 1990s, television had broadcast detailed coverage and analysis of politics. But in the 2000s, it was entertainment, rather than news, that attracted viewers. And it was entertainment that became the main focus of business development. As early as 2003, the Russian news magazine *Kompania* wrote: "On the whole Russian TV has become about entertainment. From a business perspective that's justified since the TV companies have begun to draw profit. From the standpoint of public good that's questionable: electronic media will no longer be able to control the government's performance."[3] Television had become, according to Aleksandr Rodniansky, Russia's leading entertainment TV manager, "no longer a missionary, but a sort of leisure."[4]

Channels quickly moved from buying foreign TV series to producing highly popular ones targeted at different domestic audiences. Russian-made reality shows became "one of the trendiest genres."[5] Crime shows and tabloid talk shows that focused on private affairs, such as divorcing couples engaged in fierce fights, attracted gigantic audiences. Major media companies expanded to include telecommunications, printing, and distribution businesses. Besides renovating its lineup of shows, Channel One and its top manager, Konstantin Ernst, engaged in film production. Ernst's works—which, as of 2013, included four of the ten top-grossing Russian films of all time—benefited from promotion on the station.[6] More and more niche thematic channels appeared, along with cable and satellite networks.

From the mid-2000s on, these trends coincided with rapid penetration of the Internet, especially among Russians under forty years of age.[7] Although many users were concentrated in Moscow and St. Petersburg, re-

3. "Realiti shou vmesto realnosti [Reality show instead of reality]," *Kompania*, June 30, 2003, http://ko.ru/articles/7317.

4. Ibid.

5. Ibid.

6. Romodanovsky (2013). On Ernst, see also Yaffa (2014).

7. The share of people using the Internet daily increased from about 10 percent in 2007 to 27 percent by late 2010 (it doubled again by late 2015, reaching 55 percent). Public Opinion Foundation (FOM), "Internet v Rossiji: dinamika proniknovenia.

searchers also noted the appearance of local Twitter groups and blogs in regional centers, focused on regional news (Alexanyan and others 2012). To appeal to this new audience, most major print and radio outlets developed online platforms. Indeed, print, audio, video, and Internet were increasingly merging. This period also saw a spectacular rise of social networks (Razumovskaya 2011).

Dmitry Medvedev, who served as president from 2008 to 2012, turned "modernization" into a ubiquitous slogan, posted his iPhone photographs online, and hosted his own video blog. During this period, new publications emerged catering to sophisticated urbanites ("hipsters," as they referred to themselves). Some of these publications grew politicized, as among this group interest in politics and civic life began to emerge. A range of bloggers achieved huge popularity, attracting tens of thousands of regular readers with all varieties of satire and critique. In 2010 businessman Aleksandr Vinokurov and his wife, Natalia Sindeeva, launched TV Rain, an Internet television channel that ignored the political restrictions that guided coverage on the state-managed channels. TV Rain was soon included in cable packages, increasing its audience and revenues. By 2011 a striking gap had emerged between the tightly controlled agenda of national television and the discussions of lawlessness and abuse that were becoming increasingly common on the web.[8]

CONSOLIDATING CONTROL

Even as the media modernized—professionally, economically, and technologically—a second trend was simultaneously reshaping the landscape. A process of consolidating state assets had begun even before Putin took power. During the 1990s, the eighty-nine regional subsidiaries of the state-owned All-Russia State Television and Radio Broadcasting Company (VGTRK) had come under the de facto command of the country's regional governors. As the 1999 parliamentary election approached, Boris Yeltsin's government set about recapturing them. Within a few years, the subsidiaries

Osen' 2015 [Russian Internet: Penetration dynamics. Fall 2015]," http://fom.ru/SMI-i-Internet/12497.

8. Bruce Etling, Hal Roberts, and Robert Faris (2014) showed that the content and opinion of most Russian blogs in 2012 differed consistently from the information provided by TV and other pro-Kremlin media sources.

were stripped of legal, financial, and economic autonomy—not to mention programming independence—and reduced to tame branches of the state-owned holding.

After Putin's election, the major national television companies soon became targets. Gusinsky had taken out a huge loan from the state gas company Gazprom to finance the development of his fast-growing media empire. In 2000 Gazprom insisted on early repayment. Gusinsky could not raise the money and, under intimidation, was forced to flee the country, surrendering to Gazprom his media group with its key asset, NTV. Later that year, the Kremlin forced another mogul, Boris Berezovsky, to give up control of the Russian Public Television (ORT) channel and, following Gusinsky's example, go into exile.[9]

Formally, the Kremlin was merely reasserting its legitimate control rights. Gazprom could claim to be motivated only by commercial interest (the government referred to the takeover of Gusinsky's media holding by Gazprom as a "dispute of economic entities" [*spor khozyaistvuyushchikh sub'ektov*], thus emphasizing that there was nothing political about it, just business; *Itogi.ru* 2000), and ORT, over which Berezovsky had managed to establish great influence, was majority state-owned. But the result was the consolidation under the Kremlin's direction of all three major national television channels. By the end of Putin's first term, a powerful "information vertical," connected him to all Russian households.

Throughout the 2000s, the authorities also increased pressure on independent local TV channels that had developed in the regions. Most such companies soon grew more cautious and loyal. But the most defiant, Tomsk TV-2, continued to exercise editorial independence long after others had adjusted to the new environment. TV-2 made profit and was economically viable, but eventually, in 2015, the government destroyed it: the station was reduced to a small, money-losing online operation (see Super 2015).

As the decade progressed, more and more broadcasting and other media ended up under the sway of a group of old Putin associates, the main media holder among them being banker Yuri Kovalchuk.[10] In 2005 Kovalchuk became the main shareholder of a major television station, Channel Five,

9. For a detailed account of Gusinsky's and Berezovsky's rise and fall, see Hoffman (2002, chaps. 6, 7, and 16).

10. For, a detailed description of Kovalchuk's rise and his assets, see Kozyrev and Sokolova (2008).

which then acquired an unprecedented package of several dozen regional broadcasting licenses (previously, the frequencies packages put on auction had been much smaller) (Borodina and Pushkarskaya 2007). After that, Channel Five, which was now broadcasting in over half the Russian regions and had news coverage, was granted the status of a national channel (previously assigned only to the "big three"—Channel One [formerly ORT], Rossia-1 [which belongs to VGTRK], and NTV), entitling it to state subsidies for signal transmission to smaller towns.

In 2006 business structures related to Kovalchuk acquired a large stake in REN-TV, a private channel with news coverage, originally owned by its founders, the Lesnevsky family.[11] In 2008 the creation of the National Media Group (NMG) brought together, first and foremost, the media holdings associated with Kovalchuk, as well as those of a few other business magnates. NMG included a prominent daily, *Izvestia*, REN TV, and Channel Five. As the 2007–08 election season approached, REN TV's independent editorial policy apparently raised Kremlin concerns; after NMG took over, the channel's editorial line changed quite significantly.[12] One weekly review show, *The Week with Marianna Maksimovskaya*, was allowed to practice editorial independence for several more years, but it too was eventually closed in August 2014 after the annexation of Crimea (Dergachov and Galimova 2014).

By the late 2000s, media assets under control of Kovalchuk's business structures vastly surpassed the oligarchic "media empires" of the 1990s. In 2016 the value of his NMG holding was estimated at 150 billion rubles (US$2.2 billion) (RBC 2016). In addition to media assets, Kovalchuk's Bank Rossiya bought a share in Russia's largest advertising sales house, VI.[13]

11. RBC (2006). The Lesnevskys were forced to sell their TV asset a bit earlier; among the buyers were Severstal and Surgutneftegaz. Neither of the two companies had a prior interest in media. Arguably, this was an example of an earlier-mentioned practice when big business tycoons are entrusted to hold an important political resource as a service to the Kremlin.

12. During Medvedev's presidency, as the control over media content partially softened, REN TV experienced a "second wind" of sorts: its editorial line grew more independent and its political coverage more critical. This new opening ended when the regime hardened again after Putin's return to the Kremlin.

13. Bank Rossiya acquired VI (formerly Video International). See Boletskaya (2010).

The Russian media sector, as of the late 2000s, was a tight-knit oligopoly. Almost all the federal TV channels—that is, the "big three" and about two dozen other channels with political coverage or just entertainment—were in the hands of only three entities: the state itself, Gazprom media (GPM), and NMG. These three groups also include a range of print, radio, and Internet assets. Ownership ties among them are complex. For instance, Bank Rossiya, in which Kovalchuk was the main shareholder, also indirectly owned a significant stake in GPM, giving Kovalchuk influence over two of the three entities.[14] Meanwhile, in 2016 GPM also bought 7.5 percent of NMG (Boletskaya 2016a). Two other oligarchs retain relatively minor involvement in national TV broadcasters. Roman Abramovich formally owns 24 percent of Channel One—the rest is shared between the state (51 percent) and NMG (25 percent)[15]—but Abramovich (in another example of holding a media asset as a service to the Kremlin) has in practice long ceded his control rights to the state. Another pro-Kremlin billionaire, Alisher Usmanov, the owner of the *Kommersant* group, has stakes in the major entertainment network CTC and a number of entertainment TV stations.[16]

As the Kremlin and its allies tightened control over national television, editorial policy also fell into line. The change that occurred during Putin's first term can be seen in the contrasting coverage of three major tragedies.

- In August 2000, before the Kremlin had taken control of national TV, the Kursk submarine sank in the Barents Sea. The reporters did their best to cover the disaster, investigate its causes, and expose the officials' lies about the details and eventual failure of the rescue operation. Putin

14. For detail on ties between GPM and NMG, see *Kommersant* (2012a).

15. The state's share in Channel One is formally divided among the Federal Agency for State Property Management (Rosimushchestvo) (38.9 percent), state news agency ITAR-TASS (9.1 percent), and TV Technical Center "Ostankino" (3 percent). *Kommersant* (2012b).

16. CTC Media, one of the two major Russian entertainment networks, owns four television channels. Its biggest shareholder used to be Sweden's Modern Times Group (MTG). In 2015, to comply with a new Russian law that prevents foreigners from owning more than 20 percent of media companies, MTG sold 75 percent of CTC for about US$200 million to a company half-owned by Usmanov's holding company. The remaining 25 percent stake is held by a company controlled by Yuri Kovalchuk (Mance 2015). For more details, see Boletskaya (2016d).

was furious and did not conceal his anger. Shortly afterward, he forced Berezovsky to give up his role at ORT, and the state took firm control over the channel.

• In 2002 terrorists seized Moscow's Dubrovka Theater, taking more than eight hundred people hostage. Coverage by the two major channels already under state control was driven by the interests of the government rather than public accountability. Although NTV had already been acquired by Gazprom, its journalists were not yet fully reined in, and they did not prioritize the interests of the government. NTV's coverage infuriated Putin, and he accused it of doing "publicity on blood." A few months later, the station's management was replaced.[17]

• In 2004 terrorists occupied a school in Beslan, North Ossetia, and held more than one thousand people hostage, most of them children. By then, all three national TV channels were under tight state control. The coverage was limited and aimed at playing down the tragedy, in particular, dramatically understating the number of hostages and hiding the details of the bungled rescue operation. Putin made no comments, apparently satisfied with the coverage.[18]

By 2004 political broadcasts on the "big three" were reliably progovernment and uniform from channel to channel, with a strong focus on footage of formal events involving high-ranking officials (visits, meetings, and so forth). Putin became a virtually daily presence, newsworthy or not. Although the main aim was to demobilize the population, coverage did pursue some political goals. The main one was to project the image of Putin as firmly in charge—a guarantor of social and political stability and the country's ultimate problem solver—while destroying faith in any alternative. During federal election campaigns, TV sought to win over voters to the pro-Kremlin United Russia party.[19] At other times, coverage had narrower aims—to boost or play down events or to discredit individuals and

17. For a detailed account of the Dubrovka terrorist attack and its aftermath, see Baker and Glasser (2005, pp. 156–78).

18. Print was not as tightly controlled; *Izvestia* published shocking, full-page photos of wounded children, but after that its chief editor was forced to quit.

19. The head of the Organization for Security and Co-operation in Europe (OSCE) mission observing the 2003 parliamentary campaign said: "We have serious con-

groups. Special TV "documentaries" were broadcast nationwide to smear those who aroused the Kremlin's ire. In 2010, before then president Dmitry Medvedev fired Moscow's highly popular mayor, Yuri Luzhkov, two scandalous exposés of Luzhkov's alleged wrongdoing softened up the target. Since Putin's return to the Kremlin, similar "documentaries" have regularly attacked foreign-funded nongovernmental organizations, anti-Putin protesters, and a range of civic and political activists.

The Kremlin's TV management relied on co-optation, not compulsion. From the early 2000s on, Putin's media handlers gathered the national channels' executives at briefings in the Kremlin every Friday to discuss with them how the week's news should be covered. Top TV minders included, at various times, the political operatives Vladislav Surkov and Gleb Pavlovsky and Putin's successive press secretaries, Aleksey Gromov and Dmitry Peskov (Baker and Glasser 2005). Around 2002 Mikhail Lesin, then minister of the press, raised the technology to a new level. According to Svetlana Mironyuk, the former top manager of the government news agency RIA Novosti, Lesin had special phone lines installed in the offices of all top editors of state-controlled media—and even in that of the head of the nominally independent Interfax news agency (Gatov 2015). Each was given a yellow phone without a dial—it could receive but not make calls—that the president's press secretary could use to contact them at any time.

The TV executives did not require any coercion to cooperate. According to Mironyuk: "There has never been any . . . direct intimidation of editors and owners. [They did it] themselves" (Gatov 2015). Or, as a former VGTRK manager explained in 2008, "The TV channels themselves want to be close to the Kremlin" (quoted in Fishman and Gaaze 2008). In Mironyuk's view, the government classified media players into three groups: "foes," "friends," and "semi-foes–semi-friends." Dealings with "friends" (certain television channels, news agencies, and a few newspapers) were based on personal relationships between the editors and Putin's press secretary and involved barter deals of sorts: "We grant you an exclusive interview and you reciprocate with a favor."

On the margins of the Kremlin-controlled media, islands of free expression continued to exist in print, radio, smaller-scale TV, and, later, the Internet. Such outlets continued to report news, voice critical opinions, and even

---

cerns regarding the lack of media independence. State media failed to provide balanced coverage of the campaign" (OSCE 2003).

engage in investigative reporting, despite the obstacles (Lipman 2005, 2016c). In the 2000s, as the public seemed overwhelmingly supportive of Putin, the Kremlin tolerated a degree of self-expression, so long as alternative media remained small-scale and did not stir up passions among the broader public. Given the low public demand for—or trust in—nongovernment media, such outlets remained politically irrelevant and mostly ended up preaching to the converted.

As the technology of the Internet and social networks fused with the broadening worldviews of modernized urbanites during Medvedev's presidency, the model sometimes seemed to be cracking. Although national television remained controlled, journalists began to take a few more risks. At the 2010 TV awards ceremony, Leonid Parfyonov, a top presenter forced out of NTV in 2004, spoke derisively of channels on which "a correspondent is not a journalist, [but] a bureaucrat guided by the logic of allegiance and subordination." He complained that "nothing critical, skeptical, or ironic about the president or the prime minister can be aired on federal channels" (*Kommersant* 2010). In the TV coverage of the ceremony, his criticism was censored out.

PUTIN'S RETURN AND CRIMEA

Any hopes that the media might be about to open up were cruelly dispelled after Putin's return to the Kremlin in 2012. Challenged by mass protests, Putin sought to reverse the social modernization that had produced them. The mass media became a key instrument in this battle.

State television obediently smeared the protesters, branding them an unpatriotic "fifth column." More "documentaries" were slapped together alleging, for instance, that protest leaders had conspired with foreign funders to stage a violent revolution. An anti-Western, anti-liberal, and anti-modernization campaign filled the airwaves, advocating social conservatism and "traditional values." Mironyuk, the RIA Novosti executive, had become too moderate for the changed environment. She was replaced by the pro-Kremlin propagandist Dmitry Kiselev, who said in one broadcast that if gay people died in car crashes "their hearts should be buried or burned." In another, he boasted that Russia could still turn the United States into "radioactive dust."

The liberal nongovernment media, previously tolerated, now came under attack. In most cases, "market forces" could be mobilized to do the trick. Cable providers—apparently pressured by the authorities—chose to drop TV Rain, whose journalists clearly sympathized with the protesters. The channel's monthly audience of 12 million cable viewers shrank to about ninety thousand Internet subscribers (only seventy-two thousand of them paying) (Super 2016). Echo of Moscow, although owned by Gazprom media, had for years been allowed to broadcast programs of some of the most outspoken liberal Kremlin critics. Now it, too, came under pressure. On several occasions oligarchs with print or Internet publications chose to fire editors and journalists who may have displeased the Kremlin or to close or reformat outlets that had become too political.[20] Usmanov's *Kommersant* closed several publications and dismissed a number of journalists and editors. The anti-Western turn helped to justify other measures. The Duma enacted a 20 percent limit on foreign stakes in media businesses, which forced Axel Springer to sell *Forbes Russia*, one of the best political and economic publications, and other foreign companies with big stakes also to divest.[21]

And, furious at the role the web had played in the 2011–12 protests, Putin now took aim at online communication. Having initially neglected the Internet, the security services now raced to catch up. Unlike Iran and China, Russia does not have a "firewall," or a universal filtering system. Instead, the Kremlin stepped up the use of pro-regime bloggers, Internet "trolls," and denial-of-service attacks on opposition sites; most important, the Kremlin conducted co-optation of the largest Internet corporations (Soldatov 2015).[22] New legislation allowed the authorities to block almost any website without a court ruling if it published vaguely defined "extremist" content. In 2015 and 2016, some Russians were sentenced to jail terms for posting or even reposting politically inappropriate material.[23] Another effective method was, again, to exploit the concern of Internet media owners

20. For a list of the outlets affected by the crackdown, see *Meduza.io* (2016).

21. *Forbes Russia* was sold to a new publisher, who said the magazine had "too much politics"; the top editor promptly resigned (*Meduza.io* 2015; Boletskaya 2016a).

22. For an account of Kremlin policy toward the Internet, see Soldatov (2015). On pro-Kremlin trolls, see Chen (2015). Some of the methods used in Russia to constrain media freedom resemble those used in African countries (VonDoepp and Young 2012; Ogala 2016).

23. "Russian Man Sentenced to 2 Years in Prison for Social Network Repost," *Moscow Times*, May 6, 2016.

that the audacity of their outlets might cause the Kremlin's anger and harm their other, non-media businesses. Aleksandr Mamut, an oligarch who had invested in Internet media, fired the top editor of his politically independent—and highly popular—*Lenta.ru*.[24] The three top editors at RBC.ru, a leading website that had published reports and investigations on politically sensitive subjects, were also either dismissed or quit (Lipman 2016a).[25]

Although the crackdown had begun soon after Putin's return, television current affairs coverage changed dramatically with the outbreak of conflict in Ukraine. The new approach combined increasingly strident propaganda with a preoccupation with the events in Russia's western neighbor. From late February 2014, when violence erupted in Kiev, news shows began to focus almost entirely on Ukraine, leaving barely any time for Russia itself. According to Arina Borodina, Russia's leading TV analyst, during the three months after the annexation (March–May 2014) the main nightly news broadcasts on Rossia-1 and Channel One contained on average

> 10 episodes, each 7–10 minutes long, devoted to just one theme and one idea—that there is a "Kiev junta" entrenched in Ukraine, conducting a "punitive operation." And there were dozens of such shows each day! Instead of the normal 20–30 minutes (40 min maximum), news shows lasted for one hour or longer. Already in March, weekly news roundups on both channels switched to 2-hour broadcasts, and the main themes were anti-Ukrainian. (Borodina 2014)

Figure 7-1 shows the duration of Kiselev's weekly news roundup show *Vesti nedeli*. The average length jumps after Crimea and remains high through the end of 2015.

The TV channels changed their schedules, moving popular series and entertainment shows or replacing them with lengthy discussion programs with a familiar set of guests, who repeated a single message: Ukraine had

---

24. The fired editor in chief of *Lenta.ru* and part of her team moved to Latvia, where they founded *Meduza.io*, a political website in exile.

25. In another episode of media redistribution in favor of staunch loyalists, in June 2017 RBC's owner sold control of his troublesome media asset to energy tycoon Grigory Berezkin. Berezkin is not a major media holder, but he owns the pro-Kremlin tabloid *Komsomolskaya Pravda*, Russia's largest circulation daily; his loyalty to the Kremlin is not in doubt (*Financial Times* 2016).

Figure 7-1 Length of *News of the Week with Dmitry Kiselev* in Hours and Negative Attitude toward Ukraine

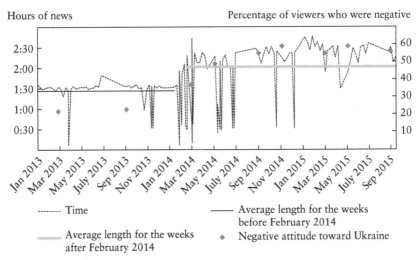

Hours of news   Percentage of viewers who were negative

------- Time

—— Average length for the weeks before February 2014

‒‒‒‒ Average length for the weeks after February 2014

♦ Negative attitude toward Ukraine

Sources: TNS Global; Levada Center, Kuryer survey.

become a fascist state. This "onslaught on the TV audience" was unprecedented, according to Borodina, more aggressive than during any past election campaign or the Georgia war. Huge audiences tuned in to news and political talk shows, as well as weekly roundup shows. In March 2014 Channel One's news broadcast *Vremya* set an amazing record by outstripping Russia's highest-ratings show of the previous three years, *Pust' govoryat* (Let'em Talk), the Russian equivalent of Jerry Springer. During the 2014–15 (September–May) TV season, Channel One's *Vremya* was the most-watched show of the week more frequently than any other regular television program.[26] Other news broadcasts also set records. Two documentaries on Rossia-1, *Crimea: Path to the Motherland,* marking the first anniversary of the region's annexation, and *The President,* celebrating Putin's fifteenth year in power, attracted 40 percent of viewers. Newspapers (traditional and web-native) as well as other mainstream media also joined the propaganda campaign (Etling, Roberts, and Faris 2014).

26. According to Borodina's analysis of the 2014–15 TV season. Echo of Moscow, "Programmnoye obespechenie [Software]," July 3, 2015, http://echo.msk.ru/sounds /1578450.html.

POLITICS OR CRONYISM?

In terms of its technology, production quality, financial management, and the merging of the Internet, film, television, radio, and print into interconnected complexes, the Russian media today is a developed modern industry, not unlike its Western counterparts. Parts of it are also highly profitable. In terms of ownership, it has become a narrow oligopoly, dominated by a few Kremlin loyalists. And in terms of news and public affairs coverage, it is more propagandistic than at any point since the 1980s. These observations raise some obvious questions.

Was the driving force behind this evolution always the administration's desire to control political information? Or was the Kremlin's campaign a more mundane attempt to grab profitable assets for its associates? The answer to these questions affects how one should understand the Putin regime. Is it an "informational autocracy" that maintains power by manipulating information flows to voters, or is it a kleptocracy, whose members seek only self-enrichment (Guriev and Treisman 2015; Dawisha 2015)?

In our reading of the evidence, political motives came first and, in case of conflict, dominated commercial impulses. But the surprising thing is that authoritarian control and the distribution of lucrative assets in favor of Putin's innermost circle fit so smoothly together. The news channels were not the main prize for the Kremlin oligarchs: news production is costly and can turn out to be a commercial liability. But favored business people could also use the political media to further their own interests. And they were simultaneously granted the opportunity to acquire profitable entertainment TV channels as a kind of bonus. Such Putin cronies could also draw on Kremlin favors (state subsidies for national news channels, credits, broadcasting licenses, and so forth) that protected them from market hazards.

Dislodging the two media tycoons, Gusinsky and Berezovsky, in 2000 was strictly political. The Kremlin wanted to wrest control of the key television channels from these two oligarchs, whom Putin viewed as too influential. At the time, the commercial upside seemed limited. To Gazprom, acquiring Gusinsky's debt-ridden media holding was arguably a net liability. As for ORT, after Roman Abramovich bought Berezovsky's 49 percent stake (or, to be more precise, paid Berezovsky to relinquish control), he ceded this property to the state and has never laid claims to it since then (later on NMG bought a 25 percent stake from Abramovich's business structures, and Abramovich's stake was thus reduced to 24 percent; *Kommersant* 2011). The harassment of Tomsk TV-2 was also political. Its owners were virtually robbed of their profitable business, but nobody gained commercially from its destruction.

When it comes to Kovalchuk's remarkable rise as a media tycoon, the story gets more complicated. By the mid-2000s, after national television had been brought into line, the commercial motive played a large role. Those with close ties to Putin were the first to benefit from media business trans- actions. Kovalchuk's reported wealth grew rapidly in this period—although mostly from his banking business rather than his media interests. By 2008, the year NMG was formed to hold his various media stakes, *Forbes* assessed his net worth at US$1.9 billion (*Forbes Russia* 2017).

The impetus for Kovalchuk's acquisition of Channel Five may have been commercial (another motive may have been his desire to raise his status and influence: there are relatively many superrich people in Russia, but very few of them own a national TV resource). Channel Five, originally a St. Petersburg channel, was the first major acquisition (see above) of what evolved into Kovalchuk's media empire. The new team managed to lure many celebrities from other channels. Commercial motives may also have played a part in the takeover of REN-TV, in which Kovalchuk's business structures have a large stake. Gradually, however, the political rationale be- came at least as important, and the channel got rid of the more audacious journalists. It is not clear, however, that this hurt the company's profitabil- ity, given the low demand for independent news and the far greater oppor- tunity to attract viewers and advertisers with entertainment shows.[27]

27. Since Channel Five was launched as a national TV channel under control of Bank Rossiya and became the "foundation stone" of the National Media Group (NMG), it has lived through several transformations. In early September 2017 it was reported that Channel Five had all but stopped its own TV production and be- came a "TV venue" for broadcasting materials made by other producers (*Kommer- sant* 2017). Despite its nominally national status, Channel Five has never come close to the outreach and influence of the "big three" and therefore could not be of primary use for the Kremlin as a political resource. It also failed to offer an attrac- tive alternative as an entertainment resource. But even if Channel Five has practi- cally stopped producing its own content, this is unlikely to negatively affect NMG. The NMG holding is currently creating a massive multimedia platform that would link together its numerous second-echelon media resources (including Channel Five) in order to avoid duplication of functions and raise the efficiency of the NMG operation.

Indeed, the nonpolitical TV channels were always the main profit centers. CTC, in which Usmanov's and Kovalchuk's structures hold stakes, and TNT, owned by GPM, are the two largest-audience entertainment channels, each with about 100 million viewers. CTC earned after-tax profits of about US$150 million in 2010.[28] Meanwhile, Kovalchuk's Bank Rossiya has a share in the main sales house VI, and in 2016 the function of audience measurement—a major index of the advertising market—was practically nationalized (Boletskaya 2016c). All in all, there seems to have been little conflict between redistributing assets to Putin friends and loyalists, tightening control over news programming, and increasing profits.

Western sanctions, however, imposed on Russia following the annexation of Crimea in March 2014 and on several occasions after that, have hurt a number of individuals and companies that had assisted the political goals of the Kremlin. In particular, Kovalchuk personally and his Bank Rossiya were put on the U.S. sanctions list, affecting his business in general and, in particular, those media companies in which he or his business structures had large stakes. In order not to harm the operation of those media companies, Kovalchuk's stakes have been significantly reduced.[29] Trusted tycoons seem always to find ways to minimize the losses (Boletskaya 2016b). They can probably also count on compensation from the government if the sanctions bar their companies from attracting investment or issuing bonds on external financial markets or cause other operational difficulties.[30]

28. Equivalent to 4.4 billion rubles at an average exchange rate for the year of 29.4 rubles per U.S. Dollar. RA Expert, "Database of Russian Media," http://raexpert.ru/database/companies/sts-media.

29. In 2016 it was reported that neither Kovalchuk personally nor Bank Rossiya any longer have control of NMG. See Boletskaya (2016b). A detailed description of the media ownership structure goes beyond the scope of this chapter. Such data are generally hard to obtain, and published reports are impossible to verify. It is also impossible to tell whether the formal reduction of Kovalchuk's shares meant that he truly relinquished control or merely redistributed assets to trusted proxies; such information, of course, is never made public.

30. Ilya Kiriya, in a recent study of the impact of international sanctions on the Russian media, points out that "the sanctions unwittingly favored the biggest players to the detriment of the smaller, protecting state-aligned media and their financial incomes." In response to the sanctions, the government "further facilitated the redistribution of market share from independent actors to particularly favored pro-state actors"; these same actors also benefited from a government-orchestrated

WHY HASN'T THE SPREAD OF THE INTERNET LED TO MORE OPPOSITION?

Early in the Internet's evolution, many saw it as a disruptive force that would break the information monopolies of unfree regimes and foster revolutions against undemocratic governments. The Kremlin's determined attacks on opposition online activity show that Putin now takes this possibility seriously. Moreover, research suggests that Internet use and social networks did, in fact, facilitate the Russian protests of 2011–12 (Enikolopov, Makarin, and Petrova 2016; Smyth and Oates 2015).

However, Internet penetration has continued to grow in the years since 2012. Russians remain active on social networks. But the protest mentality of the winter and spring of 2011–12 gave way two years later to a patriotic enthusiasm for Putin and his foreign policy. How to explain this?

In part, the weakening of opposition voices could reflect the success of the Kremlin's crackdown on civic and political activism in general and online communications in particular. The increased pressures on Internet companies and interventions of pro-Putin trolls may have reduced the impact of independent web-based news (Soldatov 2015; Etling, Roberts, and Faris 2014). But, more important, most Russians who use the Internet do not use it to obtain news. Even as Internet penetration soared, national television remained by far the most common news source. More than 80 percent of Russians still watch the national TV news at least two to three times a week.[31]

The Internet comes in second, mentioned by 33 percent of Russians.[32] But even those who get news from the web are not necessarily getting it

---

redistribution of the advertising market; in addition, they also continued to receive subsidies from the state (Kiriya 2017).

31. Figures as of June 2016. Just 4 percent said they never watch news on TV. For comparison, a tiny minority (3 or 4 percent said they follow nongovernment news outlets, such as *Echo of Moscow*, TV Rain, or RBC; about 80 percent said they never use such sources Levada Center, "Media: vnimanie i tsenzura [Media: Attention and censorship]," www.levada.ru/2016/06/06/smi-vnimanie-i-tsenzura.

32. According to the latest polling data (July 2016) as of this writing, when asked, "From where do you most often learn the news about the country and the world?," 86 percent answered "television" and 33 percent said "the Internet" (in addition, 23 percent mentioned "social networks"). The third most frequently used source, mentioned by 27 percent, was "friends, family, and neighbors," which, at least in part, must mean the same TV news, mixed up with rumors and home-brewed the-

from *alternative* sources. The most popular online source of news in Russia is Yandex Novosti, the news aggregator of the Russian search engine Yandex; it is used twice as often as the next source after it.[33] The choice of news in this aggregator is strongly affected and may even be dominated by the state-controlled TV news. Just as most Russians do not seek out independent news sources on radio or in print, most do not seek them out on the Internet. Demand for such alternative information, although it rose slightly during the Medvedev presidency, has never been high. And even when Russians visit other types of sites—from major aggregators to social networks, forums, and blogs—much of the news content on these, too, actually originates in TV programs (Nocetti 2015; Oates 2014; Orttung and others 2015). In a 2017 survey of media use by Levada Center, the number of those who consistently rely on independent sources for information (read, listen or watch two or more "independent media outlets") is estimated to be 6 percent nationally and 16 percent in Moscow (Volkov and Goncharov 2017).

Meanwhile, broadening Internet access has itself made the medium less of an opposition stronghold. With up to 70 percent of Russians—80 percent among eighteen- to thirty-year-olds—online, the profile of users has come to resemble Russian society.[34] They are not an anti-Putin minority (Greene 2013; White and McAllister 2014; Enikolopov, Makarin, and Petrova 2016; Etling, Roberts, and Faris 2014). In fact, those who got news about Ukraine and Crimea from the Internet supported Putin at rates very close to those of TV viewers (table 7-1).

Social network users also now span the opinion spectrum. The leading networks have developed distinct political personas. While Twitter and Facebook have traditionally been popular with opposition-minded elites, their homegrown Russian rivals, VKontakte and Odnoklassniki, appeal more to mainstream, pro-Putin Russians. And the latter have far more Russian users than the former. Research shows that users of Twitter and

---

ories. See Levada Center, "Trust in Media, and Willingness to Express Opinion," www.levada.ru/2016/08/12/14111.

33. For data on the Internet news audience in Moscow, see Levada Center, "Rossijsky medialandshaft: televidenie, pressa, Internet [Russian media landscape: TV, press, Internet]," www.levada.ru/2014/07/08/rossijskij-media-landshaft-televidenie -pressa-internet-3; in Russia, see Volkov and Goncharov (2015, p. 19).

34. FOM, "Interes k novostyam v internete [Interest in Internet news]," http://fom .ru/SMI-i-internet/12247.

Table 7-1. *Putin's Approval and Sources of Information about Ukraine*

| | Percent of respondents[a] | | | | | |
	One source of information	Two sources of information	More than three sources of information	Use Internet	Use social networks	Use television
Do not approve of Putin	12.2	10.7	11.3	10.9	10.9	10.1
Approve of Putin	87.8	89.3	88.7	89.1	89.1	89.9
No. of respondents	897	438	266	246	147	1,472

Source: Levada Center, Kuryer survey (June 2014).
a. All differences in approval shares are not statistically significant.

Facebook were significantly more likely to believe that electoral fraud occurred during Russia's 2011 parliamentary election (Barash and Kelly 2012; Kelly and others 2012; Reuter and Szakonyi 2015). Our analysis of Levada Center data confirms that approval of Putin is higher among VKontakte and Odnoklassniki users, especially among the young (eighteen- to twenty-four-year-olds).

HOW EFFECTIVE IS THE KREMLIN'S MEDIA STRATEGY?

Governments that use the media to manipulate the public would seem to face an obvious trade-off (Gehlbach and Sonin 2014). If the claims they propagate are too evidently false, Scott Gehlbach and Konstantin Sonin posit, they will merely drive viewers away rather than change their beliefs. Therefore, to be effective, propaganda cannot be too sharply at variance with reality.

However, Russian experience since Crimea seems to contradict this logic. State television coverage shocked Western observers with its extreme tone and far-fetched fabrications. Claims that Kiev had been overrun by neo-Nazis and the bizarre conspiracy theories offered to account for the crash of the Malaysian airliner in 2014 would seem to invite skepticism. And yet Russian viewers did not dismiss such claims and turn off their TVs. As already noted, the audience for TV news shows soared.

Why did conventional assumptions prove wrong in the Russian case? It could be that the Russian public is gullible and therefore insensitive to the implausibility of news messages. But we suggest another explanation: Russian viewers tuned into the shows of Kiselev and the like in search of not truth but emotional gratification.

"I do not think that television is the main source of information nowadays. It is simply a means of presenting particular information in a way that is convenient, pleasant, and interesting for the viewer," NTV's former top manager, Vladimir Kulistikov, said already in 2007. "Television is a form of entertainment. . . . The news is also entertainment" (Borodina 2007). The task of news producers after February 2014 was to make sure that theirs was an emotionally appealing one. To do so, they tapped into existing sentiments and told the viewers what they wanted to believe. The point was not the accuracy of the statements made but the emotional punch of the message—as Kiselev put it in an interview in the summer of 2014: "My gestures go right to the subconscious" (Remnick 2014).[35] He and his colleagues used several techniques repeatedly.

First, they played on Russians' "post-imperial syndrome," the sense of humiliation by the West, which was seen as having taken Russia for granted and exploited its weakness since the Soviet collapse. The nightly narrative turned the tables: now it was Russia that could act without asking anyone's permission; it was the West that was weak, forced to accept the annexation of Crimea as a fait accompli. A second technique was to infuse the Ukrainian drama with World War II imagery. Ukraine had been "captured" by "fascists" and "Banderites" (that is, supporters of the World War II Ukrainian nationalist Stepan Bandera, who had collaborated with the Germans).

Such techniques aimed not so much at changing beliefs as at making Russians feel pleasurable emotions—and associate them with Putin. One such pleasurable emotion was national pride. In November 2015, 68 percent said they were proud of Russia's political influence in the world, up from 46 percent in October 2012, and 85 percent were proud of the country's armed forces, up from 59 percent three years earlier. The proportion who agreed that "there are events in Russia currently that make me ashamed of the country" had fallen from 52 percent in October 2012 to just 18 percent in November 2015.[36]

35. Interviewer David Remnick (2014) described Kiselev as a "masterly, unapologetic purveyor of the Kremlin line" who with "his theatrical hand gestures and brilliantly insinuating intonation, tells his viewers that Russia is the only country in the world that can turn the U.S. into 'radioactive dust,' that the anti-gay-propaganda laws are insufficiently strict, and that Ukraine is not a real country but merely 'virtual.'"

36. Levada Center, "Pride & Patriotism," www.levada.ru/eng/pride-patriotism. More Russians than ever in post-Soviet history take pride in Russia's might, its history, its influence in the world.

Truth was redefined as a national virtue, a part of Russian identity, rather than a contingent quality of statements. "Our strength lies in truth," Putin told an interviewer, several months after the annexation of Crimea, quoting a line from a popular film. "We're stronger because we're right. . . . When a Russian is right, he is invincible."[37] After such an assertion, questioning the "truth" or "rightness" of Russian decisions seemed tantamount to weakening the nation.

The Kremlin's appeal to social conservatism and "traditional values" was also formulated to tap into an existing hostility toward gays—while conveniently avoiding Russians' more modern and tolerant attitudes on divorce, abortion, single motherhood, and pre- or extramarital sex. Discomfort with homosexuality was exploited to create the appearance of mass agreement with the Kremlin's broader agenda (see Rogov and Ananyev, this volume).

Russians seem quite aware that what TV news provides is not unbiased truth. Over 50 percent of respondents surveyed agree or mostly agree that TV is censored. About the same proportion agree or mostly agree that it would be good to have an uncensored channel that would criticize the authorities.[38] But they still remain loyal to the censored "big three" and do not defect to those minor news sources that are not controlled by the state.

Measuring how effectively Kremlin media control has shaped public opinion is extremely difficult. But some trends in polling data are at least highly consistent with a propaganda effect. Increases in the length of Kiselev's programs—which can be taken as a proxy for the increases in the total length of similar broadcasts—clearly correlate with the change over time in Russians' negative attitudes toward Ukraine (see figure 7-1). As figure 7-2 shows, moments of tension between Russia and the West—at the start of the NATO bombing of Yugoslavia, 1999; the Iraq War, 2003; the Georgia war, 2008; and the Crimea operation, 2014—all saw sharp upticks

37. Putin spoke to a TASS interviewer in November 2014. "Putin: Mi sil'neye potomu chto my pravy. Sila v pravde. [Putin: We are stronger because we are right. Strength is in truth]," www.youtube.com/watch?v=TKfeyVqL_Jg. The line "Our strength is in truth" is from *Brat-2*, a highly popular Russian movie filmed in 1999, the year of the bombing of Yugoslavia, an early peak of anti-U.S. sentiment in post-Communist Russia. The film's main character, a Russian "noble avenger," says these words before settling scores with an American mafia businessman.

38. Levada Center, "Media: vnimanie I tsenzura."

Figure 7-2   Negative Attitude toward the United States: Dynamics in Response to Major International Developments

Percent

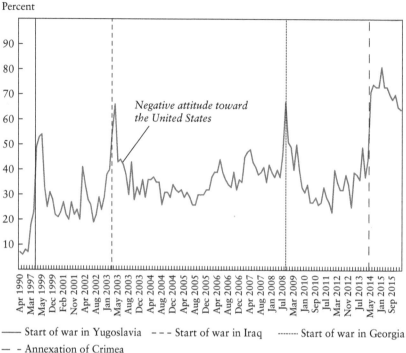

—— Start of war in Yugoslavia   – – – Start of war in Iraq   ······· Start of war in Georgia
— - Annexation of Crimea

Source: Levada Center (2014, 2016).

in anti-U.S. sentiment. For these and other foreign news events, TV is not just the primary source of information for most Russians: it is the only one.[39] While anti-U.S. sentiment quickly subsided in the first three cases, it has remained high for much longer in the fourth. Although we cannot prove a causal connection, intense anti-Western propaganda has also lasted much longer on Russian television in the case of Crimea than in the others.

Thus, it is very possible that emotionally charged propaganda influenced Russians' attitudes. Did propaganda also change their beliefs about concrete facts? One striking case is that of the Malaysian airliner that

39. In a striking demonstration of the power of centralized media, when Russians did have the accounts of family, friends, or colleagues in Ukraine to compare to those on Russian TV, they often preferred to believe the TV version; see Anastasiya (2014).

Figure 7-3   Who Downed the Malaysian Jet? Differences in Opinion in Russia and the United States

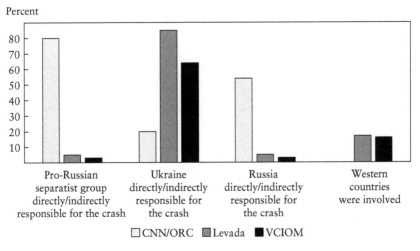

Percent

Sources: Roper Center iPOLL database (CNN/ORC poll July 17–20, 2014); Kuryer survey, by Levada Center (July 2014; September 2014); VCIOM survey (July 2014). Levada data are averaged by two surveys. CNN/ORC survey was conducted in the United States; Kuryer and VCIOM surveys were conducted in Russia.

crashed over Donbass in July 2014. While 80 percent of U.S. respondents polled shortly afterward believed that the plane had been downed by a missile fired by pro-Russian insurgents—the explanation favored by the West and international media—only 2–3 percent of Russian respondents shared this view. On the contrary, a large majority thought the Ukrainian military had shot the plane down, the version that Russian TV was pushing at the time (figure 7-3). Moreover, almost as many of those who said they used the Internet to follow news and politics believed this version in September 2014 (80.6 percent) as did those who did not use the Internet at all (89.7 percent). Alternative reports and analysis of the crash were available on the web, as well as some conventional outlets such as Echo of Moscow. But, as noted, only a tiny minority rely on such sources.

We do not believe that the Kremlin-controlled media can change public perceptions if the latter are based on people's immediate experience—for instance, on questions about rising prices. Perceptions of one's personal economic situation are obviously based on one's concrete, daily experience. As economic performance deteriorated in 2014 and 2015, so did consumer confidence, falling from 82 in March 2014 to 59 in March 2016 on an index for which 100 represents the level of March 2008.[40]

Kremlin spin doctors are wise enough not to try to convince people of things they are unlikely to believe. Characteristically, in Putin's annual call-in TV shows with the nation (*Pryamaia liniia s Vladimirom Putinym*) callers commonly share with the president their grievances, such as salaries below subsistence level, dismal housing conditions, and so on. This was especially true of the call-in show in June 2017; as Gleb Pavlovsky, a prominent Russian political analyst, remarked, the show portrayed Russia "as a poor country with disintegrating infrastructure" (Pavlovsky 2017). Instead of trying to convince people that they live well, national TV is sending a message that problems may abound, but if there is one person who can solve them, it is Putin, the leader of no alternative, above and beyond inefficient institutions and corrupt, self-seeking administrators.

Since Russians view corruption as a fact of life, the authorities did not waste time denying the opposition activist Alexey Navalny's allegations of graft among high-ranking officials. Instead, they undertook to discredit Navalny by having *him* convicted of embezzlement. He was prosecuted on the obviously trumped-up charge of stealing a large quantity of lumber from a forestry enterprise. The European Court of Human Rights ruled that "the only purpose of [this] prosecution and conviction was to curb [Navalny's] public and political activity."[41] Yet, as the case proceeded in 2011–13, state TV worked to persuade viewers that Navalny was guilty. As figure 7-4 shows, though a plurality of those who had heard of the case continued to believe that Navalny was being unjustly prosecuted, the percentage convinced of his guilt rose over time, increasing by 15 percentage points between 2011 and 2013. While people readily believed Navalny's allegations that top officials were corrupt, a mere 4 percent trusted him as a political figure.[42]

40. Levada Center, "Socioeconomic Indicators," www.levada.ru/indikatory/sotsialno -ekonomicheskie-indikatory.

41. European Court of Human Rights. "Case of Navalnyy and Ofitserov v. Russia," http://hudoc.echr.coe.int/eng#{"itemid":["001-161060"]}.

42. Levada Center, "Oppozitsiya. Neobkhodimost', uznavaemost' i doverie [The opposition: Relevance, visibility, and trust]," www.levada.ru/2016/03/14/oppozitsiya -neobhodimost-uznavaemost-i-doverie.

Figure 7-4   What Was the Reason for the Criminal Proceedings against
Alexey Navalny?

Percent[a]

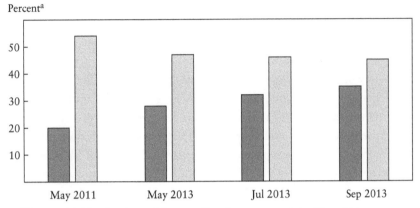

☐ Due to his illegal actions while counseling the governor of the Kirov Oblast
("Kirovles affair")

☐ Due to his work toward exposure of corrupted public officials and big corporations

Source: Volkov and Goncharov (2015, p. 19).

a. Bars show shares of answers given by those respondents who had known about the
"Kirovles affair."

CONCLUSION

Russia's media today is the product of two interweaving trends—on the
one hand, the sector's transformation into a multibillion-dollar business,
with state-of-the-art technology, products, and creative personnel, and, on
the other hand, the centralization of assets under Kremlin control. This
centralization of assets was driven primarily by political motives, but it also
served to enrich close friends of the president. When the price of oil was
steadily growing and the advertising market expanding, there was little
conflict between the two. Diverting viewers from politics to entertainment
increased both Putin's security and his cronies' profits. Moguls such as
Yuri Kovalchuk entrusted with holding major media assets could simultaneously milk the expanding advertising market and ensure positive coverage for the president and his policies.

Since 2012, as Putin struggled to reverse the social and political consequences of the country's recent economic modernization and respond to
mass protests, the media put more emphasis on political coverage; after the
annexation of Crimea and during the ensuing war in Donbass, national TV

filled with raw and aggressive propaganda. Contrary to common theories of media persuasion, however, the propaganda on state television has been both extreme in its distortions and—at least apparently—effective. Audiences were not driven away by outlandish claims—they were drawn in. And they proved quite ready to believe far-fetched fabrications about the shooting down of the Malaysian airliner as well as to follow the media's cues on attitudes toward foreign countries. Our explanation is that the media have been selling not accurate information but satisfying emotions—in particular, national pride and a sense of vindication. By constructing even distorted accounts, the media enable viewers to embrace often untrue but gratifying versions of events and to enjoy a sense of national togetherness in doing so. The most important effect of this, from the Kremlin's perspective, was a sharp rise in Putin's approval rating.

Unlike in many Western countries, where the fourth estate combined with political contestation contributes (or at least such is the normative assumption) to the accountability of government, the mainstream media in Russia, where serious challenges to the Kremlin have been eliminated, have become an instrument of undemocratic rule. On occasion—especially during Medvedev's presidency—reports by nongovernment media on the abuse of state power have gained broader resonance, even forcing officials to respond publicly. But it is hard to find a single example when the authorities have changed policies or behavior significantly in response. To take one recent case, despite credible allegations made by Alexey Navalny that the son of Prosecutor General Yuri Chaika was linked to an organized crime group, Putin dismissed the issue when questioned about it and reappointed Chaika to another five-year term.[43] In short, the media during Putin's third term play no discernible role in the making of political and policy decisions; instead, they are used by the Kremlin as a tool for publicizing and popularizing decisions.

The power of the mainstream media to shape attitudes and promote distorted narratives is not unlimited. Of course, it is easier to persuade people of a claim when they have no direct contrary evidence. Thus, foreign events are more effective foils for such propaganda than domestic issues. New technologies that encourage channel surfing and narrow niche

---

43. Navalny's allegations were made in a documentary posted online, which was watched by more than 4.5 million viewers (Anti-corruption Foundation, "Chaika," 2015, www.youtube.com/watch?v=eXYQbgvzxdM). See Lipman (2016b).

productions may in time fragment the market and make younger viewers harder to reach. If protest activity is expanding, the Internet is sure to play a large role in facilitating social organization. But, for the moment, the current model, dominated by the Kremlin-controlled mainstream media, appears solidly entrenched.

REFERENCES

Alexanyan, Karina, Vladimir Barash, Bruce Etling, Robert Faris, Urs Gasser, John Kelly, and John Palfrey. 2012. "Exploring Russian Cyberspace: Digitally-Mediated Collective Action and the Networked Public Sphere." Berkman Klein Center for Internet and Society, Harvard University.

Anastasiya, Bereza. 2014. "Semeinye voyny [Family wars]." *Novoje Vremya*, October 7. http://nv.ua/publications/semeynye-voyny-raznye-politicheskie-vzglyady-i-istochniki-informacii-rassorili-tysyachi-rodstvennikov-po-vsey-ukraine-14940.html.

Baker, Peter, and Susan Glasser. 2005. *Kremlin Rising: Vladimir Putin's Russia and the End of Revolution*. New York: Scribner.

Barash, Vladimir, and John Kelly. 2012. "Salience vs. Commitment: Dynamics of Political Hashtags in Russian Twitter." Berkman Klein Center for Internet and Society, Harvard University.

Boletskaya, Ksenia. 2010. "'Video International' smenil khozyaev ['Video International' has changed hands]." *Vedomosti*, June 28. www.vedomosti.ru/business/articles/2010/06/28/video-interneshnl-smenil-hozyaev.

———. 2016a. "'Gazprom-media' kupil 7,5% akzij 'Nazionalnoj media gruppi' ['Gazprom Media' bought 7.5% of the 'National Media Group' stock]." *Vedomosti*, March 31. www.vedomosti.ru/technology/articles/2016/03/31/635878-gazprom-media-natsionalnoi-media-gruppi.

———. 2016b. "Natsionalnuyu media gruppu vozglavit Olga Paskina [National Media Group will be headed by Olga Paskina]." *Vedomosti*, March 17. www.vedomosti.ru/technology/articles/2016/03/17/634079-nmg.

———. 2016c. "Novoye izmerenie VTsIOMa [VTsIOM's new dimension]." *Vedomosti*, July 24. www.vedomosti.ru/newspaper/articles/2016/07/24/650378-novoe-izmerenie-vtsioma.

———. 2016d. "Usmanov i Tavrin zaplatili za STS Media na $7,5 mln men'she [Usmanov and Tavrin paid $7.5 million less for STS Media]." *Vedomosti*, February 12. www.vedomosti.ru/technology/articles/2016/02/12/628802-ctc-media.

Borodina, Arina. 2007. "V Kreml' dolzhen khodit' rukovoditel' kazhdoi bolshoi korporatsii [Any head of a large corporation must consult regularly with the Kremlin]." *Kommersant*, May 25. http://www.kommersant.ru/articles/2007/kulistikov.html.

———. 2014. "Televisor Olimpiady i Ukrainy. Rekordy propagandy [TV of the Olympics and Ukraine. Propaganda records]." *Forbes Russia*, July 3. www.forbes

.ru/mneniya-opinion/konkurentsiya/261539-televizor-olimpiady-i-ukrainy
-rekordy-propagandy.

Borodina, Arina, and Anna Pushkarskaya. 2007. "'Pyatij Kanal' rvetsya v chislo
pervih ['Channel Five" wants to be number one]." *Kommersant*, May 25. www.
kommersant.ru/doc/768564.

Chen, Adrian. 2015. "The Agency." *New York Times Magazine*, June 2.

Dawisha, K. 2015. *Putin's Kleptocracy: Who Owns Russia?* New York: Simon &
Schuster.

Dergachov, Vladimir, and Natalia Galimova. 2014. "Konets 'Nedeli s Mariannoj
Maksimovskoj' [The end of the 'Week with Marianna Maksimovskaya']. *Gazeta.
ru*, August 1. www.gazeta.ru/politics/2014/08/01_a_6154997.shtml.

Enikolopov, Ruben, Alexey Makarin, and Maria Petrova. 2016. "Social Media
and Protest Participation: Evidence from Russia." CEPR Discussion Paper no.
DP11254.

Enke, B., and F. Zimmermann. 2016. *Correlation Neglect in Belief Formation*. IZA
Discussion Paper no. 7372.

Etling, Bruce, Hal Roberts, and Robert Faris. 2014. "Blogs as an Alternative Public
Sphere: The Role of Blogs, Mainstream Media, and TV in Russia's Media Ecology." Berkman Klein Center for Internet and Society, Harvard University.

Financial Times. 2016. "Mikhail Prokhorov sells control of Russian media outlet
RBC." June 16. www.ft.com/content/37fd6ob8-66b4-3b38-9286-4e7062c45229?
mhq5j=e2.

Fishman, Mikhail, and Konstantin Gaaze. 2008. "Efir dlia dvoikh [Broadcasting
for Two]." *Newsweek Russia*, August 4.

Forbes Russia. 2017. "Profile of Yuri Kovalchuk." www.forbes.ru/profile/yurii
-kovalchuk.

Gatov, Vasily 2015. "Putin, mar'jivanna i 'ukraintsy v televizore' [Putin, Maria Iva-
novna and 'Ukrainians on TV']." Radio Svoboda. https://www.svoboda.org/a
/26840571.html.

Gehlbach, Scott, and Konstantin Sonin. 2014. "Government Control of the Media."
Journal of Public Economics 118, pp. 163–71.

Greene, Samuel. 2013. "Beyond Bolotnaia: Bridging Old and New in Russia's Election Protest Movement." *Problems of Post-Communism* 60, no. 2, pp. 40–52.

Guriev, Sergei, and Daniel Treisman. 2015. "How Modern Dictators Survive: An
Informational Theory of the New Authoritarianism." Working Paper 21136.
Cambridge, Mass.: National Bureau of Economic Research.

Hoffman, David E. 2002. *The Oligarchs: Wealth and Power in the New Russia*. New
York: Public Affairs.

Itogi.ru. 2000. "Ulika nomer shest' [Evidence number six]." September 26. http://
www.itogi.ru/archive/2000/39/114667.html.

Kachkaeva, Anna, 2008. "Glamurny totalitarizm: Televizionnaia industriia v
epokhu stabil'nosti (2004–2007) [Glamorous totalitarianism: Media industry
during the era of stability (2004–2007)]." In *Teleradioefir: Istoriia i sovremennost'*
[TV and radio broadcast: History and contemporaneity]. Moscow: Elitkomstar.

Kelly, John, Vladimir Barash, Karina Alexanyan, Bruce Etling, Robert Faris, Urs Gasser, and John G. Palfrey. 2012. "Mapping Russian Twitter." Berkman Klein Center for Internet and Society, Harvard University.

Kiriya, Ilya. 2017. "The Impact of International Sanctions on Russia's Media Economy." *Russian Politics* 2, no. 1, pp. 80–97. http://booksandjournals.brillonline .com/content/journals/10.1163/2451-8921-00201005.

Kommersant. 2010. "Vysshaya vlast' predstayot dorogim pokojnikom: o nej tol'ko khorosho ili nichego [High government officials are like the dearly departed: One should speak well of them or not at all]." November 25. www.kommersant .ru/doc/1546420.

———. 2011. "Yuri Kovalchuk+1." February 2. www.kommersant.ru/doc/1581792? isSearch=True.

———. 2012a. "Kak sozdavalsya i razvivalsya 'Gazprom-media holding' [The creation and development of Gazprom Media]." February 15. www.kommersant.ru /doc/1873630.

———. 2012b. "'Pervij kanal' vzyalsya za 'Serp i Molot' ['Channel One' has taken hold of 'The Hammer and Sickle']." May 3. www.kommersant.ru/doc/1927788.

———. 2017. "'Pyaty' osvobozhdaet studii [The 'Fifth' is vacating its studios]." September 4. https://www.kommersant.ru/doc/3401865?utm_source=rnews.

Kozyrev, Mikhail, and Anna Sokolova. 2008. "Yuri Kovalchuk. Starshij po 'Rossii' [Yuri Kovalchuk. The head of 'Rossiya']." *Forbes Russia*, August 3. www.forbes .ru/forbes/issue/2008-08/7645-yurii-kovalchuk-starshii-po-%C2%ABrossii% C2%BB.

Levada Center. 2014. *Obshchestvennoe mnenie 2013* [Public opinion 2013]. Moscow.

———. 2016. *Obshchestvennoe mnenie 2015* [Public opinion 2015]. Moscow.

Lipman, Maria, 2005. "Constrained or Irrelevant: The Media in Putin's Russia," *Current History* 104, no. 684, pp. 319–24.

———. 2009. "Media Manipulation and Political Control in Russia." London: Chatham House.

———. 2016a. "The Demise of RBC and Investigative Reporting in Russia." *New Yorker*, May 18.

———. 2016b. "How Putin Silences Dissent: Inside the Kremlin's Crackdown." *Foreign Affairs*, May–June.

———. 2016c. "The Media." In *Putin's Russia: Past Imperfect, Future Uncertain*, edited by Stephen Wegren. 6th ed. Lanham, Md.: Roman and Littlefield.

Mance, Henry. 2015. "Alisher Usmanov Pays $200M for Stake in Russia Media Group." *Financial Times*, September 25.

Meduza.io. 2015. "Lannister s dolgami [Lannister with debts]." November 17. http:// meduza.io/feature/2015/11/17/lannister-s-dolgami.

———. 2016. "12 redaktsij za pyat' let" [12 publications in five years]." May 17. http://meduza.io/feature/2016/05/17/12-redaktsiy-za-pyat-let.

Nocetti, Julien. 2015. "Russia's 'Dictatorship-of-the-Law' Approach to Internet Policy." *Journal of Politics* 4, no. 4, pp. 1–19.

Oates, Sarah. 2014. "Russia's Media and Political Communication in the Digital Age." In *Developments in Russian Politics*, edited by Stephen White, Richard Sakwa, and Henry E. Hale. 8th ed. Basingstoke: Palgrave Macmillan.

Ogala, Emmanuel. 2016. "Investigation: How Jonathan Govt. Paid Companies Linked to Doyin Okupe to Hack 'Unfriendly' Websites." *Premium Times* (Nigeria), January 18. www.premiumtimesng.com/investigationspecial-reports/196964/.

Orttung, Robert, Christina Cottiero, Katherine Kucharsky, and Evgenia Olimpieva. 2015. "War of Words: The Impact of Russian State Television on the Russian Internet." *Nationalities Papers* 43, no. 4, pp. 533–55.

OSCE (Organization for Security and Co-operation in Europe). 2003. "State Duma Elections Well Organized but Failed to Meet Many International Standards." www.osce.org/odihr/elections/55878.

Pavlovsky, Gleb. 2017. "K konzu pryamoj linii Putin sovsem ischez [By the end of his call-in show Putin has entirely disappeared]." *Snob*, June 15. http://snob.ru /selected/entry/125838.

Razumovskaya, Olga. 2011. "Social Networks See Big Bucks in Inmates and Spirits." *Moscow Times*, March 24.

RBC. 2006. "Severstal i Surgutneftegaz sokratili svoi doli v 'REN TV' [Severstal and Surgutneftegaz reduced their shares in 'REN TV']." December 21. www.rbc .ru/economics/21/12/2006/5703c3a89a7947dde8eob5ae.

———. 2016. "Mediokompaniju Kovalchuka and Mordashova ozenili v 150 mlrd rub. [The value of Kovalchuk's and Mordashov's media company is estimated at 150 billion roubles]." March 31. www.rbc.ru/technology_and_media/31/03/2016 /56fcf20c9a7947dd35dbdoof.

Remnick, David. 2014. "Watching the Eclipse." *New Yorker*, August 11.

Reuter, Ora John, and David Szakonyi. 2015. "Online Social Media and Political Awareness in Authoritarian Regimes." *British Journal of Political Science* 45, no. 1, pp. 29–51.

Romodanovsky, Matvey. 2013. "Samie kassovie rossijskie filmi ot 'Nochnogo dozora' do 'Gor'ko' " [Top-grossing Russian films: From 'Night Watch' to 'Gor'ko']." *Proficinema*, December 30. www.proficinema.ru/questions-problems/articles/detail .php?ID=153052.

Smyth, Regina, and Sarah Oates. 2015. "Mind the Gaps: Media Use and Mass Action in Russia." *Europe-Asia Studies* 67, no. 2, pp. 285–305.

Soldatov, Andrey. 2015. "Ukroshchenie internet [Taming the Internet]." *Counterpoint*, no. 1. www.counter-point.org/укрощение-интернета/.

Super, Roman. 2015. "Kak umirayut telekanali [How TV channels die]." Radio Svoboda. www.svoboda.org/content/article/27433733.html.

———. 2016. "Chelovek Dozhdya [The Rain Man]." Radio Svoboda. www.svoboda .org/content/article/27561599.html.

Volkov, Denis, and Stepan Goncharov. 2015. "Demokratiya v Rossii: ustanovki naseleniya [Democracy in Russia: Population's attitudes]." Levada Center, August 11. www.levada.ru/2015/08/11/demokratiya-v-rossii-ustanovki-naseleniya-2015.

————. 2017. "Rossijsky medialandshaft: osnovnye tendentsii ispol'zovania SMI—2017 [Russian media landscape: Main trends of media use—2017]." Levada Center, August 22. https://www.levada.ru/2017/08/22/16440/?utm_source=mailpress&utm_medium=email_link&utm_content=twentyten_weekly_15291&utm_campaign=2017-08-26T13:00:05+00:00.

VonDoepp, P., and D. J. Young. 2012. "Assaults on the Fourth Estate: Explaining Media Harassment in Africa." *Journal of Politics* 75, no. 1, pp. 36–51.

White, Stephen, and Ian McAllister. 2014. "Did Russia (Nearly) Have a Facebook Revolution in 2011? Social Media's Challenge to Authoritarianism." *Politics* 34, no. 1, pp. 72–84.

Yaffa, Joshua. 2014. "Putin's Master of Ceremonies." *New Yorker,* February 5, 2014.

EIGHT

Public Opinion and Russian Politics

KIRILL ROGOV and MAXIM ANANYEV

What is the role of public opinion in Russian politics today? Does it affect decisionmaking, or is it merely shaped by state propaganda to support the decisions that are made? On this, scholars and writers—in both Russia and the West—offer radically different answers. Some view public opinion as mainly manipulated through controlled media and see the strong backing for Vladimir Putin's policies as the result of such manipulations. Rather than the demands of citizens prompting responses from the authorities, the authorities engineer support from citizens for *their* demands (Pomerantsev 2014; Lipman 2009). Others emphasize that Putin's policies are mostly consonant with mass attitudes. At the extreme of this view, some see public opinion as all-determining. The authoritarian nature of Putin's regime is attributed to deeply rooted and unchanging illiberal values among Russians (Pipes 2004).

In between these two poles, some see public opinion as driven—at least in part, and especially in the long run—by forces that change over time and that are not entirely controlled by those in power. Some consider economic factors to be important. In the shorter run, the ups and downs of economic performance are said to have affected support for the incumbent authorities, making it either easier or harder for them to achieve their goals, whether these were institutional reforms or policies (Treisman 2011, 2014; Rose, Mishler, and Munro 2006, chap. 8). But these shifts are not the only way that the economy affects public opinion. In the long run, economic development is seen as having promoted an evolution of values and attitudes in Russia, in a pattern observed previously in other countries and associated with "modernization theory" (Dmitriev 2015; Inglehart and Welzel 2005).

From an examination of polls taken in Russia over the past twenty-five years, we derive a number of conclusions. First, Russians are not wedded to an immutable conservative outlook that favors authoritarian government and explains Putin's rise. In fact, public opinion started out liberal enough in 1991 and has changed dramatically and in a nonlinear fashion over the years since then. Second, the changes over time can, for the most part, be understood as reactions to three phenomena: the experience of transition, economic modernization, and the evolution of political institutions (including the level of control over the media). Although we cannot completely rule out the influence of cultural legacies, it is hard to prove or disprove their importance with existing data, and, in any case, the three factors already mentioned do a good job of explaining how post-Soviet public opinion has evolved.

The experience of transition—an initial, extended economic crisis and simultaneous weakening of the state, followed by a revival of the economy and a recentralization of power—prompted an opposite dynamic in public attitudes. As the economic crisis deepened, while new political and state institutions remained weak, Russians came to desire more order and centralization; later, as Putin consolidated power and the economy recovered, the aspiration for more freedom, autonomy, and government accountability revived. This second trend culminated at the end of Dmitry Medvedev's presidency of 2008–12, when the most modern segment of the population mobilized to demand greater integrity and openness in public life. Nevertheless, Russian public opinion remains transitional—modern in some respects, quite conservative in others, such as in the continuing support for state intervention.

Finally, addressing how Putin's Kremlin has reacted to the evolving pattern of public opinion, we propose a more complicated model of what is generally regarded as manipulation. The Kremlin has neither ignored public opinion nor managed to completely manipulate it. For most of the period since 1999, Putin's approach has been a kind of selective responsiveness. The Kremlin monitors public opinion closely, paying particular attention to the president's approval rating and adjusting policy in the attempt to keep it high, responding to and amplifying some public demands. This allows the Kremlin to ignore other public demands not consistent with its goals. Of course, this pattern of manipulation is based on an increasing level of control over the national media and the cultivation of authoritarian institutions that marginalize or silence opposition voices. This selective responsiveness seems to be characteristic of how modern authoritarian regimes interact with mass public opinion.

Since 2012, Putin's strategy has become more ambitious. Reinforcing authoritarian institutions and control over the media, he now seeks to create the kind of conservative traditionalism and autarchic anti-Westernism that historians such as Richard Pipes thought existed all along. Emphasizing confrontation with the West serves to strengthen some trends in public opinion and suppress others. This strategy is both selectively responsive and manipulative at the same time. Its short-run success is striking on the surface but may be shallower than it appears, for reasons we discuss.

A BLOCK OF ICE FLOATING BACKWARD OR THAWING HERE AND THERE?

In one common view, already mentioned, Russia's politics are the outgrowth of a unique set of traditional values and institutions. A distinctive brand of Orthodox-fueled conservatism supposedly prevents Russians from adopting liberal or Western ways. Putin is popular, according to Pipes (2004, p. 15), "precisely because he has re-instated Russia's traditional model of government: an autocratic state." The conservatism of Russian society is taken to embrace not just political arrangements but social values as well. To the novelist Vladimir Sorokin, "Russia is like a block of ice floating back into the 16th century."[1]

How accurate are these views? In fact, sociological research provides little support for them. On several occasions since 1990, the World Values Survey (WVS) has questioned Russians—as well as respondents in various other countries—on a variety of social and political issues (see table 8-1). The

1. Quoted in BBC, "How Putin Is Inspired by History," http://news.bbc.co.uk/2/hi /europe/7262661.stm.

Table 8-1. *Russians' Preferences on Political and Social Issues*

	Russia		World Average	
	Early 1990s	*Early 2010s*	*Early 1990s*	*Early 2010s*
Political system				
Support for democracy	45	68	77	82
Support for "strong leader"	43	67	32	42
Social issues				
Men should have priority for jobs	38	28	38	39
Homosexuality never justifiable	83	54	65	48
Abortion never justifiable	18	23	37	45

Source: World Values Survey.

results suggest that Russian society is neither particularly conservative nor desirous of autocracy in comparison with others. Contrary to the common belief that Russians are strongly influenced by the Orthodox Church, only about 31 percent in 1990 said they considered religion important in their lives. Of course, communist regimes stigmatized religious belief and practice; religiosity did rise somewhat in subsequent decades, but it remained low relative to the world average. Even in 2011, a time when the country's leaders openly expressed respect for the Orthodox faith, only about 42 percent of Russians told the WVS that religion was important in their lives. In both 1990 and 2011, the rate was far below the average across countries the WVS polled (56 percent in the early 1990s, and 72 percent around 2011).[2]

When it comes to social issues, Russia's culture in the early 1990s was mostly relatively liberal. In 1990, 81 percent of Russians said they supported the "women's movement," compared to 70 percent in the average country polled. Russians' acceptance of abortion and divorce was above the WVS average. Only a minority of Russians—the same proportion as in the average WVS country—thought that men should have priority over women in

2. Here and elsewhere, see World Values Survey database (www.worldvaluessurvey .org/wvs.jsp). Russian data fall within four periods: 1990–94, 1995–98, 2005–08, and 2010–14.

access to jobs.[3] Tolerance for homosexuality was an exception—this was unusually low in Russia in 1990.

On a range of social values, Russians appeared more liberal and tolerant in 2011 than in the 1990s. Support for gender equality in the workplace and education—already quite high at the start of transition—rose a bit more, as did acceptance of divorce. The proportion who thought homosexuality was never justifiable fell by almost 30 percentage points in the twenty-one years after 1990 (WVS).[4] Acceptance of premarital sex rose from 42 percent in 1992 to 58 percent in 2013; in 2013, only 21–26 percent think the government should do something to limit divorces and abortion.[5]

Putin's efforts since 2012 to promote social conservatism based on Orthodox values seem to have had limited success. While the Kremlin managed to mobilize fears of "homosexual expansionism"—the prohibition of "homosexual propaganda" is widely supported—it failed to win support, for example, for more involvement of the church in setting policy. In the mid-2000s, about 35 percent agreed that the church should influence government decisions, while 55 percent opposed this. By the mid-2010s, the share of supporters of church intervention had fallen to 25 percent, while the proportion of opponents had grown to 66 percent (LC).[6]

3. Also, see Grigore Pop-Eleches and Joshua Tucker (2017), who argue that, in general, the experience of communism did not increase the support for gender equality.

4. By 2011 the proportion was only slightly above the global average and close to the levels found in the United States and Japan in the early 1980s.

5. Levada Center (2016, p. 27); Levada Center (LC) monthly Kuryer survey, June 2013. If another source is not mentioned, we use VCIOM / Levada Center survey data for 1990–2013 from Yediny Arkhiv Economicheskyh i Sociologicheskikh Dannykh [Unified Archive of Economic and Sociological Data] (http://sophist.hse .ru/db) and, for the period 2014–16, from the Levada Center's monthly Kuryer surveys. Note that the center's methodology for weighting observations changed in the 1990s; we therefore sometimes use unweighted data for comparability. But the difference between weighted and unweighted results is never more than 1–2 percent, less than the observational error of 3.6 percent for a sample of 1,600–2,000 respondents. Our analysis is mostly based on VCIOM (until 2003) / Levada Center data for three reasons: (1) it is the oldest, the most well-known and independent sociological center; (2) all of its data for 1989–2013 are available in free access (see the link above); and (3) it provides long-term series of results on the same or comparable questions.

6. Levada Center (LC) surveys in 2005, 2007, 2012, 2013, and 2016.

Although Russian society looks less tolerant than societies in high-income countries, conservative values and institutions (the traditional family, church influence on politics) have low support. Moreover, one sees a tendency toward the modernization of attitudes. In some regards, this started already in the 1990s, but it was during the long boom of the 2000s that modernization took off. As GDP per capita rose from under US$13,000 in 1999 to US$24,000 in 2011, Russians became noticeably more tolerant, individualistic, and focused on self-expression.[7]

TRANSITIONAL CYCLING TOWARD MODERNITY

If they have become more modern in their social attitudes, are Russians nevertheless conservative in their political preferences? Traditional values and institutions (the traditional family, the church) were destroyed and repressed by the Soviet regime, but in terms of political culture Russians had an extremely painful and negative experience. While in what the WVS project defines as "secular values" (Welzel 2013) Russians were above average in 2011 (0.49 against 0.35), in so-called emancipative values (those dealing with personal freedom, self-expression, equality, and political participation) Russians were about average (0.40), and on the voice subindex (reflecting the disposition to political participation) Russians were below the average (0.28 against 0.40).[8]

WVS data give some evidence that Russian public opinion is distinctive in the political sphere. Russians have relatively low support for democracy. In the countries surveyed by the WVS in 2010–14, on average 83 percent of people thought that "having a democratic political system" was "very good" or "fairly good." In Russia, the share—67 percent—was lower, but still a majority, and a big increase from the mid-1990s, when only around 45 percent of respondents had supported democracy.[9] In Russia, the pro-

---

7. World Bank estimates, at purchasing power parity and in constant 2011 U.S. dollars. World Bank Open Data, https://data.worldbank.org/.

8. WVS data at www.worldvaluessurvey.org/.

9. Other countries with a low level of support for democracy in this wave are South Africa (69 percent), China (70 percent), and Japan (72 percent), while other obviously nondemocratic countries have very high levels of support—for example, Nigeria (95 percent) and Belarus (85 percent). (WVS data at www.worldvaluessurvey .org/).

portion of respondents who said it was "very good" or "fairly good" to have a "strong leader who does not bother with the parliament or elections" was 67 percent in 2011, compared to an average across all WVS countries of 45 percent. Russia's level on this was close to those of Kazakhstan (64 percent), Brazil (65 percent), Romania (70 percent), and Ecuador (70 percent). However, such support for a "strong leader" does not seem to result from long-established cultural preferences. In 2006, the previous time that the WVS had asked the question, only 47 percent of Russians thought having such a leader was "very good" or "fairly good," and in 1995 the figure was 43 percent.

Strangely enough, many who favored such unconstrained leadership also favored democracy: 70 percent of those who considered a democratic system "very good" or "fairly good" said the same about having a strong leader, and 70 percent of those who endorsed strong leadership also endorsed democracy. One might understand this contradiction as a case of what Guillermo O'Donnell calls "delegative democracy," in which voters freely elect leaders but do not seek to impose accountability in between elections or to limit their authority with checks and balances (O'Donnell 1994; Hale, McFaul, and Colton 2004).

While supporting democratic government, albeit with a strong executive, the majority of Russians are less sanguine about the market economy. More Russians than inhabitants of the average WVS country viewed competition and private ownership of businesses as harmful. In our view, this paradoxical pattern of favoring *both* free elections and unconstrained leadership, as well as the comparatively low support for the market economy, reflects mostly Russians' experience of the troubled postcommunist transition and intense economic recovery of the 2000s.

Observing the dynamics of public opinion in post-Soviet Russia, one sees a cyclical pattern of change related to the experience of transition, superimposed on the modernization trend. Russia's impetuous transition to electoral democracy and a market economy in 1991–92 was more a consequence of the collapse of the Soviet empire than the result of elite agreement or a strong and consolidated popular demand. The supporters of democracy and the market economy had a slight advantage at that moment, and the proportion answering poll questions on these topics with "don't know" was relatively high. While about 50 percent supported a multiparty system in 1990–91, 30 percent favored keeping the one-party system or thought that parties were unnecessary (LC). As of 1992, almost 50 percent preferred a market economy, while about 25 percent favored one based on state planning, and the rest could not say (LC). These figures are lower than the levels of support for the market economy in central Europe and in the Baltic States but very close to those in Ukraine and Romania.[10]

The protracted and confrontational path of Russia's transition can be attributed largely to this lack of agreement on key issues and elite polarization that led to the violent constitutional crisis of fall 1993 (McFaul 2001). In 1994–96 the share favoring market institutions fell to roughly equal those preferring state planning, while brutal elite clashes increased the demand for "strong leadership." Pro- and anti-reform groups were roughly equal in the mid-1990s, and by the end of the decade the anti-reform agenda had consolidated. A conservative consensus emerged in the late 1990s and changed little in the early 2000s. The share of proponents of "strong-hand leadership" rose from 40 percent in 1989 to 60 percent in the mid-1990s and more than 70 percent in the early 2000s (LC). Twice as many supported the centralization of power as opposed it (60 and 30 percent, respectively). Therefore, Putin's political reforms of 2001–04, aimed at consolidating power and enhancing hierarchical control, were likely a response to this demand.

Surprisingly, these reforms were not regarded by the majority as antidemocratic. The parliament, political parties, and other democratic institutions had been discredited by their inability to provide either the rule of law and democratic order or economic growth. By contrast, Putin's antidemocratic reforms coincided with the economic recovery of the early 2000s. This explains why many more Russians than before reported "democratic development" in politics at that time (on average 34 percent in 2005–09 against 11 percent in 1993–99) and why a growing majority said that they felt personally free (58 percent in the 2000s against 32 percent in the 1990s).

The years 2008–12 witnessed a dramatic and previously underappreciated shift in Russian public opinion. The statist, politically deferential consensus of the early 2000s gave way to increasing demands for a more open and responsive public life, demands that were at first encouraged by the rhetoric of the Medvedev presidency. Support for a multiparty system rose to more than 60 percent, its highest level on record. The proportion of

10. See Central and Eastern Eurobarometer 1990–97 (www.gesis.org/eurobarometer-data-service/survey-series/central-eastern-eb).

Figure 8-1 The Most Important Rights and Freedoms

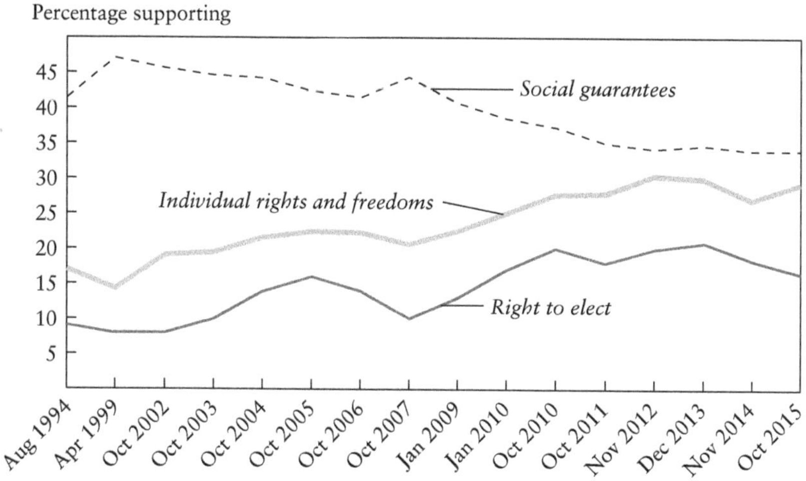

Percentage supporting

Sources: Levada Center; authors' calculations.

those who thought the country needed a political opposition increased to 70 percent in 2011–12, up from 47 percent in 2000. Support for centralizing political power fell from 60 to 40 percent, while backing for decentralization rose from 30 to 45 percent. The share of Russians who saw the regime moving in an undemocratic direction approached the share who saw democratic development (27 percent and 34 percent, respectively, in 2011–13). Fewer favored the "current regime," and more favored the "Western model."

At the same time, in assessing the relative importance of different human rights, respondents placed increasing weight on freedoms of speech and the press and elections, and less on social guarantees (figure 8-1). The paternalist predisposition, although still present, weakened. The proportion who thought that government should guarantee all citizens a decent level of well-being fell from 45 percent in 2002 to 34 percent in 2015. Meanwhile, the share who thought that government should only establish common rules of the game doubled from 20 to 40 percent.[11]

When hopes for a political opening were dashed by Putin's decision to return to the Kremlin, the disappointment climaxed in the street politics

---

11. All data in this paragraph and the previous three come from Levada Center polls.

of 2011–12, as the most modernized elements in Russian society rebelled against the Putin consensus that they had outgrown. However, modernization had not generated a stable majority in favor of a more open political system. Rather, it had created an equilibrium between liberal and conservative parts of the population. While on average 46 percent of respondents did not support the demands of the anti-Putin demonstrators in 2012, 38 percent said that they did in several surveys throughout the year, despite intense criticism of the protesters on the official TV channels (LC).

Looking over more than twenty years of post-Soviet development, one can see several phases: (1) 1990–93, the majority supports political and economic liberalization; (2) 1994–99, disillusionment with the results of reforms leads to consolidation of an antireformist agenda; (3) the 2000s, intense economic recovery, coinciding with Putin's state consolidation, produces a pro-authoritarian consensus; and (4) the late 2000s to early 2010s, erosion of the pro-authoritarian consensus amid emerging demands for political modernization. Taking support for a multiparty system as an indication of changing political attitudes between the early 1990s and the early 2010s, one sees this U-turn or even J-curve.[12] It reflects, in our view, the traumatic experience of transition and economic modernization (suggested roughly by the trend in GDP per capita; see figure 8-2) and is mirrored by a range of attitudinal variables (see more evidence and discussion on transitional cycling in Rogov 2013).

THE ACHILLES HEEL OF RUSSIAN MODERNIZATION

Popular attitudes toward market economics have changed significantly over time. In the early 1990s, Russians were quite hopeful that radical economic reforms would quickly improve their standard of living. As of 1990, a larger proportion of Russians wanted to increase private ownership in business and industry than was the case in Spain, Chile, or Turkey (WVS). By the mid-1990s, amid falling wages, an epidemic of nonpayments, and the spread of crime and corruption, free markets had lost much of their al-

---

12. We use support for a multiparty system as an indicator for the preference for democracy because the term *democracy* became itself controversial in the transition period.

Figure 8-2   Support for Multiparty System and GDP per Capita

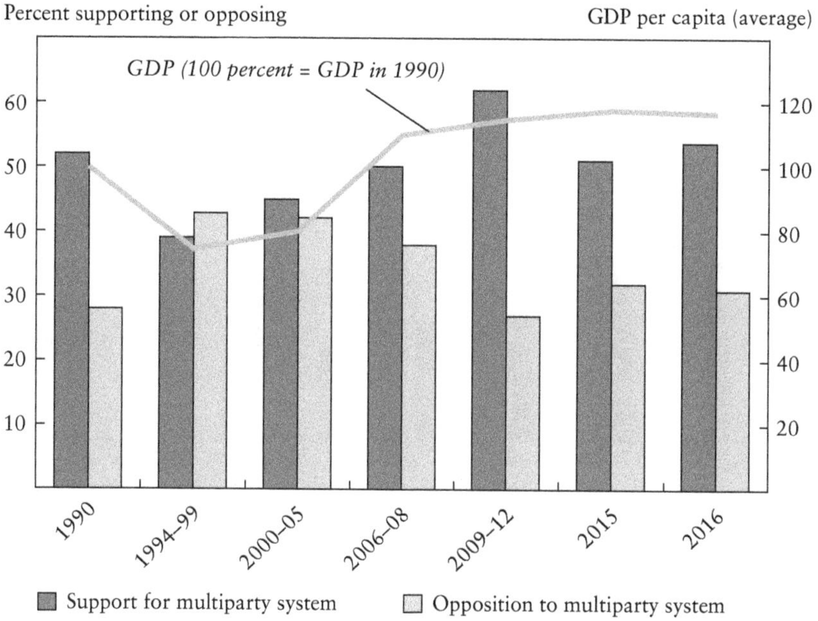

Percent supporting or opposing   GDP per capita (average)

GDP (100 percent = GDP in 1990)

■ Support for multiparty system   □ Opposition to multiparty system

Sources: Levada Center; World Bank.

lure. At that point, more Russians than inhabitants of the average WVS country viewed competition and private ownership of businesses as harmful. Nevertheless, support for increasing private ownership was now much lower than in Spain, Chile, or Turkey.

As figure 8-3 demonstrates, even as political attitudes liberalized in the late 2000s and early 2010s, economic preferences remained conservative or extremely ambivalent. According to the WVS, by 2011 backing for private ownership had risen from its mid-1990s lows but was still below the level at the start of transition in 1990. According to Levada Center data, only slightly more than 30 percent said that a market economy was "the right type of system [*pravilny*]," compared to a little more than 50 percent who said this of state planning (the mirror image of the situation in the early 1990s).

But while support for the market economy was very low, that did not mean that respondents actually wanted to return to Soviet socialism. Two-thirds of respondents in 2014–15 nevertheless agreed that Russia "needed" a

Figure 8-3   What Economic System Is Better: One Based on State Ownership and Planning or One Based on Private Property and the Market?

Percent

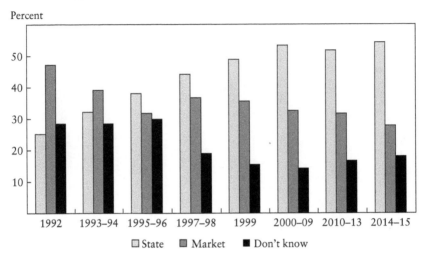

State   Market   Don't know

Source: Levada Center.

market economy (LC, Kuryer, June 2013 and June 2015). Russian respondents appear to differ from Western ones in that they see the market economy not as a source of prosperity but as a necessary evil.

This skepticism also manifests itself in other answers. Although Russians have supported private ownership of small firms and land since the start of the transition, the proportion that opposed large-scale private capital even grew during the period—from 50 percent in the early 1990s to 70 percent in the 2000s (LC). This increase suggests that Russians' ambivalence about the market economy is as much a result of recent experience with distorted market institutions as of historically rooted cultural predispositions. The combination of unfair market rules, corruption, high concentration of assets and wealth, and oil-fueled growth meant that the huge benefits from economic growth in the 2000s did not significantly improve people's trust in the market economy and competition. This distrust, in turn, seems to weaken the demand for political liberalization—many regard state-managed wealth distribution as a more appropriate model. While economic growth advanced modernization, the rent redistribution policies increased the role of the state and clientelism in the economy and suppressed market incentives and market competition. These contradictory trends formed the ambivalent pattern of Russian modernization.

PUBLIC OPINION, AUTHORITARIAN INSTITUTIONS, AND DECISIONMAKING

Putin's outstanding personal popularity seems to be one of the main pillars of the current political regime in Russia and of Putin's ability to stay in power for so long, ignoring claims of opposition and elite groups, as well as dismantling checks and balances and institutional constraints on his power. Between January 2000 and December 2015, Putin's approval rating averaged 75 percent (LC). For comparison with U.S. presidents, Bill Clinton, in his successful second term, averaged 61 percent, and George W. Bush, in his first term, averaged 62 percent.[13] For Putin, 61 and 62 percent are the lowest levels his rating has ever fallen to.

Sophisticated statistical analysis demonstrates the overwhelming importance of economic performance (Treisman 2011; see also Colton and Hale 2009). But one more feature of Putin's rating needs to be mentioned—the gap between Putin's approval and the proportion of respondents who agree that the country is "going in the right direction." This gap widens and narrows over time, averaging about 33 percentage points (the average level of satisfaction with the situation in the country is not more than 42 percent in these fifteen years; see Rogov 2015). The gap exists at times for U.S. presidents—especially in "honeymoon" months early in their terms or during periods of national or partisan mobilization—but in Putin's case the gap is larger and durable. Were Putin's delta just 10 percentage points, as under Clinton and Bush, his approval rating would fluctuate around 53 percent.[14] While Putin is generally supported by 90–95 percent of those who think the country is going in the right direction, Putin also picks up 60–80 percent of the undecided and 30–75 percent of those dissatisfied with Russia's direction (LC). In other words, his astronomical ratings depend not just on the share of those satisfied with the country's situation but also on others who support him despite their dissatisfaction.

A similar increasing delta between the level of satisfaction and approval characterizes the surges of approval U.S. presidents have experienced during "rally around the flag" episodes. As some scholars argue, the "rally"

13. "Presidential Approval Ratings—Gallup Historical Statistics and Trends," www .gallup.com/poll/116677/presidential-approval-ratings-gallup-historical-statistics -trends.aspx.

14. "Satisfaction with the United States: Gallup Historical Trends," www.gallup .com/poll/1669/general-mood-country.aspx.

phenomenon is based on the fact that in situations of international crises the opposition stops criticizing the government, and the unity of elite discourse drives the president's approval to outstanding heights (Brody 1991). But while such effects disappear when opposition politicians and the media resume criticism of those in power, Putin's ability to divert blame for extended periods reflects the authoritarian constraints his regime places on such independent voices, which are unable to focus public attention on the government's failures.

In short, a lack of public criticism of Putin by the elite could explain the enormous gap between the level of satisfaction with the situation in the country and presidential approval. Authoritarian institutions preventing criticism of the leader create a stable supermajority in favor of Putin. In its turn, the scale of this majority, which is promoted by the national media, presses poll respondents to succumb to the "social desirability bias," opting to conform to what they perceive to be the dominant opinion in society and to address their dissatisfactions or hesitations not to the popular leader but to other factors and actors. So the consistency of Putin's exclusively high levels of approval could be attributed to the effects of authoritarian institutions, in particular and foremost—control over media.

Not only Putin himself but also his policies and decisions seem to be mostly supported by the majority of Russians during his leadership. Is this the result of media manipulations or the result of Putin's responsiveness to people's aspirations? Do Russians approve of what Putin is doing or does Putin do what people want?

The image of Putin's regime in the West is certainly one of unresponsive detachment. Some in high Russian circles concur. The former head of the analytical department of Putin's administration, Simon Kordonsky, when interviewed, could not recall a single case in which survey results had influenced any tangible policy choice. At the same time, he testified to the Kremlin's deep interest in polls results.[15]

Indeed, the Kremlin is an avid consumer of survey data—and has been for a long time. For years, the Kremlin has commissioned weekly nationwide surveys from two firms, the Russian Public Opinion Research Center (VCIOM) and the Public Opinion Foundation (FOM), founded by Alexander Oslon. An impressive sign of the importance Putin's team attaches to

15. Interview, Moscow, December 15, 2015.

opinion polls was the scandalous dismissal in 2003 of Yury Levada, the founder and director of VCIOM, and his replacement by Valery Fedorov, who, like Oslon, had been a Kremlin sociological analyst. Besides the weekly polls, FOM periodically conducts regionally representative surveys with a sample of sixty thousand respondents, and both companies perform numerous special polls as Kremlin need arises.

If public opinion is irrelevant to decisionmaking, why the considerable investment in monitoring it so closely? Another long-serving Kremlin official, Aleksei Chesnakov, explains that the Kremlin uses surveys as a diagnostic aid to reveal when and where propaganda needs to be intensified (Guriev and Treisman 2015). However, a closer look at key decisions made by Putin's administration suggests a more complicated picture. Putin's actions exhibit a mix of popular and unpopular elements. According to Fedorov, the VCIOM director: "There are some examples when polls had a lot of influence on policy and others where they had none at all."[16]

Putin's policies of centralizing power to "restore order," reducing the authority of regional governors (2001–02), and attacking oligarchs (2003–04) all matched public preferences at the time. So did his move to restore the Soviet-era national anthem, as well as two negative decisions: the choice not to reform the pension system or to remove Vladimir Lenin's body from the Red Square mausoleum, both of which were favored in the Kremlin but unpopular outside it.[17] Yet some other key decisions—the introduction of a flat income tax and the replacement of pensioners' benefits in kind with a cash equivalent—contradicted public preferences (Treisman 2011, pp. 590–609; data from LC). Putin was receptive to the popular demand for political centralization and on issues of symbolic politics (for example, the Soviet anthem, Lenin's body). But—although there were exceptions—he was less responsive on economic issues.

Having started his public political career on the wave of political mobilization after terrorist attacks in Moscow in August–September 1999, Putin used the pattern of political consolidation in the face of external or internal threat for the nation and national interests real or alleged, exploiting it to concentrate political power. The abolition of gubernatorial elections in

16. Daniel Treisman, "Interview with Valery Fedorov, Moscow, January 2016," University of California, Los Angeles, unpublished.
17. Ibid.

2004 was unpopular with both the public—in 2000, 80 percent favored such elections—and regional elites. Pitching the change as a response to the shocking terrorist attack in Beslan, North Ossetia, seems to have temporarily swung opinion behind the reform (46 percent said they approved of it in October 2004). However, over the next six years around 60 percent of respondents said they would prefer direct elections, and only slightly more that 20 percent opposed them (LC). Putin did eventually give in and reinstate gubernatorial elections—but only when the decline in his popularity and the antigovernment protests of 2011–12 motivated him to compromise. After the protests were suppressed and Putin's popularity soared again, the Kremlin introduced new restrictions and reinforced informal control over the governors.

To generalize, one could say that the Kremlin exploits certain popular demands—the restoration of order, the fight against terrorism and extremism, the prosecution of corruption, and the defense of Russian international interests and traditional values—to organize political campaigns in the controlled media and consolidate public support. It uses this support to marginalize critics, presenting its policies as the choice of society, while often including in the package some less popular measures that actually serve only Kremlin interests. Thus, the model of manipulation of public opinion that the Kremlin used for most of Putin's period is based on selective responsiveness. And as it tightened control over the media—in particular TV—the Kremlin turned more and more to managing rather than satisfying public demands.

Returning to the Kremlin in 2012, Putin sought to build an antiliberal coalition around social conservatism. Warning of the danger of "homosexual propaganda," the national media created the image that "traditional values" were under attack and needed to be protected. The protection initiatives, amplified by a vigorous media campaign, had considerable public appeal. But, as after the Beslan terrorist attack in 2004, the Kremlin packaged crowd-pleasing planks, which were supported by 45–65 percent of Russians, together with a set of prohibitive measures that reduced individual freedoms and that were supported by a minority of 20–35 percent. Because intense Kremlin propaganda emphasized the socially conservative elements, and the opposition had no access to TV to contest the proposals, the less popular measures largely slipped below the radar. When asked about measures such as the law on "foreign agents," notorious in the West, a great many Russian respondents did not know whether they approved of it,

Figure 8-4 Support for Putin's Restrictive Policies, 2013

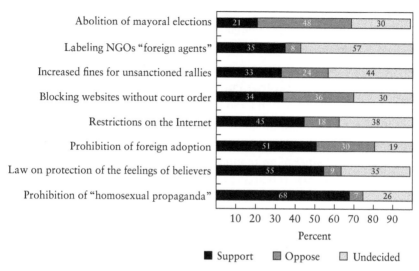

Abolition of mayoral elections	21	48	30
Labeling NGOs "foreign agents"	35	8	57
Increased fines for unsanctioned rallies	33	24	44
Blocking websites without court order	34	36	30
Restrictions on the Internet	45	18	38
Prohibition of foreign adoption	51	30	19
Law on protection of the feelings of believers	55	9	35
Prohibition of "homosexual propaganda"	68	7	26

10 20 30 40 50 60 70 80 90

Percent

■ Support   ▨ Oppose   ☐ Undecided

Source: Levada Center, Kuryer Survey.

and this reflects the lack of discussion on the issue while more popular is-sues were broadly discussed (see figure 8-4).

If asked whether they prefer a state that protects "traditional values" or one that supports liberal values including equal rights for homosexual couples, a large majority of Russians would favor the first. But if asked whether the government should take away free access to information and the right to demonstrate peacefully, the answer would definitely be no. In a competitive system, the government might try to focus discussion on ho-mosexual rights, but the opposition would insist on discussing the other, less popular parts of its package. In today's Russia, with opposition voices banned from nationwide TV, it wrongly appears that a large majority sup-ports the whole set of restrictive initiatives. Just as media control leads to an exaggerated sense of Putin's popularity, it also misleads citizens into think-ing conservative policies are more popular than they are.

In short, public opinion still matters for the political process and decisionmaking in Russia—but in a very different way than in competi-tive political systems. The Kremlin aims—and often manages—to use support on some particular issues to silence public criticism on others, ma-nipulate people's attention, and create an image of huge support for all its initiatives.

THE KREMLIN'S COUNTERATTACK

The trend toward social modernization reflected in significant changes of preferences distribution, essential decline of the support for the regime, and mass protests of 2011–12 undermined the image of overwhelming support for Putin and his policies.

The ambitious project that Putin initiated on his return was nothing less than to reverse this trend and to replace it with a conservative, statist culture that would reject Western ideas and rally behind his traditionalist policies—to reconstruct the kind of Russia that the historian Richard Pipes imagined. The politics of promotion of "traditional values" and pressure on the opposition in 2012–13 that included the famous Pussy Riot trial, a broad campaign stigmatizing gays, and the law against nongovernmental organizations still had limited success. Putin's famous rating remained on its lowest levels until the end of 2013, and the opposition succeeded in local elections in September 2013 in some important cities. As mentioned above, the level of religiosity and the influence of the church in Russia are lower than the world average, and the idea of extended influence of the church on public life remained unpopular.

Annexing Crimea, Putin replaced the main emphasis on traditional values with the emphasis on nationalist, postimperial sentiments and anti-Westernism. At the time of the USSR's downfall, Russia managed to avoid the "Yugoslavian scenario" of the collapse of the empire. Annexing Crimea, Putin revived the postimperial syndrome and political potential of this scenario that was blocked in previous decades. The annexation of Crimea and war in eastern Ukraine could be seen as a postponed and light Yugoslavian scenario that not only launched the "rally around the flag" effect in Russia but also stirred up the idea of deeply rooted antagonism of "national interests" and Western politics and values.

At first sight, this maneuver had outstanding success in terms of reshaping public opinion. Putin's approval rating shot up to over 80 percent, where it has remained since then. In April 2013, only 26 percent of Russians had said they wanted to see Putin continue as president after the 2018 election. By November 2015, 57 percent wanted him to stay.[18]

Enthusiasm over Crimea seemed, at least initially, to affect Russians' evaluations of almost everything and to reverse the trends in public opin-

18. Levada Center (2016, p. 125).

Figure 8-5 Positive Attitudes toward the United States, the European Union, and Ukraine

Percent

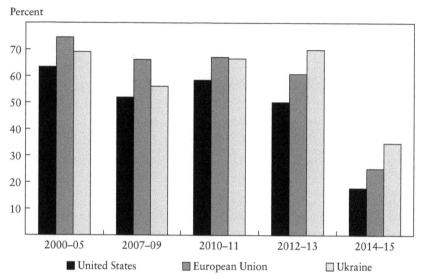

■ United States   ■ European Union   □ Ukraine

Source: Levada Center.

ion observed in the previous period. Not only the president's rating but also respondents' assessments of all levels and branches of government surged, and economic evaluations also grew much rosier (although, objectively, the first quarter of 2014 was the worst since the start of the postcrisis recovery). National pride swelled, and hostility toward Western countries soared (see figure 8-5). The previous trend toward greater tolerance—toward homosexuals, homeless people, drug addicts, and other social undesirables—reversed slightly.[19]

This syndrome of positivity raises certain questions. Did the Crimean operation activate a latent strain of conservative nationalism, deeply lodged in the Russian psyche? And if so, why did this lead to more positive assessments of the regime on issues that had nothing to do with Crimea, Ukraine, and the West, such as the perception of corruption? In 2004–09, about 23 percent said there was more corruption in Russia than before, almost the same share answered there was less corruption, and the rest considered corruption to be on the same level. In 2011–13, 51 percent said there was

19. Levada Center (2016, pp. 28–29). However, there was no significant toughening of attitudes toward the disabled.

more corruption, 35 percent thought corruption was on the same level, and only 7 percent said there was less corruption. After Crimea in 2014–16 the first group dropped to 31 percent, the second enlarged to 47 percent, and the third increased to 11 percent (LC).

No doubt the annexation of Crimea, war in eastern Ukraine, and confrontation with the West revived and reinforced the revanchist pattern of postimperial traumatic sentiments. But how to explain the general rise of loyalty to the authorities reflected in the changing perception of corruption in particular? Indeed, both the nationalistic consolidation after Crimea and this sudden surge of loyalty after the period of rising dissatisfaction are easier to understand as a sort of rally around the flag than as the manifestation of a long-term shift in public attitudes. Yet this raises additional questions. In democratic regimes, such rallies occur when the country is involved in external conflict and the competing political forces suspend their rivalry and unify their positions, drawing the public along with them. In authoritarian regimes, by contrast, the elite discourse is already mostly one-sided and political competition muted, so a different mechanism must be at work.

Carefully checking the changing attitudes after Crimea, one can detect a sharp shift in the level of mass attention to the official news media. To measure Russians' attentiveness to the news media, we use a Levada Center monthly poll that asked respondents to name five to six memorable events that had occurred in the previous four weeks. For each month, we identified the five events most frequently singled out by respondents and then added up the percentages that mentioned each of these five events. Since the vast majority of Russians get their news primarily from the Kremlin-controlled national TV channels, the news broadcasts of these channels are the only plausible source of coordination among respondents on which events are important. This index, therefore, captures the extent to which respondents in the aggregate were paying attention to the national news.[20]

The index shows a sharp jump in the public's attention to official news broadcasts in the period of the Crimean operation and war in eastern

---

20. This approach is based on the framework of John Zaller (1992), which postulates that the effectiveness of elites in shaping mass opinion is largely determined by people's exposure to the elite's discourse (usually translated through the national media).

Ukraine. In the second half of 2012 and in 2013, the index's monthly value averaged 125 points. In the first six months of 2014—as events in Ukraine unfolded—it leapt to 190 points. The informational intensity faded somewhat in later months, but the index still was averaging 172 points in 2014 and 152 points in 2015. That means that the level of informational involvement of people into the official news agenda in 2014–15 was about 30 percent higher than in the eighteen months before this. These findings correspond to TNS Russia, which measures the TV audience. Between the 2007–10 period and the 2011–13 period, the average audience of the two main news programs on Russian TV (*Vremia* and *Vesti*) shrank by 17 percent. But in 2014 it returned to the 2007–10 level. In 2015 the audience was 92 percent of the 2007–10 level.

Change in Russians' attention to the official news helps one understand the significant changes in public opinion. The fall in support for the regime, its institutions, and main doctrines (such as "the vertical of power") in 2011–13 coincided with a fall in attention to the news. The sharp rise in attention to the news in 2014–15 synchronized with rising support for the regime and for the conservative, revanchist values it was promoting through controlled media and TV first and foremost. Even Russians who had been avoiding political news earlier were captivated by the Ukrainian events—and simultaneously indoctrinated into the official version, as well as Kremlin-favored points of view on other political and social issues.

Another issue is that rallies around the flag after international incidents usually proved short-lived. But the rally behind Putin over Crimea has already lasted for years. Why the difference? Not rejecting the hypothesis that events in Ukraine, conflict with the West, and the intense media campaign provoked a conservative shift in Russian public opinion, we suppose that authoritarian institutions may have exaggerated the extent of this change in underlying opinion. There are several reasons to believe this. Although we lack data to test the hypothesis, it is likely that critics of the regime have increasingly dropped out of pollsters' samples, either because they fear negative consequences for expressing dissent or simply to avoid the social awkwardness of disagreeing with what they presume to be the majority opinion. When the opinion climate becomes hostile to minority views, polls may fail to reflect them (see Elisabeth Noelle-Neumann's [1984] "spiral of silence" theory).

Those who *do* answer polls lend some support to this conjecture. When asked in 2013 whether they felt free to talk about their attitudes toward the government, only 30 percent of respondents said they felt fully free to do so. Another 30 percent felt partly free, and 40 percent said they chose not to disclose their opinions of the government, either because they feared retribution or because they "did not feel the need" (LC).

Fewer respondents thought that *other* people talked openly about their attitudes toward the government and Putin in 2013 (30 percent) than had thought this in the mid-2000s (50 percent). One quarter of respondents thought people might face retribution for voicing critical opinions in anonymous polls, and one quarter said that they themselves had reservations about answering sincerely in such surveys. Moreover, if in 2009 the fear of retribution was the same among Putin's supporters and critics, in 2015 it slightly raised among supporters (26 percent) and jumped to 37 percent among his opponents (all figures from LC database).

Because of a range of technical, financial, and political problems, most polls in Russia have response rates no higher than 30–40 percent.[21] And as the intensity of propaganda increases, people with more critical views may become more reluctant to participate. Our hypothesis differs from the more frequently discussed problem of the "social desirability bias"—the probability of preference falsification in the course of interviews (there are controversial findings about the desirability bias in Putin's Russia; see Kalinin 2016 and Frye and others 2017). Indeed, it seems much easier to refuse to participate in a poll when such refusals are almost a social norm than to lie during the interview. And we can suppose that, under a worsening opinion climate, the probability of such refusals for those who feel discontent or disagreement with common attitudes would be higher than for those who are captured by the TV campaign and feel themselves to be in the mainstream. All this suggests that survey results could end up significantly distorted—and all in a pro-government direction. That does not mean polls are irrelevant, but those that cover politically sensitive topics are probably becoming less precise, especially when propaganda is intense and opposition is stigmatized and repressed.

Yet there is some evidence in polls that not all of the trends associated with modernization have reversed. Some continue, or at least have stayed

21. In the late 1990s, when Russian politics and media coverage were much more competitive, people's readiness to participate in polls was higher, so lower response rates reflect the distortion of the public sphere under progressing authoritarianism.

constant. Paternalist attitudes continued to weaken. Those favoring a state that sets fair rules for all rather than providing for citizens materially rose from 34 percent in 2011 to 41 percent in 2015.[22] The proportion saying that an individual's well-being depends most of all "on the person himself [or herself]" rose from 46 percent in 2012 to 61 percent in 2015; the share saying that it depended "on how just the society is" fell from 51 to 36 percent.[23]

In short, we interpret Russia's anti-Western "consensus" since Crimea not as the manifestation of some deeply rooted cultural phenomenon but as a rally around the flag, which has been amplified by a relentless propaganda campaign in the official news media and by the "spiral of silence" effect. Like electoral campaigns that aim not to change people's minds so much as to mobilize supporters and discourage opponents, the Kremlin's propaganda offensive may have triumphed by activating potential backers and intimidating holders of alternative views. Yet the polling data available suggest that the attempt to stop modernization in its tracks has at most only partly succeeded. And the poll results themselves probably exaggerate the degree of agreement on a reactionary agenda since fewer and fewer critics of the regime may be willing to express their opinions even in anonymous polls.

While the loss of Crimea and Sevastopol was always symbolically important and sensitive, their return was never a major issue on the national political agenda, because of the supposed costs. The annexation of Crimea (see Treisman, this volume) was used to generate a "rally around the flag." A huge propaganda campaign aimed to stigmatize opposition and present an image of unity, although in fact society in the preceding years (2011–13) had looked less consolidated than it had been at any point since the beginning of Putin's rule.

CONCLUSION

Rather than the reflection of some historically rooted cultural predispositions, Russian public opinion today is primarily an outgrowth of the recent past and current political institutions. Two trends characterize its evolution. First, the trauma of transition produced a cycle of fall and rise, economic collapse and recovery, chaotic decentralization and recentralization. The

22. Levada Center (2016, p. 63).
23. Levada Center (2016, p. 20).

polarization of elites in the 1990s generated sometimes violent clashes and deadlock, prompting a backlash. Second, the modernization of economy and society, particularly after 1999, produced the kind of value shift seen in many other modernizing countries—toward a greater priority on self-expression, tolerance, openness, and accountable government. However, the economic boom of the 2000s, besides fueling modernization, also secured a base of enthusiastic support for Putin, allowing him to concentrate power, while restricting the media and political competition. This trend toward tightening Kremlin control eventually came into conflict with the demands thrown up by modernization, resulting in a confrontation in the snow-covered streets of Moscow in the winter of 2011–12.

Since 2000, Putin's administration has neither ignored public opinion nor succeeded in completely manipulating it. His regime has used a repertoire of techniques that combines selective responsiveness to public demands, control of information via the state-controlled media, and some more overt repression. The Kremlin became an avid consumer of polling data, using them to monitor Putin's rating, target television propaganda, and construct packages that exploit public support on certain policies to suggest consensus behind less popular ones. All this provided the impression of overwhelming support for Putin and his policies, convincing ordinary people and the elites that Putin's huge supermajority exists and is stable (for a discussion of similar effects in Mexico under the Institutional Revolutionary Party [PRI], see Magaloni 2006). This picture was shaken by the 2011–12 mass protests.

Since returning to the Kremlin, Putin has sought to turn back the clock on social modernization and construct the kind of deferential, Orthodox-based, socially conservative culture that some historians thought already existed. This turn coincided with the start of a slowdown in the Russian economy—economic improvement is no longer the reliable bedrock of regime popularity as it was in the 2000s. Manipulation and repression have come to dominate responsiveness, along with mobilization of the public through confrontations with the West. Since the annexation of Crimea, the strategy has seemed remarkably effective.

However, survey evidence suggests that the turn to social conservatism is more shallow than it seems and that modernized values often remain under the surface. Even the shift to hostility toward the West may prove hard to sustain. Polls, taken in an unfree information environment, may exaggerate support for the incumbent. While the Kremlin's grip seems stronger now than five years ago, the strategy requires a high degree of mobilization. How long this can be maintained remains to be seen. Two factors—reinforced authoritarian institutions that prevent coordination among the discontented and consolidation of opposition, on the one hand, and worsening economic conditions that undermine confidence in the stability and effectiveness of the political regime, on the other—will determine the future oscillations of Russian modernization.

REFERENCES

Brody, Richard. 1991. *Assessing the President: The Media, Elite Opinion, and Public Support*. Stanford University Press.

Central and Eastern Eurobarometer. 1990–97. www.gesis.org/eurobarometer-data-service/survey-series/central-eastern-eb.

Colton, Timothy J., and Henry E. Hale. 2009. "The Putin Vote: Presidential Electorates in a Hybrid Regime." *Slavic Review* 68, no. 3, pp. 473–503.

Dmitriev, Mikhail. 2015. "Evolution of Values and Political Sentiment in Moscow and the Provinces." In *Putin's Russia: How It Rose, How It Is Maintained, and How It Might End*, edited by Leon Aron. Washington, D.C.: American Enterprise Institute for Public Policy Research.

Frye, Timothy, Scott Gehlbach, Kyle L. Marquardt, and Ora John Reuter. 2017. "Is Putin's Popularity Real?" *Post-Soviet Affairs* 33, no. 1, pp. 1–15.

Guriev, Sergei, and Daniel Treisman. 2015. "How Modern Dictators Survive: An Informational Theory of the New Authoritarianism." Unpublished Paper. University of California, Los Angeles.

Hale, Henry E., Michael McFaul, and Timothy J. Colton. 2004. "Putin and the 'Delegative Democracy' Trap: Evidence from Russia's 2003–04 Elections." *Post-Soviet Affairs* 20, no. 4, pp. 285–319.

Inglehart, Ronald, and Christian Welzel. 2005. *Modernization, Cultural Change, and Democracy: The Human Development Sequence*. Cambridge University Press.

Kalinin, Kirill. 2016. "The Social Desirability Bias in Autocrat's Electoral Ratings: Evidence from the 2012 Russian Presidential Elections." *Journal of Elections, Public Opinion and Parties* 26, no. 2, pp. 191–211.

Levada Center. 2016. *Obshchestvennoe mnenie 2015* [Public Opinion 2015]. Moscow.

Lipman, Maria. 2009. "Media Manipulation and Political Control in Russia." London: Chatham House.

Magaloni, Beatriz. 2006. *Voting for Autocracy: Hegemonic Party Survival and Its Demise in Mexico*. Cambridge University Press.

McFaul, Michael. 2001. *Russia's Unfinished Revolution: Political Change from Gorbachev to Putin*. Cornell University Press.

Noelle-Neumann, Elisabeth. 1984. *The Spiral of Silence: A Theory of Public Opinion— Our Social Skin*. University of Chicago Press.

O'Donnell, Guillermo. 1994. "Delegative Democracy." *Journal of Democracy* 5, no. 1, pp. 55–69.

Pipes, Richard. 2004. "Flight from Freedom—What Russians Think and Want." *Foreign Affairs*, May–June.

Pomerantsev, Peter. 2014. "How Putin Is Reinventing Warfare." *Foreign Policy* 5 (2014).

Pop-Eleches, Grigore, and Joshua Tucker. 2017. *Communism's Shadow: Historical Legacies and Contemporary Political Attitudes.* Princeton University Press.

Rogov, Kirill. 2013. "Forty Years in the Desert: The Political Cycles of Post-Soviet Transition." In *Russia 2025: Scenarios for the Russian Future*, edited by Maria Lipman and Nikolay Petrov. Basingstoke: Palgrave Macmillan.

———. 2015. "Triumphs and Crises of Plebiscitary Presidentialism." In *Putin's Russia: How It Rose, How It Is Maintained, and How It Might End*, edited by Leon Aron. Washington, D.C.: American Enterprise Institute for Public Policy Research.

Rose, Richard, William Mishler, and Neil Munro. 2006. *Russia Transformed: Developing Popular Support for a New Regime.* Cambridge University Press.

Treisman, Daniel. 2011. "Presidential Popularity in a Hybrid Regime: Russia under Yeltsin and Putin." *American Journal of Political Science* 55, no. 3, pp. 590–609.

———. 2014. "Putin's Popularity since 2010: Why Did Support for the Kremlin Plunge, Then Stabilize?" *Post-Soviet Affairs* 30, no. 5, pp. 370–88.

Welzel, Christian. 2013. *Freedom Rising: Human Empowerment and the Quest for Emancipation.* Cambridge University Press.

Zaller, John. 1992. *The Nature and Origins of Mass Opinion.* Cambridge University Press.

NINE

The Courts, Law Enforcement, and Politics

ELLA PANEYAKH and DINA ROSENBERG

Over the past twenty years, some journalists and scholars in both Russia and the West have converged on a conventional view of the Russian legal system. In this view, the courts and law enforcement agencies are highly corrupt, repressive, non-transparent, politicized, and mistrusted by citizens.[1] Rather than rule of law, Russians are said to live under "telephone justice" (*telefonnoe pravo*), a term borrowed from Soviet times that means

---

Most interviews used in this article were conducted by researchers from the Institute for the Rule of Law (Institut Problem Pravoprimeneniya) of the European University at St. Petersburg as part of the research projects "The Trajectory of a Criminal Case: Institutional Analysis" and "Russian Judges as a Professional Group." Ella Paneyakh, who worked at the institute as director in 2009–10 and as leading researcher in 2010–14, is grateful for the opportunity to use its primary data.

1. Some scholars go as far as to call courts "one of the biggest corruption markets in Russia" (for example, Satarov 2006). On corruption in Russian courts, see Pastukhov (2002); Solomon (2005); Barber, Buckley, and Belton (2008); Transparency International (2008); Bureau of Democracy, Human Rights, and Labor (2007).

that political orders from above matter more than legal norms.[2] During elections, the courts are seen as tools for eliminating opposition candidates and validating electoral fraud.

In the common Western media narrative, this system is typically explained with reference to history—both that of the Joseph Stalin–era Soviet Union and that of the troubled transition of the 1990s. Russian courts are depicted as combining the undesirable features of both periods. Current miscarriages of justice elicit references to Stalin's repressions and opaque court rulings. Attempts at reform under President Boris Yeltsin in the 1990s are seen as having been subverted by the explosion of corruption associated with market reforms and the capture of the judiciary by business. Under Vladimir Putin, the story goes, business lost out to the country's political leaders. Law enforcement and courts were now captured by the president and slotted into his executive "vertical of power." The courts became subservient to law enforcement, and the whole system became an instrument for crushing political opposition and enriching top Kremlin circles.

Western media tend to cover those aspects of Russia's legal environment that fit this picture. A quick search of top world publications turns up articles in several categories. First, there are *political and other high-profile cases* (Mikhail Khodorkovsky, the oil tycoon with antigovernment political views, who was jailed for ten years for tax evasion and embezzlement; Alexey Navalny, the crusading anticorruption activist and opposition leader, who was charged with several allegedly fabricated economic crimes). Second, there are *selected human rights violations* (the feminist punk band Pussy Riot, whose members were jailed for hooliganism; Sergei Magnitsky, a whistle-blowing lawyer, who was charged with tax evasion and died in prison) (Barry and Roth 2012; Elder 2013). Politically motivated murders of journalists also fall into this category (Paul Klebnikov, editor of the Russian edition of *Forbes*, murdered in 2004; Anna Politkovskaya, a journalist at *Novaya Gazeta*, shot in 2006). Third, articles cover the *introduction of shameful laws* ("Herod's law," passed in 2012, banned U.S. families from adopting Russian orphans). Fourth, court-ruled *disqualifications of opposition*

2. On telephone justice in the Western media, see Schwirtz (2009); Lipman (2009); *The Economist* (2008). Telephone justice is equally germane to the regional and municipal level (see, for example, Lambert-Mogiliansky, Sonin, and Zhuravskaya 2007).

candidates are also a hot topic (for instance, the barring of former prime minister Mikhail Kasyanov from the 2008 presidential election under the pretext of invalid signatures).[3] Fifth, and finally, the Western media also often reports on cases of "raiding"—the corrupt expropriation of business people by politically connected rivals who use fabricated cases and bribed judges to seize their target's assets.[4] From such cases, authors often extrapolate to the entire judicial system and draw conclusions about the authoritarian drift of the country's political order and the obstacles to democratization (Antonova 2012; Reevell 2014; Balmforth 2013; Ledeneva 2008; Rose 2009).

Some academic writers draw a more nuanced picture of modern Russian law, recognizing the different ways it handles high-profile political cases and mundane cases (for example, Hendley 2009, 2011; Yakovlev and Kazun 2015), the overemphasis on internal incentives (Paneyakh 2015b; Solomon 1987; Titaev and Shkliaruk 2015), and the decreasing popularity of legal nihilism (Hendley 2012). Others have documented peoples' increasing willingness to actually file claims in the courts—and their frequent victories against some government agencies, although usually the less powerful ones (Hendley 2009; Solomon 2008; Trochev 2012).

We argue here that the conventional wisdom—although articulating one element of reality—misses a big part of the picture. We base this claim on analysis of formal statements, internal documents, and official data of law enforcement agencies, as well as in-depth, unstructured interviews with a number of judges and law enforcement figures. Although the capture of courts and law enforcement agents by business and the politicization of them by the Kremlin are serious problems, an even more widespread defect of the system relates to perverse incentives within it. Highly formalized rules for performance evaluation combined with the inconsistency of promotion policy in practice, both largely inherited from the Soviet period, motivate police, prosecutors, and judges to pick easy cases, prosecute the most defenseless targets, and ignore the more serious crimes that are hard to close quickly. Since internal rules and procedures are almost impossible

3. Newburg (2000); Tsukanova (2002); Chivers (2008). For many such examples at both federal and regional levels, see Fish (2005).

4. For scholarly accounts, see Firestone (2010); Gans-Morse (2012); Nazrullaeva, Baranov, and Yakovlev (2013); Rochlitz (2014); Volkov (1999, 2002); Yakovlev, Kazun, and Sobolev (2014).

to follow consistently, legal professionals are forced to violate laws not just for corrupt gain but simply to do their jobs.

As in other spheres of Russian life, there is an everyday system that functions by its own logic and there is a separate system that kicks in when cases—rarely—attract the attention or affect the interests of top Kremlin decisionmakers.[5] That some of the most serious failures of the legal system derive not from its capture by business or political elites but from the system's own internal pathologies suggests that increasing its independence from higher political authorities may not—by itself—result in much improvement. (By contrast, increasing the independence of courts from *law enforcement agencies* would help.) One must also reform the system's incentive scheme.[6]

This conclusion is not more reassuring than the conventional wisdom. But an additional goal of this chapter is to challenge the universally negative view of Russia's judiciary. Although the law enforcement system, on balance, has been an obstacle to the country's modernization, it has itself nevertheless recorded significant progress in certain respects. Statistics show a marked improvement in the work of Russia's commercial courts over the past fifteen years, although the trend may now be reversing. More generally, government, civil society, and the professional community have come together to modernize some aspects of judicial practice—humanizing criminal sentencing, reducing the prison population, and easing access to civil litigation. In the past decade, the courts have provided some support—more than usually recognized—for citizens in conflicts with the state. Record numbers of Russians have sued the authorities and won.

Much less successful were attempts to increase judicial independence, equality of the parties in court, and the impartiality of judges in general (both in terms of prosecutorial bias in criminal trials and of social bias in

5. Scholars have pointed to a similar dualism between mundane and political cases in various political eras (see Sharlet [1977] about the Stalin times; Feifer [1964] and Gorlizki [1997] about the Khrushchev times; and Burbank [2004] about peasants' litigation in nineteenth-century Russia). For similar conclusions about the Chinese system, see Peerenboom (2002) and Woo and Wang (2005).

6. The idea that internal stimuli influence outcomes is not new or unique to Russia's system (see, for example, Eisenstein and Jacob [1977] on courts; Mastrofski, Ritti, and Hoffmaster [1987] on police in the United States), but in Russia this impact is much more profound and important (Paneyakh 2015b; Solomon 1987; Titaev and Shkliaruk 2015).

all kinds of litigation). And, at times, technological innovations, introduced without changing underlying incentives, made things worse. Computerization of police work, for example, increased the paperwork burden on already overloaded detectives, leaving even less time for other aspects of their jobs. It also led to "copy-paste investigations," in which police officers craft evidence to fit reused electronic templates, and "copy-paste justice," in which judges literally copy and paste content provided by the prosecution into their verdicts.

We also contest the view that Russia's courts are completely subservient to the country's top political leaders. In fact, if the courts are subservient, it is generally not to Moscow but to the local branches of law enforcement agencies. At the same time, the courts have often acted as constraints on political decisionmaking—for instance, obstructing repeated attempts to reform them. Law enforcement agencies have proved even more resistant to central politicians' attempts at reform.

Examining the complete trajectory of Russia's judicial system since the end of communism, the story is a mixed one, with serious lingering problems, perverse incentives, and entrenched resistance to change, but also some notable progress. In some respects, the years since 2000—and especially those during Dmitry Medvedev's presidency—saw pressures for modernization, which resulted in a huge fall in the prison population, some humanization of sentencing, and a rapid increase in the use of commercial courts. Since 2012, with the return of Putin to the presidency, such positive trends have been frozen or reversed.

That said, in general we see the Russian court system as an obstacle for the country's modernization, rather than a driving force for it, and the law enforcement system as a leading countermodernization force.

WHAT THE CONVENTIONAL IMAGE MISSES

Although one would not guess this from much media coverage, high-profile political cases probably constitute much less than 1 percent of the total. Most—although not all—political crimes are classified as cases "of an extremist nature." In 2015, 1,329 such crimes were registered. Although that represents an astonishing jump of 48 percent over 2013—we return to this below—such cases still constituted only about 0.05 percent of all those registered. While the average citizen has a low opinion of the legal system, Russians do not consider the high-profile political cases as at all typical.

When Kathryn Hendley questioned focus group participants in Moscow and Saratov in 2007 about the Khodorkovsky prosecution, almost all agreed that it was a kind of show trial, designed—most thought—to threaten other oligarchs (Hendley 2009).[7]

The scale of raiding and other corrupt uses of the legal system to advance business interests is harder to measure. Often, the targeted business silently cooperates with the authorities in the hope of salvaging something. The consensus seems to be that hundreds or even thousands of such attacks occur each year (Rochlitz 2014; Zhang 2010). In 2015 Russian law enforcement agencies registered 112,445 economic crimes (Procuracy 2015). However, this total will miss many cases of raiding in which business people surrender before they are charged with fabricated crimes or in which they are charged with noneconomic crimes, and it will include cases of genuine economic crimes with no raiding. One study, which gathered information about raider attacks from Russian newspapers, concluded that the number increased rapidly after 2003, peaking in 2005–06, and then fell by 2010 back to the level of 2002 (Rochlitz 2014). Although press reports probably identify only a fraction of the total—the study found fewer than sixty in the peak year—the change over time may capture the dynamic.

Besides raiding and corruption, the law enforcement system's prosecutorial bias imposes costs on firms by rendering them continually vulnerable and depressing economic activity (Yakovlev, Kazun, and Sobolev 2014). Experts estimate that about 15 percent of all business people were subjected to criminal prosecution in 2000–10, resulting in the closure of businesses each year with total income of about 1.8 percent of GDP (Center of Legal and Economic Studies 2010). However, although such cases seriously weaken the country's property rights system, they still constitute a small percentage of the total activity of law enforcement agencies and the courts.

As well as focusing on a nonrepresentative subset of cases, the common image entirely ignores some positive aspects of the system's evolution. If Russian courts were uniformly politicized and corrupt, one would expect businesses to find other ways to resolve their disputes. Yet they flocked to

7. That does not mean they do not influence judges' decisions on more mundane cases; our interviews suggest that judges take cues from such public trials on what shortcuts are allowed.

Figure 9-1   Petitions Received by Russia's Commercial Courts[a]

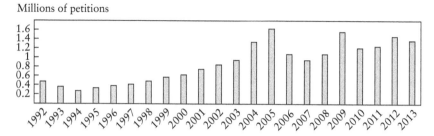

Millions of petitions

Source: Results of *arbitrazh* courts' activity, federal *arbitrazh* courts of the Russian Federation, archive (www.arbitr.ru/press-centr/news/totals/index_ar.htm).

a. In Russian, commercial courts were referred to as *arbitrazh* courts at the time.

the commercial (*arbitrazh*) courts in precisely the period in which raiding and political penetration of the judiciary were increasing (Hendley 2009). The number of times businesses initiated cases in these courts more than quadrupled between 1994 and 2013 (see figure 9-1).

Such figures do not mean these courts were clean of corruption, but it does suggest their rulings were sufficiently predictable to make businesses want to use them (Dmitrieva, Titaev, and Chetverikova 2012, p. 3). The *arbitrazh* system was widely considered more professional, just, and modern than the courts of general jurisdiction, mostly because of its smaller size, its higher professional requirements for judges, and the greater resources of its litigators. However, in February 2014, the two systems were merged, ending the *arbitrazh* courts' autonomy and threatening their reputation for relative competence.

Besides fighting raiders in the courts, some businesses have managed to enlist the media (Yakovlev, Kazun, and Sobolev 2014). After two scandalous incidents—the seizure of 167,000 Motorola phones by customs agents in 2006 and a raid by the Federal Drug Control Service on a number of medium-size chemical companies "in the hope of gaining access to elements needed to manufacture narcotics" (Fedorin 2008, as quoted in Yakovlev, Kazun, and Sobolev 2014, p. 176)—the targeted companies chose not to give up, attracted major publicity, and won their cases. Curiously, after the Motorola case the head of the Federal Tax Service, Aleksandr Zherikhov, and Prosecutor General Vladimir Ustinov were dismissed (Myers 2006). Unfortunately, these two cases are a drop in the bucket; most raider attacks succeed.

Do the courts always take the authorities' side, as the "telephone law" image suggests? In fact, the answer is no. As one expert noted in 2008: "Various courts, including military tribunals and arbitrazh courts, have satisfied citizen complaints against officials at well above the fifty percent level. Even complaints against the legality of normative acts of ministries come out in favor of the complainant (and against the government) around thirty percent of the time" (Solomon 2008, p. 69).

Unlike in the United States, the Russian state does not enjoy sovereign immunity. And, in fact, citizens sue government agencies hundreds of thousands of times a year—and often win. In 2008 alone, 137,359 Russian plaintiffs won damages totaling US$1.1 billion in successful suits against the government on just two grounds: wrongful actions by government officials and failure of federal agencies to fulfill their contractual obligations (Trochev 2012, p. 18). Quite amazingly, success rates for citizens who sued the government in courts of general jurisdiction between 2007 and 2011 never fell below 87 percent (Trochev 2012, p. 22). Even on highly political topics, citizens often prevailed: "Between 2008 and 2011, litigants won about one-third of lawsuits filed against election commissions, which have been under the tight control of the ruling United Russia party" (Trochev 2012, p. 22). The courts have often sided with human rights activists who sued the government for wrongful prosecution of their clients and have ordered the government to pay significant compensation.

The explanation is that Russian courts overwhelmingly side with the accuser—whoever that is. In civil cases, government agencies suing citizens win 88 percent of the time, and citizens suing government agencies win 86 percent of the time (Dmitrieva, Titaev, and Chetverikova 2012). (In criminal and administrative lawsuits, this bias in favor of the accuser always favors the state: the acquittal rate is only 6 percent in administrative cases and less than 0.001 percent in criminal cases where law enforcement agencies are involved.) Courts also differentiate among government agencies: judges are not afraid to rule against municipalities and civil agencies. They are much more timid about ruling against more powerful agencies such as the Ministry of Internal Affairs (MIA), even in civil cases such as workplace disputes.

Businesses also often prevail against the state. One study that examined a representative sample of ten thousand commercial cases from the *arbitrazh* courts in 2007–11 found that when private entrepreneurs opposed state agencies over nontrivial sums of money, the two sides had equal chances of winning. Moreover, entrepreneurs could improve their odds by participating more actively in the court proceedings (Dmitrieva, Titaev, and Chetverikova 2012).

Perhaps most surprising, this phenomenon of Russians successfully suing their government and winning damages is almost entirely a product of the Putin years. Most of the procedures for obtaining redress against unlawful government action were introduced during Putin's first term (Trochev 2012, p. 20). The amount of money paid out by the federal government, under court order, to compensate victims of wrongful government actions was seventy times larger in 2010 than in 2001 (Trochev 2012, p. 30).[8]

Siding with plaintiffs in many cases against government is only one form of judicial resistance. As in other undemocratic regimes, some Russian courts choose to go public and post on their websites "special requests" from officials regarding certain cases (Trochev and Ellett 2014). Russian attorneys also hold public meetings where they discuss the perverse system of incentives and corruption (Trochev and Ellett 2014).

Statistics also show a progressive humanization of criminal sentencing since the 1990s, although this tendency has now reversed. The number of Russians sentenced to prison fell from a peak of around 389,000 in 1999 to 312,000 in 2008 and then 206,000 in 2012 (Judicial Department of the Supreme Court 2006–15). In the early 1990s, judges hardly ever gave probation. Between 1997 and 2011, probation became significantly more frequent than sentences for actual prison time. Interviews with judges suggest that some were consciously trying to find humane options, within limits imposed by the law enforcement apparatus.

In short, the Western image of the Russian judiciary and law enforcement extrapolates from a limited number of high-profile and political cases and abusive expropriations of businesses and ignores much data about the increasing successes that firms and citizens have had over the past two decades in using the courts to defend themselves against the state. We certainly do not mean to exaggerate those successes, but nor should one ignore them. Still, the greatest problem with the conventional image is something

---

8. Despite such a high success rate in suing the government, public trust in the courts has fallen since 1995 (Levada Center 2015). This could be because people-friendly decisions are not always enforced or because the public is uninformed about the success rate (Trochev 2008).

else: it mischaracterizes the real cause of the deep problems in Russia's criminal justice system.

PERVERSE INCENTIVES

The way crimes are investigated and punished in Russia is inefficient and unjust. But the main reason for that is not corruption or capture of law enforcement by business interests. It is the internal logic of the system, which has been left virtually untouched since the end of communism.

Throughout its operation, the criminal justice system exercises an extreme form of socioeconomic discrimination. Police, prosecutors, and judges go after the poor and those considered "marginal" (the homeless and unemployed), not because the rich pay, but because the rich have the skills and resources to defend themselves—and the system values easy victories.

Russian official statistics on law enforcement are rightly considered problematic. However, although inadequate for measuring the incidence of crime, say, they are nevertheless useful—combined with insights from interviews and understanding of the context—for our purpose: analyzing how the law enforcement system works. For all their weaknesses, Russian law enforcement agents collect a great quantity of bureaucratic indicators about work flow and so on, which are likely to be roughly accurate.

At least 60 percent of those tried for a crime in Russia are unemployed (table 9-1) as well as 73 percent of those imprisoned (Paneyakh 2013). Across the board, the acquittal rate is extremely low—0.7 percent in 2011. But 49 percent of these acquittals go to five high-status groups—law enforcers, top managers, civil servants, entrepreneurs, and office workers—who make up only 7 percent of defendants (table 9-1), and about half of them to private accusation cases, where the law enforcement agencies are not involved (about 8 percent of all cases). Such disparities do not prove discrimination. But regression analysis, controlling for a variety of other factors and taking into account the type of crime, confirms that the likelihood of conviction and the severity of punishment are strongly linked to socioeconomic status (Volkov 2014).

Interviews with practitioners suggest a simple explanation for the targeting of marginal members of society. Police have discretion in picking crimes to register, and prosecutors decide for themselves which cases to pursue. In the extreme hierarchy of Putin's "power vertical," local commu-

Table 9-1. *Defendants by Status Group: Court Outcomes, 2009–10*

Percent, unless otherwise indicated

Status Group[a]	All defendants	Acquitted	Acquitted, private	Acquitted, public	Sentenced to prison	Probation	Average time served in prison, years
Law enforcer	0.2	13.9	54	4.5	25.3	31.7	4.2
Civil servant	1.2	10.1	33	2.9	11.8	29.0	4.0
Top manager	1.2	8.8	32	3.4	13.8	27	4.6
Entrepreneur	1.6	7.5	27	1.6	15.1	24.5	4.7
Office worker	3.2	4.7	24	0.5	18.6	28.8	4.0
Manual laborer	20.9	2.7	14	0.2	21.6	31.4	3.8
Student	2.3	2.2	16	0.1	17.2	35.1	4.1
Unemployed	60.1	1.7	15	0.3	32.8	29.4	3.7
Prisoner	1.0	1.52	25	0.4	78.9	7.5	3.9

Source: Volkov (2014).

a. The category "others" (8.3 percent) is not included.

nities, local authorities, and even other government agencies have no legal means to influence how law enforcers do their jobs. Such agents are motivated by the performance evaluation systems within their own bureaucracies (Paneyakh 2014). And these systems—changed little since Soviet times—give strong incentives to pick cases that seem easy to win and rush the process whenever possible.

Performance is evaluated on the basis of (1) how many cases are processed, (2) how serious are the crimes, and (3) what percentage of cases advance to the next stage in the prosecution chain (for example, the "clearance rate" for police or the number of cases won in court for prosecutors). A typical case passes from the police officer who registers it to a field detective who conducts a preliminary investigation, to an investigator who decides whether to proceed, to a prosecutor who oversees the case in court. At each stage, those earlier in the chain are judged on whether the case proceeds—and ultimately results in a guilty verdict. After the field detective records evidence, no one subsequently dealing with the case is able to check if it is true and was collected appropriately. The investigators cannot themselves search for material evidence or additional witnesses—that would require a bureaucratically complicated departure from usual procedures. The prosecutor who represents the case in court has generally not participated in the investigation and knows mostly what is written on the bill of indictment.

In all regards, quantity trumps quality. All are strained to the limit by the need to fulfill quotas, and courts are swamped in paperwork. Seeking to increase their promotion chances, law enforcers favor easy and standard cases, as well as those with more serious charges. Police officers do their best not to register "inconvenient" crimes. When difficult cases nevertheless materialize, lower-level agents falsify documents, exert pressure on witnesses, and torture defendants to push the cases through (Gilinskiy 2011). Even judges prefer to take the prosecutor's side since their job evaluation suffers when their rulings are overturned (and prosecutors have more time, skills, resources, and leverage to appeal to superior courts than other parties). All collude to cover up misconduct. Curiously, even defense lawyers, who supposedly represent the interests of their clients, often collaborate with the prosecutors since the chance of acquittal is minuscule and collaboration is often the only path to a milder verdict (Khodzhaeva and Rabovski 2015).

Socially marginal defendants are easy to railroad through the system. However, if defendants are wealthy and can mobilize resources to protect themselves, those at all levels think twice. Such individuals can produce evidence that is harder for the judge to ignore and can stretch out the process or appeal the verdict.

On paper, law enforcement looks remarkably effective: in the United States in 2011, the clearance rate for property crimes was 19 percent and that for violent crimes 48 percent; in Russia, the rates were about 60 and 90 percent, respectively (Paneyakh 2013). Far more robberies are registered in the United States than in Russia, yet Russia records far more homicides per capita than the United States (Volkov and others 2012). One possible explanation is that robbery cases are hard to solve (so the police do not open cases and the public does not bother to report incidents), whereas murders are hard to hide (Yakovlev and Kazun 2015). In Russia, police register relatively few cases of rape, which is a difficult crime to prosecute. But those rapes they do register usually get "solved." The Russian clearance rate for rapes is an unprecedented 91 percent, compared to just 34 percent in the United States.[9]

If, as we argue, the most widespread problems of the Russian legal system result not from the penetration of it by political and business interests but from the system's own internal pathologies, then increasing the independence of judges and prosecutors will not solve them. Making legal practitioners more independent will merely enable them to respond to the existing perverse incentives with even greater vigor. Instead, the system of promotions and work evaluations needs to be thoroughly reformed.

An additional concern is the low quality of legal personnel. The number of Russians working in the courts and Procuracy doubled between 2000 and 2015 (from 113,700 to 233,000) (Rosstat 2015). Unfortunately, the competence of judges did not improve. Fewer than one-half of Russia's law schools are accredited, and two-thirds of judges received their legal education by distance learning (Burnham, Maggs, and Danilenko 2004; Volkov and Dmitrieva 2015). As of 2013, an estimated 30 percent of judges had risen from clerical positions within the judicial system. (The younger the cohort, the higher the percentage of former clerical workers, which means that the problem is getting worse.) Another 38 percent had a background in

9. Rapes are underreported, underregistered, and hard to clear in all countries (see, for example, Bryden and Lengnick 1997). But the discrepancies in Russian statistics point to the unusually broad discretion that police have there.

law enforcement and prosecution, and many—as in the Soviet period—had come from careers in the security services (Volkov and Dmitrieva 2015).

THE COURTS, LAW ENFORCEMENT, AND CENTRAL POLITICAL DECISIONS

To what extent do law enforcement agents and judges influence and constrain the decisionmaking of Russia's political leaders? One way to investigate that is to examine attempts made over the years to reform the legal system. If, on the one hand, police, prosecutors, and judges are—as many perceive—subservient tools of top executive officials, reforming the system should pose no particular difficulty. If, on the other hand, such actors can shape and block attempted reforms, that would suggest a more complicated relationship.

Reforming the Courts

How the Russian court system developed in 1990–2016 largely mirrors the preferences of the top political decisionmakers. Some reforms were initiated from below and aimed at strengthening judicial power and autonomy. But, as we show, such reforms succeeded only when consistent with power holders' priorities. Factionalized, embedded in a hierarchical structure of career incentives, and not immune from corruption, judges rarely managed to unite to push for reforms and were only occasionally able to resist a determined offensive by the Kremlin. Also, in some cases reforms were compromised simply due to external factors such as corruption and organized crime.

The nature of the Russian judicial system is inherently hierarchical, with lower courts dependent on higher courts both in terms of review of their work (lower-level judges are evaluated based on how many of their decisions are overturned by higher courts) and organizationally (in practice, the chair of a higher court manages subordinate courts and appoints lower-level judges, although these must also pass an examination and selection process to be appointed to the bench by the president). Judges depend on the chair of their own court as much as any employees in a government agency depend on their direct supervisor.

Amid early enthusiasm for liberal democracy in the 1990s, Yeltsin introduced Western-style judicial reforms. Judges won life appointments (after a three-year probationary period). A constitutional court was created, and administration of the courts was transferred from the executive branch to a department under the Supreme Court. A new Criminal Procedure Code increased adversarialism, while new justice of the peace courts (regional courts that could resolve civil cases through mediation and criminal ones through reconciliation) were established. At this time, a broad consensus among judges, many business people, and officials favored strong, independent courts. The main constraints were lack of financial resources, the weakness of the transitional state, and organized crime, which had little interest in strong judges. In Russia's provinces, criminalized businesses colluded with local elites to weaken judicial autonomy.

Putin at first saw stronger courts as a way to foster economic growth. By this point, entrepreneurs were themselves realizing that resolving disputes in court might be cheaper and more efficient than employing mafias. In his first two terms, Putin's government got new criminal and civil codes enacted, in 2002 and 2003, respectively; increased judges' salaries, as well as the number of judges and assistants; introduced jury trials; made data public; and repaired and computerized court buildings (Solomon 2008). However, Putin also sought to re-impose executive control, supposedly to break up corrupt cabals of judges, governors, and oligarchs in the regions. This agenda was backed by certain relative outsiders—the Ministry of Economic Development and Trade and the High Arbitrazh Court—and opposed by the judicial mainstream.

The judges won some battles in 2002–04, rebuffing proposals to remove their life tenure and reduce their number. But such victories were exceptions. Putin was able to stack the regional qualifications commissions that regulate the procedure for selecting judges with people from the executive branch, often with security backgrounds (Remington 2011). The desire to keep courts available for political use in rare, handpicked cases apparently outweighed for Putin the goal of improving the business climate.

President Medvedev, during his term (2008–12), repeatedly criticized the legal nihilism in Russia. He initiated several reforms, such as the adoption of a new Code of Ethics for judges (which had little practical effect) and a broad humanization of the Criminal Code. He particularly sought to improve treatment of business people accused of white-collar crimes, and criminal investigations of those in business did fall after 2008, although enforcement agents may have found other ways to target firms.

Thus, from the early 1990s until the end of Medvedev's presidency, a large number of reforms were introduced that aimed at modernizing and improving the efficiency of the courts. Although judges were sometimes part of a coalition backing these reforms, what really mattered was that the president favored them. Judicial opposition did sometimes succeed in blocking even some reforms the Kremlin favored—as in the fight over life tenure—but this was unusual. In the 2000s, moves to modernize the court system increasingly lost ground to the Kremlin's efforts to ensure its control over all powerful public actors.

Reforming the Police and Procuracy

The Soviet Union was "the world's largest-ever police state" (Kotkin 2001, p. 173). After it collapsed, Russia's leaders aimed to replace Soviet-era law enforcement structures with more modern, professionalized alternatives. Communist Party cells within the Russian Ministry of Internal Affairs (MIA) were abolished and most departments were reshuffled or renamed (for example, the Department against Misappropriation of Socialist Property became the Department for Economic Crimes (Favarel-Garrigues 2011). A 1991 "law on militia" created a local "public order police," separate from the criminal police, with partial subordination to regional authorities. Governors often co-opted local branches, creating problems for the federal authorities and prompting Putin to recentralize control in the 2000s. In 1998 the prison system was transferred from the MIA to the Justice Ministry, and in 2003 the MIA received some functions from the Tax Police, when this was abolished. The system for appointing regional police chiefs was modified several times (Taylor 2014).

Yet these reforms are widely regarded as cosmetic. They did not change the internal practices and mind-sets inherited from the Soviet era, and—while removing the external control previously exercised by the Communist Party—they did not replace it with any new accountability mechanism. Corruption flourished (Favarel-Garrigues 2011). The greatest concern for the enforcement agencies in the 1990s was not to protect the citizenry but to outflank organized crime in the competition for control over private business. They won (Volkov 2012). In the 2000s, the Kremlin's main goal was not to reform the police but merely to recentralize control over it.

Only in 2009 did more serious reform make it onto the agenda, largely due to the appalling performance of the police, who had been implicated in not just corruption but contract murders, torture, excessive violence, and even mass shootings of random citizens. In 2006, 80 percent of police officers were involved in unofficial activities, ranging from corruption to working as security guards for private businesses on the side (Gudkov and

Dubin 2006). Officers responsible for shocking abuses often enjoyed impunity because of personal connections (Zagorets 2009). Responding to a flood of embarrassing news and public criticism of the police, President Medvedev announced reform as a priority in December 2009 (Taylor 2014).

Medvedev's December 2009 decree listed a number of objectives, including (1) cutting MIA personnel by 20 percent, (2) centralizing financing of the public order police, (3) increasing police salaries, (4) reorganizing administration, (5) improving police education with ethical and anticorruption measures, and (6) improving hiring procedures (Taylor 2014, p. 235). While items 5 and 6 would help to address the issues we have argued were important, others would not. Cutting staff was in part aimed at making possible the salary increases—which were supposed to reduce incentives for corruption. Needless to say, such salary increases were welcome to MIA insiders. Item 2 was part of Putin's agenda of recentralizing control.

Most observers saw the eventual outcome—codified in a 2011 law—as a failure from the point of view of improving policing. The personnel cuts and wage increases were retained, as was the provision for centralizing financing of the public order police. An impressive-sounding 42 percent of MIA jobs were eliminated, but many of these were currently vacant positions or technical staffing (for example, cleaning personnel). Higher-level bureaucrats mostly survived, at the expense of street-level officers, who had been stretched thin even before the reform. Nothing in the new law changed the routine practices of police officers. The old system for professional evaluation remained intact, and the number of quantitative indicators actually increased from 65 to 72 (Volkov, Paneyakh, and Titaev 2010b). Hiring remained highly discretionary and random, with prestigious jobs filled on the basis of connections.

Why the failure? Some attributed it to Medvedev's vagueness about what type of reform was needed. Others blamed his decision to entrust responsibility for drafting the law to a committee dominated by current and former MIA officers (Taylor 2014). The Russian Lawyers' Association, headed by former prime minister Sergei Stepashin and supported by several think tanks and human rights groups, had proposed a radical liberalization and decentralization of the MIA. But this contradicted Putin's centralization priority and was opposed by the Federal Security Service (FSB), the Federal Drug Control Service, the Finance Ministry, and other influential executive branch players (Taylor 2014). Even Medvedev appears to have decided against decentralization early on (Taylor 2014, p. 236). In the face of MIA resistance, the reformers left police with the right to engage in commercial activities and with controversial powers to investigate economic crimes, known to facilitate corruption (Taylor 2014; Volkov, Paneyakh, and Titaev 2010a; Novikova 2011).

Yet the MIA did not get exactly the law it would have preferred. Either for public relations purposes or in a sincere attempt to outmaneuver the police generals, Medvedev opened up the draft to Internet discussion. This led to the insertion of certain humanizing elements that police insiders cannot have favored. For example, two young activists from Transparency International and the Youth Human Rights Movement initiated an online campaign in support of five police reform components, two of which—a new right for detainees to make one phone call within three hours of being detained and the requirement that police wear a badge with their identification number—became law (Taylor 2014). Other notable measures included the right to a lawyer from the moment of detention and the responsibility of police to inform detainees of their rights. In some sense, these concessions are a response to the vocal public discontent, expressed in the media and in opinion polls, with the police's awful performance.

In short, when it comes to police reform, the notion of an unconstrained dictatorship simply announcing decisions does not fit well. On the contrary, the MIA managed to defend its corporate interests even against a seemingly determined offensive by the country's president. It is possible that Putin—the true top decisionmaker—backed the MIA behind the scenes. Public opinion and mobilized civil society (human rights groups, Internet activists) also scored small victories, perhaps because of backing from Medvedev.

One observes a similar ability to block reform at times on the part of the Procuracy and FSB (for the latter, see Soldatov and Rochlitz, this volume). During the 1990s, the Procuracy beat back several attempts to limit its power. However, in the 2000s, it fell victim to turf wars (Remington 2015). Despite resistance from Prosecutor General Yuri Chaika, Putin gave the Procuracy's Investigative Committee considerable autonomy in 2007, freeing investigators from following orders of the prosecutors. Four years later, the Investigative Committee became completely independent, responsible only to the president. Separating prosecution from investigation was in line with President Medvedev's liberalizing political discourse and also usefully reduced the power of the Procuracy, which had excelled at business raiding and political tricks. Still, the Procuracy retained a certain veto, as the sole agency that can prosecute a case. The Investigative Committee can arrest defendants, seeking to pressure them for some reason, but, without the Procuracy's cooperation, it cannot bring the matters to court.

Reviewing Laws

Another way to judge the legal system's impact on political decisionmaking is to explore whether—and, if so, when—the courts strike down laws and executive branch decrees. We already discussed the courts' underappreciated role in supporting citizens in lawsuits against the state. But what about court review of legislation?

The Russian Constitutional Court has had a turbulent history. First, the court survived the suspension of its activity for two years (1993–95) under Yeltsin. Second, in 2001 the court successfully resisted an attempt by the Kremlin to transform it into a council with mere advisory powers. However, after the court's relocation to St. Petersburg in 2008 (as decreed by Putin), its efficiency and prestige declined (Paneyakh 2015a).

Over the past twenty-five years, constitutional judges have often shown deference toward the executive, especially on salient political matters (for example, backing the use of military force in Chechnya in 1994 and supporting abolition of gubernatorial elections in 2004). Yet, in other cases, they have overruled federal and regional executive and legislative decisions. For instance, in 2002 the court declared the existing standards for invalidating election results unconstitutional (it made such invalidation virtually impossible) (Solomon 2004, p. 568). In 2010 the judges ruled unconstitutional seven out of twenty-two bills submitted to them for review, and in 2014, twenty out of thirty-three. The story does not always end there—the court sometimes reverses itself or fails to ensure enforcement, and recently judges have voiced concerns about officials' noncompliance with the law. Still, the knowledge that the court can rule against the political elite—or, at the least, give government agencies a hard time proving their case—affects political decisionmaking to some extent.

The Supreme Court also reviews executive branch decisions—and sometimes strikes them down. The frequency of such rulings falls the higher up the state one goes. Between May 2001 and August 2009, the Supreme Court "checked the legality of 541 edicts of the Federal Cabinet of Ministers and overturned provisions of 85 . . . a 16 percent success rate." This fell to 8 percent in following years (Trochev 2012, p. 22). Overruling the president has always been very rare—between June 2002 and July 2012, the Supreme

Court overturned only two presidential decrees out of sixty-five cases, and both had been passed by Yeltsin in the 1990s. Still, the possibility of such losses affected Putin's actions, at least in the early 2000s. When faced in 2004 with a likely Supreme Court challenge to his right to detain homeless people, he repealed the offending decree (Trochev 2012, pp. 20–21).

The impact of the Russian Constitutional Court and Supreme Court on political decisionmaking has been changing over time. Although these courts have never been truly independent in postcommunist Russia, the early 2000s saw them rule against ministers, and they have continued to overturn many legislative bills. Unfortunately, the recent turn to authoritarianism suggests a further weakening of the role of both courts.

PUTIN'S THIRD TERM

Since Putin's return to the presidency in 2012, a series of counterreforms have entrenched Kremlin control over the legal system and weakened pockets of independence. Most dramatically, Putin merged the regular and *arbitrazh* courts in 2014, subordinating both to a newly beefed-up Supreme Court. The High Arbitrazh Court was reduced to a thirty-member Economic Collegium. At the same time, the powers of the Supreme Court chair were expanded: the term is no longer limited to twelve years, and the chair is basically responsible for appointing and replacing all judges. Putin entrusted this key role to the serving Supreme Court head, Vyacheslav Lebedev, who had been a judge since the 1970s.

The Kremlin claimed that this change was needed to unify the often conflicting practices of the general and *arbitrazh* courts. However, the reform clearly targeted the *arbitrazh* system, always considered to have the fairest, most efficient, and competent judges. Their more modern and democratic procedures came under threat. Meanwhile, the firing of many judges during the reform contradicted the constitutional principle of life tenure and reminded all of their vulnerability.

The real reason for this reform can only be political. Amid economic hard times and the protest movement of 2011–12, the Kremlin sought to domesticate any actors that could potentially threaten its plans. *Arbitrazh* courts, with their high-quality judges, were one of many targets. In creating the enhanced role for the Supreme Court chair, Putin established a pivotal go-between at the top of the judiciary, whom the Kremlin could hold personally responsible for the actions of all judges.

Despite its previous successes, the MIA proved powerless to block another recent reform that stripped it of all its militarized units. In April 2016 Putin announced the creation of a new National Guard, officially to fight terrorism. With about four hundred thousand troops, formed by conscription and contract, this body is, in fact, a second army, subordinate directly to the president. Perhaps as compensation for its losses, the MIA got to absorb both the Federal Drug Control Service and the Federal Migration Service.

The Procuracy, oddly enough, benefited from Putin's latest shake-up, probably because previous reforms had left it too weak to pose any credible threat. On the one hand, the president got to appoint not just the prosecutor general but also the deputy prosecutor generals, bringing the institution even more tightly under Putin's personal direction. On the other hand, Putin returned to it almost all the powers it had lost vis-à-vis the Investigative Committee. Together with several unexpected firings and replacements of prosecutors, this probably served the same purpose as the de-modernizing reorganization of the courts: to disorient all potentially independent groups within the elite.

Finally, the Russian Constitutional Court, rather than constraining the Kremlin, has become its most dependable enabler. The court approved the merger of the Supreme Court and the Higher Arbitrazh Court; the right of the president to appoint 10 percent of the parliament's upper chamber for life; the annexation of Crimea and Sevastopol; legislation requiring nongovernmental organizations that receive foreign funding to register as "foreign agents"; and the law banning propaganda aimed at lesbians, gays, bisexuals, and transsexuals. It has ruled that in certain cases Russia has the right to disregard decisions of international organizations of which it is a member. And it decided that judges, rather than acquitting a defendant, could return cases to the Procuracy to dig up more evidence (Solomon 2015).

Putin's return also halted or reversed most positive trends in the legal statistics, while strengthening the negative ones. In 2015 the total number of criminal convictions increased for the first time in many years (figure 9-2). In 2011–12 more than five thousand people were detained for political reasons after protests in Moscow and adjacent territories. Law enforcement agencies are opening more criminal investigations, requesting pretrial detention for more defendants, and being granted hundreds of thousands of warrants to tap phones and read mail each year (for example, the number of

Figure 9-2   Number of Defendants Found Guilty, All Types of Sentences

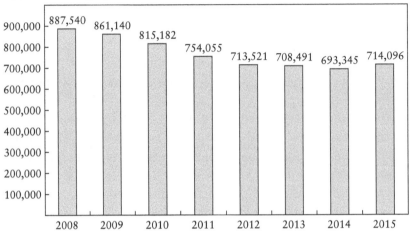

Defendants found guilty

Source: Paneyakh (2016).

permissions for wiretapping granted by courts grew from 117,000 in 2006 to 608,000 in 2015, with 99 percent of requests approved). The number of prison sentences stopped falling—the share of those sentenced to actual jail time has risen by 16 percent since 2012—and the frequency of suspended and other more humane sentences fell (figure 9-3). As of 2015, the prison population was still in slow decline, but only because of an unprecedented amnesty in 2015 to celebrate the seventieth anniversary of the World War II victory, along with another smaller one in 2014 (Paneyakh 2016).[10] If not for these amnesties, the prison population would have grown by 6–7 percent in 2014–15, with an estimated extra thirty thousand prison sentences handed down in 2015 (Paneyakh 2016).

The figures show a startling growth in prosecutions for "extremist" crimes, which increased from 896 in 2013 to 1,024 in 2014 and 1,329 in 2015. Law enforcers were given greater powers, including the right to open

10. We only consider criminal cases of public and private-public prosecution here, excluding private prosecution (about 8 percent of all cases). The reason is that we want to account for activity of the law enforcement system and its interaction with the judicial system. Private prosecution cases, where law enforcement agencies do not have to be involved, are solved by courts in a very different way, with many more acquittals and dismissals of cases by reconciliation (Paneyakh 2014).

Figure 9-3 Shares of Different Judicial Outcomes in Guilty Verdicts

Percent

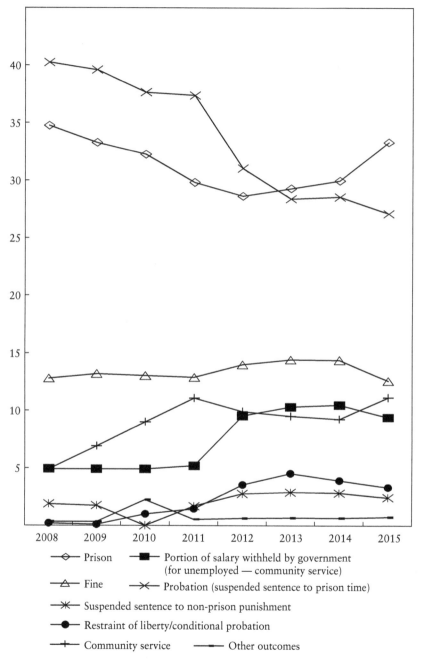

Source: Paneyakh (2016).

Figure 9-4 Dynamics of Acquittal Rates in Russia, 2008–14, Public and Private-Public Accusation

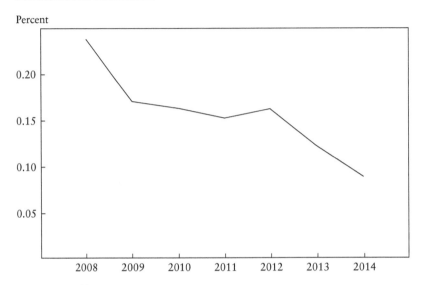

Source: Paneyakh (2015a).

criminal cases on taxation issues without involvement of the tax services. Interrogators won additional leverage to abuse suspects in their charge. The acquittal rate, microscopic to begin with, fell still further between 2012 and 2014 (figure 9-4), as did share of settlements with the injured party, which fell from 16.7 percent of all criminal cases heard by courts in 2012 to 15 percent in 2015.

Courts currently approve 97–99 percent of enforcement agencies' requests to encroach on citizens' privacy, but only 39.5 percent of requests for release on parole (compared with 56 percent in 2011 and 41 percent in 2014). By contrast, only 6 percent of citizens' complaints about the unlawful behavior of law enforcement personnel during criminal investigation were decided by courts in favor of the complainant in 2015.

CONCLUSION

Many Western writers tend to see corruption, business capture, and politicization as the greatest defects of the Russian court and law enforcement systems. In our view, these systems are less corrupt and politicized than usually assumed. Their critical flaw is internal institutions, especially the system of evaluation of employees' performance, which create perverse incentives. The pressure to fulfill quantitative targets and avoid being overruled leads to a conspiracy among the various actors to target the poor and defenseless and cover up the shoddy quality of most legal proceedings.

Despite various attempts at top-down reform over the past twenty-five years, none have succeeded in significantly improving the quality of criminal justice—or, for that matter, reducing corruption and politicization. Indeed, the trend under Putin has been toward consolidating presidential power over the legal system and making further reforms even less feasible. In exchange, the law enforcement agencies were granted a high degree of bureaucratic autonomy and greater power vis-à-vis the courts. As a result, most cases—that is, typical and non-politicized ones—are processed in a way that serves enforcers' interests rather than those of the ruling group or elites in general. The criminal justice system in Russia is not captured by the Kremlin; it is captured by law enforcement agencies themselves.

Throughout the past twenty-five years, the greatest obstacles to reform in this sphere have been the law enforcement bureaucracies themselves, which—for instance, in the 2011 police reform—sought to protect their interests. The resistance of these bureaucracies has checked the power of top decisionmakers, who apparently fear to push the law enforcement chiefs too far and lack instruments for systematic intervention into enforcement agencies' modus operandi on the everyday level. At the same time, the courts—by ruling quite often for citizens in suits against the government, and by sometimes striking down legislation on constitutional grounds—have posed a more significant, albeit limited, constraint than is sometimes recognized. While submissive to the law enforcement agencies in criminal justice (and administrative cases where law enforcement is involved), the courts are far less timid toward civilian government organizations, especially on the local level and in civil cases (and administrative cases where the state is represented by civilian authorities).

That said, some modernization did occur over the past fifteen years. The commercial courts made notable progress; judges overwhelmingly backed citizens in a growing number of suits against state authorities; and humanizing impulses—both in the Kremlin under Medvedev and among many judges—led to a sharp drop in the prison population and to milder sentencing. Yet these impulses were overshadowed in the 2000s by the combination of political opportunism at the top and inertia at the bottom. And since 2012, all positive trends have been frozen or reversed by the campaign to use law enforcement to protect the regime against possible civil unrest. Today, the law enforcement system is the main instrument of Putin's countermodernization.

Why have Russia's leaders settled for less than complete control over the courts? Carlos Menem, the president of Argentina in 1989–99, once asked: "Why should I be the only president in fifty years who hasn't had his own court?" (quoted in Walker 2006, p. 784). All strong leaders in authoritarian and hybrid states would surely like to have "their own courts," and many get them. At the same time, if Russia's political leaders do have some interest in the quality of the legal system, why have they for so long disregarded the perverse incentives at its heart? Why have they done so little to reduce day-to-day corruption?

Our answer is that the status quo we describe here represents a kind of bargain. It serves the Kremlin's interests to have a legal system that—while not dangerously incompetent—is systematically compromised. The political authorities allow the courts and law enforcement autonomy to continue with their flawed everyday routines because this keeps the judges and agents vulnerable to scrutiny. The Kremlin can use the legal system itself to punish any judge or police officer who steps out of line, using the flaws of that system against recalcitrant individuals. Knowing this, legal professionals give the authorities the results they want on rarely occurring politically loaded cases. Russia's leaders may prefer such a system to having completely dependent, rule-governed courts: by forcing judges and bureaucrats to bend or break rules, the Kremlin keeps them vulnerable and loyal, while they remain just as effective instruments of political manipulation.

REFERENCES

Antonova, Natalia. 2012. "The Pussy Riot Trial Exposes a Russian Court System in Crisis." *The Guardian*, July 30.

Balmforth, Tom. 2013. "Putin's Legal Vertical: Kremlin Seeks to Consolidate Court System." Radio Liberty, October 9. www.rferl.org/content/russia-judicial-reform -arbitration-court/25131950.html.

Barber, Lionel, Neil Buckley, and Catherine Belton. 2008. "Laying Down the Law: Medvedev Vows War on Russia's 'Legal Nihilism.'" *Financial Times*, March 24.

Barry, Ellen, and Andrew Roth. 2012. "Punk Band Feels Wrath of a Sterner Kremlin." *New York Times*, July 20.

Bryden, David P., and Sonja Lengnick. 1997. "Rape in the Criminal Justice System." *Journal of Criminal Law and Criminology* 87, no. 4, pp. 1194–384.

Burbank, Jane. 2004. *Russian Peasants Go to Court: Legal Culture in the Countryside, 1905–1917*. Indiana University Press.

Bureau of Democracy, Human Rights, and Labor. 2007. "Country Reports on Human Rights Practices: Russia, 2007." March 11. www.state.gov/j/drl/rls/hrrpt /2007/100581.htm.

Burnham, William, Peter B. Maggs, and Gennady M. Danilenko. 2004. *Law and Legal System of the Russian Federation*. Huntington, N.Y.: Juris Publishing.

Center of Legal and Economic Studies. 2010. "Sotsial'no-ekonomicheskiye posled-stviya ugolovnoy politiki gosudarstva v otnoshenii biznesa [Socio-economic consequences of state criminal policy toward business]." www.lecs-center.org/index .php?option=com_content&view=article&id=162%3Acriminal-policy-report& catid=34&Itemid=29&lang=ru.

Chivers, Christopher J. 2008. "Russia Bars Opposition Candidate from March 2 Ballot." *New York Times*, January 28.

Dmitrieva, Arina, Kirill Titaev, and Irina Chetverikova. 2012. *Russian Arbitrazh (Commercial) Courts: A Statistical Study*. St. Petersburg: Institute for the Rule of Law, The European University at Saint Petersburg.

The Economist. 2008. "A Matter of Judgment." November 27.

Eisenstein, James, and Herbert Jacob. 1977. *Felony Justice: An Organizational Analysis of Criminal Courts*. Boston: Little, Brown.

Elder, Miriam. 2013. "Sergei Magnitsky Verdict 'Most Shameful Moment since Stalin.'" *The Guardian*, July 11.

Favarel-Garrigues, Gilles. 2011. *Policing Economic Crime in Russia: From Soviet Planned Economy to Privatization*. Columbia University Press.

Fedorin, Vladimir. 2008. "Biznes pod pressom [Business under pressure]." *Forbes*, March 3.

Feifer, George. 1964. *Justice in Moscow*. New York: Dell Publishing.

Firestone, Thomas. 2010. "Armed Injustice: Abuse of the Law and Complex Crime in Post-Soviet Russia." *Denver Journal of International Law and Policy* 38, no. 4, pp. 555–80.

Fish, Steven. 2005. *Democracy Derailed in Russia: The Failure of Open Politics*. Cambridge University Press.

Gans-Morse, Jordan. 2012. "Threats to Property Rights in Russia: From Private Coercion to State Aggression." *Post-Soviet Affairs* 28, no. 3, pp. 263–95.

Gilinskiy, Yakov. 2011. "Torture by the Russian Police: An Empirical Study." *Police Practice and Research: An International Journal* 12, no. 2, pp. 163–71.

Gorlizki, Yoran. 1997. "Political Reform and Local Party Interventions under Khrushchev." In *Reforming Justice in Russia, 1864–1996: Power, Culture, and the Limits of Legal Order*, edited by Peter H. Solomon Jr., 256–75. Armonk, N.Y.: M. E. Sharp.

Gudkov, Lev, and Boris Dubin. 2006. "Privatizatsiya policii [Privatization of police]." *Vestnik Obshchestvennogo Mneniya: Dannyye, Analiz, Diskussii* 1, no. 81, pp. 58–71.

Hendley, Kathryn. 2009. "'Telephone Law' and the 'Rule of Law': The Russian Case." *Hague Journal on the Rule of Law* 1, no. 2, pp. 241–62.

————. 2011. "Explaining the Use of Russian Courts." Legal Studies Research Paper 1166. Madison: University of Wisconsin.

————. 2012. "Who Are the Legal Nihilists in Russia?" *Post-Soviet Affairs* 28, no. 2, pp. 149–86.

Judicial Department of the Supreme Court of the Russian Federation. 2006–15. Reports on criminal convictions. www.cdep.ru/index.php?id=79&item=2040.

Khodzhaeva, Ekaterina, and Julia Rabovski. 2015. "Strategii i taktiki advokatov v usloviyah obvinitelinogo uklona v Rossii [Strategies and tactics of criminal defenders in the context of 'accusatorial bias' in Russia]." *Sotsiologiya Vlasti* 27, no. 2, pp. 135–67.

Kotkin, Stephen. 2001. *Armageddon Averted: The Soviet Collapse, 1970–2000.* Oxford University Press.

Lambert-Mogiliansky, Ariane, Konstantin Sonin, and Ekaterina Zhuravskaya. 2007. "Are Russian Commercial Courts Biased? Evidence from a Bankruptcy Law Transplant." *Journal of Comparative Economics* 35, no. 2, pp. 254–77.

Ledeneva, Alena. 2008. "Telephone Justice in Russia." *Post-Soviet Affairs* 24, no. 4, pp. 324–50.

Levada Center. 2015. "Institutsionalnoe doverie [Trust in institutions]." www.levada.ru/2015/10/07/institutsionalnoe-doverie/.

Lipman, Masha. 2009. "Medvedev's Promises on Trial in Russia." *Washington Post*, April 8.

Mastrofski, Stephen D., R. Richard Ritti, and Debra Hoffmaster. 1987. "Organizational Determinants of Police Discretion: The Case of Drinking-Driving." *Journal of Criminal Justice* 15, no. 5, pp. 387–402.

Myers, Steven Lee. 2006. "Putin Fires Prosecutor, Providing Grist for Kremlinologists." *New York Times*, June 3.

Nazrullaeva, Eugenia, Alexey Baranov, and Andrei Yakovlev. 2013. "Criminal Persecution of Business in Russia's Regions: Private Interests vs. 'Stick' System." *Research Projects* 22. Working Paper. Moscow: Higher School of Economics.

Newburg, Paula L. 2000. "Corrupt Elections: What's an NGO to Do about It?" *St. Petersburg Times*, December 8.

Novikova, Asmik. 2011. "Politsiya s mentovskim oskalom [Police with a cop's grin]." *Gazeta.ru*, February 10. www.gazeta.ru/comments/2011/02/10_a_3519594.shtml.

Paneyakh, Ella. 2013. "Zaregulirovannoye gosudarstvo [Regulated state]." *Pro et Contra* 17, nos. 1–2, pp.79–92.

————. 2014. "Faking Performance Together: Systems of Performance Evaluation in Russian Enforcement Agencies and Production of Bias and Privilege." *Post-Soviet Affairs* 30, nos. 2–3, pp. 115–36.

————. 2015a. "Evolyutsiya rossiyskoy sudebnoy sistemy v 2014 godu [Evolution of Russian judicial system in 2014]." *Counterpoint*, no. 1. www.counter-point.org /эволюция-российской-судебной-систем/.

————. 2015b. "The Practical Logic of Judicial Decision Making: Discretion under Pressure and Compromises at the Expense of the Defendant." *Russian Politics and Law* 54, nos. 2–3, pp. 138–63.

———. 2016. "Sudy I pravookhranitelnye organy: repressivnoe pravoprimenenie [Courts and law enforcement agencies: Repressive law enforcement]." In *Politicheskoye razvitiye Rossii, 2014–2016: instituty i praktiki avtoritarnoĭ konsolidatsii* [Political development of Russia, 2014–2016: Institutions and practices of authoritarian modernization], edited by Kirill Rogov, pp. 154–64. Moscow: Fund "Liberalnaya Missiya." http://liberal.ru/upload/files/Prakticheskoe_razivitie_Rossii.pdf.

Pastukhov, Vladimir. 2002. "Law under Administrative Pressure in Post-Soviet Russia." *East European Constitutional Review* 11, no. 3, pp. 66–74.

Peerenboom, Randall. 2002. *China's Long March toward Rule of Law.* Cambridge University Press.

Procuracy. 2015. *Crime Rate in Russia: January–December 2015.* http://genproc.gov.ru/upload/iblock/d07/0112_2015.pdf.

Reevell, Patrick. 2014. "Legislation Merging Russia's 2 Top Courts Stokes Worries." *New York Times,* February 6.

Remington, Thomas. 2011. *The Politics of Inequality in Russia.* Cambridge University Press.

———. 2015. *Politics in Russia.* New York: Routledge.

Rochlitz, Michael. 2014. "Corporate Raiding and the Role of the State in Russia." *Post-Soviet Affairs* 30, nos. 2–3, pp. 89–114.

Rose, Richard. 2009. *Understanding Post-Communist Transformation: A Bottom-Up Approach.* London: Routledge.

Rosstat. 2015. *Number of State Employees at the Federal and Local Level of the Russian Federation.* www.gks.ru/wps/wcm/connect/rosstat_main/rosstat/ru/statistics/state/.

Satarov, Georgii, ed. 2006. "Corruption Process in Russia: Level, Structure, Trends." In *Diagnostics of Corruption in Russia: 2001–2005.* INDEM Foundation. www.indem.ru/en/Publicat/2005diag_engV.htm.

Schwirtz, Michael. 2009. "New Trial for Tycoon Is a Test for Russia." *New York Times,* March 5.

Sharlet, Robert S. 1977. "Stalinism and Soviet Legal Culture." In *Stalinism: Essays in Historical Interpretation,* edited by Robert C. Tucker. New York: W. W. Norton.

Solomon, Peter H., Jr. 1987. "The Case of the Vanishing Acquittal: Informal Norms and the Practice of Soviet Criminal Justice." *Europe-Asia Studies* 39, no. 4, pp. 531–55.

———. 2004. "Judicial Power in Russia: Through the Prism of Administrative Justice." *Law and Society Review* 38, no. 3, pp. 549–82.

———. 2005. "The Criminal Procedure Code of 2001: Will It Make Russian Justice More Fair?" In *Ruling Russia: Law, Crime, and Justice in a Changing Society,* edited by William Pridemore, pp. 77–100. Lanham, Md.: Rowan and Littlefield.

———. 2008. "Assessing the Courts in Russia: Parameters of Progress under Putin." *Demokratizatsiya* 16, no. 1, pp. 63–73.

———. 2015. "Understanding the History of Soviet Criminal Justice: The Contribution of Archives and Other Sources." *Russian Review* 74, no. 3, pp. 401–18.

Taylor, Brian D. 2014. "The Police Reform in Russia: Policy Process in a Hybrid Regime." *Post-Soviet Affairs* 30, nos. 2–3, pp. 226–55.

Titaev, Kirill, and Maria Shkliaruk. 2015. "Investigators in Russia: Who Creates Practice in the Investigation of Criminal Cases?" *Russian Politics and Law* 54, nos. 2–3, pp. 112–37.

Transparency International. 2008. *Annual Report 2007*. www.transparency.org /whatwedo/publication/transparency_international_annual_report_2007.

Trochev, Alexei. 2008. *Judging Russia: The Role of the Constitutional Court in Russian Politics, 1990–2006*. Cambridge University Press.

———. 2012. "Suing Russia at Home." *Problems of Post-Communism* 59, no. 5, pp. 18–34.

Trochev, Alexei, and Rachel Ellett. 2014. "Judges and Their Allies: Rethinking Judicial Autonomy through the Prism of Off-Bench Resistance." *Journal of Law and Courts* 2, no. 1, pp. 67–91.

Tsukanova, Liubov. 2002. "Few Guarantees on Elections." *Novoe Vremya*, June 23. www.eng.yabloko.ru/Publ/2002/papers/nv-230602.html.

Volkov, Vadim. 1999. "Violent Entrepreneurship in Post-Communist Russia." *Europe-Asia Studies* 51, no. 5, pp. 741–54.

———. 2002. *Violent Entrepreneurs: The Use of Force in the Making of Russian Capitalism*. Cornell University Press.

———2012. *Silovoe predprinimatelstvo, XXI vek: ekonomiko-sotsiologicheskiy analiz* [Violent entrepreneurship, twenty-first century: Economic and sociological analysis]. 3rd ed., corrected and extended. European University at Saint Petersburg Publishing House.

———. 2014. "Socioeconomic Status and Sentencing Disparities: Evidence from Russia's Criminal Courts." Working paper. St. Petersburg: Institute for the Rule of Law, The European University at Saint Petersburg.

Volkov, Vadim, and Elena Dmitrieva. 2015. "Istochniki rekrutirovaniya, gender i professional'nyye subkul'tury v rossiyskoy sudebnoy sisteme [Sources of recruitment, gender and professional subcultures in the Russian court system]." *Sociologia Vlasti* 27, no. 2, pp. 94–134.

Volkov, Vadim, Ella Paneyakh, and Kirill Titaev. 2010a. "Proizvolnaya aktivnost pravookhranitelnykh organov v sfere borby s ekonomicheskoy prestupnostyu [Arbitrary activities of law enforcement authorities in the sphere of combating economic crime]." St. Petersburg: Institute for the Rule of Law, The European University at Saint Petersburg.

———. 2010b. "Reforma MVD v Rossii: Chetyre problemy i vosem mer po ikh resheniyu [Reform of the Ministry of Internal Affairs in Russia: Four issues and eight ways of tackling them]." St. Petersburg: Institute for the Rule of Law, The European University at Saint Petersburg.

Volkov, Vadim, and others, eds. 2012. *Kak sudyi prinimayut resheniya* [How judges make decisions]. Extra Jus. Moscow: Statut.

Walker, Christopher J. 2006. "Toward Democratic Consolidation? The Argentine Supreme Court, Judicial Independence, and the Rule of Law." *Florida Journal of International Law* 18, no. 3, pp. 745–806.

Woo, Margaret Y. K., and Yaxin Wang. 2005. "Civil Justice in China: An Empirical Study of Courts in Three Provinces." *American Journal of Comparative Law* 53, no. 4, pp. 911–40.

Yakovlev, Andrei, and Anton Kazun. 2015. "Advokatskoye soobshchestvo i kachestvo pravoprimeneniya v Rossii [Attorneys' community and quality of law enforcement in Russia]." *Ekonomicheskaya Politika* 10, no. 5, pp. 7–37.

Yakovlev, Andrei, Anton Kazun, and Anton Sobolev. 2014. "Means of Production versus Means of Coercion: Can Russian Business Limit the Violence of a Predatory State?" *Post-Soviet Affairs* 30, nos. 2–3, pp. 171–94.

Zagorets, Yaroslav. 2009. "God menta [Year of the cop]." *Lenta.ru*, December 30. http://lenta.ru/articles/2009/12/30/finalmilitia.

Zhang, Xin. 2010. "Scramble for Control: Market, Law, and Corporate Property Conflicts in Russia." Ph.D. dissertation, University of California, Los Angeles.

TEN

Civic and Political Activism in Russia

ANTON SOBOLEV and ALEXEI ZAKHAROV

What role have civic and political activism played in Russian political de-cisionmaking over the past twenty-five years? What role do they play today? By civic and political activism, we mean the actions of citizens who organize to pursue collective and humanitarian goals or to demand changes in state policy. Civic activists focus mainly on social issues (including local affairs, ecology, human rights, and the defense of vulnerable social groups), while political activists aim to change both government policies and, often, government personnel. At times, they may seek to participate in political institutions themselves, either to accomplish policy objectives or to advance their own careers. (We exclude from both categories registered political parties and state-organized structures—although, of course, civic and po-litical activists may interact with such bodies.)

A common opinion among scholars is that civil society in Russia is weak and that this constitutes an obstacle to the development of democracy. To quote Debra Javeline and Sarah Lindemann-Komarova (2010, p. 173): "Most western analyses offer comparable assessments of Russian civil society as browbeaten and unable to play a meaningful role in mediating between individual interests and the state." The perceived weakness of civil society is attributed to a variety of causes—from the cultural legacies of imperial and Soviet Russia, which have supposedly left Russians atomized and distrustful (Rose 2000; Howard 2002; Flynn 2006; Ledeneva 2008), to the authoritarian repression of the current regime (Evans, Henry, and Sundstrom 2006; McFaul and Treyger 2004). As a result, political leaders are today unconstrained—and their policies unaffected—by those who represent particular social interests.[1]

We examine the evidence and argue that this view does not offer a full picture of Russian civil society. Russians are not more distrustful than citizens of comparable countries; trust has been trending upward in recent years, and its short-term volatility is inconsistent with the view that it is determined by distant historical experiences. The evidence does suggest a low level of civic participation after the end of communism—in part because membership in the discredited Communist Party and pro forma membership in official labor unions were not quickly replaced by other involvements—but we also note an apparent increase in civic activity in the past five years, despite the tightening of political controls. At the same time, nongovernmental organizations (NGOs) have improved their capacity to mobilize supporters and volunteers and to raise cash through contributions. We show that in two key regards—the petitioning of officials at all levels of the state and election monitoring—Russian citizens have affected political outcomes and policy decisions, albeit to a limited extent. Indeed, the rise of civic and political activism recently explains why the authorities have reached for more repressive responses.

RUSSIA'S "WEAK" CIVIL SOCIETY

Decades of communist rule, preceded by centuries of autocracy in a peasant society, are thought by various scholars to have hampered the formation of trust and social capital in Russia. That, in turn, prevented the emergence of a Western-style civil society after the Soviet collapse. Consequently, scholars argue, political leaders—and especially the executive branch—are unconstrained by NGOs and other civic groups, and the political opposition is

---

1. Some studies are less skeptical about the role and perspectives of civic activism in Russia. See, for example, Gibson (2001); Javeline and Lindemann-Komarova (2010); Aron (2012, 2013); Greene (2014); Salamon, Benevolenski, and Jakobson (2015).

unstructured and weak. After coming to power, Vladimir Putin systematically clamped down on any civic or political activism, destroying even that little which did exist (see, for example, Evans, Henry, and Sundstrom 2006).

Although many Russia experts agree on this image of weakness, they differ on its causes. Some emphasize characteristics of Russian society, others implicate the state. Taking society-focused explanations first, a common claim is that generalized trust is too low in Russia to support a vibrant civic sphere. Centuries of harsh imperial rule and then communist dictatorship have supposedly left citizens mutually suspicious and fearful of being exploited if they contribute to collective endeavors. Not just Western scholars but many leaders of Russian NGOs themselves give similar explanations for the paucity of civic activism (Evans 2002). Russians are slow to join NGOs because of the discrediting of such organizations under communist rule, when citizens were forced to "volunteer" in state-run bodies that maintained a façade of independence, such as professional organizations (Howard 2002). Private networks of family and friends reduce the need for—and crowd out—formal organizations (Howard 2002; Flynn 2006; Ledeneva 2008). Finally, the social stratification between Soviet elites and the rest persisted into the 1990s and beyond, resulting in "hourglass"-shaped social networks, with few connections between the state and population at large (Rose 2000).

Other scholars view Russian NGOs as distorted by the influx of foreign aid, which created competition for the flow of dollars and entrenched "patron-client ties between donors and recipients rather than horizontal networks of civic engagement among Russian NGOs and their domestic audience" (Henderson 2002, p. 139; Sundstrom 2006). Russia's extreme size is also seen as an obstacle to successful civic activities. With enormous, sparsely populated territories, Russia's geography constitutes a challenge for forming nationwide groups of any kind. Political protests tend to be larger and more frequent in large cities than in rural communities.

Besides arguments that focus on society, some blame the Russian state for blocking the growth of civic organization. Michael McFaul and Elina Treyger (2004, p. 136) argue that the Putin regime's policies to curb international funding and suppress independent groups and media are responsible. Samuel Greene (2014), while skeptical about the impact of repression, finds that Putin's success in demobilizing activists can be partially attributed to co-optation. In 2001 Putin convened a civic forum, "including 4,000 NGO representatives from around the country" (Greene 2014, p. 103) and later he created national and regional public chambers—permanent bodies of NGO representatives. The civic activists involved in these chambers became dependent on funds provided by the authorities, which may have softened their criticism of the country's leadership (see also Evans 2008).

Others point to the role of the state in controlling the media and thus preventing citizens from converting private grievances into public ones: "In the absence of such information, individual grievances remain too compartmentalized to fuel collective action" (Pfaff and Kim 2003, p. 408; Greene 2014, p. 51; Oates 2006; Mickiewicz 2008). Greene (2014) argues, meanwhile, that the Russian state's very unpredictability forestalls the emergence of civil society, since civic campaigns face a constantly changing pattern of state intrusions.

Other sources paint a more complicated picture. Russian civil society is functional, while motivations for civic participation are evolving (Aron 2012, 2013). While the government is hostile to some types of civic groups, partnership relations with other types of NGOs exist (Salamon, Benevolenski, and Jakobson 2015). The models of interaction with state authorities are also heterogeneous and subject to change (Salmenniemi 2010).

IS RUSSIA SHORT ON TRUST?

Are Russians less trusting than people elsewhere in the world? One way to assess that is to use the responses to a standard survey question that has been asked in many countries: "Generally speaking, would you say that most people can be trusted or that you need to be very careful in dealing with people?" Between 2010 and 2014, the World Values Survey (WVS) posed this question to representative samples of the populations of sixty countries. Figure 10-1 shows the proportion of respondents who said that, generally speaking, "most people could be trusted" plotted against the proportion of respondents who said that they participated in at least one social, civic, or political group. Focusing first on just countries' positions on the horizontal scale, which measures trust, we see that Russians are by no means unusually suspicious. In fact, the country is slightly above average on trust: 27.8 percent of Russians thought that most people could be trusted, compared to 23.2 percent in the average country surveyed. The proportion of Russians who trusted others was higher than that in Poland, Spain, or South Korea.

Figure 10-1 Trust and Civic Involvement in Different Countries, Based on Group

Percent of members of at least one group

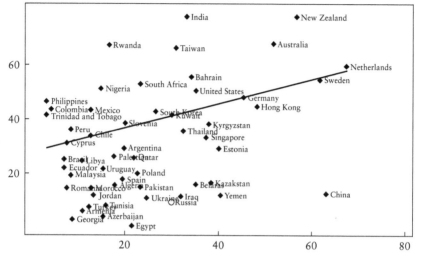

Percent agreeing most people can be trusted

Source: World Values Survey / European Values Survey. Groups include educational or music organizations; labor unions; political parties; environmental, sport, or recreational organizations; and professional associations.

How has the level of trust—measured in this way—changed over time? Available evidence suggests that trust in Russia fell sharply during the early 1990s. There is no agreement on the dynamics, but data suggest that trust began to recover in the late 1990s and rose through the 2000s. Trust appears to have dipped in 2009, but to have subsequently recovered (see figure 10-2).

The dynamics of trust closely resemble the trend in Russia's economy, and research suggests that it was indeed the economic crises of the 1990s and then 2009 that reduced Russians' confidence in the honesty of their peers.[2] The relationship seems particularly clear around the 2009 crash. Our data on this come from the Public Opinion Foundation (FOM). FOM

2. In particular, Maxim Ananyev and Sergei Guriev (2016) find that the decline in trust between 2008 and 2009 was larger in regions with a big share of heavy industry that were harder hit by the 2009 economic crisis. One possible explanation is that economic crises cause people to become more risk averse and therefore less willing to give their peers the benefit of the doubt.

Figure 10-2   Interpersonal Trust in Russia

Percent agreeing most people can be trusted

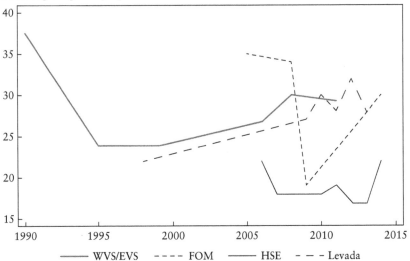

Sources: World Values Survey / European Values Survey (WVS/EVS); Public Opinion Foundation (FOM); Higher School of Economics (HSE) Center for Studies of Civil Society and the Nonprofit Sector; Levada Center.

posed a question about trust—allowing for more differentiated answers than the WVS—to nationwide samples in four waves of surveys (2005, 2008, 2009, and 2014).[3] The proportion who agreed "completely" or "somewhat" that most people could be trusted fell from 36.4 percent in 2005 to 33.5 percent in 2008, and 18.9 percent in 2009, before rebounding to 29.5 percent in 2014.

Moreover, reactions to the economic crisis and the decline in trust were much larger and more persistent for younger birth cohorts. Among those born in the 1980s, the percentage saying others could generally be trusted fell by almost 10 percentage points between 2005 and 2014; among those

3. The study asked the following question: "Some people say that people can be trusted, while others think that one should be careful with people. Which of these two opinions—the first one or second one—do you agree with?" There were five possible answers: "Definitely the first one," "The first one rather than the second one," "The second one rather than the first one," "Definitely the second one," or "Can't tell." The variable was set to 1 for the first two answers, to 0 for the second two answers, and to missing for the final answer.

Figure 10-3   Trust during Different Years, for Different Birth Cohorts

Percent agreeing most people can be trusted

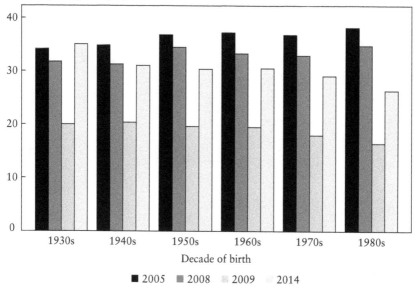

Decade of birth

■ 2005   ■ 2008   2009   2014

Source: FOM.

born in the 1930s, trust was actually slightly higher in 2014 than in 2005 (see figure 10-3). In 2005 the 1980–89 cohort was the most trusting age group, and those born in 1930–39 the least trusting; by 2014 this pattern had reversed.

The plunge in trust among the young during the crisis raises concerns given the findings of various scholars that attitudes acquired in youth can last for life. Indeed, some have found that economic conditions in early adulthood have a persistent impact on an individual's subsequent values and beliefs.[4] Besides age—which had a changing effect—income and higher education consistently correlated with higher trust. Somewhat surprisingly, levels of trust were higher in large cities (with population above one million) than in small towns and rural areas.

4. Alberto F. Alesina and Paola Giuliano (2009), Giuliano and Antonio Spilimbergo (2014), and Yotam Margalit (2013) all show that adverse economic experiences can have an impact on social capital and political preferences.

Figure 10-4   Interpersonal Trust and GDP in Russia, Compared to Other Countries

GDP per capita, constant 2010 U.S. dollars

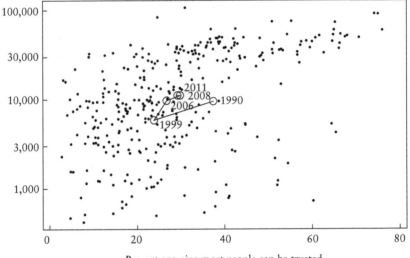

Percent agreeing most people can be trusted

Sources: World Values Survey / European Values Survey; World Bank, 1980–2014. Three hundred thirty-three observations from 100 countries. Russian data shown for 1990, 1999, 2006, 2008, and 2011.

In sum, Russia does not have a particularly low level of interpersonal trust for a middle-income country; indeed, Russians trust each other more than citizens in some more economically developed countries. The level of trust has changed significantly over the past twenty-five years, most likely in response to economic performance, with booms building social capital and crises eroding it; across all countries, higher levels of trust are generally characteristic of more economically developed countries, although the relationship is not perfect, and the cause-and-effect mechanism remains poorly understood (see figure 10-4 for dynamics of interpersonal trust and per capita GDP in Russia, compared to other countries).

While economic conditions may have long-lasting effects on people in early adulthood, these findings are not at all consistent with the conventional view that trust is determined by deeply rooted historical and cultural factors and that Russia's legacies from Soviet communism and even the imperial era rule out a civic path of development.

IS RUSSIA SHORT ON CIVIC PARTICIPATION?

Although Russians are not unusually distrustful, the rate of participation in social, civic, and political groups that they report on the WVS is today somewhat low. The WVS asks respondents whether they are members of a range of types of organizations. Since 1990, the survey has consistently asked about participation in sport or recreational groups; art, music, or educational organizations; labor unions; political parties; environmental organizations; and professional associations. We calculate the proportion that said they were members of at least one of these. In the 2010–14 wave, Russia came forty-ninth out of the sixty countries surveyed, with 18.5 percent of those respondents who answered the question saying that they were members of at least one of the named groups (see figure 10-1).

As figure 10-1 shows, there is a positive association between higher trust and participation. However, participation in Russia is lower than that predicted from trust alone; based on their level of trust, Russians should be participating more actively. We need to seek other explanations.

The level of participation has changed over time. Judging by the WVS, it appears that Russians belonged to fewer and fewer organizations in the 1990s. The proportion of respondents who said they were members of the groups listed above fell from 69 percent in 1990 to 45 percent in 1995, and then to 16 percent in 2008, before reaching 18.5 percent in 2011 (figure 10-5). However, this mostly reflected the very high membership in the old Communist Party and in Soviet-era "labor unions." The first of these disappeared along with the Soviet order; membership in the second was never truly voluntary and declined when quitting became easy. Excluding parties and labor unions, group membership changed from 13.3 percent in 1990 to 7 percent in 1999, and 9.8 percent in 2011.

Several points follow from this. First, as of the early 1990s, Russia did not have a particularly low participation rate. Indeed, with 69 percent of respondents saying that they belonged to at least one of the named groups, Russia was the second highest out of the eleven countries where the WVS asked these questions. However, this was due to pressures to participate in communist organizations in the old Soviet system. Excluding membership in labor unions and political parties, Russia had the second-lowest participation rate—above Turkey's and a little below Spain's.

Although Russia's participation rate in 2008 was higher than those of Hungary, Bulgaria, Romania, Turkey, and Portugal, it remained below

Figure 10-5 Trust and Civic Participation in Russia

Percent who belong to at least one group

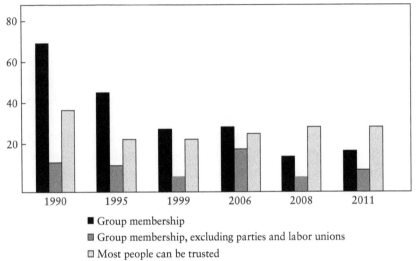

■ Group membership
▨ Group membership, excluding parties and labor unions
☐ Most people can be trusted

Source: World Values Survey / European Values Survey. Groups include educational or music organizations; labor unions; political parties; environmental, sport, or recreational organizations; and professional associations.

average among the countries surveyed. Yet, here again, a caveat is needed. The last iteration of the WVS survey in Russia occurred in 2011. And some evidence suggests that some forms of civic activity—after declining markedly as the global financial crisis sent Russia's economy crashing—increased in subsequent years.

One such form of civic activity is the collective management and oversight of multi-apartment buildings, in which a majority of the urban Russian population resides.[5] Most residential buildings are maintained by state-assigned utility companies, but various oversight decisions (and ultimately the decision to change utility companies) can be made if a residential council is convened. A residential council can also vote to form a housing association that requires a more regular involvement on the part of residents; the

5. According to PropertyExperts.ru, private accommodations made up 80 percent of the housing stock in 2013. http://propertyexperts.ru/info/115-skolko-kvartir -privatizirovano-v-moskve.html.

Table 10-1. *Rates of Civic Participation*

Which of the following did you do within the past year?	Percent
Took part in *subbotnik* (community work)	24
Took part in residential council meetings	20
Voiced my opinion on meetings and state institutions	6
Petitioned state institutions over a personal matter	6
Took part in a collective action helping people in a difficult life situation	5
Signed a collective petition to a state institution over a nonpersonal matter	4
Organized a group to solve a personal or nonpersonal problem	4
Took part in public hearings	3
Participated in an NGO	2
Voluntarily took part in a protest action, rally, or picket	2
Voluntarily took part in a peaceful demonstration	2
None of the above	57

Source: Mersiyanova and Korneeva (2013).

number of such associations shot up in the mid-2000s—from about ten thousand in 2004 to almost sixty thousand in 2010.[6]

Another popular type of collective activity consists of participation in a *subbotnik*—a neighborhood action that usually involves cleaning garbage, landscaping, or other community service. Two sociologists who conducted a representative survey of Russians in 2013 found that 20 percent had participated in residential council meetings and 24 percent had taken part in a *subbotnik* (see table 10-1). Table 10-1 also shows rates of participation in a variety of other civic and political activities.

Participation on a regular, more institutionalized basis is rarer. For example, while up to 20 percent of Russians may have taken part in residential council meetings (which often require a majority of homeowners to be present to arrive at some decision), only 4.3 percent indicated that they had participated in the initiative groups that usually organize such meetings. Table 10-2 reports participation rates for some types of organizations.

In another indicator of civic consciousness, a large share of Russians report making donations to those in need. In one survey, 31 percent said they had given cash handouts in the street within the past year, and 17 percent

6. See Polishchuk, Borisova, and Peresetsky (2010).

Table 10-2. *Voluntary Participation in Organizations*

In which organizations did you voluntarily, and without compensation, participate within the past year?	Percent
Labor unions	6.7
Municipal/street/residential councils, local initiative groups	4.3
Parents' groups	3.7
Sport, tourism, hunter, auto groups/clubs	3.0
School/student self-governing bodies	2.7
Cultural/environmental movements and initiative groups	2.3
Charity funds/organizations	2.0
Religious communes/organizations	1.5
Veterans organizations	1.3
Political parties	1.3
Associations of people with disabilities	1.0
Other	2.3
None/can't remember	75.0

Source: Mersiyanova and Korneeva (2013).

had donated personal items. The proportion reporting having made such contributions has remained stable over the past decade, while giving money has become more popular than giving personal items. At the same time, the popularity of institutionalized donations, such as those made through charity funds, has remained low, at some 6 percent (Volkov and Goncharov 2014), while the number of people who have taken part in organizing such efforts is smaller still (table 10-2).

One way to gauge the extent of civic activity in Russia is to look at how the number of registered civic organizations has changed over time. We collected information on all noncommercial organizations that had ever been included in the official registry of NGOs by the Ministry of Justice. As of early 2016, the list contained about 256,000 such organizations, of which approximately 148,000 were still operative. Among the roughly 50 percent of groups whose mission we could identify, trade unions, religious groups, and sports groups predominated, along with charitable organizations and business associations. In addition, almost 7 percent were organizations of army, police, and special services veterans. Human rights and environmental groups appeared much less common (slightly more than 1 percent).

The overall dynamics of registered NGOs have remained stable during the past twenty years. The Ministry of Justice registers around ninety-five hundred new NGOs—and liquidates six thousand—each year. However, the characteristics of newly created and liquidated organizations have changed over time. In the 1990s the majority of new organizations consisted of trade unions, business associations, and religious organizations. By the end of 2015, the composition of Russia's third sector had become much more diverse, with sport and charity organizations recording the highest rates of new openings.

While the overall rate of NGO liquidations has also remained stable, two important patterns have emerged since 2011. First, almost one quarter of all liquidations after 2011 were due to court decisions—compared to no more than 1 percent in previous years. This most likely reflects the impact of new anti-NGO legislation, including the laws on "foreign agents" and "undesirable organizations" discussed below. Second, human rights organizations as well as ecological ones proved four times more likely than others to close.

Those organizations that survive today increasingly fund themselves either from private contributions or from the increased flow of Russian government funds (federal, regional, and local). Some—especially charities—can use crowdfunding to raise money for particular high-profile projects. Few receive money from abroad—in one 2015 survey of 850 NGOs, only 2 percent reported having received funds from foreign nonbusiness sources; however, this percentage is much higher for environmental and human rights organizations.

Why do some Russians participate in civic and political activities? According to one study, Russians become active in order to defend their rights and to communicate with like-minded individuals. Those who did not participate most often said that this was because they did not believe collective civic action would achieve anything. Far fewer gave as a reason a lack of trust in social and political institutions or leaders, while a small minority of respondents feared for their personal safety.

A data set containing information about more than nine thousand people in nine Russian regions, collected in 2011 by the Higher School of Economics Laboratory for Comparative Social Research, offers hints about what types of individuals participate most in a range of civic activities. Characteristics that correlated with more civic activity included interest in politics, urban residence, higher education, greater national pride, and being a student. Retirees were notably less active in civic causes.

Even those who do not participate are often aware of civil society. Over 80 percent of respondents had heard of some locally organized civic group or initiative within the past three years. But the focus is local: very few organizations achieve national recognition.[7] The single best-known NGO is the Committee of Soldier's Mothers, an organization that aims to defend the rights of Russian army conscripts; 29 percent of people surveyed said they "knew well" about this group. It was followed, with 8 percent, by City without Drugs, a Yekaterinburg-based NGO dedicated to helping police fight the drug trade and rehabilitating drug addicts.

Public interest in civic activities can be measured using Google search data. Google allows one to calculate an index of "interest over time" for each search term, which shows how the frequency of searches for that term has varied over the past twelve years. Specifically, the index measures the number of searches (within Russia, in our case) for the given term in the given month, as a percentage of the highest monthly search volume for that term (within Russia) in the period since 2004 (that is, volume in the peak month is normalized to 100).[8] We classify all practices (and corresponding search terms) as formal (involving various degrees of interaction with the state) or informal. In the formal category, we include "registration of NGOs," "registration of housing associations," "public hearings," and "petitions." All these activities involve interaction with state agencies. Among informal practices, we include "donate money," "donate organ," "donate blood," "help animal shelter," and "become volunteer."

Figure 10-6a shows the time trends in the popularity of these topics. Searches involving "registration of NGOs" and "housing associations" peaked in 2004–07 and gradually declined thereafter. Indicators for "petitioning" and "public hearings" have gone the other way, increasing since 2004 and reaching a maximum in recent years. In particular, public interest in petitions has grown very significantly. We return (in the section "Strategies of Civic Activism") to the question of what explains the striking increase in interest in petitioning in 2016.

Figure 10-6b shows trends in public interest toward informal civic practices. On average, the frequency of these requests has increased fivefold,

---

7. The failure of many NGOs to reach the general public was noted by several scholars (Crotty 2009; Lyall 2006). For some, the problem may have been exacerbated by the reliance on Western donors, leading to more centralized decisionmaking and the prioritization of donor interests over broad public appeal (Richter 2002).

8. Unfortunately, at the time of this writing Google search data did not allow us to compare the relative interest in different terms at a given time.

Figure 10-6   Public Interest in Civic Activities[a]

Public interest index

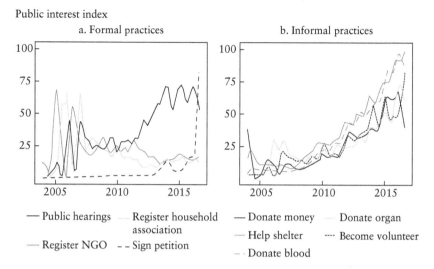

a. Formal practices

b. Informal practices

— Public hearings   — Register household association

— Register NGO   – – Sign petition

— Donate money   — Donate organ

— Help shelter   ···· Become volunteer

— Donate blood

Source: Google Trends data.

a. Graphs show frequency of Google searches (within Russia) for the given term in the given month as a percentage of the frequency of searches for that term in the peak month for that term since 2004. (Thus, levels for one term cannot be compared to those for others.) Series are smoothed, so the peaks at 100 do not show.

reaching a maximum in 2016. Some local peaks in the data can be linked to specific events. In particular, the peaks in "volunteering" searches in 2010 and 2013 correspond to a wave of severe forest fires in the summer of 2010 and to the Student Olympic Games of 2013, respectively.[9]

The growing interest in volunteering, making donations, attending public hearings, and signing petitions—as suggested by the pattern of Internet searches—is consistent with the spread of post-materialist values, which tends to occur as countries modernize.[10] From around 2008 on, Russians appear to have become more interested in contributing to society, building community, and improving their immediate environments. However, we see a divide between less institutionalized forms of civic behavior—which were apparently spreading—and more institutionalized

9. A related study by Sergei Guriev and Nikita Melnikov (2016) finds that interest in several civic practices—in particular, blood donations—was driven by the ongoing conflict in the Donbass region of Ukraine.

10. Inglehart (1997).

forms, which have remained relatively stable and, in some cases, stagnated. This is especially true regarding participation in, and registration of, NGOs. The main reason for this change is probably the increasing state pressure, reporting requirements, and restrictions on these (as we discuss later in the chapter).[11]

IS RUSSIA SHORT ON PROTESTING?

Russians are believed to be reluctant to join social movements or participate in mass protests (Greene 2014). Some survey evidence supports this. According to data from the WVS in 2004–09, only 12 percent of Russians reported that they had ever participated in a lawful demonstration, compared to 20.5 percent for member countries of the Organization for Economic Cooperation and Development.

Since the end of the Soviet era, Russia has witnessed several large-scale protest events: waves of anticommunist demonstrations in the early 1990s, protests against the substitution of cash transfers for in-kind benefits (*monetizatsya l'got*) in 2004–05, and rallies following parliamentary and presidential elections in 2011–12. These three waves gathered hundreds of thousands of participants in total and were widely covered in the Russian and international press. Though these campaigns had different goals, each was either directly connected to economic issues (such as *monetizatsya l'got*) or followed an economic crisis. Indeed, the Levada Center polls reveal that the share of Russians considering joining protests peaks at times of economic turmoil (figure 10-7a). From one-fourth to one-third of respondents considered that they might take to the streets during the financial crises of 1998 and 2008–09.[12]

According to surveys, citizens' willingness to protest declined over the past twenty years (see figure 10-7a), with the share of people considering taking part in mass protest actions falling from 25 to 15 percent, although with some zigzags along the way. Systematic data on the occurrence of protests, available only since 2007 (figure 10-7b), generally match the poll data

---

11. Most of the Russian civic activists we interviewed in 2015–16 for this project did not believe that officially registering an NGO is a viable option, preferring to operate unregistered to avoid potential legal issues.

12. The Levada Center's data on participation in protests with political goals are available for a shorter period and basically reproduce the same pattern.

Figure 10-7a Protest Sentiment of Russians

Percent of respondents

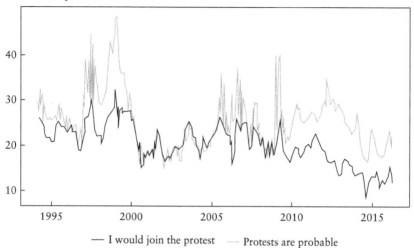

— I would join the protest — Protests are probable

Source: Levada Center (www.levada.ru/2016/05/04/protestnyj-potentsial-3).

Figure 10-7b Number of Protests in Russia

Protests by quartile

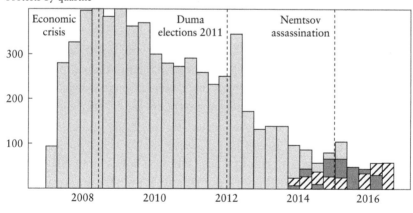

Site: ☑ Activatica.org ☐ NaMarsh.ru ■ PoliticalActions.info

Source: Authors' calculations based on news reports on protest activity from Activatica.org, NaMarsh.ru, and PoliticalActions.info.

for this period.[13] The number of protests peaks around the economic crisis of 2008–09 and then falls from eleven hundred in 2009 to one hundred in 2015.[14]

There are also significant changes in protest turnout. Most of the collective protests of 2008–09 were small, gathering around a hundred participants on average. In contrast, the overall protest turnout of 2011–12 was around 1 million, suggesting an average number of thirteen hundred participants per demonstration. However, protest turnout has fallen almost to zero since 2013.[15] Indeed, the data in figure 10-7b suggest that the surge in urban protests after the 2011 election was just an aberration around a consistent downward trend. Tomila Lankina's (2015) estimates of protest turnout in Russia between 2007 and 2013 also support this interpretation.

Data on search requests for the Russian words *"miting"* (political rally) and *"protest"* (protest) are not consistent with the downward trend in actual participation in demonstrations since 2008 (figure 10-7c). Searches for *"miting"* appear to trend up slightly from 2008 to 2016, with a huge spike at the time of the urban protest wave of 2011–12, and smaller spikes in early 2014—perhaps associated with certain antiwar rallies at that time—and 2016. Searches for *"protest"* trend upward until about 2013, with spikes in the global economic crisis and then in 2013; however, as in English, the word could also refer to non-collective acts such as letters of protest or personal expressions of protest.

Several processes may have contributed to the downward trend in protests—although not necessarily in interest in them—since 2009. Among the elderly, some survey data suggest that greater economic well-being and, perhaps, the rise in aggressive pro-regime propaganda, may have reduced

---

13. Here we use a data set constructed from the 7,464 protest events reports from the websites NaMarsh.ru, Activatica.org, and PoliticalActions.info.

14. In this chapter we use data on collective protest actions, including meetings, demonstrations, and pickets. Some scholars have used a broader sampling of events collected by the Center of Social and Labor Rights, which also includes strikes and work disruptions. The trend in these is not identical. Overall labor conflict activities (including, for example, work stoppages and individual hunger strikes) increased from 241 per year (on average in 2008–14) to 409 in 2015.

15. Authors' calculations based on data from NaMarsh.ru and Lankina (2015, p. 39).

Figure 10-7c Russian Interest Using *"Miting"* (Political Rally) and *"Protest"* (Protest), as Reflected in Google Searches[a]

Public interest index

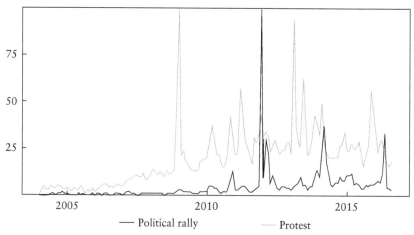

Source: Google Trends data.

a. Graph shows frequency of Google searches (within Russia) for the given term in the given month as a percentage of the frequency of searches for that term in the peak month for that term since 2004. (Thus, levels for one term cannot be compared to those for others.)

protest sentiment.[16] Stepped up repression since 2012 probably helps to explain the decline since then. According to one estimate, the proportion of demonstrations that were suppressed by the police rose from one-fifth in 2008 to one-third in 2012 (Lankina 2015, p. 38). Participating in several unsanctioned rallies can now lead to a prison term, and a number of people have been sentenced since 2015. The growing gap between respondents' belief that a protest will occur and their self-reported readiness to participate in one may reflect such repression.

The grievances of protesters have changed in recent years. Since 2010, the share of economically motivated protests has been falling, giving way to those with political or civic goals (Lankina 2015). Indeed, the moral demands of Russian protests in 2011–12 sometimes recalled famous civil rights campaigns such as those in the United States (1945–70), Mahatma

16. By contrast, lower-income groups, industrial workers, and residents of small and medium-size towns have remained more ready to take to the streets. Men are more protest-prone than women, and students are in some years but not in others.

Gandhi's India (1917–47), and Solidarity-era Poland (1979–81) (Aron 2013, p. 69). Observers reported that during the 2011–12 demonstrations Russians frequently used words such as *honor, dignity,* and *conscience* to describe why they chose to join collective actions (Aron 2012). Surveys conducted at protest sites also found that participants in 2011–12 were primarily motivated by a sense of civic duty.[17] Yet, unlike their historical precursors, these protests were short-lived and lacked cohesion and a strategy. Between 2012 and 2014, protest sentiment declined sharply, and attitudes toward protestors became less positive and more indifferent.[18]

In 2016 some evidence suggested that public interest in protests was, once again, increasing. Both the protest count data from Activatica.org and searches for the words *"miting"* and *"protest"* were trending up. It is too early to tell whether this constitutes a change in the long-term dynamic.

STRATEGIES OF CIVIC ACTIVISM: PETITIONS

In the late twentieth century, petitioning the authorities became an ever more common strategy for citizens in advanced democracies. According to the WVS, about three quarters of residents of Sweden, Switzerland, Canada, and the United States had signed a petition as of 2006 (Sriprasit 2014). With the spread of the Internet, e-petitioning has recently caught on.

In Russia, Soviet dissidents pioneered the use of petitions in the postwar period to demand that the Communist Party respect human rights. Unable to publish their appeals, groups of courageous activists would deliver open letters to the reception desk of the Central Committee of the Communist Party. Petitioning has continued in the post-Soviet period. Recently, more than sixty thousand Russians signed a petition on the website Change.org calling for the release of two members of the punk band Pussy Riot, who had been sentenced to jail for singing and dancing in Moscow's main Orthodox cathedral in 2012. They were amnestied in 2013.

Data on petitioning in Russia are hard to interpret. The proportion of Russians who said in the WVS that they would consider signing a petition fell from 77 percent in 1990 to 38 percent in 2011, suggesting a major decline in interest. Yet something may have changed since that time. The frequency of Google search requests made by Russian Internet users containing the

17. See also Smyth, Soboleva, Shimek, and Sobolev (2015).
18. Based on FOM polls.

words "petition" and "sign petition" has drastically increased since 2012. At the same time, actual petitions attract impressive numbers of signers. In 2012–15 Russian civic activists initiated 5,172 petitions on the petitioning platform Change.org, receiving around 17 million signatures. About half of these were addressed to executive, legislative, and judicial authorities at federal, regional, and municipal levels. (The rest were mostly addressed to commercial enterprises, requesting that they change some features of their products.) Initiators of 150 petitions reported that they were successful. Although this success rate is not high, it shows that public campaigns do sometimes achieve their objectives.

What predicts which petitions succeed and which fail? As one might expect, a greater number of signatures increases the odds of a positive response—the average successful petition had sixteen thousand signatures, while the average failing one had three thousand. Still, a lot of signatures is not enough by itself—one with 358,863 signatures failed.[19] The topic of the petition did not in itself distinguish winners from losers: all topics had similar success rates. It did help to deliver the petition to more than one addressee. And, in general, petitions delivered to lower-level authorities— regional or municipal officials, rather than federal ones such as the president or prime minister—had better odds of success. Petitions related to criminal prosecutions were more likely to succeed when addressed to the regional government than when sent to the prosecutors.

In 2016 public interest in online petitioning grew exponentially, driven by three petitions. The first called for the dissolution of the Russian national football team after its disappointing performance in the European championship tournament and attracted one million signatures. The second demanded the dismissal of Russia's children's rights ombudsman, Pavel Astakhov, who had made callous comments after a boating accident (it received 160,000 signatures). The third called on Putin to fire Prime Minister Dmitry Medvedev, after he offended teachers by dismissing their calls for salary increases (210,000 signatories). Although the Russian authorities made no reference to the petitions, the football team was formally dissolved and Astakhov was dismissed soon after they were initiated. Internet

19. This petition requested that President Putin organize an additional murder investigation for a schoolgirl, Katya Soboleva, who was hit by a car in St. Petersburg. The public campaign organized by Katya's parents and civic activists received significant media attention, but no investigation was organized.

petitions appear to be becoming a popular way for the public to express dissatisfaction with the government. It remains to be seen whether this serves as a pressure valve for discontent, a mechanism for further civic mobilization, or a new tool that state officials can use in the intra-elite struggle.

STRATEGIES OF CIVIC ACTIVISM: ELECTION MONITORING

Volunteer election observers had a significant impact on the country's political and civic landscape during and after the 2011–12 elections. On the eve of the 2011 Russian Duma vote, activists formed the group Citizen Observer with the goal of recruiting several hundred volunteers to monitor about 150 of Moscow's over 3,000 polling stations. Large-scale fraud had been suspected in prior elections (such as the 2007 State Duma vote and, especially, the 2009 Moscow City Duma election). About nine core activists recruited and trained about 530 volunteers and negotiated with political parties and media outlets to get the monitors mandates to observe the vote and vote count. The project operated on a zero budget, relying on the efforts of volunteers and friendly NGOs, which provided space for organizational and training sessions.

The exposure of massive electoral fraud by Citizen Observer and other, smaller civic initiatives sparked the 2011–12 wave of protests and led to a massive increase in volunteer election monitoring. During the March 2012 presidential elections, the number of volunteer observers equaled ten thousand or perhaps twenty thousand in Moscow alone. This large-scale mobilization may have had a deterrent effect as the level of fraud in the March elections was much lower than in those in December 2011, at least in Moscow.

The Russian authorities' response to the growth in volunteer electoral monitoring has been twofold. On the one hand, they took steps to increase the legitimacy of the 2012 presidential elections, limiting the level of fraud in large cities and providing most polling stations in the country with web-linked video cameras. Although increasingly authoritarian, the Russian regime has also become more averse to outright electoral fraud, preferring other methods such as limiting the registration of undesired candidates and gerrymandering to achieve its objectives. On the other hand, recent regulations aim to limit the impact of volunteer electoral monitors by making it much more difficult to register as one.

Although a large number of monitors can be mobilized for some high-profile elections (such as federal elections or regional ones in which well-known opposition candidates run), fewer volunteer to work in most regional and local elections. Perhaps two dozen Moscow-based monitors regularly travel to observe small elections across the country, participating in what one activist termed electoral tourism. In their words, such deeply committed activists seek more to educate electoral commissions and apply regular public pressure on them than to influence the outcomes of the elections per se: "What we can really achieve in those regions that are cooperative . . . is the education of electoral commissions. They listen to us. You wouldn't believe it, but in one region United Russia regularly consults with us; in another, they try to make sure that the electoral commissions work flawlessly, to avoid possible complaints."[20]

STATE COUNTERMEASURES

Russia's authorities have responded to the pressures coming from civic activists with a mixture of tactics that include repression, co-optation, and imitation.

Since the late 1990s, repression has increased, slowly at first, then accelerating more recently. In 1999–2003, the Ministry of Justice required all NGOs to reregister. The goals were to learn the size of the sector, unify reporting rules, and eliminate nonfunctioning entities. However, some environmental and human rights organizations were denied registration, partly due to lobbying by regional and municipal authorities.

In 2005 the Duma passed several amendments to laws regulating NGOs, restricting foreign funding, and giving regulators more discretion.[21] Perhaps the greatest blow to Russia's civic sector was the Law on Foreign Agents, signed on July 20, 2012.[22] The law requires all NGOs that participate in political activity and receive monetary assistance from abroad to register as "foreign agents"—a term that in Russian connotes espionage. Since the law did not explicitly define what constitutes "political activity," this left

20. Interview with civic activist, Moscow, November 2015.

21. The forced nationalization of Yukos, the country's largest private firm, in 2003 led to an erosion of corporate giving. Businesses became more reluctant to fund political and increasingly social causes without explicit approval of the authorities (see, for example, Aron 2012).

22. See the text of the Law on Foreign Agents published at Garant.ru, http://base .garant.ru/70204242/.

many organizations vulnerable. A new law, signed on June 2, 2016, classifies almost any public activity (including public statements on state policy and public petitions) as political. Although an exception for charities and other socially oriented causes is provided, the wording of the new law is still vague enough for it to be applied arbitrarily to almost any organization receiving contributions from abroad.[23]

Initially, NGOs that received foreign funding did not comply with the new regulation, but they were later forced to do so by court action or were assigned this status directly by the Ministry of Justice. As of September 2016, the list of "foreign agents" included 104 organizations. A further twenty-four were removed from the list after having closed down, and thirteen more successfully appealed their status, usually on the grounds that foreign funding had ceased. At the same time, some foreign-funded NGOs that specialize in the provision of social services are allowed to operate without the foreign agent status.

The Law on Undesirable Organizations, signed on May 23, 2015, targets Russian branches of foreign NGOs. It makes it a crime (punishable with a fine or imprisonment) to head or participate in an undesirable organization. As of September 2016, seven organizations had been declared undesirable, but no individuals had been prosecuted under the law.

While restricting some NGOs in these ways, the Russian state set about co-opting others. It significantly increased its own funding for civic organizations. Federal government spending on support for socially oriented NGOs shot up from US$170 million in 2011 to US$310 million in 2014. Most of this increase reflected the growth in federal "presidential grants," distributed through several Kremlin-connected operators. Activists see such grants as a means by which the authorities establish political control; some choose to avoid state funding altogether: "State finance of NGOs works like drug addiction. . . . The first dose is for free. Then, as the NGO builds some infrastructure that needs to be maintained, the state begins dictating its terms to continue support. Gradually, without realizing it, the NGO loses its strength, cohesion, and sense of mission and becomes another information phantom that we see on TV screens but not in real life."[24]

23. See the updates to the law on NGOs published at the Russian parliament website, http://asozd2.duma.gov.ru/main.nsf/%28SpravkaNew%29?OpenAgent&RN =1000884-6&02.

24. Interview with civic activist, Moscow, December 2015.

Federal funding is becoming increasingly concentrated in fewer hands. While the average sum of a presidential grant increased from US$50,000 in 2012 to US$110,000 in 2015, the number of recipients dropped from approximately fifteen hundred to fewer than five hundred. Meanwhile, a significant proportion of grant winners are ideological or political allies of the Kremlin, such as patriotic organizations, groups affiliated with the Russian Orthodox Church, and unions of special services veterans.

Finally, the authorities seek to control and disrupt the autonomous civic sphere by creating their own imitation civic bodies and paying agents to interrupt civic communication. The Russian government employs paid commentators (trolls) to inject themselves into online political conversations, express pro-government views, and challenge the narratives of the political opposition.

An example of imitation is the Moscow City Administration's online platform. Launched in 2014, the Active Citizen website supposedly offers Muscovites a forum to express preferences on city policy decisions, such as how to allocate funds to the construction and maintenance of roads. The site has 1.2 million registered users, and hundreds of thousands participate in its online votes. However, a recent investigation by Alexey Navalny's Anti-Corruption Foundation claims that the local authorities control most of the active accounts and bribe other users to vote as they are told in online ballots. For instance, in 2015 a proposal to rename the Voykovskaya Metro Station, whose name commemorates one of the people who murdered the Russian royal family in 1918, was defeated by "public" voting on the Active Citizen website, amid reports of suspicious patterns in the timing of the voting. With Active Citizen occupying the space, it is hard to create an alternative site to host authentic discussion of city policies.

CONCLUSION

Evidence presented in this chapter suggests that Russia's civil society is in the process of modernization. Russians do not appear historically conditioned to distrust each other and reject collective action; increasing numbers of them have been engaging in civic activities that are typical for post-materialist societies (charity, volunteering, petitioning), along with actions to improve their immediate surroundings. Since 2010, the ability of civic activists to mobilize supporters (including volunteers) and finance campaigns and initiatives appears to have increased, driven in part by new information technologies. While participation in protests has fallen sharply since 2012, interest in them has not. Motivations for protests have also changed, especially during the 2011–12 wave, with more participants driven by moral concerns rather than just economic needs.

Activist attempts to influence policies of the Russian authorities sometimes succeed. In response to protests, the Russian government reintroduced gubernatorial elections in 2012. The ease of information dissemination via the Internet and mobile phones sometimes constrains bureaucrats and politicians. However, even the ability to mobilize supporters and attract media attention does not guarantee the success of civic action. For example, the protests of truckers against the introduction of new road taxes were largely unsuccessful, despite a fair amount of media attention. It remains to be seen to what extent civic action will limit the large-scale urban redevelopment program that was launched in Moscow in 2017 and that is opposed by a significant minority of the residents involved.

At the same time, Russian authorities have sought to contain and control civil society. The concessions made by the Kremlin after 2011–12 were mostly short-lived. New repressive laws and practices, in addition to existing ones, were enacted to target undesirable NGOs and individual activists. Funding was channeled to co-opt others, promote an agenda of loyal patriotism, and create the impression that the state enjoys the support of civil society as well as of the public at large. In the years to come, Russia's civil society will be shaped by the interaction between these two forces—modernization and the repressive state responses it provokes.

REFERENCES

Alesina, Alberto F., and Paola Giuliano. 2009. "Preferences for Redistribution." Technical report. Cambridge, Mass.: National Bureau of Economic Research.

Ananyev, Maxim, and Sergei Guriev. 2016. "Effect of Income on Trust: Evidence from the 2009 Crisis in Russia." Working Paper. Paris: Sciences Po.

Aron, Leon. 2012. *Russia's Protesters: The People, Ideals, and Prospects.* Washington, D.C.: American Enterprise Institute for Public Policy Research.

——. 2013. "The Long Struggle for Freedom." *Journal of Democracy* 24, no. 3, pp. 62–74.

Crotty, Jo. 2009. "Making a Difference? NGOs and Civil Society Development in Russia." *Europe-Asia Studies* 61, no. 1, pp. 85–108.

Evans, Alfred B. 2002. "Recent Assessments of Social Organizations in Russia." *Demokratizatsiya* 10, no. 3, pp. 322–342.

————. 2008. "The First Steps of Russia's Public Chamber: Representation or Co-ordination?" *Demokratizatsiya* 16, no. 4, pp. 345–362.

Evans, Alfred B., Laura Henry, and Lisa McIntosh Sundstrom, eds. 2006. *Russian Civil Society: A Critical Assessment.* New York: M. E. Sharpe.

Flynn, Moya. 2006. "Formal and Informal Strategies of Migrant Populations: Migrant Activity in Post-Soviet Russia." In *Russian Civil Society: A Critical Assessment,* edited by Alfred B. Evans, Laura Henry, and Lisa McIntosh Sundstrom, pp. 246–65. New York: M. E. Sharpe.

Gibson, J. L. 2001. "Social Networks, Civil Society, and the Prospects for Consolidating Russia's Democratic Transition." *American Journal of Political Science* 45, no. 1, pp. 51–68.

Giuliano, Paola, and Antonio Spilimbergo. 2014. "Growing Up in a Recession." *Review of Economic Studies* 81, no. 2, pp. 787–817.

Greene, Samuel. 2014. *Moscow in Movement: Power and Opposition in Putin's Russia.* Stanford University Press.

Guriev, Sergei, and Nikita Melnikov. 2016. "War, Inflation, and Social Capital." *American Economic Review* 106, no. 5, pp. 230–35.

Henderson, Sarah L. 2002. "Selling Civil Society Western Aid and the Nongovernmental Organization Sector in Russia." *Comparative Political Studies* 35, no. 2, pp. 139–67.

Howard, Marc Morjé. 2002. "The Weakness of Postcommunist Civil Society." *Journal of Democracy* 13, no. 1, pp. 157–69.

Inglehart, Ronald, 1997. *Modernization and Postmodernization: Cultural, Economic, and Political Change in 43 Societies.* Princeton University Press.

Javeline, Debra, and Sarah Lindemann-Komarova. 2010. "A Balanced Assessment of Russian Civil Society." *Journal of International Affairs* 63, no. 2, pp. 171–88.

Lankina, Tomila. 2015. "The Dynamics of Regional and National Contentious Politics in Russia: Evidence from a New Dataset." *Problems of Post-Communism* 62, no. 1, pp. 26–44.

Ledeneva, Alena. 2008. "Blat and Guanxi: Informal Practices in Russia and China." *Comparative Studies in Society and History* 50, no. 1, pp. 118–44.

Lyall, Jason. 2006. "Pocket Protests: Rhetorical Coercion and the Micropolitics of Collective Action in Semiauthoritarian Regimes." *World Politics* 58, no. 3, pp. 378–412.

Margalit, Yotam. 2013. "Explaining Social Policy Preferences: Evidence from the Great Recession." *American Political Science Review* 107, no. 1, pp. 80–103.

McFaul, Michael, and Elina Treyger. 2004. "Civil Society." In *Between Dictatorship and Democracy: Russian Post-Communist Political Reform,* by Michael McFaul, Nikolai Petrov, and Andrei Ryabov, pp. 135–73. Washington, D.C.: Carnegie Endowment for International Peace.

Mersiyanova, Irina, and Irina Korneeva. 2013. "Charity and Participation of Russians in Civic Activities: Regional Dimension." Working paper, Civic Society Series. Moscow: Higher School of Economics.

Mickiewicz, Ellen. 2008. *Television, Power, and the Public in Russia.* Cambridge University Press.

Oates, Sarah. 2006. "Media, Civil Society, and the Failure of the Fourth Estate in Russia." In *Russian Civil Society: A Critical Assessment,* edited by Alfred B. Evans, Laura Henry, and Lisa McIntosh Sundstrom, pp. 57–69. New York: M. E. Sharpe.

Pfaff, Steven, and Hyojoung Kim. 2003. "Exit-Voice Dynamics in Collective Action: An Analysis of Emigration and Protest in the East German Revolution." *American Journal of Sociology* 109, no. 2, pp. 401–44.

Polishchuk, Leonid, Ekaterina Borisova, and Alexey Peresetsky. 2010. "Management of Collective Ownership in Russian Cities: An Economic Analysis of Housing Associations." *Problems of Economics,* November, pp. 115–135.

Richter, James. 2002. "Promoting Civil Society? Democracy Assistance and Russian Women's Organizations." *Problems of Post-Communism* 49, no. 1, pp. 30–41.

Rose, Richard. 2000. "Uses of Social Capital in Russia: Modern, Pre-Modern, and Anti-Modern." *Post-Soviet Affairs* 16, no. 1, pp. 33–57.

Salamon, Lester M., Vladimir B. Benevolenski, and Lev I. Jakobson. 2015. "Penetrating the Dual Realities of Government-Nonprofit Relations in Russia." *VOLUNTAS: International Journal of Voluntary and Nonprofit Organizations* 26, no. 6, pp. 2178–214.

Salmenniemi, Suvi. 2010. "Struggling for Citizenship: Civic Participation and the State in Russia." *Demokratizatsiya* 18, no. 4, pp. 309–328.

Smyth, Regina, Irina Soboleva, Luke Shimek, and Anton Sobolev. 2015. "Defining Common Ground: Collective Identity in Russia's Post-election Protests and Rallies." In *Systemic and Non-systemic Opposition in the Russian Federation: Civil Society Awakens,* edited by Cameron Ross, pp. 51–77. London: Ashgate.

Sriprasit, Siriluk. 2014. "The Mobilization Effects of Online Campaigns: An Experimental Study of Online Environmental Petitions." Ph.D. thesis, University of Amsterdam.

Sundstrom, Lisa McIntosh. 2006. *Funding Civil Society: Foreign Assistance and NGO Development in Russia.* Stanford University Press.

Volkov, Denis, and Stepan Goncharov. 2014. "Russian Media: TV, Press, Internet." [In Russian.] Moscow: Levada Center.

ELEVEN

Crimea

Anatomy of a Decision

DANIEL TREISMAN

President Vladimir Putin's decision to seize the Crimean peninsula from Ukraine and incorporate it into Russia was the most consequential of his first fifteen years in power. It had profound implications for both foreign and domestic policy as well as for how Russia was viewed around the world. The intervention also took most observers—both in Russia and in the West—by surprise. For these reasons, it is a promising case from which to seek insight into the concerns and processes that drive Kremlin decision-making on high-stakes issues.

One can distinguish two key questions: *why* Putin chose to do what he did, and *how* the decision was made. In fact, as will become clear, the answer to the second question helps one choose among different possible answers to the first.

This chapter draws heavily on Daniel Treisman, "Why Putin Took Crimea: The Gambler in the Kremlin," *Foreign Affairs*, May–June (2016), pp. 47–54. I thank *Foreign Affairs* for permission to reuse this material. I also thank Alberto Alesina for his help in scheduling one of the research trips.

Why did Putin order his military intelligence commandos to take control of the peninsula? In the immediate aftermath, four explanations dominated discussion in the Western media and academic circles. A first image— call this "Putin the defender"—saw the Russian intervention as a desperate response to the perceived threat of NATO enlargement. Fearing that with President Viktor Yanukovych gone Ukraine's new government would quickly join the Western military alliance, so the argument goes, Putin struck pre-emptively to prevent such a major strategic loss and to break the momentum of NATO's eastward drive (see, for example, Mearsheimer 2014).

A second image—"Putin the imperialist"—cast Crimea as the climax of a gradually unfolding, systematic project on the part of the Kremlin to recapture the lost lands of the Soviet Union. In this view, Putin never accepted Moscow's diminished status and territory. Although at times artfully concealing his purposes, he was determined to push Russia's borders outward and restore the state's lost prestige (see, for example, Grigas 2016). He merely used the opportunity provided by Kiev's political crisis to advance a long-standing plan.

Third, there was "Putin the populist." Perhaps grabbing the former Russian territory, while thumbing his nose at the West, was intended to rally public support behind him at a time when the economic underpinnings of his previous popularity were fading. This third Putin sought a short victorious war to burnish his image. And, indeed, his ratings quickly soared to above 80 percent, making this version seem plausible.

The fourth perspective crosses over from the "why" question to the question of "how." In this version—"Putin the improviser"—there was no consistent, long-term goal. Instead, the intervention represented a victory of tactics over strategy. Putin was a leader preoccupied with day-to-day choices, pulled in different directions, and reacting to events with no model to guide him. Crimea, in this view, was an accident into which he stumbled in the heat of a particular disorienting crisis. There was no "why" beyond short-term advantage, the determination to seize opportunities and to create problems where possible for those perceived as hostile.

How plausible are these interpretations of the Russian leader's motivation? I use a variety of evidence, from interviews in Moscow, published analyses, and detailed press accounts. Of course, certain facts remain unknown and participants may aim to mislead. The truth could combine elements from more than one of the common views. While these points dictate caution, close examination of the record does suggest some conclusions.

THE OFFICIAL LINE

An obvious place to start is with the Kremlin's official explanation—but, not surprisingly, it turns out to be little help. A collage of disparate elements, it seems designed to appeal simultaneously to different groups of Russians. All four of the images find support somewhere in Putin's public comments.

On the one hand, he emphasizes improvisation. The intervention, he has said, was an impromptu response to the chaos unleashed by President Yanukovych's fall from power. At a reception in Sochi in October 2015, I asked Putin in person whether the operation had been planned long in advance. "Not at all. It was spontaneous," he replied. "We saw what was happening in Kiev and I made a decision."

At other times, Putin has hinted at a deeper motivation. Rather than a snap reaction to fast-moving events, the operation was an overdue correction of a historical injustice. "In people's hearts and minds, Crimea has always been an inseparable part of Russia," he told the Russian parliament in March 2014. It is the place where Prince Vladimir adopted Christianity in the tenth century and where Russian soldiers from the Crimean War lie buried. In losing the peninsula to Ukraine in 1991, Putin insisted, Russia "was not simply robbed, it was plundered."[1]

Concern about military encirclement also shows up. In the same speech, Putin complained that he had "already heard declarations from Kiev about Ukraine soon joining NATO." NATO sailors were mostly "wonderful guys," he added, but he did not want to have to visit them in Sevastopol, from where their guns would threaten "the whole of southern Russia."[2]

And a little later, he turned to Russian public opinion. According to Putin, 86 percent of Russians saw Crimea as "still being Russian territory," and almost 92 percent supported the region's "reunification with Russia." In short, bringing Crimea "home" was popular. That was lucky for the

1. "Address by President of the Russian Federation," March 18, 2014, http://en.kremlin.ru/events/president/news/20603.
2. Ibid.

Kremlin, since, as Putin put it, "any decision here can be based only on the people's will, because the people are the ultimate source of all authority."[3]

Putin has also mentioned several other motives—to protect Crimea's Russian population against violent Ukrainian nationalists and to respect the community's right to self-determination. But since the threat from Ukrainian nationalists in Crimea was almost entirely fictitious and since Putin had shown little interest in the Crimeans' self-determination during his previous fourteen years in power, these points look more like an effort at justification than like true causes.

So was it an act of imperial expansion, an attempt to halt NATO's spread to the east, a populist move to shore up his approval rating? Or was it merely an improvised response to a particular short-run crisis, hastily initiated with no particular long-run objective in mind?

KEEPING NATO OUT

Consider first the idea that the intervention aimed to prevent Ukraine's entry into NATO. The way that the West had enlarged the alliance, without more than token attempts to integrate Russia, clearly helped to poison the relationship between the two over the preceding decades. The Kremlin was determined to prevent Ukraine from becoming a NATO member. But was that really a key factor in this case?

One problem is that Ukraine was *not* heading toward NATO membership at the time. Under Yanukovych, Ukraine had passed a law committing the country to non-bloc status (Moshes 2013). It had settled for partnership with the alliance rather than membership, an outcome Russia seemed to accept. When, in his March speech, Putin mentioned the "declarations from Kiev" about joining NATO, he failed to mention one important detail—all such recent declarations had come *after* Putin's troops appeared in Crimea.

The Russian leader might still have feared that Ukraine's new government would reverse course—as President Viktor Yushchenko had done after the Orange Revolution. It was quite reasonable to anticipate that the new pro-Western leaders would revisit the issue. Yet, even if Ukraine wanted to join, NATO was not about to let it in. Putin had won that battle at the 2008 Bucharest Summit. At the urging of the leaders of Germany,

3. "Address by President of the Russian Federation."

France, and the United Kingdom, the organization had rejected the proposal to give Ukraine and Georgia membership action plans (BBC 2008).

Moreover, although NATO refused to say "never," German chancellor Angela Merkel remained opposed to practical steps in that direction, and U.S. president Barack Obama, unlike his predecessor, George W. Bush, took no action to advance Kiev's membership. Moreover, NATO's secretary-general, Anders Fogh Rasmussen, had announced just months earlier, in October 2013, that Ukraine would definitely not be joining NATO in 2014, and there was little reason to expect that to change in subsequent years (Lekic 2013).

In fact, Putin's Crimea intervention—along with his support for separatist rebels in Ukraine's east—precipitated just the kind of military buildup near Russia's borders that he ostensibly hoped to avoid. To deter challenges to its members, NATO created a rapid reaction force of four thousand troops to rotate among Estonia, Latvia, Lithuania, Poland, Romania, and Bulgaria and stationed four warships in the Black Sea (Garamone 2015; Shankar 2016). In early 2016 the White House proposed a quadrupling of U.S. military spending in Europe (Lyman 2016). If Putin's goal was to break out of containment, his actions were predictably counterproductive.

Even if objectively Ukraine was not heading toward NATO in 2013, Putin might still have believed otherwise. In that case, one might expect him to have raised the topic in his interactions with Western leaders. But did he? For three years—from 2009 to 2012—Michael McFaul served as special assistant to President Obama on Russia, and for the following two years he was the U.S. ambassador in Moscow. During that time, he was present for all but one of the meetings between President Obama and Putin or Dmitry Medvedev. From the White House, he listened in on all the phone conversations between Obama and either Russian leader. In all those exchanges, McFaul (2015) said recently, "I can't recall once that the issue of NATO expansion came up."

In January 2016 I asked a source close to the commander of the military operation in Crimea, Vice Admiral Oleg Belaventsev, if decisionmakers had been afraid of Ukraine joining NATO in the months preceding the intervention. "They weren't afraid of Ukraine joining NATO," he said. "But they were definitely worried that the Ukrainians would cancel the lease on Sevastopol and kick out the Black Sea Fleet."[4]

4. Interview with source close to Oleg Belaventsev, commander of Crimean operation, Moscow, January 2016.

This seems plausible. The Black Sea Fleet is crucial to Russia's ability to project force into the Black and Mediterranean Seas, and many of Ukraine's opposition leaders had criticized Yanukovych for extending Moscow's lease on the base. But it still leaves a puzzle. With a contingent of twenty thousand highly armed troops in Sevastopol, a mostly pro-Russian local population, and many other sources of leverage over a weak regime in Kiev, Russia would always have been difficult to evict. Its old mode of pressure and negotiation had worked consistently to protect its interests. Annexing the territory—at the cost of international isolation, economic sanctions, a reinvigoration of NATO, and the alienation of most of the Ukrainian population— seems an extreme reaction to a real but probably manageable threat. The costs appear out of proportion to the expected benefit.

REBUILDING THE EMPIRE

To those who see Putin as an imperialist, his move in Crimea seems almost *too* easy to explain. A former State Security Committee (KGB) spy, he notoriously characterized the Soviet disintegration as "the greatest geopolitical catastrophe of the century."[5] In a private conversation with President Bush in 2008, he seemed to question Ukraine's right to exist: "You understand, George, that Ukraine is not even a state! What is Ukraine? Part of its territory is eastern Europe, and a significant part was given by us!" (quoted in Allenova, Geda, and Novikov 2008). Russia has periodically used gas shut-offs to pressure Kiev and other dependent clients, and it has handed out passports to residents of contested territories, creating a pretext to intervene later to protect "Russian citizens."

In 2008 Russian forces invaded Georgia, and Moscow then recognized the independence of the separatist territories Abkhazia and South Ossetia. After Estonia moved a memorial to Soviet World War II soldiers in 2007, Russia was accused of inciting deadly riots, and in 2014 its soldiers crossed the border to kidnap an Estonian security officer.

---

5. "Poslanie Federalnomu Sobraniu Rossiiskoy Federatsii [Message to the Federal Assembly of the Russian Federation]," www.kremlin.ru/events/president/transcripts /22931. Some controversy surrounds the correct translation of Putin's words— "krushenie Sovetskogo Soyuza bylo krupneyshey geopolitisheskoy katastrofoy veka." The word *krupneyshey* can mean either "the greatest" or "a very great" something. This matters little for my point here.

Given all this, one might suppose that Russia had been planning to annex Crimea for years, if not decades. Other signs hint at active preparations in the six months before Yanukovych's fall. In September 2013 Putin appointed his political guru Vladislav Surkov to handle relations with Abkhazia and South Ossetia, as well as—unofficially—Ukraine. Surkov, who hung a prerevolution map in his office on which Crimea appeared as a Russian province, visited Kiev and Simferopol, the Crimean capital, numerous times in the following months (Mazaeva 2014). Teams of Russian police and secret service officers were also seen around Kiev. Among other projects, Surkov was promoting the construction of a bridge across the Kerch Strait to connect southern Russia to Crimea—an essential transportation link in case of annexation.

The chair of the Crimean parliament, Vladimir Konstantinov, was making frequent trips to the Russian capital. In December 2013, according to the journalist Mikhail Zygar, he met in Moscow with Nikolai Patrushev, the secretary of Russia's Security Council. According to Zygar's source, who witnessed the meeting, Patrushev was "pleasantly surprised" to learn from Konstantinov that Crimea would be ready to "go to Russia" if Yanukovych were overthrown (Zygar 2015, p. 337). Konstantinov was back in Moscow on the eve of Russia's intervention, meeting with senior politicians.

In February 2014, according to the newspaper *Novaya Gazeta*, a memorandum circulated in Russia's Presidential Administration that prefigured subsequent developments. Apparently composed by consultants working for a well-connected nationalist businessman, Konstantin Malofeev, it proposed a strategy for annexing Crimea and other eastern Ukrainian regions. If Yanukovych fell, the memo warned, Ukraine would split into western and eastern parts, with the European Union swallowing up the west. Moscow should then move fast to promote referendums in Crimea and Kharkov on uniting the regions with Russia. The memo's authors claimed that they could organize such referendums within two weeks (Lipsky 2015).

These details seem at first to indicate a long-prepared plan to seize Crimea. However, on examination, the case weakens.

One cannot be sure what Surkov discussed with local leaders on his visits to Crimea. But if he was preparing the republic's annexation, then Putin's next move seems bizarre. Rather than sending Surkov to Simferopol to implement his "plan," Putin took him off the case. Surkov apparently spent March in Moscow, where he found time to attend a gallery opening on March 6 and publish a short story on March 12.[6] He even managed, around March 20, to fit in a vacation in Sweden with his wife (*Znak* 2014). According to the journalist Zygar, Surkov's real assignment had been not Crimea but keeping Yanukovych in power. To Putin's displeasure, he failed, which explains his temporary sidelining. As for the police and secret service teams, had they been planning the Crimea operation, they would have visited Crimea, not Kiev. Their role was more likely to advise Yanukovych's staff on how to crush the Maidan protests.

Russia's interest in a bridge across the Kerch Strait seems at first consistent with an imperial design. Yet if Moscow had *really* been scheming for years to annex Crimea, it would not be just talking about such a bridge—it would have built it. In fact, negotiations had crept along for more than ten years. Since 2010, when Yanukovych and then president Medvedev signed an agreement, the Russians had not even managed to complete a feasibility study (Lyutova 2014). Construction began in 2015.

Indeed, many supposedly incriminating details actually point to the absence of any plan until shortly before the event. The *Novaya Gazeta* memorandum shows that there was a lobby in the Kremlin for more assertive action. But that such a speculative document was circulating less than a month before the operation suggests that no concrete plan had yet been adopted. And why was Patrushev, the top security official in Russia and reportedly one of the strongest backers of intervention, "surprised" to hear in December 2013 that the Crimean elite would approve unification with Russia? If he were already contemplating a Russian occupation of the territory, he should have seen intelligence reports on this.

That same month, Russia lent Ukraine US\$3 billion as part of a deal under which Yanukovych agreed to postpone signing the EU association agreement. Had Putin suspected that Yanukovych would be gone in two months, he would have found some pretext to delay the disbursement. "It's not Putin's style to make such presents," Aleksei Chesnakov, a former Kremlin official, told me. Ukraine defaulted on the bonds in December 2015.[7]

Overall, it seems that until shortly before the end the Kremlin was preoccupied with events in Kiev. Although the Russians were coming to see

6. See Buro 24/7, "'Chitay po gubam' v galeree art-podarkov 'Shaltay-Boltay' ['Read lips' in the art-gifts gallery 'Shaltay-Boltay']," www.buro247.ru/events/photo-reports/proekt-chitay-po-gubam-v-galeree-art-podarkov-shal.html.

7. Interview with Aleksei Chesnakov, Moscow, January 2016.

Yanukovych as hopelessly ineffective, Putin was still trying to save him. Only in Yanukovych's final days did the focus shift from Kiev to Crimea.

RAISING THE RATINGS

Between May 2010 and November 2013, according to the Levada Center, President Putin's approval fell from 80 to 61 percent—equaling the lowest point of his entire time in office. The Crimean adventure is the only explanation for the dizzying leap that occurred in the subsequent months, driving his rating back up to 88 percent in October 2014. Given the close attention that Kremlin operatives are known to pay to the president's popularity, it is easy to conclude that securing this leap was the motive behind the annexation (Barry 2011).

Based on previous experience—in the war with Georgia in 2008 and the second Chechen war, from late 1999 on—the Kremlin could have anticipated a robust "rally around the flag" after Russian troops went into action. Given the gross disparity in military capacity between Russia and Ukraine, and the disorientation of the authorities in Kiev, a quick victory was likely. As Putin revealed in his triumphant March 2014 speech, after the intervention the Kremlin had polled Russians to see if they would welcome Crimea's annexation. Chesnakov, the former Kremlin official, confirmed to me that both the main pro-Kremlin polling agencies, the Public Opinion Foundation (FOM) and the Russian Public Opinion Research Center (VCIOM), had done enormous nationwide surveys that had yielded similar results—overwhelming support for Crimea's merger with Russia.[8] All this is consistent with a populist motive.

Besides boosting the president's ratings, the Crimea operation could also be seen as part of a broader strategy to cement Kremlin control over Russia's affluent elite by halting its integration into the West. Along these lines, Putin had previously sought to force oligarchs and bureaucrats to "repatriate" their foreign assets. Reversing the Europeanization of Russian society could complement the drive to freeze the country's modernization in order to eliminate domestic political threats.

But there are problems with this explanation. First, although Kremlin insiders could be dissembling, they dismiss the notion that Putin's political team was seriously concerned in late 2013 about his falling rating. "They

8. Interview with Chesnakov.

were hoping for the Olympics to raise it," one Kremlin-connected pollster recalled. "There wasn't panic."[9] That the Kremlin would hope for—and expect—the Sochi Olympics to rally the public makes sense; and the first polls after Russia's victory in the gold medal count did show an uptick in Putin's support.[10] Could the goal of boosting Putin's approval have factored into the Crimea decision, I asked Chesnakov, who had been part of Surkov's team at the time. "Perhaps if it had been a pre-election period, that would be more plausible," he replied. "But it was not."[11] According to Chesnakov: "They don't worry in the Kremlin when the president's rating falls to 60 percent because there's no alternative; no one else has support."[12] Such insiders might seek to present a false image of confidence. But with his rating already rising again after Sochi—and outstripping those of almost all his Western peers—Putin hardly needed to resort to extreme measures to restore his popularity.

Second, although a leap in Putin's rating was predictable, nobody could have foreseen how long this rating would, in fact, remain above 80 percent. According to the Kremlin-connected pollster, the political team did not anticipate this: "They were expecting Putin's rating to fall in the summer of 2014. They would not have been alarmed if it had."[13] After the immediate rallies associated with the wars in Chechnya and Georgia, Putin's rating had drifted downward, giving up much of the advance in subsequent months. In 2000 the economic recovery had offset the decline, while in 2009 the economic crisis had accelerated it.

Although it could perhaps have contributed, the notion that Putin deliberately sought self-isolation to break the elite's ties to the West seems more like a rationalization after the fact than a cause of the Crimea intervention. The imposition of sanctions seems to have surprised the Kremlin. Vice Premier Igor Shuvalov, speaking in late March 2014, said the government had only begun analyzing the risk of sanctions after the Crimean events

9. Interview with Valery Fedorov, director of VCIOM polling agency, Moscow, January 2016.

10. A Levada poll taken in late February 2014, before Crimea but right around the end of the Sochi Olympics, showed Putin's ratings rising to 69 percent (www .levada.ru/2014/02/26/fevralskie-rejtingi-odobreniya-i-doveriya-3).

11. Interview with Chesnakov.

12. Ibid.

13. Interview with Fedorov.

when "we started to receive signals from foreign governments that if Russia behaved in this way there would be economic complications" (*Interfax.ru* 2014). The immediate concern seemed to be to preserve economic ties to the West rather than to sever them. As Shuvalov put it: "We will not leave traditional markets and slam the door unless we are pushed out of them." Putin made a point of meeting with Siemens's CEO on March 26 to signal business as usual (Bryant 2014). The project of repatriating the elite, although floated rhetorically in the previous two years, had never been implemented very seriously.

Domestic political factors may have weighed on the scale, but they do not seem to have been decisive. Had there not been other powerful motives to intervene in Crimea, it is unlikely Putin would have taken such a risk for a bump in his ratings that all expected to be ephemeral. Having sent in the "little green men" and provoked a furious response from the West, he clearly decided that milking nationalist euphoria and accentuating confrontation was the best short-term strategy. But he does not seem to have settled on that before the operation began. The lack of a clear decision on Crimea's ultimate status (see below) suggests that at first he hoped to negotiate with the West, resulting in a less drastic break in relations. But he underestimated the strength of the Western reaction.

MUDDLING THROUGH

The clearest evidence against a consistent plan for territorial expansion—and for Putin as improviser—is the chaotic way in which the Crimea operation unfolded. *How* the decisions were made—or, at least, what is known about this—says a lot about *why* they were made. The military component ran smoothly; a detailed military contingency plan had clearly been prepared, perhaps long in advance. By contrast, the political aspects revealed an almost farcical lack of preparation.

Putin has said that he gave the first order on the morning of February 23, after Yanukovych's flight from Kiev. In fact, according to my source close to the commander of the operation, Russia's special operations forces in the southern port of Novorossiysk and in the Black Sea Fleet's base at Sevastopol were already put on alert on February 18. Then, on February 20, they received an order from the president to begin a "peacekeeping operation" to blockade Ukrainian military installations in Crimea and prevent bloodshed between pro-Russian and pro-Kiev groups.

Although it contradicts Putin's account, the earlier date is consistent with other evidence. For instance, medals that the Kremlin awarded to participants were engraved with the dates of the operation: "20/2/14–18/3/14" (Kates 2014). Russia's "little green men" did not begin blockading buildings until at least February 23, so the mission could still have been aborted if the agreement that Yanukovych signed on February 21 with opposition leaders and EU foreign ministers had held. A Crimean Internet portal reported that on February 23 and 24 several military aircraft flew Russian marines into the peninsula and that on February 25 ships delivered eleven thousand more Russian marines to Sevastopol (*Sobytia Kryma* 2014).

How was this decision made? The official line is that Putin acted alone, without consulting any of his aides. "It was a personal decision of the head of state. He was the only person who could and had to make it and who made it," Putin's press secretary Dmitri Peskov told the TVC television channel.[14] This is consistent with what Putin told me at the reception in Sochi and with the account in the propagandistic movie broadcast on Russian state television, *Crimea: Path to the Motherland*.[15]

Some press accounts reported that Putin reached the decision in a meeting with three key associates—his chief of staff, Sergei Ivanov; the head of the Security Council, Nikolai Patrushev; and Federal Security Service (FSB) chief Alexander Bortnikov (Myers 2014). However, the *New York Times* account said that this meeting occurred on February 25 or 26—at least five days after the original order was given, according to the source close to Belaventsev and the dates on the medals. This meeting might have been when Putin decided to progress from preparations to the actual blockading of installations. Of course, the occurrence of such a meeting in no way demonstrates that the participants influenced Putin's decision; he could simply have been giving them orders.

If others influenced Putin's decision, it was probably by shaping the flow of information to him. As explained by Andrei Soldatov and Michael Rochlitz (this volume), Putin was by this point receiving briefings primarily from the security service chiefs—in particular, Bortnikov. How such reports framed and shaped the facts must have affected how imminent the loss of Sevastopol looked to the president as Yanukovych fled Kiev. Nothing from

14. TVC, April 19, 2014.

15. When I asked if he had consulted aides, he replied: "No, I told them we will do this and then that. I was even surprised at how well it went!"

the briefings has leaked into the press, so one cannot check exactly what was communicated.

Ordering the troops into action in the "peacekeeping operation" was only the first step. That left open the political leadership and status of the region. The commander of Russian forces, Vice Admiral Belaventsev, arrived in Crimea on February 22, according to my source. A longtime aide to Russia's defense minister, Sergei Shoigu, Belaventsev was unfamiliar with Crimea's political scene. After consulting locals, he pressured the incumbent prime minister, a Yanukovych appointee disliked as an outsider, to step down. To replace him, he chose an elderly Communist, Leonid Grach, who had been known in Moscow since Soviet times. Shoigu himself spoke to Grach on a secure line on the evening of February 26 to urge him to take the job and, according to Grach, told him that Putin had personally approved his appointment (Bonet 2015).

As Grach tells it, the security services, acting separately from the Defense Ministry, had also settled on him as their candidate. As he was dining with Belaventsev and two other naval officers, he got a call from an FSB general in Moscow, who asked Grach to meet his local representative. After dinner, Grach drove to a Simferopol hotel to meet the local FSB person, who he says told him that the FSB and the Main Intelligence Directorate (GRU) also wanted him to become Crimea's prime minister (Bonet 2015).

Unfortunately, as Belaventsev soon found out, Grach did not have the backing of important local power brokers. To his embarrassment, Belaventsev had to retract the offer. He then turned to Sergei Aksyonov, a local pro-Russian businessman and former semiprofessional boxer, known to locals by the underworld nickname "Goblin" (*Japan Times* 2015).

If Grach's account is accurate, the security services and the Defense Ministry team seem to have been operating in parallel. That they would both separately seek to recruit Grach to lead the republic suggests a lack of coordination except at the highest levels in Moscow. That Belaventsev would later take back the offer, apparently under pressure from Konstantinov and Aksyonov, shows a shocking lack of intelligence and reliance on improvisation. Grach got the impression that his local FSB interlocutor had not been informed of the change of plans (Bonet 2015).

Even more surprising than this leadership musical chairs, the Kremlin apparently did not yet know what it wanted to do with the region. The Crimean parliament, after voting to confirm Aksyonov, agreed to hold a referendum on May 25. Residents would be asked whether they agreed that

Crimea "is a self-sufficient state and is a part of Ukraine on the basis of trea-
ties and agreements"—in other words, whether Crimea should have stronger autonomy while remaining in Ukraine. At that point, Putin had apparently not decided on full-fledged unification.[16]

The following week, as planeloads of Russian notables flocked to the
peninsula, obeying a Kremlin instruction to go down and counteract Ukrai-
nian propaganda, a secret debate raged in Moscow over the next move. On
March 1 Crimea's parliament rescheduled the referendum forward from
May 25 to March 30. Then, five days later, the deputies advanced it again, to
March 16, and they changed the question to: "Are you for the unification of
Crimea with Russia with the rights of a subject of the Russian Federation?"[17]

Why did Putin raise the stakes from autonomy within Ukraine to full
unification with Russia? It is possible that the whole series of events was a
smoke screen, that the decision to annex had been made long before. But
then why not, from the start, announce that the referendum would be on
unification with Russia? And why change the date twice? It is hard to find
any secret logic in these changes. The evolution was certainly welcomed by
the pro-Russian Crimean leaders. Konstantinov feared ending up in a
semi-recognized statelet like Abkhazia or South Ossetia. "That would be
pure adventurism, which would ruin us all," he said (quoted in Galimova
2015). But it is hard to believe that Putin took the preferences of such minor
figures seriously. More important, it seems that Putin found himself

16. Grach, in the *El Pais* interview (Bonet 2015), said that Shoigu had already told
him on February 26 that Putin had decided to annex Crimea, but this could have
been misinformation aimed at persuading Grach, a longtime advocate of reunification, to serve as prime minister. It is not consistent with the repeated
changes in the referendum details described below. Konstantinov later recalled
that in the early days "no one knew that there would be this exact resolution [that is,
annexation]" (quoted in Galimova 2015).

17. The involvement of the Kremlin was confirmed by a leak of documents hacked
by the group Anonymous International from the e-mail of one Presidential Administration official, Aleksei Anisimov, whose e-mail attachments included a copy of
the final referendum wording a day before it was voted on by the Crimean parliament and released to the public. The involvement of the domestic politics department of the Presidential Administration is also suggested by analysis of who received medals for their participation in the operation. The head of the domestic
politics department, Oleg Morozov, two of his deputies, Anisimov and Viktor Seliv-
erstov, and an adviser to the department, Dmitri Kiryukhin, were all rewarded.

trapped. Having plunged in, he discovered there was no acceptable exit option.

To simply withdraw, allowing Ukrainian troops to retake the peninsula and prosecute Moscow's supporters there, would make him look intolerably weak. And then Kiev might well cancel the lease for the Black Sea Fleet. The only way Russia could leave safely would be if the West recognized the proposed referendum vote for Crimean autonomy as legitimate and persuaded the Ukrainian government to accept it. Western leaders—outraged by Russia's invasion—made clear that they would do nothing of the sort.

That meant Russia would have to continue to defend the pro-Russian government in Crimea against Kiev's attempts to restore order—a complicated task, given the twenty-two thousand Ukrainian military personnel on the peninsula. Were Russia to expel these soldiers and defend Crimea militarily against a Ukrainian counteroffensive, that would arouse almost as much condemnation and pushback from the West as if Russia annexed the territory outright. By March 4, the advocates of annexation had won.

CONCLUSION

Closely examined, Russia's Crimea operation does not look like the climax of a revanchist campaign. Any halfway competent imperialist would know whom to appoint as local agent after the invasion and would have already decided whether the population was to "vote" for independence or annexation. Such an imperialist would have built a bridge to the target territory rather than fiddling around in planning for ten years. This does not mean that there was not a group in the Kremlin with imperial appetites and that the commander in chief did not also get twinges of temptation. But that is not the same as a concerted plan.

NATO enlargement was a chronic irritant and a rhetorical rallying point. But in the years before Crimea, Putin seemed less concerned about it in his talks with Obama than one might guess from his speeches. As his sources of information and analysis narrowed more and more to just the security services, the notion that the West would use any opportunity to weaken his regime was being regularly reinforced. He was primed to see the hand of the United States in any crisis around his borders. But this had little to do with NATO expansion per se. A more plausible fear was that a post-Yanukovych government would cancel the lease on the Sevastopol base and demand that Russia's Black Sea Fleet leave.

Although the recapture of Crimea proved extremely popular with the Russian public, that does not mean that increasing Putin's popularity was the main motivation. His political team would have expected the operation to give him a boost in the polls, but for six months to a year, a significant but limited benefit. The associated risks—of international isolation, military and economic reactions by the West, capital flight, and the definitive refusal by Ukraine to join Putin's Eurasian Union—seem so much greater that it is hard to believe that Putin would have struck were popularity the only motive. Nor does it seem that Putin deliberately engineered a decisive break with the West in order to discipline the Russian elite. The Kremlin seems to have underestimated the Western reaction and to have initially hoped to negotiate a less severe rupture.

Although other factors must have set the stage, the initial intervention seems most likely to have been prompted by a panicked attempt to rule out the loss of the Black Sea base at Sevastopol, with the potential risks and costs either poorly understood or disregarded. The subsequent decision to annex the territory appears to have been made because at that point all options involved heavy costs and annexation would at least provide a concrete and highly symbolic benefit.

What can one learn from the details of the Crimea case about Russian political decisionmaking? How did the various actors this book examines contribute to the process? Even in such a high-stakes case, many familiar features appear.

First, the initial decisionmaking seems to have been extremely centralized. It was a clear case of "System 2" taking over. There is no evidence that Putin consulted anybody before ordering the operation. That is what he says, and no one else has even hinted at broader involvement. Second, we see an extreme reliance on the security services, both for information and execution of decisions, even those of a political nature. Those with useful experience or genuine expertise were sidelined and ignored at key points. The government was treated not as a source of policy or even advice so much as an instrument for solving problems after the fact.[18]

---

18. Circumstantial evidence suggests that Prime Minister Medvedev, although in Sochi with Putin, was not kept in the loop. On February 24, in a press conference, Medvedev complained that the only authorities in Kiev after Yanukovych's flight were people "in black masks with Kalashnikovs"—a strange image to emphasize if

Third, although the military side of the operation ran smoothly, subsequent political events suggest chaotic improvisation. This, in part, resulted from the disregard of local expertise and apparent lack of political planning. Adding to the confusion, different sets of siloviki competed to influence the operation, with the FSB and GRU weighing in on political appointments themselves in parallel to the operation's nominal commander. Perhaps out of frustration with earlier failures of the security services, Putin also made use of informal allies and freelancing agents—from the Orthodox businessman Malofeev, with his network of ultranationalist volunteers, to the Night Wolves motorcycle gang, who turned up in Crimea to help blockade buildings, and odd Cossack units. Even Belaventsev himself was picked out of nowhere to lead the intervention, presumably on Shoigu's recommendation.

The Russian parliament's main contribution was to provide legal cover. First, the Federation Council approved—after the fact—the use of Russian troops in Ukraine. Then the Duma ratified the treaty to incorporate Crimea and Sevastopol into the Russian Federation, and the Federation Council approved the necessary constitutional amendment. Does this imply that, contra Ben Noble and Ekaterina Schulmann (this volume), the Duma was acting as a mere "rubber stamp"? In fact, the parliament seems to have been an important arena in the behind-the-scenes struggle over Crimea's future. On February 28, before annexation was even being mentioned, Sergei Mironov, the leader of the Just Russia faction, introduced a bill to simplify procedures for Russia to absorb foreign territories (the proposal was to no longer require the agreement of the country the territory was leaving). This bill was reported to have been drafted in the Kremlin (Galimova 2015). But did it come from Putin? Had this been so, one might have expected it to fly through. In fact, it was initially buried. Sources told journalists of a fierce battle being fought among insider factions. "The decision [on annexation] was not easy to take," Konstantinov explained. "There were various visions of the status of Crimea" (quoted in Galimova 2015). Mironov's gambit looks very much like the kind of "sneaky bureaucratic gamesmanship masquerading as parliamentary politics" that Noble and Schulmann (this volume) describe.

---

he knew that Russia's own men in black masks with Kalashnikovs were preparing to seize the Crimean parliament (*Interfax.ru* 2017).

Turning to regional elites, the immediate aftermath of intervention saw an influx of central federal actors, in a more extreme manifestation of the process Nikolay Petrov and Eugenia Nazrullaeva (this volume) observe elsewhere. Muscovites descended on the peninsula to manage the transition. Yet, again as elsewhere, the outsiders proved ready to work with local elites, including those like Aksyonov whose reputations were not unblemished. Another similarity was the quick resumption of conflict over rents. As central attention moved on, local power brokers and siloviki battled it out, fighting corruption or using corruption as a pretext to fight each other. To the chagrin of the security services, Crimean premier Aksyonov seemed to be appealing for the kind of personalized relationship with Putin that Ramzan Kadyrov enjoyed in Chechnya. "No one, except the president [Putin], will tell me what to do," he said in July 2015. "I will not be pushed around and no services [likely a reference to the FSB] can force me to change my position on anything" (EurasiaNet 2015). Like Kadyrov, he offered in return a kind of embarrassing hyper-loyalty, insisting publicly that Putin should be anointed president for life (Reuters 2017).

With respect to business, Crimea manifested two tendencies noted elsewhere—favoritism toward cronies and the use of businesses as proxies for the state, providing services that Putin did not trust the ministries to manage. To build a US$3.5 billion bridge across the Kerch Strait, Putin contracted the company of his childhood judo partner, Arkady Rotenberg (Hille and Seddon 2016). In itself, this project, which required difficult engineering in treacherous conditions, might not be profitable—indeed, no other contractor would bid on the project (Yaffa 2017). Yet Rotenberg, who was included on the U.S. and EU sanctions lists over Crimea, clearly benefited from the state in other ways. In 2015, after sanctions were imposed, he won state contracts worth US$9 billion, up from US$3.5 billion the previous year (Yaffa 2017).

Finally, the Crimea operation and the insurgency in eastern Ukraine served as a testing ground for the regime's strategy of manipulating information—both to the Russian public and as a weapon against foreign targets. Russian fake news sources worked overtime to create the impression that Russian speakers were fleeing the region in fear for their lives, while those who remained were being persecuted by Ukrainian neo-Nazis (Bigg 2014). As a reward for their efforts—and to keep them co-opted— three hundred Russian journalists and media executives secretly received medals from Putin for their Crimean coverage, some of which came with monthly monetary allowances (Bigg 2014). In the initial hours of the assault, Russian media distortions helped to confuse and disorient Western governments (Herszenhorn 2014). Subsequently, the "raw and aggressive propaganda" served—quite effectively, in Maria Lipman, Anna Kachkaeva, and Michael Poyker's view (this volume)—to mobilize Russian public opinion behind the annexation and the Kremlin.

In a broader perspective, Crimea—along with the Russian interference in the 2016 U.S. presidential election—exemplifies an apparently growing affinity for Pyrrhic victories. Seduced by the attraction of its tools for hybrid conflict, the Kremlin scores tactical successes, while neglecting potential costs. In the Crimean case, the benefits included securing the base in Sevastopol against a highly uncertain threat and earning a long-lived but superficial boost in domestic popularity; the costs consisted of international isolation, economic sanctions, capital flight, increased desire among Ukrainians to join the EU and NATO, and a reinforcement of NATO defenses around Russia's perimeter. The Kremlin's election meddling might have helped marginally to weaken Hillary Clinton's campaign at key moments. But the massive, unfolding scandal it provoked has made any short- or medium-term improvement of relations with the United States and Europe less likely. Rather than helping Russia break out of isolation, the Kremlin's tactics have prompted a search in the West for a new model of containment. Given the trends noted in this book—of centralization, informational narrowing, cronyism, and the personalization of policy implementation—it is hard to see what could cause a major reorientation in Moscow under the current leadership. At the same time, pressure on the regime is likely to grow, as the current economic stagnation interacts with the ongoing social modernization that the Kremlin has only managed to restrain superficially. One should not be surprised to see additional gambles, Pyrrhic victories, and perhaps also defeats.

REFERENCES

Allenova, Olga, Elena Geda, and Vladimir Novikov. 2008. "Blok NATO razoshelsya na blokpakety [The NATO bloc separated into bloc fragments]." *Kommersant*, April 7. www.kommersant.ru/doc/877224.

Barry, Ellen. 2011. "Before Voting, Russian Leaders Go to the Polls." *New York Times*, August 16.

BBC. 2008. "NATO Denies Georgia and Ukraine," April 3. http://news.bbc.co.uk/2 /hi/europe/7328276.stm.

Bigg, Claire. 2014. "Putin Awards 300 Journalists for 'Objective' Crimea Coverage." Radio Free Europe / Radio Liberty, May 5. www.rferl.org/a/putin-awards -journalists-objective-crimea-coverage/25373844.html.

Bonet, Pilar. 2015. "La misión del Kremlin para elegir a su hombre en Crimea [The Kremlin's mission to choose its man in Crimea]." *El Pais*, March 18. http:// internacional.elpais.com/internacional/2015/03/17/actualidad/1426620920 _045185.html.

Bryant, Chris. 2014. "Siemens CEO Meets Putin and Commits Company to Russia." *Financial Times*, March 27.

EurasiaNet. 2015. "Crimea: Corruption Fueling Feud between Local and Federal Elites." July 16. www.eurasianet.org/node/74266.

Galimova, Natalya. 2015. "Kak Rossia prisoyedinyala Krym: Rassledovanie Gazety. ru [How Russia annexed Crimea: Gazeta.ru's investigation]." *Gazeta.ru*, March 12. https://www.gazeta.ru/politics/2015/03/11_a_6503589.shtml.

Garamone, Jim. 2015. "NATO Responding to Russia's Actions against Ukraine." U.S. Department of Defense, March 23. www.defense.gov/News-Article-View /Article/604333/nato-responding-to-russias-actions-against-ukraine.

Grigas, Agnia. 2016. *Beyond Crimea: The New Russian Empire*. Yale University Press.

Herszenhorn, David. 2014. "Russia Is Quick to Bend Truth about Ukraine." *New York Times*, April 15.

Hille, Kathrin, and Max Seddon. 2016. "Bridge to Crimea: Putin Strives to Complete a Historic Mission." *Financial Times*, September 23.

Interfax.ru. 2014. "Shuvalov predupredil ob opasnosti 'skrytykh' sanktsii protiv Rossii [Shuvalov warned of the danger of 'hidden' sanctions against Russia]." March 26. www.interfax.ru/russia/367312.

———. 2017. "Medvedev usomnilsya v legitimnosti vlastey Ukrainy [Medvedev doubted the legitimacy of Ukraine's authorities]." February 24. www.interfax.ru /russia/360727.

Japan Times. 2015. "The 'Goblin' King: Crimea Leader's Shady Past." March 9. www.japantimes.co.jp/news/2014/03/09/world/the-goblin-king-crimea-leaders -shady-past.

Kates, Glen. 2014. "The Online Debate over a Mysterious Russian 'Medal.'" Radio Free Europe / Radio Liberty, April 24. www.rferl.org/content/the-online-debate -over-a-mysterious-russian-medal/25361367.html.

Lekic, Slobodan. 2013. "Ukraine Abandons Bid to Join NATO." *Stars and Stripes*, October 23. www.stripes.com/news/ukraine-abandons-bid-to-join-nato-1.248630.

Lipsky, Andrei. 2015. "Predstavlyaetsya pravilnym initsirovat prisoedinenie vostochnykh oblastey Ukrainy k Rossii [It seems right to initiate the annexation of the eastern regions of Ukraine to Russia]." *Novaya Gazeta*, February 24. www.novayagazeta.ru/politics/67389.html.

Lyman, Rick. 2016. "Eastern Europe Cautiously Welcomes Larger U.S. Military Presence." *New York Times*, February 2.

Lyutova, Margarita. 2014. "Most k sosedyam [A bridge to neighbors]." *Vedomosti*, February 14. www.vedomosti.ru/newspaper/articles/2014/02/14/most-k-sosedyam.

Mazaeva, Darya. 2014. "Boris Rapoport: 'Surkov vsegda byl i ostaetsya storonnikom doktriny 'Moskva—Trety Rim' [Boris Rapoport: 'Surkov has always been and remains an adherent to the doctrine that Moscow is the Third Rome']." *Moskovsky Komsomolets*, December, 16. www.mk.ru/print/article/1137993.

McFaul, Michael. 2015. "A New Cold War? Russia's New Confrontation with the West." Talk at the University of California, Los Angeles, May 12. www.international.ucla.edu/media/podcasts/McFaul-Podcast—edit-v5-llj.mp3.

Mearsheimer, John J. 2014. "Why the Ukraine Crisis Is the West's Fault." *Foreign Affairs,* September–October, pp. 77–89.

Moshes, Arkady. 2013. "Zhdat li Natovskie tanki pod Kharkovom? [Should We Wait for NATO Tanks to Appear near Kharkiv?]" *Yezhednevnyy Zhurnal*, November 13.

Myers, Steven Lee. 2014. "Russia's Move into Ukraine Said to Be Born in Shadows." *New York Times*, March 7.

Reuters. 2017. "Russia-Backed Crimea Chief Says Putin Should Be President for Life." March 18. www.reuters.com/article/us-ukraine-crisis-russia-crimea-idUS KBN16P0SI.

Shankar, Sneha. 2016. "Russia Boosts Military Presence in Response to Increasing NATO Drills in Eastern Europe." *International Business Times*, January 22. www.ibtimes.com/russia-boosts-military-presence-response-increasing-nato -drills-eastern-europe-2275977.

Sobytia Kryma. 2014. "V Krym styagivayutsya rossiyskie voyska [In Crimea Russian troops are being pulled together]." February 26. www.sobytiya.info/news /14/38891.

Yaffa, Joshua. 2017. "Putin's Shadow Cabinet and the Bridge to Crimea." *New Yorker*, May 29.

Znak. 2014. "Surkov udivil Runet, sfotografirovavshis v Stokgolme, nesmotrya na sanktsii ES [Surkov surprised the Russian internet, having photographed himself in Stockholm, despite the EU sanctions]." March 24. www.znak.com/2014 -03-24/surkov_udivil_runet_sfotografirovavshis_v_stokgolme_nesmotrya_na _sankcii_es.

Zygar, Mikhail. 2015. *Vsya Kremlevskaya rat* [All the Kremlin's men]. Moscow: Intellektualnaya Literatura.

About the Contributors

MAXIM ANANYEV is a Ph.D. student in the Department of Political Science, University of California, Los Angeles.

ANNA KACHKAEVA is a professor in the Faculty of Communications, Media, and Design at the Higher School of Economics, Moscow, and a well-known media analyst. From 1994 to 2012, she hosted and participated in programs on Radio Svoboda.

NATALIA LAMBEROVA is a Ph.D. student in the Department of Political Science, University of California, Los Angeles.

MARIA LIPMAN is editor in chief of *Counterpoint* (George Washington University) and a regular contributor to the *New Yorker* online. A former analyst at the Carnegie Moscow Center, she was a cofounder and deputy editor of the weekly magazines *Itogi* and *Ezhenedelny Zhurnal*.

EUGENIA NAZRULLAEVA is a Ph.D. student in the Department of Political Science, University of California, Los Angeles.

BEN NOBLE is a junior research fellow at New College, University of Oxford, and senior researcher at the Higher School of Economics, Moscow. He is the recipient of the 2017 Walter Bagehot Prize in Government and Public Administration, awarded by the Political Studies Association.

ELLA PANEYAKH is a docent in the Department of Sociology, Higher School of Economics, Moscow. Previously, she was a professor in the Department of Political Science and Sociology and the director of the Institute for the Rule of Law, European University at St. Petersburg.

NIKOLAY PETROV is a professor and laboratory head at the Higher School of Economics, Moscow, and the director of the Center for Political-Geographic Research. Previously he served as director of the Society and Regions project at the Carnegie Moscow Center and as an advisor to the Russian parliament, government, and Presidential Administration in the early 1990s.

MICHAEL POYKER is a Ph.D. student in the Anderson School of Management, University of California, Los Angeles.

MICHAEL ROCHLITZ is a research fellow in the Institute of Sociology at the Ludwig-Maximilian University, Munich, and a former assistant professor in the Department of Politics, Higher School of Economics, Moscow.

KIRILL ROGOV is an expert on Russian politics and economics and a member of the boards of the Liberal Mission Foundation (Moscow) and the Levada Center. A cofounder and editor in chief of *Polit.ru* and deputy editor in chief of *Kommersant*, he is a regular columnist for *Vedomosti, Novaya Gazeta,* and *RBC*.

DINA ROSENBERG is an assistant professor in the Department of Politics, Higher School of Economics, Moscow.

EKATERINA SCHULMANN is a senior lecturer at the School of Public Policy of the Russian Presidential Academy of National Economy and Public Administration. A former expert in the Russian State Duma's Analytical Department, she is the author of *Zakonodatelstvo kak politicheskiy protsess* [Legislation as a political process] (2014) and a regular contributor to *Vedomosti, New Times,* and *Republica*.

ANTON SOBOLEV is a Ph.D. student in the Department of Political Science, University of California, Los Angeles.

ANDREI SOLDATOV is the founder and editor of *Agentura.ru*, an information hub on Russia's intelligence agencies. A frequent commentator on terrorism and intelligence topics for the national and international media, he is a coauthor of *The Red Web* (2015) and *The New Nobility* (2010).

KONSTANTIN SONIN is a professor in the Harris School of Public Policy, University of Chicago, and a research fellow at the Centre for Economic

Policy Research. A columnist for *Vedomosti* and *The Moscow Times*, he was previously a professor and vice-rector at the Higher School of Economics and the New Economic School, both in Moscow.

DANIEL TREISMAN is a professor of political science at the University of California, Los Angeles, and research associate at the National Bureau of Economic Research. He is the author of *The Return: Russia's Journey from Gorbachev to Medvedev* (2011).

ALEXEI ZAKHAROV is an assistant professor of economics at the Higher School of Economics, Moscow, and a columnist for *Vedomosti*.

Index

Lightning Source UK Ltd.
Milton Keynes UK
UKHW011136020322
399453UK00001B/10